Keeping the Dream Alive
The Survival of the Ontario CCF/NDP, *1950–1963*

Keeping the Dream Alive examines a crucial era in the evolution of the CCF/NDP in Ontario when, after almost a decade of unprecedented popularity, the party experienced a significant decline in support. Dan Azoulay chronicles the party's difficult but inspiring struggle to survive and to regain its status as a major player in the political arena.

Azoulay delineates the central themes and determining factors of the party's development during the 1950s and early 1960s. The CCF/NDP had to contend with not only a booming postwar economy and a very popular premier but also a Cold War-induced phobia toward the Left and serious intraparty divisions. Despite this the party slowly recovered, led by a core of dedicated activists and employing an array of strategies, including the much publicized transformation of the CCF into the NDP in the early 1960s.

The author counters allegations that the CCF/NDP opportunistically abandoned its essential qualities (such as its socialist ideology or democratic structure) for the sake of electoral gain and that organized labour played a leading role in the party in these years, contributing to the dilution of the movement. Although the party sought new alliances among the province's less privileged groups, especially organized labour, it did so cautiously and even hesitatingly, always conscious of the need to preserve its basic identity.

DAN AZOULAY is an instructor of history, Atkinson College, York University.

Keeping the Dream Alive

The Survival of the Ontario
CCF/NDP, 1950–1963

DAN AZOULAY

McGill-Queen's University Press
Montreal & Kingston · London · Buffalo

© McGill-Queen's University Press 1997
ISBN 0-7735-1634-4

Legal deposit third quarter 1997
Bibliothèque nationale du Québec

Printed in Canada on acid-free paper

Publication of this book has been made possible by
funding from the Douglas-Caldwell Foundation.

McGill-Queen's University Press acknowledges the
support received for its publishing program from the
Canada Council's Block Grants program.

A modified version of chapter 2 appeared originally in
Ontario History 84, no. 2 (1992).

All photographs courtesy of Queen's University
Archives.

Canadian Cataloguing in Publication Data

Azoulay, Dan André, 1960–
    Keeping the dream alive : the survival of the Ontario
CCF/NDP, 1950–1963
    Includes bibliographical references and index.
    ISBN 0-7735-1634-4
    1. Co-operative Commonwealth Federation. Ontario
Section – History. 2. New Democratic Party of
Ontario – History. 3. Ontario – Politics and
government – 1943–1985. I. Title.
    JL279.A5A93 1997   324.2713'07   C97-900375-X

Typeset in Sabon 10/12
by Caractéra inc., Quebec City

To my mother and father, and my wife, Raya

Contents

Acknowledgments

I incurred numerous debts in the production of this study, the bulk of which stems from my doctoral dissertation. I wish to acknowledge, first and foremost, the members of my supervisory committee at York University – Peter Oliver, Jack Granatstein, Robert Drummond, and Michiel Horn – whose candid and helpful comments through several drafts of the dissertation made this a better study. My supervisor, Peter Oliver, was especially valuable. Apart from his meticulous and time-consuming scrutiny of what were – and still are – very long chapters, he was always careful to balance his criticisms with words of praise and encouragement. He has been a friend as well as a mentor. I am grateful, as well, to Alan Whitehorn of Royal Military College in Kingston, Desmond Morton now at McGill University in Montreal, and the publisher's reviewers and editors for their helpful suggestions. Needless to say, I take full responsibility for any of the book's short-comings or mistakes.

I also wish to thank the Douglas-Coldwell Foundation in Ottawa for its generous financial assistance in the preparation and publication of this study. Its faith in the merits of this project and in my ability to undertake it, especially when these were not always evident to other funding bodies, will not be forgotten. I am grateful, too, for the generous donations from the following members of the Ontario NDP: the Honourable Shelley Martel; the Honourable Gilles Bisson; the Honourable Howard Hampton; Dr Dan Geagan of McMaster University; June Caskey of Hamilton; and Charlotte Sheriff of Toronto. The periodic assistance of the York University Faculty of Graduate Studies is hereby acknowledged as well. Apart from these benefactors, and in the spirit of sacrifice described in the following pages, this work was largely self-financed.

For the intangible assistance received over the years, however, I owe my deepest gratitude to persons too numerous to mention here. I think in particular of John Wadland of the Canadian Studies Program at Trent University, who reduced my teaching load so that I might complete the study; the former party activists who kindly consented to speak with me; the individuals and organizations who allowed me to use their papers; and my family, friends, and colleagues, who have been patient and understanding throughout. Of the latter, I must single out the assistance of my good friend and fellow educator Phillip Buckley, who not only rendered invaluable assistance in raising money for the project, but, more importantly, helped raise my at times flagging spirits.

My greatest debt, however, is to my wife, Raya. She, like the players in this historical drama, came to understand only too well the meaning of the word sacrifice; nevertheless, she was unfailing in her support and advice. This study is as much hers as it is mine.

Abbreviations

TLC   Trades and Labour Congress
TUC   Trade Union Committee
UAW   United Auto Workers
UFO   United Farmers of Ontario
USA   United Steelworkers of America

Ted Jolliffe addressing 1949 CCF convention. Morden Lazarus seated on left.

Bill Temple

C.C. "Doc" Ames

CCF gathering, 1950s. From left to right: True Davidson, Ted Jolliffe, Ted Isley, Morden Lazarus, Tommy Thomas.

Lyal Tait

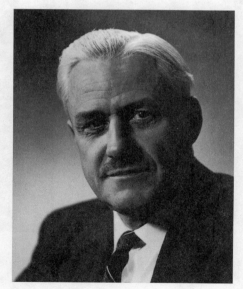

Fred Young

Donald MacDonald and Peg Stewart chatting at CCF's twenty-fifth anniversary celebration, 1957.

CCF's twenty-fifth anniversary celebration, 1957. From left to right (back row): Stanley Knowles, Jack Henry (federal CCF candidate for Halton), Sam Lawrence, Reg Gisborn, Bill Scandlan (candidate for Hamilton West); (front row): James Stowe (Hamilton and District Labour Council president), May Gisborn (Women's Committee president), Dave Lawrence (candidate for Hamilton South), Marjorie Pinney, and Joan McIntosh.

Art Shultz, United Auto Workers representative, canvassing for New Party memberships in Toronto, 1961.

Ontario Committee for the New Party. From left to right (seated): OFL vice-presidents Scotty Liness and Mike Fenwick, M.P. Murdo Martin, New Party Club representative Lewis Hanley, Donald MacDonald, Peg Stewart, OFL vice-presidents George Watson and Bill Punnett, and UAW's Art Shultz; (standing): Morden Lazarus, New Party Club representatives Walter Basciewicz and Roy Battagollo, "Doc" Ames, OFL vice-president George Barlow, M.P.P. Reg Gisborn, Henry Weisbach, and OFL president David Archer.

Newly elected NDP leader Donald MacDonald waving to delegates at provincial founding convention, 1961.

NDP election leaflet, 1963.

Keeping the Dream Alive

Introduction

The following is a history of Ontario's democratic socialist party, the Co-operative Commonwealth Federation/New Democratic Party (CCF/NDP), for the years 1951 to 1963. In truth, the study was originally meant to extend into the mid-seventies. Convinced by the paucity of scholarly research on the party for the fifties and early sixties that the period was not fertile ground for the political historian, and persuaded by at least one leading figure in the CCF/NDP that it was not worth spending too much time on these "stagnant" years, I looked forward to moving swiftly through this uneventful decade and into the party's exciting "take off" phase, beginning in the mid-sixties. What I discovered, instead, was a period in the CCF/NDP's history as compelling and dramatic as any other and which, as a result, warranted a more in-depth examination. Devastated by the results of the 1951 provincial election and reeling from several years of declining membership and funds, the party underwent a painstaking, innovative, and, at times, heroic rebuilding process – one which was to culminate in the CCF's metamorphosis into the NDP almost exactly ten years later, but which would only begin to bear fruit after 1963. These were, it is true, years of stagnation. This study hopes to make clear, however, that there is as much to be gained from studying failure as from studying success. Unlike so many other political histories, therefore, this is not a story of triumph. It is, rather, a story of struggle and survival, of people fighting to save an institution that they believed had been, and could still be, a force for positive social change in a province that had traditionally accepted change in only measured doses.

Another reason for focusing on the history of the party over this relatively short period is, as mentioned, the scarcity of secondary literature available for these years. At present, only four book-length studies deal directly with the Ontario CCF/NDP or aspects thereof: Gerald Caplan's *The Dilemma of Canadian Socialism*, a history of the party from its inception in the early thirties to its sudden rise and fall in popularity during the Second World War; Gad Horowitz's *Canadian Labour in Politics*, an account of the relationship between organized labour and the CCF up to the mid-sixties; Leo Zakuta's *A Protest Movement Becalmed*, a brief analysis focusing largely on the immediate postwar years; and J. Terence Morley's *Secular Socialists*, the only broad survey of the Ontario party from its foundation through to the 1970s.[1]

Of the four, only the Zakuta and Morley studies discuss, albeit briefly, the history of the CCF/NDP during the 1950s and early 1960s. Their main failing, however, is the lack of genuine historical analysis. As works of social science, their approach tends naturally to be more analytical and theoretical than evolutionary or descriptive. Different aspects of the party, whether that be structure, ideology, or leadership, are lopped off and analysed separately over a number of years in order to confirm a predetermined hypothesis-model; they are very much, as Zakuta's subtitle declares, "studies of change." While this approach provides useful generalizations about these party aspects, the reader too often learns little about the "how" and "why" of the changes. Morley, for example, imposes a rather dubious theoretical model – called the "secularization" hypothesis – upon a complex morass of data in order to prove that the CCF/NDP has developed in a manner analogous to the human personality: that is, from a phase of immaturity, or isolation from the world around it, to one of maturity, in which it successfully adapts to its sociocultural milieu while maintaining its distinct character. It is this supposedly non-deterministic process, marked above all by the interaction of the stable party personality with the surrounding environment, to which Morley attributes the development of the CCF/NDP. But in trying to link that development to the evolution of the human personality, which on an intuitive level alone is difficult to accept, Morley obscures the true nature of the changes that the party underwent. Without giving more than a vague outline of the psychological dynamic, he identifies the period 1951–1964 as the CCF's "Quest for Respectability." However, as with his other so-called stages of growth, this so-called "Quest for Respectability" is inadequate as a category for organizing and making sense of the variety of phenomena in this period; indeed, it is so amorphous that it can easily characterize almost any other phase of the party's growth. Furthermore, for a book that also claims to explain the development of the CCF with reference to its "external world," there is surprisingly little development of the historical context, including the party's ongoing relationship with organized labour. In short, because Morley substitutes a theoretical strait-jacket for solid historical analysis, his study sheds little light on the reasons for the CCF/NDP's evolution.

Zakuta's study is better, although it, too, suffers to some extent from a lack of historical analysis, as well as a fair degree of personal bias.[2] The general thesis – that by 1961 the CCF had become a "becalmed" protest movement insofar as it "developed much of the outlook and structure of the 'old parties'" – is only partially convincing. Zakuta presents little analysis to indicate a rightward shift in party ideology, and although the central leadership did play a more prominent role in party affairs during the fifties and early sixties (for reasons other than those presented by Zakuta), it is not clear that over the decade as a whole the party devoted more of its time and resources than before to winning elections and less time to discussing socialism. Zakuta's secondary thesis – that this alleged transformation was due to the strong influence of a small, informal "administration" or "unofficial leadership" of about a dozen individuals, known for their "right wing orientation and close connections with the trade unions" – is even less persuasive. His description of this powerful inner circle, lurking in the shadows, determining the composition of the official leadership, and moving CCF policy to the right in accordance with the labour movement's wishes, is at best vague; little solid evidence is offered to substantiate the charge of domination.[3] Even if we assume the existence of these two phenomena – an informal leadership clique dominated by the trade unions, and a more moderate, conservative party – Zakuta does not demonstrate a causative connection between them.

Clearly, therefore, the usefulness of the above studies as histories *per se* of the Ontario CCF/NDP is rather limited, whether because of their narrow scope or the particular scholarly method employed. Hence, the method chosen for the present study emphasizes, chronologically and precisely, those developments between 1951 and 1963 that appear to have been the most significant, in terms of the party's survival, and the most prominent, in terms of their relevance to the party's everyday concerns. In other words, rather than dissect the party's "anatomy" and give equal emphasis to its standard components, I have chosen to deal holistically with the CCF/NDP: to treat it as a unit in which changes to one component, such as party ideology, are related to changes in other components or to important external factors, such as economic

vicissitudes and world events. The goal, of course, is to better understand how and why the CCF evolved as it did during this period.

In adopting this approach I have been forced to concentrate heavily
on a single theme: the role of the provincial leadership in trying to
rebuild, maintain, and expand the party's membership, finances, and
public support, that is, its *basic* organization. There are two reasons
for this. Because of the decision to highlight the significant and salient
events in the CCF/NDP between 1951 and 1963, and because basic
organization was clearly the main activity of the CCF in this period,
and *had* to be given the uncertainty of the party's very survival, hence
the emphasis on leadership-directed organization. Other themes were
present and will be discussed in turn, but the overriding theme of the
period 1951 to 1963, simply because it consumed so much of the time
and energy of the party, particularly its leaders, was this business of
basic organization.

A more academic reason for focusing on the theme of organization
is that the subject of party organization in general has been neglected
by historians and social scientists alike. Writing at the turn of the
century, the renowned political theorist James Bryce observed that
"although political parties are as old as popular government itself,
their nature, their forces, and the modes in which they have been
organized have received comparatively little [scholarly] attention."[4]
Unfortunately, almost a century later, this is still largely the case. Until
very recently, political histories have dealt almost exclusively with the
legislative activities of parties, their electoral performance, and their
leading public figures. Even in studies of the CCF/NDP, where one
might expect to find a treasure trove of information on something as
vital to the party as organization, the focus has been on elections,
ideology, leadership, and party structure. Some of these subjects are
related to the question of organization, to be sure, but the topic itself
has rarely been given the detailed attention it deserves.

There are, of course, exceptions. Several articles have been written
about CCF organization at specific moments in its history, primarily
during pivotal elections or by-elections, and several dissertations
examine party organization at the local level, although in cursory
fashion.[5] In addition, Seymour Martin Lipset's classic study of the CCF
in Saskatchewan, *Agrarian Socialism*, looks in some detail at the organizing activities of cooperatives and other agrarian bodies in building
the foundation for the CCF's impressive organization in that province.
Bits and pieces of information on the nature of CCF organizing activities can also be found in several political memoirs. For example,
David Lewis's, *The Good Fight*, provides a lively insider's view of
membership recruitment, fund-raising, and political education at the

federal level from the author's unique vantage point as CCF national secretary between 1936 and 1950. As well, Donald MacDonald, leader of the Ontario CCF/NDP between 1953 and 1970, has recently issued his memoirs. Although they deal primarily with his years as leader of the CCF caucus at Queen's Park, the earlier chapters detail his travels across Canada in the immediate postwar years as the party's national organizer and treasurer, and his work in creating the NDP in the late 1950s.[6] Generally speaking, however, most of the work on party organization has focused on other third parties and, to a lesser extent, on the Liberal and Conservative parties. So in addition to outlining the driving force behind the CCF/NDP's evolution in these years, this present study should shed some much needed light on the question of party organization.

The account that follows has as its starting point the provincial election of November 1951. In many ways, this event was a dramatic turning-point for the party. Going into the campaign, the CCF had held the position of Official Opposition for five of the previous nine years and had averaged a popular vote of 26 percent over the last three elections. But when the dust settled and the votes were counted, the party found itself reduced to a mere two seats in the legislature, one ahead of the fourth-place Communist party. Shocked and disillusioned with the sudden turn of events, party leaders and rank-and-file members alike searched frantically for answers; they concluded that the problem was largely one of weak basic organization. With membership, finances, and the number of CCF clubs having fallen dramatically in a number of ridings since 1949, it was clear that the party lacked an organization strong enough to convey its message, raise much needed funds, or get its supporters to the polls on election day. But the party was also aware that the organizational decline was merely symptomatic of a more serious and less easily solved problem: the severe disillusionment and apathy a growing number of party members had suffered after the CCF's plunge in popularity, following the heady years of the mid-forties. The fear of postwar recession and the warmer feelings toward Canada's wartime Communist allies in the Soviet Union, both of which had fueled support for the party during World War Two, quickly gave way in the late forties to a complacency borne of unprecedented prosperity, as well as a fear of left-wing movements based on the perceived threat of international communism. The quick reversal in the party's fortunes proved too difficult for many of the rank and file to endure, and they either allowed their membership to lapse or allowed themselves to fall into inactivity.

One thing was certain, particularly in the minds of party leaders: if the disintegration of the party's basic organization was not reversed, the CCF would not survive as a political entity. The party had to be rebuilt and, given the general feeling of lethargy at the local level, the reconstruction had to be directed by the central leadership. In 1952, therefore, the Provincial Office shifted its organizational emphasis from promoting membership education and recreation to recruiting new members, renewing old ones, and raising money. The new emphasis on money and members, however, created a strong backlash in the party from the individuals opposed to those so-called purely "organizational" concerns. For the CCF to regain its popularity and organizational strength, argued the dissidents, it had to talk more about basic socialism. This would foster a core of well-versed socialists, who would then embark on a mission to convert others to socialism. The newly converted would, in turn, join the party and become recruiters themselves; through this essentially educative process, the problem of membership and finances would be solved. In the end, the issue was decided by the membership in convention, where the Provincial Office's "organize first, educate later" method prevailed. This, too, was an important turning point for the Ontario CCF. The forces of organizational conservatism and reform battled it out, with the new emphasis on membership recruitment and finances (directed by the Provincial Office) accepted as an essential element in the party's quest to revive its fortunes. It was a decision that was to shape the party's organizational activities for the next twelve years and beyond.

However, many dissidents, unhappy with the decision, accused the leadership of attempting to increase its control over party affairs, at the expense of internal democracy and socialist principles. Here, once again, the "iron law of oligarchy" was thought to be at work.[7] But these critics, along with their intellectual mouthpieces, people such as Frank Underhill and Leo Zakuta, were seeing demons where none existed. The provincial leadership's decision to take responsibility for reviving the movement was not part of the inevitable, machiavellian drive for power that political theorist Robert Michels and others insist is endemic to all parties. Rather, the decision was purely pragmatic. Given the widespread lethargy at the local level, CCF leaders reasoned that unless they initiated the process of rebuilding, no one else would. They desired not to aggrandize or consolidate their power; quite the opposite, in fact. They hoped to restore the strength and power of the constituency associations so that *less* responsibility for organizing and financing the party would rest on their shoulders. Nor was the democratically sanctioned decision to find new members and raise money based on either political opportunism or personal enrichment, for the CCF was far from power and most CCF leaders received no remuneration for their services. It was based, instead, on a straightforward and earnest desire to save the party. The centralization of responsibility and the marginally larger "bureaucracy" needed to administer the new organizational program, in the form of two full-time provincial organizers, were seen as the necessary means to that very basic end. In short, whatever relevance the "iron law of oligarchy" may have had in the context of European socialist politics at the turn of the century, it was not a factor in the CCF's important first step along the road to recovery.

The evolution of the party in the dozen or so years that followed, therefore, can best be understood as a series of increasingly innovative and sophisticated attempts to rebuild the party's basic organization, *including* the encouragement of socialist discussion among the rank-and-file members. Zone and poll committees; annual membership and finance drives; regional educational conferences; new program statements; the concentration of resources in key ridings; the election of a new, more vigourous provincial leader – all were attempts to attract members and funds to the party, so that the party could enter the next election campaign with a stronger organizational base and perhaps make some gains at the polls. All were functions of the "mass" organizing impulse that drove the leadership and consumed most of the party's time and resources.

But for the most part the CCF fought a losing battle, as perpetual rank-and-file apathy thwarted the vigourous efforts of the Provincial Office to stimulate the riding associations into assuming greater organizational responsibilities. Many of the new members who entered the party in the mid-fifties through such gimmicks as the "CCF Brigade," a blatant effort to lengthen the party's membership list, were offset by an even larger number who left the party as a result of the failure of complacent riding associations to renew memberships. If Whitaker's "government party" concept[8] can be applied to the Ontario CCF in the 1950s, the party had become the "leadership party," a largely extra-parliamentary political organization in which most of the fund-raising, publicity, and other organizational duties were combined in the highest levels of the party's organizational structure – not by choice, but by necessity.

By 1956, after a nationwide soul-searching exercise, the national CCF decided to introduce a new organizing technique into the Ontario CCF's bag of tricks: image. To some extent, the question of image had always been a concern of the party; but in the last half of the decade, image manipulation had become the party's main method of rebuilding its organization. The goal was to transform the CCF's image from that of a doctrinaire, Depression-inspired "class" party, to that of a liberal-minded, modern, and broadly based "people's party." This subtle but significant shift in the national CCF's approach to political

organization gave birth to the Winnipeg Declaration of 1956, achieving its highest expression in the creation of the New Democratic Party
exactly five years later. The Ontario CCF, although initially reluctant
to change its ways, was by 1961 a master practitioner of the politics
of image. Beneath the carefully cultivated image of a "new" party,
with strong representation from organized labour and the progressive-
minded middle class, lay yet another attempt by the CCF to rebuild its
basic organization. But in the end, this latest technique was also a
failure. By late 1963, the NDP was no further ahead in its membership
levels, popularity, or proportion of legislative representation than it
had been twelve years earlier as the CCF.

Certainly, other themes appear in the history of the CCF during this
period: its repeated failure to advance at the polls, the recurrence of
internal dissent, and the often strained relations with organized labour.
But the main theme remains that of an innovative, leadership-directed
drive to keep the party alive by rebuilding and expanding its basic
organization; almost all of the major initiatives and developments in
the CCF in this period can be linked to this imperative. The proposition
that the CCF evolved as it did largely because it sought to rebuild and
expand its basic organization may nevertheless appear a bit specious,
especially when placed alongside the standard interpretation of the
CCF/NDP – Walter Young's attractive, even mesmerizing "movement/
party" thesis. According to this view, the party is said to have been
shaped by the essentially antagonistic interaction of the movement and
party elements of the CCF, with the party elements prevailing over time.
As the party aged, states Young, "the increasing attention that was paid
to electoral activity, the increasing emphasis on organization, and the
lessened emphasis on education marked the decline of the movement
aspect of the CCF and the predominance of the party aspect. This development reached its zenith in the formation and subsequent political
activity of the New Democratic Party."[9] Few studies of the party have
wandered far from this interpretation.[10]

The problem with the movement-to-party model in relation to the
Ontario CCF/NDP, however, is that it either contradicts or sheds little
light on a variety of historical phenomena. The party's socialist ideology, for example, does not appear to have been diluted during the
period 1951 to 1963. The CCF remained committed throughout this
period to creating a more equitable social order through wealth redistribution and the advancement of civil liberties. Nor was there an
increasing neglect by the party leadership of educational matters.
When the circumstances called for intense membership discussion of
policy, such as after the Winnipeg Declaration was issued and during
the formation of the New Party, party leaders encouraged this as a

way of stimulating membership interest in the party or creating publicity to attract new members. In fact, the degree of membership education, measured by the amount of party literature ordered from the Provincial Office by the riding associations, was substantially higher in the mid-fifties than earlier in the decade. At other times, particularly when membership figures and revenues took a sudden turn for the worse, fund-raising and membership recruitment would receive priority. It is not clear, furthermore, that the CCF paid more attention to "electoral activity" over time. The party simply did what it could with the resources, always insufficient, that it had at its disposal. As a result, much more money and effort went into the 1951 campaign, for instance, than into the subsequent election, because of the party's weaker financial state by 1955. Finally, to say that the party gave more attention to "organization" over time, is not really saying much at all; that is, if one defines "organization" as it should be defined – in broad terms – since the primary task of all political organizations is to organize support by whatever means they consider most effective, including membership education. All of this is not to suggest that the movement/party thesis is invalid. Perhaps a wider chronological framework would substantiate it. What it does suggest is that such a model fails to shed much light on the evolution of CCF/NDP at a time of rising prosperity and Cold War anti-communism – when one might indeed have expected a more party-oriented transformation.[11]

Instead, the best explanation for the numerous party phenomena of this period is the concern of the provincial leadership with basic organization – with simply keeping the party alive under adverse circumstances. If this seems too mundane, perhaps it is because the existing literature on the party is so deterministic, so firmly attached to ascribing the party's evolution to natural "laws" of institutional behaviour of one sort or another – whether Michel's law of oligarchical control, Young's movement-to-party model, or Morley's secularization thesis – that the most persuasive explanation turns out to be the most obvious. The methods devised by the leadership to rebuild, maintain, and expand the party became more complex and innovative as time went on, to be sure, but the object was always the same: to preserve the CCF as a viable political entity so that it might one day win the prize and bring Ontario one step closer to the cooperative commonwealth. The following is an account of this struggle.

1 Into the Wilderness

"It's a landslide!" came a shout from the crowded floor of the premier's campaign headquarters, to which a more restrained, but equally pleased, Leslie Frost replied with a grin, "You know, you might be right about that!"[1]

As the results poured in on that unusually mild but rainy evening in late November 1951, it became quite clear that Leslie Frost's Progressive Conservatives were indeed on their way to a massive victory, the most resounding in the province's history. By 10:30 P.M., the newly elected premier had humbly accepted his party's overwhelming mandate and graciously thanked all those who had worked on his behalf. Within minutes, he found himself atop a large, red fire truck, smiling and waving at the throngs of jubilant supporters who cheered and honked their horns in celebration as the traditional victory procession inched its way through the rain-soaked streets of Lindsay, Ontario, his home town.

The scene was a much more somber one some one hundred kilometres to the southwest. There, in the riding of York South, a black cloud loomed over the small campaign headquarters of CCF leader Ted Jolliffe, signalling the end of his party's "Golden Age." A tired Jolliffe had spent most of the evening huddled in a chair beside a little radio, smoking one cigarette after another and saying very little as he listened attentively to the grim electoral returns. "It doesn't look good," was his only comment to a reporter's query. In a nearby committee room his wife, Ruth, and party M.P. Joe Noseworthy tabulated election results, while party workers waited anxiously for further news. But as the results became known, any hope party supporters may have had when the polls closed at 7:00 P.M. quickly waned. Hope turned to anxiety, which soon became shock and despair. The party had suffered near annihilation.

Uncertain of his own fate in York South, Jolliffe nevertheless made his way to the Boys' Band Hall on Eversfield Avenue, where his supporters were assembled for what they had hoped would be a victory speech. As he entered the hall and began advancing through the throng, someone shouted "Are we downhearted?", to which the crowd responded emphatically, "No!" Upon reaching the podium, Jolliffe apologized for being late and, showing no signs of disappointment, launched into a brief pep talk. "My faith in the CCF cause was never greater than it is tonight," he told his listeners. "We've had our ups and downs, and we'll have more. But as sure as day follows night, the people of Ontario will some day come to see the need for a movement of democratic socialism such as ours, not only in opposition but in government." That day must have seemed a long way off to all who heard Jolliffe that evening, especially after the media announced that their leader had been beaten in his own riding.[2]

On 22 November 1951, Ontario voters gave the Conservative party the largest majority ever given to an Ontario political party – seventy-nine of a possible ninety seats. The Liberal party, led by Walter Thomson, fell from thirteen seats to seven, becoming the new Official Opposition. As for the CCF, it was able to salvage only two of the twenty-one seats it had won in 1948. The two remaining seats were won by the Labour Progressive Party (LPP, i.e., Communist), and by a candidate running on a Liberal-Labour ticket.[3] To add insult to injury, the leaders of the Liberals, CCF, and LPP all lost their seats in the Tory landslide.

Even the Tories were surprised at the number of seats they had won, many at the expense of CCF candidates in urban-industrial ridings which the latter had been expected to win. The CCF lost three seats in Hamilton and one in Windsor. In Toronto and the Yorks, a party stronghold, it lost all eleven of the seats it had held in the last legislature and, along with them, some key party figures, including labour leaders Charles Millard and Eamon Park, as well as the long-time farm spokesperson, Agnes Macphail. Indeed, the only successful CCF candidates were Bill Grummett in Cochrane South and Tommy Thomas in Ontario. "A lot of things happened that I didn't expect to happen," commented Frost on the night of his tremendous victory. "A lot of pretty nice people have fallen by the wayside."[4]

No one was more surprised at the outcome than the CCF, for it had approached the election with much confidence. Although Jolliffe had refused to predict publicly how the party would fare, he had been less reticent among the party faithful. In May he told the province's largest labour organization, the Ontario Federation of Labour (OFL), that "there is a total of 57 seats which are potential CCF wins, or 11 more than the number necessary to form a government"; several months later, he was declaring before party members that "there will soon be another provincial election, and when it comes, the possibility of electing a CCF government in Ontario is greater than most people realize." Most CCFers had been inclined to believe him. After all, they reasoned, the party had gained sizeable representation and formed the Official Opposition in two of the last three provincial elections; furthermore, with the articulate and forceful Jolliffe at the helm, the party had performed well in the legislature.[5]

Two more immediate factors, though, had fed the CCF's feeling of impending success. The first was the election campaign itself. Led by Jolliffe, a veteran of four campaigns, the CCF ran a spirited, issue-oriented campaign. Officials from all levels of the party undertook a hectic schedule of speeches before CCF-nominating conventions and groups of party supporters across the province. But Jolliffe was by far the most active. He delivered talks on a multitude of subjects, such as subsidies to municipalities, hospital care, housing, education, old age pensions, and party financing – all of which were highlighted in the party's election manifesto, "Twelve Steps to a Better Ontario," and several of which were quite timely. With the tremendous growth in Ontario's urban areas after the war, and the accompanying demands for essential social services, municipalities had been forced to raise taxes to meet their higher expenditures. During the campaign, therefore, Jolliffe criticized the Tories for not helping to ease the municipal tax burden with larger provincial subsidies, and promised an immediate subsidy amounting to 10 percent of existing municipal expenditures if elected. As well, the province's rapidly growing population required greater health care facilities, and the CCF was quick to make the most of this too. Both leader and candidates stressed the need for more hospital facilities, as well as a public hospital insurance plan to ease access to these facilities. The Saskatchewan CCF government's record in this area was used over and over as an example of what the CCF would do if given the opportunity.[6]

The weak performance of the Liberal party's cocky and occasionally bombastic leader, Walter Thomson, had added to the CCF's optimism. The fifty-six-year-old Pickering, Ontario, lawyer and former Liberal M.P., with his endless promises and unsubtle wooing of the *Toronto Star* (he had echoed its call for the repeal of the Charitable Gifts Act of 1949), had raised the ire of political and media opponents alike and done much to undermine his credibility with the voters. During the course of his campaign, Thomson was further handicapped by a number of imprudent and contradictory statements. On the one hand, he promised to reduce government spending significantly, by slowing down the construction of schools, for example; on the other, he blamed Frost for the deaths and insanity of elderly persons who could not be accommodated in existing health care facilities, which he promised to expand. At one point, he broadened his charge of negligence to include the entire health care community. Moreover, his portrayal of the affable and avuncular Leslie Frost as a callous penny-pincher (when he wasn't accusing him of squandering tax dollars) was probably difficult for the average Ontario voter to swallow. Also, the Tories and CCF made much of the fact that, as an M.P., Thomson had voted against many of the same things he was now promising to implement. Thomson's performance, in turn, alienated many traditional Liberal supporters, thereby reducing the pool of campaign workers and donations for the party.[7] Overall, Walter Thomson was perhaps the CCF's greatest asset.

The CCF campaign was also helped by the fact that in spite of the Cold War hysteria gripping much of the Western world at the time, red-baiting was not common during the campaign, not even in the staunchly conservative *Globe and Mail*. Perhaps it was thought redundant under the circumstances, or perhaps the unconscionable antics of United States Senator Joe McCarthy fostered an aversion in Canada to such tactics. In any case, the absence of anti-socialist rhetoric was in marked contrast to the campaigns of the war years, which had contributed significantly to the party's dramatic decline in the mid-forties.[8] Also, very few instances occurred in which the LPP tried to align itself with the CCF. Such associations, whether deliberate or not, had proven lethal to the party in the past.

Overall, the CCF's skilled performance and good luck during the campaign were reflected in the opinion polls. A poll taken early in the campaign gave the Conservatives 48 percent support of decided voters, with the Liberals and CCF garnering 40 percent and 11 percent respectively. A poll released several weeks later, however, revealed that the CCF's popularity had more than doubled, at the expense of both parties, especially the Liberals. Some of this swing was no doubt due to the party's stronger canvassing efforts, which accompanied all elections, but much of the credit belonged to the CCF's campaign performance and the weak showing of the Liberals under Thomson.[9]

The second reason for the CCF's hopeful spirit in 1951 was the close cooperation between itself and the OFL just prior to the election, as well as the substantial assistance it received from the OFL's Political

Action Committee (PAC). Formal cooperation at the executive level between the CCF and the OFL began in February. At that time the party's Provincial Council instructed the secretary "to take whatever steps necessary to further the relationship between the trade unions and the CCF." This was followed three months later by the establishment of a Joint Committee consisting of OFL-PAC and CCF executive officers who met informally each month to coordinate political activities and foster closer CCF-union relations at the local level.[10]

Insofar as it represented a departure from the ad hoc, sporadic cooperation of the past, the Joint Committee seemed to herald a new beginning in CCF-labour relations. It also served as a model for cooperation at the local level. One of the first instances of such cooperation, and one of the more successful, was a conference in Niagara Falls in June, at which representatives from three CCF riding associations and local unions in the region agreed to establish their own joint committee. In the following months, this committee coordinated efforts to increase individual membership in the party and appointed a subcommittee to oversee the activities of local unionists and CCFers during the election campaign. In particular, both sides agreed that "there should be consultation between the CCF and trade unions about all matters affecting the [upcoming provincial] campaign, including the nomination of candidates." This pattern of cooperation, starting with a joint conference and leading to the formation of joint committees, was duplicated in a number of areas across southwestern Ontario over the summer and fall of 1951, mostly in such places as Windsor, Hamilton, Toronto, and Oshawa, where CCF and union members were concentrated in large numbers and where a tradition of labour-CCF cooperation existed. Even in some of the less industrialized areas, such as the ridings of Lambton West and Waterloo North, unionists and CCFers were meeting one another for the first time.[11] The degree of cooperation between the CCF and the OFL at all levels, therefore, was impressive and unprecedented.

Although the CCF made the first move in this process of *rapprochement*, its eagerness to establish closer ties with organized labour was easily matched by the OFL's desire to help the party through its PAC. The PAC, comprised of representatives from all affiliated unions in the province, had been established in 1948 to implement the CCL's 1943 endorsement of the CCF as "labour's political arm." To this end, the PAC had two main functions: to educate OFL members about any political matters that could affect their interests, such as the workings of government, the CCL's legislative demands, and the nature and performance of Canada's political parties; and, more importantly, to secure the financial and electoral support of its members for the CCF.

The OFL-PAC thus played a leading role on behalf of the CCF during the provincial and federal elections of the late 1940s, after which responsibility for political action in Ontario shifted to the OFL's parent body, the CCL. In April 1951, however, the CCL shifted responsibility for political action back to the provincial federations of labour, who were now free to re-establish their own PACs. Shortly after, the OFL appointed Henry Weisbach, secretary-treasurer of the United Steelworkers of America (USA) and also chair of the CCF's Organization Committee, as PAC director for the province.[12]

Led by Weisbach, the PAC began preparing for the upcoming provincial election in July. It launched a drive among local unions and labour councils to raise money for the campaign; then, in the months that followed, it sent out staff representatives not only to assist labour councils and local unions in establishing PACs, but also to arrange meetings between local PACs and CCF riding associations for discussions of election activity.[13] Once the election was announced, the PAC intensified its efforts. It distributed over $20,000 to local PACs, primarily in the cities and towns between Windsor and Oshawa, to pay for CCF publicity, cover the election expenses of candidates, and hire organizers. The strongest local effort was made in Windsor. Here, PACs of the United Automobile Workers (UAW) locals, representing over 25,000 workers, joined with the Windsor CCF to form a joint committee to coordinate the city-wide campaign. The UAW also assigned several high-ranking staff members from its Windsor locals to promote the CCF within their unions, while providing free radio air-time to the party during the last week of the campaign. The PAC's main contribution, however, was the provision of union candidates for the CCF, particularly in ridings where the party had little or no organization. Forty-two, or more than half, of the party's seventy-seven candidates, in fact, were CCL union members. In short, all indications confirmed the *Globe*'s observation that "this has been the most intense political campaign put on by the OFL" and strongly suggested that the OFL-PAC would deliver the labour vote to the CCF.[14]

As a result, the CCF's expectations of labour support were high. "The contribution of PAC to this campaign is on a much broader scale than in either 1948 or 1949," the *CCF News* told its readers. "The union locals themselves are participating more actively in most centres, and this may turn the scales in a number of industrial centres." Party president Miller Stewart told his colleagues on the council that "there was a good possibility of winning 3 out of 4 Windsor seats as UAW participation and cooperation with the CCF was very high." Nor did the OFL say much to dampen these expectations. Art Shultz, the UAW-PAC representative, informed party officials that "the potential for CCF support [in Windsor] was very good," while other PAC leaders assured the CCF that, unlike the 1949 federal election, when most OFL members voted Liberal, on election day organized labour would vote CCF.[15]

The CCF had many reasons, therefore, to feel confident about its chances. Past success, a decent legislative performance, a solid campaign led by a well-known and respected leader, and the strong backing of the labour movement all pointed to substantial electoral gains. Yet by no means did party documents for the period reflect an overwhelming sense of optimism. Even the usually irrepressible CCF News was reluctant to herald an inevitable victory too loudly. Despite the positive signs, the party was also receiving some rather ominous signals concerning its organizational strength, the actual extent of labour support, and the mood of the public during the campaign – signals that were difficult to ignore.

The CCF began its election preparations well in advance of the government's official announcement. Shortly after the establishment of the CCF-OFL Joint Committee in May, the party established an Electoral Committee, headed by the chair of the CCF Executive, David Archer, as well as subcommittees on election program, publicity, and financing. More importantly, it hired Fred Young to work as a full-time party organizer. Young, who had been a United Church minister in Prince Edward Island and Nova Scotia in the 1930s, had done some voluntary organizing for the nascent CCF in the Atlantic region. His strong social gospel beliefs had led him to Halifax during the war, where, as general secretary of the YMCA, he provided aid to destitute servicemen, before being recruited by the CCF's national secretary, David Lewis, to be the party's Maritime organizer. But after "beating his head against a stone wall for ... a good ten years in all of the Atlantic provinces," as the then national organizer, Donald Mac-Donald, put it, a frustrated Young had been persuaded by the former to relocate to Ontario, where CCF prospects were better.[16] For the 1951 campaign, he was assigned to work alongside Ken Bryden. Bryden, the son of a famous University of Toronto theologian, brought equally impressive credentials to his work with the party. Trained as an economist, he worked for the federal Department of Labour during the war before joining the first CCF government in Saskatchewan: there, as Deputy Minister of Labour, he drew up and implemented a highly progressive package of labour reforms. In 1949, convinced that the key to the party's national success lay in the heavily industrialized province of Ontario, he returned to become the Ontario CCF's caucus research director. Never known to suffer fools quietly, Bryden was nevertheless a tireless and intelligent socialist; he would eventually replace Morden Lazarus as provincial secretary and later serve nine years as M.P.P. for Toronto-Woodbine.

Young and Bryden's primary objective in the summer of 1951 was to help the CCF find between seventy-five and eighty candidates. What they discovered, however, was that in many parts of the province the organizational machinery necessary to achieve this goal was in terrible disarray. In late July, the Electoral Committee told the Executive that "50 or 60 nominations could be obtained on short notice"; they warned, however, that "there are about 30 ridings which would require a great deal of attention before nominations could be held." This diagnosis, though, only obscured the true severity of the CCF's organizational woes. A comprehensive riding report of April 1951 indicates that, in almost every riding, membership had fallen dramatically since 1948 – from 8,164 at the end of 1948 to 4,128 at the close of 1950 – and that in a large number of ridings the constituency associations had all but disappeared.[17] In others, interest was at such a low level that members rarely participated in such basic party functions as fund-raising, meetings, and membership drives. Overall, at least thirty-seven – or close to half of all – ridings, most of which were located in eastern and north-central Ontario, fell into the intensive care category. About thirty-three ridings were borderline cases, often in the process of rebuilding their membership with the help of the provincial organizers, while the remaining twenty, mostly in south-western Ontario and the far North, were in fairly good condition, insofar as membership levels had fallen at a slower pace and riding associations were still meeting occasionally. Membership levels recovered slightly in 1951, by about 500 members; but by year's end the CCF had still lost approximately 43 percent of its members since 1948.[18]

Why, then, did membership levels fall so precipitously after 1948? The party certainly expected some loss of members after the provincial election of that year, as supporters left the party to pursue other activities until the next campaign, but the severe blood-letting which the CCF suffered in this period requires further explanation. To begin, it is clear that the party lacked competent leadership at the constituency level and, as a result, had to sometimes settle for mediocre riding officers who often cared more about their own personal advancement and gain than about the party or its members. Naturally, this had the effect of driving out dedicated members and keeping potential members away. The Cornwall CCF was a case in point. When the Provincial Office sent part-time organizer Ron Cheffins to investigate the state of affairs in Cornwall during the summer of 1951, the subsequent report noted that neither the president nor secretary of the riding association were carrying out their normal executive duties. Neither one, for example, had called a membership meeting for some time; as a result, they had fallen from favour, leaving a very disillusioned membership who no longer wanted anything to do with the leadership or the party. Nor was the Cornwall CCF alone in its experience. The riding of South Renfrew was also plagued with leadership problems. "Never have I seen the CCF since its inception at such a low ebb in South Renfrew," complained one CCFer to Donald MacDonald, the national treasurer, in April. "McManus [the former riding president] killed the CCF and those [who] worked for him."[19]

One reason for the shortage of talented local leaders was the labour movement's preoccupation with struggles against employers over the issue of the union check-off. In northern Ontario especially, this diverted many capable potential union leaders from the CCF. As a result, the comment "lack of effective leadership; situation complicated by trade union conflict" appears again and again in CCF riding reports to the Provincial Office. Lack of organizational leadership may have been a problem at the provincial level as well. Donald Mac-Donald states flatly that Jolliffe must bear part of the blame for the party's weakened organization in those years. "The party, from 1948 to 1951, was extremely neglectful of the basic organizational needs," he asserts, "and to be frank, part of the problem ... was that Ted Jolliffe did not give the necessary leadership on organization." Mac-Donald acknowledges that the provincial leader was very busy with his legislative duties, but believes that there was "too much of a focus on, and ... glorification of the legislative role." Jolliffe's inability to retain his own seat, says MacDonald, was evidence of this organizational neglect at the top.[20]

A more important reason for the shortage of talented leaders, and for the members' lethargy in general, was the strong feeling of disillusionment that beset the party after the 1949 federal election. Part of this was due to the election itself, in which the CCF lost sixteen seats and elected only one member from Ontario. But a more important factor was the onset of the Cold War. As left-wing movements around the world came under attack – thereby destroying the dream of postwar international cooperation, peace, and harmony cherished by many socialists during the bleak days of World War Two – party members became increasingly disillusioned and apathetic. This problem was discussed at a Provincial Council meeting in February 1951. "People generally have a sense of futility because of the international situation," remarked one member, whose comment prompted another to insist that the party "must start getting the will to win if we are going to have to face an election." By September, though, party leaders were still trying to lift both leaders and the rank and file out of their doldrums. "An important ingredient in the formula for a successful campaign," the Executive told the Council, "is confidence. Council members can help to develop a winning spirit among our supporters if they themselves realize our potentialities for victory." But even the most dedicated party workers became frustrated and indifferent when their efforts to expand, or just maintain, the movement in the face of the growing apathy met with only minimal success. Many could not carry the heavy strain of rebuilding or maintaining a constituency organization with little or no help from other members. One frustrated CCFer in Smiths Falls complained to Donald MacDonald in April 1951: "I haven't time to do all the necessary calling and telephoning and I don't know anyone here who will. I will definitely not call another meeting, as I have not the evenings to waste when no one cooperates ... Last week I was busy every night and I will now leave it to someone else."[21]

The unusually low level of interest within the party placed an added burden on the Provincial Office as well. The latter had to continually send in its busy organizers to jump-start local riding associations. With the party unable to afford to hire enough organizers to ensure that each riding association could continue to perform its necessary functions, such as renewing memberships, collecting money, nominating candidates, and distributing party literature, many riding clubs stagnated or simply fell apart. "It is obviously impossible for [our provincial organizers] to cover all 83 federal constituencies every year or even to do a thorough job in a majority of them," complained the Provincial Council. "This is one of the dilemmas the organizing committee has always faced: if we concentrate on the strong ridings, the weak ones almost disappear; if we work in the weaker ridings, the stronger ridings let up." Organizational stagnation or voids, in turn, meant fewer dollars flowing into the Provincial Office from the ridings; thus it was that much more difficult to hire the organizational staff needed to sustain momentum at the local level. Hence the vicious circle.[22] So while local stagnation was not unheard of even in the best of times, the growing rank-and-file indifference toward the CCF in the period 1949 to 1951 exacerbated the problem.

Nevertheless, the CCF did what it could to reverse the situation before the 1951 election. During the spring and summer, both the provincial and national CCF dispatched a number of temporary organizers around the province to recruit members, revive local riding associations, and, most importantly, find candidates. The work of husband and wife team

Dudley and Denise Bristow in northern Ontario is especially noteworthy. The Bristows managed to obtain close to 500 general and family
memberships worth over $1,200 and succeeded in setting up new riding
association executives in Sudbury, Temiskaming, Nippising, and Timmins, "such that nominations in these areas were now likely," reported
the Organization Committee. Their efforts and those of several others,
including Bryden and Young, led the Organization Committee to conclude, in September, "that on the whole, the organizational picture was
brighter than it has been for a long time."[23]

But the situation in certain parts of the province was still extremely
poor. The party was having a particularly hard time finding candidates,
even token ones, in eastern Ontario, an area not known for its left-
wing sympathies. Earlier that month, the provincial secretary, Morden
Lazarus, informed his federal counterpart, Lorne Ingle, that "generally
speaking ... eastern Ontario is in no better position than it was last
spring" and persuaded the National Office, in conjunction with the
Ottawa CCF Council, to assume the task of finding candidates in that
region. Logistically, this was a good move, but it did not pay dividends.
In many eastern ridings, the party could persuade no one – not even
mediocre candidates – to run under its banner. "I am afraid that the
Eastern Ontario nomination picture is not too bright," wrote a disillusioned Ingle to Lazarus several weeks later. "All efforts at obtaining
candidates in Leeds, Grenville-Dundas and Renfrew East have failed
... [and] we made no effort in Glengarry since we had no contacts
there." He added, perhaps with a note of strained optimism, "Workers
are few in all of these ridings, including Ottawa, this year, but I have
a feeling that nevertheless the campaigns are gathering steam." The
nomination picture was equally grim for the area along Lake Huron
and Georgian Bay.[24] All things considered, the fact that the party was
eventually able to field seventy-seven candidates, albeit with substantial
help from the labour movement, was quite remarkable.

As the party suffered organizationally, so did it suffer financially. A
declining and increasingly apathetic membership resulted, quite naturally, in lower revenues, first from a drop in dues-paying members,
and second, from a decline in membership contributions over and
above general membership fees. Even if members wished to make an
additional contribution, chances were that because party workers in
their ridings were less eager than ever before to work for the party,
the money would never be collected. The Provincial Office was already
having a great deal of trouble persuading local riding leaders to collect
money owing from earlier pledges. An obviously impatient national
treasurer, referring to the Toronto CCF Council's failure to follow up
on pledges made during its spring membership drive, asked Lazarus

whether "somebody, or preferably a committee of two or three, [could] be assigned the specific responsibility of contacting the various Toronto ridings and reviving their enthusiasm so that this is carried through?"[25]

The same lack of grass-roots interest had been evident during the CCF's second annual National Expansion Drive (NED) in the spring of 1951. The NED was devised by the CCF's National Office in 1950 to keep the federal party solvent in the face of declining membership figures. Its prime goal, therefore, was to raise money from party members across Canada; but it was also to sign up new members and renew old ones. The program had not been very successful in its first year, and party leaders were not too optimistic about prospects in 1951. "We will have to make a much greater effort to reach our objective this year," Lazarus warned MacDonald. "I am sure that the money is there but you may find it more difficult to get key workers in these places to spend the time on the planning and preliminary organization [for the drive]." And he was right. Several weeks into the drive, a dejected Lazarus informed Macdonald that "there is so little effective membership canvassing that I am seriously thinking of 'dunning' our ex-members with a series of 'high-pressure' sales talks in letter form." Only a few ridings showed any interest at all in the drive and enthusiasm overall was lower than that of the previous year. As a result, contributions were down 20 percent from 1950.[26]

The shortage of funds in 1951 meant that less money was available for hiring organizers and additional office staff, printing and distributing party literature, and, most important, financing a strong election campaign. In August, the Executive Committee noted that funds were "urgently needed to do enough organizing work to obtain nominations in 20 or 30 of the more difficult ridings as well as to assist the established ridings." It subsequently sent an urgent memo to the ridings, requesting money: "NOW IS THE TIME WE NEED MONEY. Printing and advertising costs are way up and it takes real money to get value and service. Try to send us 10% or 20% of your [election] quota right away." Despite this plea, the party fell $10,000 short of its modest goal of $50,000. Although the underlying cause of the CCF's financial weakness was organizational, the end result was the same: insufficient funds to rebuild the movement and conduct a strong election campaign.[27]

Even the party's closer relationship with the labour movement, one of the more encouraging developments for the CCF in 1951, had its less auspicious side. First, although the degree of CCF-union cooperation in southwestern Ontario was impressive, the situation elsewhere was very different. CCFers in Timmins and Temiskaming, for example, complained that they were "not receiving the cooperation from PAC or the union leadership and that the CCF workers and leadership were being drained off by the unions." One reason, according to Henry Weisbach, secretary-treasurer of United Steelworkers of America (USA) and chair of the CCF organization committee, was that many of the unions in that area were newly formed; they "could not participate too openly in political action at the moment" for fear of creating internal divisions along political lines. Another was that pro-CCF union leaders, who would otherwise be concentrating on CCF activities, were too busy organizing workers and preparing for a possible strike against regional mine owners over the issue of the union check-off. Finally, unionists and CCFers were still bitter over the party's lack of success in the 1949 federal elections; as a result, observed Donald Macdonald, "There has tended to be some back-biting as between trade union organizations and CCFers, growing primarily out of the failure to achieve what appeared to be a sure victory" in that election. Mutual recrimination and lack of cooperation were evident, too, in several eastern Ontario ridings, usually for the same reasons. Even in southwestern Ontario, the eagerness of union members to support the CCF, either actively or otherwise, may have been overstated by OFL and CCF leaders. Shortly after the election, the Provincial Council could note only that "the initial attempt at CCF-union co-ordination both at executive and riding level was ... *reasonably* successful," a far cry from earlier pronouncements and one that was confirmed by the election results, which saw most of the union vote go to the Conservatives.[28]

But labour's less than overwhelming support for the CCF had been foreshadowed in several ways. According to one union member from Brantford, speaking at an NED planning meeting in February, the PAC was spending insufficient time educating workers politically, and too much time pressuring them to join the CCF. As a result, "PAC was not effective in its own union and only succeeded in making rank-and-file workers feel they were being pushed into the CCF." In response, the provincial secretary explained that "PAC was only two years old and had not had time to re-educate the trade unionists" and, further, that "more emphasis on education should be given by PAC." This, plus the fact that the PAC had had trouble raising money for the election from local unions and had had to rely heavily on large loans from the head offices of its international unions, demonstrated that serious political education was needed before organized labour would rally to the CCF banner. That organized labour had swung strongly behind the CCF in the 1943 and 1948 elections was largely due to exceptional circumstances, not to any successful imparting of democratic socialism to the working class; in the first instance, the CCF's promise of postwar security, full employment, and collective bargaining was the drawing card; in the second, Premier George Drew's insensitive treatment of the CCL's annual delegation to the Premier's Office forced labour temporarily back into the CCF camp.[29]

The final bad omen for the CCF was the state of public opinion prior to, and during, the 1951 election campaign. Before the election was announced, the CCF was running at only 8 percent in the polls; before the 1948 campaign, in contrast, its popularity had been double that. And during the campaign itself, despite an increase in CCF popularity, there were unmistakable signs that Ontario voters were quite satisfied with the status quo, the most ominous sign being the absence of controversy or excitement. "Unless there is a sharp change in the short time remaining," observed the *Globe and Mail* a week before voting day, "the campaign should rate as one of the calmest ever. What little heat there has been does not seem to have communicated itself to the great bulk of the voters … The lack of public excitement attending the election would seem a more favourable sign for the government than for the opposition parties. It suggests there is no demand for a change."[30] This complacency was reflected in the low voter turnout, as only 64.6 percent of eligible voters went to the polling booth in 1951, compared to 71.5 percent and 67.0 percent, respectively, in the two previous contests.[31]

How, then, did all these negative factors account for the CCF's poor showing in the 1951 election? Actually, if one disregards the party's meagre legislative representation – a misleading indicator of popularity in a single-member plurality electoral system in any case – and looks only at its popular vote (19.1 percent, compared to 26 percent in 1948), the decline in CCF support does not appear to be that serious. Nevertheless, the results were a near-fatal blow to an already faltering party, and CCF stalwarts were determined to find out what had gone wrong. The most common explanation articulated by party leaders in the days following the election was that the CCF had been beaten by a low voter turnout. "The vote that stayed at home," declared the CCF *News* in December, "beat the CCF members in 14 out of (the) 19 seats which the CCF lost in the recent election." The evidence was straightforward: in these fourteen ridings the Tory vote stayed the same as in 1948, but the CCF vote declined. Therefore, the reasoning went, if the party had been able to get its supporters to the polls, it would have won these seats again. Unfortunately, this explanation makes little sense. It assumes that those who stayed at home on election day would have voted for the CCF, when in fact they could, and probably would, have voted for the Tories, or perhaps the Liberals. Underlying this assumption was the belief that Ontario voters' party preferences were fixed and that it was just a matter of getting people to the polling booths, a rather naive belief, and one that distracted the party, at least initially, from a more realistic and insightful analysis of its defeat. Moreover, it is difficult to discern any correlation between voter turn-out and CCF success in this period. In 1943, when the party won a record thirty-four seats and formed the Official Opposition, the turn-out was a meagre 57.9 percent. In 1945, when it was reduced to eight seats, the turnout was a phenomenal 71.5 percent. And in 1955, when it captured only three seats, the turnout was only 60.6 percent.[32]

A slightly better analysis of the results came once the party had had time to recover from the initial shock of defeat. Some suggested that the string of federal and provincial elections since 1943 had virtually exhausted the energy and resources of the party. Others felt that insufficient publicity was the cause, or that the CCF had not stressed its democratic socialist philosophy enough to distinguish itself from the two old parties.[33] However, in view of some of the more glaring weaknesses within the party as well as certain external factors, these problems appear to have been of secondary importance at best.

Clearly, the main factors in the party's defeat were those that had plagued the party throughout 1951 and into the election campaign: the failure of the PAC to deliver the labour vote and the organizational weakness caused largely by the apathy and indifference of the membership. The results of the election in urban-industrial ridings such as Windsor, Hamilton, and Toronto decisively showed that the OFL-PAC had failed to deliver the rank-and-file vote to the CCF, even when candidates were well-known, respected union leaders with political experience. According to Weisbach, "Trade union Political Action was not effective enough in getting out the trade union vote. While I believe that in the industrial ridings we have been able to bring out a large number of trade union members, we were not able to translate the plant sentiment for Political Action into a strong desire to come out and vote for labour representatives."[34] Despite the strong backing of the PAC, therefore, most union members were not ready to follow their leaders in support of the CCF.

It is equally clear that the CCF's declining and increasingly apathetic membership, particularly in eastern Ontario, had a great deal to do with the party's electoral misfortune. The election returns show that where the CCF's membership had fallen most and where apathy was greatest – that is, in eastern and north-central Ontario – the party either fielded no candidate or did very poorly. Indeed, it follows that if a significant portion of a party's membership no longer exists or cares, the effect on party popularity apart from these so-called lost individuals is bound to be negative. This is particularly true of protest parties, which, because they are viewed as being different and more or less marginal, cannot count on the automatic support of a large segment of voters and are therefore that much more dependent on their members to find recruits, raise money, and spread the "good word." When these members disappear or lose the will to fight, the party inevitably declines electorally, which results in even more departures, still greater disillusionment, and a more entrenched marginal status.[35] Not all CCF members were apathetic, however. The CCF in St. David riding, for example, had "never had as many new and enthusiastic workers" according to the riding's president. But judging from reports flowing into the Provincial Office before the election, St. David was an exception; the CCF News was to note that, even here, "the old workers were apathetic."[36]

The widespread apathy that infected the CCF before the election was further reflected in the surprising absence of open and prolonged introspection that usually follows in the aftermath of such setbacks. The CCF News, the traditional forum for this therapeutic self-examination, contained very little leadership or rank-and-file discussion of the defeat, prompting an angry letter from Bill Temple, a CCF candidate and former M.P.P. from High Park. "The result of the provincial election was dealt with in a casual, almost flippant manner," he told readers of the News in January 1952. "Surely it must be obvious that the movement has suffered a very serious setback that will have a damaging effect upon the CCF in Ontario and throughout the entire Dominion?"

Several of the party's top leaders looked beyond internal factors to explain the defeat. They argued that economic prosperity and the Cold War, insofar as one or the other bred complacency, apathy, and fear among many voters, were hurting socialist parties everywhere. Economically, Ontario enjoyed unprecedented growth in this period. Driven by postwar consumerism, European reconstruction, and a growing demand for war-related materials, the level of output, productivity, and wages rose quickly, while inflation and unemployment remained low. The resulting increase in standard of living for most people, however, was matched by an increase in complacency.[37] Donald MacDonald recalls that "as you moved into the fifties, you moved into what is sometimes referred to as the Eisenhower era – a desperate yearning to get back to normalcy. [And] in that kind of an atmosphere, public interest in something new in politics dwindles." The Western world's growing hatred of the Soviet Union and communism also undermined CCF support. "It is a period (in) which, throughout the whole of the Western world," Jolliffe told delegates to the 1952 convention, "constructive popular interest in social welfare, in social ownership, in all forms of social progress, is increasingly overshadowed by the clouds of international uncertainty. Domestic issues, national, provincial and local, do not receive the attention they deserve because the world is living in fear – not so much fear of poverty at this time as the fear of war." During World War Two, he observed on another occasion, "we received a lot of support ... for a strange reason, that of sympathy on the part of the public to Russia. Every time the Red Army won a battle our stock went up. Since then, the trend has been the other way." As a result, voters in New Zealand, Australia, and Britain had recently tossed out labour governments. The CCF was simply the latest victim in this worldwide pattern.[38]

Closer to home, some credit must be given to the Tory party, and especially to its popular leader, Leslie Frost, for achieving such an overwhelming victory in 1951. The Tories conducted a smart, if somewhat uninspiring, campaign. Frost ran on his government's record of unprecedented economic growth and good government and, in contrast with his Liberal opponent, who, according to one tally made 116 promises during the campaign, promised only more of the same. Nor was the premier less than a gentleman throughout. Only infrequently did he criticize his opponents, leaving this "dirty" task to his cabinet ministers. Even his opponents were reluctant to attack him personally, focusing instead on gaps in his government's record. Overall, the image that emerged was that of a benign, non-partisan leader looking out for the best interests of all Ontarians. Under normal circumstances, this sort of campaign would have guaranteed victory. In the presence of a brash and incredible Liberal leader, a CCF party riddled with internal problems, and a prosperous but increasingly anxious electorate, however, it guaranteed a landslide.

The 22nd of November, 1951, marked the CCF's lowest point since becoming a political contender in the early forties. With only two seats in the legislature (neither of which belonged to the party leader), a heavy budgetary deficit, a dejected membership, and an organization desperately in need of revitalization, the future did not look bright. Before the election, party leaders had maintained an air of cautious optimism, based on several encouraging factors and developments: the success of the party in contests dating back to the early 1940s; the effectiveness of its caucus (although the media had paid little attention to this); the pledge of total support given by the OFL; and the strong party campaign, led by a dedicated and well-respected leader. Where the party did well on election day, it was largely for these reasons.

Where it did poorly, it was for reasons that had persisted for months, even years: a declining, demoralized membership; insufficient finances; a labour movement whose rank and file were as yet uncommitted to the party; and a popular premier who was right for the times.

While many CCFers were deeply disappointed with the election results, some remained undeterred. "Are we defeated?" asked one member in the CCF *News*, who then continued: "The answer is a confident 'No.' The spirit of socialism stands unchanged. Its aim is still to build a just and free society and a world at peace ... The disappointment will pass. Meanwhile, in greater determination than ever we shall go on." Others, such as Gwen and Stewart Cooke of Hamilton, sent financial contributions to the Provincial Office to help keep it solvent. And Ted Jolliffe, who looked confidently to a future in which organized labour would tie its flag to the party, tried to rouse members with the declaration, "Labour is itself in the process of being born as an organized force in Ontario." He argued, "We have only just begun to do the work which requires to be done among our fellow citizens in industrial Ontario."[39] Time would tell, of course, whether such signs of bravado were justified. But for the moment, they were the only stirrings of hope from a party that had just been banished to the political wilderness.

2 A Party Divided

If the 1951 provincial election left many CCF supporters in shock, for others it simply confirmed long-held suspicions that something was very wrong with the party. Declining popularity, membership, and morale in recent years had made some CCFers restless with the status quo. But as long as the CCF was the Official Opposition, as it had been from 1948 to 1951, critics of the party were reluctant to openly challenge the leadership or demand change. With the recent election disaster, however, the lid came off. The dissent that had been brewing in certain quarters of the CCF since 1949 could no longer be contained, with the result that provincial party leaders and their backers found themselves under attack from disgruntled members on two fronts – both inside and outside the party. The dissidents, driven largely by a nostalgic desire to restore the "movement" dimension to the CCF, in terms of a more decentralized, discussion-oriented, and spirited party, presented a critique based on their perception of actual developments within the party as well as on certain misperceptions fostered by the Cold War anxiety of the period. The end result was a power struggle of near epic proportions.

In the months following the 1951 election, party leaders decided that the answer to the CCF's woes lay in a more continuous organizational effort. "A rash of activity at election time is not good enough in a movement such as ours," the Provincial Council told delegates at the party's annual convention in April. Members had to build the party between elections as well. But because of the low level of interest among the rank-and-file members, especially after the election defeat, the leadership also decided that the initiative for reviving the movement had to come from the top, in the form of paid organizers, directed by the Executive. These organizers would tour the province and try to revive or assist CCF riding associations. But this required money, a commodity in short supply after the election. The financial situation was aggravated by the fact that with only two M.P.P.s in the new legislature, fewer donations could be expected from caucus. Although some CCFers felt money could be saved by reducing office and organizing staff, the majority of the Council and Executive believed this would damage plans to resuscitate the movement. The answer, they agreed, was to use the sympathy created by the party's recent defeat to first establish a more solid financial foundation. "We must not lose sight of the primary job this winter," Morden Lazarus told the party's national treasurer, Donald MacDonald, shortly after the election, "which is to try to build up a steady source of income so that the work on organization can go ahead. If we don't, the so-called work on organization will just be work on money-raising all year round."[1]

Having thus decided that the party's top priority for the next few months would be fund-raising, the Executive adopted a concept devised by Lazarus and the Finance Committee called the "500 Club." The idea was to entice 500 party members to pledge regular contributions of five to ten dollars per month, over and above sustaining and regular membership fees, in return for which they would receive a few "frills," such as free party literature and tickets to party social functions. Ken Bryden and Fred Young began working on the scheme in the new year and by April had signed up 160 members.[2] A further indication of the Executive's short-term emphasis on fund-raising was its decision to allow the Finance Committee to devise the general organizational plans for the year (to no one's surprise, it contained a strong element of fund-raising). In addition to the main task of finding "500 Club" members, Bryden and Young were instructed to help with the annual Sustaining Membership drive in February and the Toronto Membership drive in March. Only when this work was complete were they free to undertake their usual organizing activities.[3]

Although the organizers received their general instructions from the Finance Committee, their *specific* duties for the year were based largely on a set of organizational proposals drawn up by the national treasurer, Donald MacDonald, in January 1952. MacDonald was undoubtedly the strongest proponent, at the federal level of the CCF if not throughout the movement, of "organizing" for success. In March,

having told the National Council quite emphatically that "at this stage
in the history of our movement, no single thing is as important as an
effective meeting of our organizational needs," he recommended the
acquisition of more full-time, paid provincial organizers, using funds
that he hoped to obtain from the labour movement. This would eventually happen, but for the immediate future MacDonald proposed the
establishment of "poll organization," which involved the creation of
"poll committees" for each poll within a riding, either in place of, or
in addition to, regular CCF clubs.[4] The committees, which would act
as local contact points or tentacles of the party, would consist of CCF
supporters within the poll whose main responsibility would be to
attract new members, renew old memberships, and raise money.
"Where [CCF] clubs already exist," explained MacDonald, "the
approach will be that these clubs continue as educational, recreational,
etc., centres, but that henceforth they assume a major responsibility
building poll committees within the area from which their membership
is drawn"; where no club existed in a riding, only poll committees
would be set up. MacDonald assured party members that educational
and recreational activities, which constituted an important part of the
traditional riding club, would not disappear under the poll committee
set-up. In fact, he was hopeful that "if periodic meetings of poll committees, drawing in all or most of the members in the immediate area,
can be developed, this provides a real opportunity for more extensive
educational work than we have ever had before." Nevertheless, for the
short term at least, the more traditional club activities would figure
less prominently, and the main goal of the poll committee structure
would be to help *in this year's Drive to renew memberships and build
the budget.* With an average of 100 polls in each riding, it was clear
that the poll organization plan, if successful, would have meant a
much more complex and extensive party organization, one in which
members of the smallest unit – the poll committee – would, in the
short run at least, focus primarily on expanding membership and raising money.[5]

The CCF also adopted MacDonald's suggestion that the annual
National Expansion Drive (NED) for funds and membership renewals,
a rather unsuccessful event in 1951, be replaced with a "CCF Week"
in each riding. Although the goals of CCF Week were identical to
those of the NED, the duration and methods were new. "The idea,"
MacDonald explained, "is merely to concentrate the [canvassing]
activity into a single week, rather than let it drag on with the result
that often it never gets finished." Expectations were that the combi-
nation of a specific week, with poll organization and extensive
advance publicity, would help achieve optimal results. A successful

canvass, in turn, meant that attendance at the riding association's annual convention – recommended for just after the riding's CCF Week – would be higher, the upshot being sustained enthusiasm among old and new members and more qualified people available for election to the riding executive.[6]

These proposals, then, formed the basis of the instructions the CCF gave to its provincial organizers, and with the help of MacDonald, who toured southern Ontario in February and March, Bryden and Young devoted much of their time during the winter of 1951–52 to promoting poll organization and CCF Week. They also encouraged riding associations to nominate candidates for the next federal election, to study the draft of the federal CCF's new policy statement and, if possible, to begin preliminary canvassing for membership renewals. Where riding associations were dormant or did not exist, Bryden, Young and MacDonald tried to establish contacts with individual party supporters who might form the basis of a poll committee.[7]

But not everyone in the CCF agreed with the leadership's diagnosis of the party's problems or with the resulting prescriptions. In fact, the idea that the party should try to rebuild on the basis of salaried organizers, financial drives, and poll committees – in other words, through what were derided as bureaucratic organizational means directed by the Provincial Office – was anathema to many CCF members. Many blamed the CCF's recent decline on the current leadership's emphasis on these very techniques. The main opposition came from the so-called "Ginger Group," a collection of about twenty-five party members, centred primarily in the Toronto area.[8] Taking its name from the even smaller band of left-wing farmer and labour M.P.s led by the CCF's founder, J.S. Woodsworth, in the 1920s, the Ginger Group was formed in the summer of 1950 in response to the events of the CCF's national convention of that year. At that time, a handful of delegates from Ontario, relying to some extent on distorted media accounts of the convention proceedings, concluded that the party was becoming less democratic in structure and less socialist in philosophy. They criticized, for example, the National Council's *appointment* of many delegates (versus their election by riding associations), the new policy announcements of the National Leader shortly before the convention, and the excessive power of the convention's Resolutions Committee. These developments, they argued, were slowly shifting control over party policy from the rank and file to the national leadership, who were using the new power to dilute CCF principles. Moreover, they were convinced that the members themselves were largely to blame, insofar as many had lost the vigilance which in the past had led to an active interest in policy formation and an undying determination to convert new recruits to socialism; this vigilance and determination would, they felt, have prevented the new trends from arising. But they blamed the leadership, too, for supposedly doing little to revive the party's spirit, preferring instead to aggrandize its power and shift party policy to the right – all of which only served to reinforce rank-and-file apathy and disillusionment.[9]

The dissidents consequently decided to organize all those within the party who shared their concerns. Calling themselves the "Ginger Group of the Ontario CCF," it elected a six-person executive and issued a newsletter. The declared purpose of the Group was, "to arouse the members who are apathetic and bewildered to do some concrete work in their clubs, and in this way encourage critical thinking by our members toward building a stronger CCF Party which will take a clearer socialist stand on foreign and domestic policies."[10] Members were encouraged not only to run for office in the CCF, but also to persuade their respective riding associations to take action along the lines suggested by resolutions passed at meetings of the Ginger Group. Some of these resolutions called for changes in convention procedures, to make the party more democratic, but most dealt with foreign policy. Here, the CCF was asked to support such things as a strong and independent United Nations, a seat for Communist China on the United Nations' Security Council, increased foreign aid to east European countries, and the concept of World Government; opposition to the rearmament of West Germany was also suggested. In general, neither the CCF leaders, nor the OFL seemed very concerned about the emergence of organized dissent within the party, and perhaps with good reason.[11] After several meetings in the fall and winter of 1950–51, at which numerous resolutions were passed and forwarded to the CCF's National Office, little more was heard from the Group until the spring of 1952.

In March of 1952, some of the Group's remaining members, including three original executive members, decided to regroup because they "were alarmed by certain trends in the movement and ... feared that unless those who were opposed to these trends were organized they would be steamrollered at the [Ontario CCF's annual] convention" in early April. All of the Group's members would be attending the convention as delegates, and each of what appeared to be its four main leaders – Bill Temple, Mary Ramsay, True Davidson, and Avis McCurdy – was, or had recently been, a member of either the CCF Executive or the Provincial Council and felt that their views had been continually ignored by their colleagues. The Ginger Group met four times in the month before the 1952 convention to prepare a plan of action.[12]

In general, members of the revived Group were opposed to what they saw as the bureaucratization of the CCF movement. That is, they wanted a return to the days when party workers, including staff and executive officers, were not salaried administrators preoccupied with raising money and signing up new members, but self-sacrificing, dedicated volunteers. Volunteers, they argued, would focus their efforts on educating members in the principles of democratic socialism and on spreading the socialist message among the public at large, all the while maintaining the intellectual independence salaried workers were less likely to enjoy.[13] At a meeting of the CCF Executive Committee in early January, at which members discussed the organizational plans for the coming year, True Davidson emphasized that "the solution to our problems is not more paid workers. We need to revivify the movement. Instead, our tendency seems to be to emphasize money-raising." Mary Ramsay, chair of the CCF's Membership Education Committee, added that "the situation would be more satisfactory if the [organizational] staff spent as much time on educational as on organization work." According to the Ginger Group, the CCF had done poorly in the last election because it had spent too little time discussing and teaching socialism, and too much time "organizing." The dedicated core of long-time party members, they contended, tired of the uninspiring emphasis on membership recruitment and fund-raising over the past few years, had become apathetic and left the party. Thus, the necessary pre-election organizing had not been accomplished.[14]

Members of the Ginger Group were also concerned with what they saw as growing concentration of power in the hands of the party's Executive Committee. This, too, they believed, was a symptom of the cold, mechanical bureaucratization that had infected the CCF in recent years and which, in their view, accounted for the party's overall decline. They suspected that the Executive was exercising excessive control over the general direction of the party and that legitimate democratic dissent and multiplicity of opinion at the grass-roots level were being suppressed. Party policy, to take but one example, was no longer being created by the membership, but by an increasingly intolerant Executive intent on discouraging the unfettered discussion of policies by the rank-and-file members.[15]

The main culprit in this alleged conspiracy was the provincial secretary, Morden Lazarus. Some Ginger Group members felt that Lazarus was simply taking too much upon himself, but most, sensing more sinister motives, accused him of deliberately excluding capable people from key positions on Executive committees so that he could retain ultimate control through obedient stooges. "Morden is the king-pin of the provincial set-up," stated one dissident, "and ... all committees function as he sees fit." As a result, the necessary educational and organizational work of the committees was not being carried out properly. The Ginger Group therefore passed a resolution calling for a limitation and redistribution of the provincial secretary's powers, as well as a motion supporting "the autonomy of the Education Committee" from the Executive.[16]

In what would become a common feature of party dissent in the future, the Ginger Group partly blamed the trade union leadership for the CCF's problems. According to Mary Ramsay, labour leaders did not tolerate a diversity of opinions and were intent on creating a party adhering rigidly to a fixed set of ideas. "They do not believe in flexibility," she told her fellow dissidents, "but in a kind of monolithic party, and they are intolerant of differences of opinion within the CCF." It was because of the unions, several members alleged, that the Ginger Group's views were not widely accepted in the party. Consequently, although the Ginger Group did not call for the exclusion of trade union leaders from the CCF, "because the CCF needs the labour movement," it did advocate the installation of "more progressive people" on the Provincial Council and Executive.[17]

It appears, therefore, that differences between the new and the old Ginger Group were those of emphasis only. Both complained about the apparent centralization of power in the movement, the inattention to membership education, and the general loss of energy at the local level. But while the original Group blamed the situation primarily on the rank-and-file members themselves and seemed more concerned with the so-called moderation of CCF policy that resulted from membership apathy, their successors focused to a greater extent on the Executive's alleged autocracy and inattention to socialist discussion and were less reluctant to blame the leadership for the party's decline. If the watchword of its predecessor was "Keep Left," that of the new Group was "Keep Talking."

The reasons for these subtle differences are not entirely clear. To some extent, they reflected changed circumstances. The disappointing results of the 1951 election no doubt emboldened critics to seek more concrete reasons for the party's precipitous decline, thereby replacing the rather vague notion of rank-and-file "apathy" articulated by their predecessors. Naturally enough, they pointed a finger at the leadership. Moreover, their resolve was likely stiffened, and their criticism focused, by the leadership's decision to pursue remedies that many dissidents believed, now more than ever, had been discredited. The important point, however, is that both sets of dissidents were determined to resist what they perceived to be a tendency toward increased centralization and formalization of the movement, in the form of less rank-and-file discussion of socialism, and a disproportionate emphasis on the soulless mechanics of organization and fund-raising.

How valid were the criticisms and suspicions of the revived Ginger Group? This is a difficult question to answer because the charges themselves were somewhat vague, with the accusers providing few examples. Nevertheless, the main allegation – that for several years the CCF had neglected to promote membership discussion of socialism or current issues – seems to have been accurate. In 1950, for example, the Provincial Office focused exclusively on the provision of leadership schools or workshops to train local leaders in the techniques of setting up viable riding associations; meanwhile, the generally low level of membership education was reflected in the small number of requests received by the CCF Literature Committee, from the ridings, for party literature. As well, in September of that year, the Executive received a letter from the Eglinton CCF – supporters of the Ginger Group – complaining that "the lack of membership education is a major contributing factor in the decline of the CCF" and strongly opposing the fact that the Membership Education Committee had been recently relegated to a subcommittee of the Organization Committee.[18]

Early the following year, the Provincial Office organized a series of lectures entitled "Socialism at mid-century" and planned a number of regional and local study sessions for the fall pertaining to the national CCF's forthcoming draft statement of principles. Because of the election, however, only one session took place and sales of party literature to ridings remained low.[19] After the election, as noted, the party made fund-raising and membership recruitment its top priority.

To some extent, the low level of membership education between 1950 and 1952 was due to the demise during World War Two of the party's former brain trust, the League for Social Reconstruction, which used to provide the CCF with ample material for membership discussion. This, plus the CCF's shortage of funds by the early fifties, and its unwillingness to divert human resources from the party's basic organizational requirements to research, meant a shortage of new educational materials with which to stimulate membership discussion. In any case, the decline in educational activities by 1952 was unmistakable.[20]

Although the charge that the Executive, and specifically the provincial secretary, was "controlling" the party and stifling dissent did contain some measure of truth, the plaintiffs in the dispute cited only a few examples to substantiate this charge. Bill Temple complained that because Lazarus kept a tight rein on who chaired the important Executive committees, "it was difficult to get action on committees," with the result that "the organization and finance committees had done little this year, and ... Morden had done everything." This was certainly true for the post-election period at least. Lazarus, in collaboration with Donald MacDonald, almost single-handedly formulated the party's fund-raising and organizing plans for the year to follow, leaving the chairpersons normally responsible for these tasks with little to do. Before the election, however, most of this work had been done by the capable and independent chairpersons of the Organization and Electoral committees, Henry Weisbach and David Archer, with little intervention from the provincial secretary. Avis McCurdy, the former chair of the Membership Education Committee, also complained of Executive interference, telling her fellow dissidents that at the last minute Lazarus had imposed a "completely new agenda" on a weekend educational conference her Committee had been planning for some time. There is some evidence, too, that the views of dissidents on the Executive were being ignored or played down. Mary Ramsay was correct in noting, for example, that, at the Executive meeting at which the 1951 election results were discussed, the views of those who disagreed with the majority view of the election were not recorded; moreover, when this oversight was raised at a subsequent meeting, the dissidents were treated contemptuously. Several in the Group blamed such intolerance on the behind-the-scenes influence of the trade union leadership.[21] It should be noted, however, that the majority views had not been recorded at the meeting in question either, and that, generally speaking, party meetings recorded all opinions. That members of the Ginger Group were unable to cite further, more serious instances of Executive tyranny, and given that most committees were chaired by respected and capable party members who were not easily pushed around, suggests that the charge was greatly exaggerated.

When assessing the validity of the Ginger Group's numerous accusations, it is also important to keep in mind the essentially democratic structure within which leaders of the party were forced to operate. Sovereignty lay in the annual convention, the "supreme governing body of the movement in Ontario," with "power to make decisions, rules, and regulations which shall govern and regulate the policies and activities of the movement." The convention, in turn, was composed of incumbent Provincial Council members and of delegates elected by riding associations and affiliated organizations. The Council consisted primarily of members elected by the convention and the riding associations, its main function being to carry out the wishes of the membership as expressed in convention resolutions. To assist in this function, the Council elected committees, including the Executive Committee, which managed party business in between Council meetings; it also elected the chairpersons of the committees (until 1952, when this task was left to the Executive, "subject to ratification by Council)." Committees reported their activities to Council regularly, and Council reported to the annual convention. These reports could be referred back for further investigation, and whether accepted by the members or not, were always accompanied by ample discussion. In short, power flowed from the bottom up. The Executive was simply a creature of the Council, which was itself a creature of the membership gathered in convention. In proper democratic fashion, the Executive, Council, and Council committees were obliged to implement resolutions initiated in large part at the riding level and were annually called to account before the membership in convention. Nor was this structure at all threatened by a self-perpetuating clique of party leaders, for the turn-over rate from one year to the next was quite substantial.[22] In this context, then, the power of a single committee or individual should not be exaggerated. With reference to the Ginger Group's allegations specifically, all that can be said for certain is that the CCF was placing less emphasis on political education than in the past, and that after the 1951 election the provincial secretary may have exercised slightly more control than was necessary or desirable.

Nevertheless, the Ginger Group was quite convinced of its beliefs and, as a result of its deliberations, devised a plan of action for the 1952 annual convention. The primary goal was to gain control of the party, by getting as many of their number and supporters as possible elected to the Provincial Council or Executive. From there, the Ginger Group would be able to secure the appointment of favoured candidates to the all-important chairperson positions of the Executive committees, thus ensuring that their views on organization and political education would finally prevail. For the position of party leader, the Ginger Group decided, albeit reluctantly, to support Jolliffe, but agreed that "if a motion were introduced that the post of provincial leader be left vacant for a year, we should support it." For the position of party president, it decided to support Bill Temple over the "administration's" candidate, Ted Isley, because it was felt that Isley, as chair of the CCF Farm Committee, "had followed the official line in almost all cases." True Davidson agreed to stand for vice-president, and the rest of the Ginger Group vowed to run for Council. Not wishing to miss any opportunity to exert influence or get its message across, the Ginger Group also decided who among them would speak to which resolutions and make which amendments.[23]

The showdown between the Ginger Group and the leadership took place at the CCF's eighteenth annual convention in April at Toronto's King Edward Hotel. For the dissidents this was the moment of truth.

They had agreed on their targets and had carefully chosen their torch-bearers. The real test of their support would be the election of officers, and the whole convention edged tensely towards this moment. On the surface, however, all appeared calm. Reports from CCFers at the convention indicate that the debate over resolutions, which always preceded the elections, demonstrated no basic divisions among members over party policy, with one observer lamenting that "the policy resolutions incline to a monotonous pattern." The real battles, it is safe to say, took place behind closed doors, in the closed panel sessions, where according to one insider, the hottest fight was over the role of political education in the CCF, with McCurdy leading the fight for the dissidents.[24]

Nevertheless, it was difficult to hide the party's long-simmering dissatisfaction entirely from public view. The numerous instances of procedural wrangling and confusion which finally forced a weary, gavel-wielding convention chairperson to make way for someone else, signalled that all was not well. This was confirmed when a reporter approached Bill Temple, who happened to be standing within earshot of the party brass at the time, and asked whether he was the Ginger Group leader. "I don't know that I am the leader of, or represent, any particular group," a cautious Temple replied, to which CCF President Miller Stewart turned and snapped, "Will you say you are not a member of any dissident group now?" Still composed and tight-lipped, Temple gave his answer. "I represent, I hope, a broad cross-section of opinion which is not satisfied with the way things are going."[25] It was a prophetic reply.

In the elections that followed, the first position to be filled was that of party leader. Jolliffe let it be known that he would stand, once again, if the party wished. But no sooner had he accepted the nomination when the president of the East York CCF and a Ginger Group member, Phillip Moore, sent shock waves through the convention with his proposal that no provincial leader be elected for the coming year. Oddly enough, Moore explained that because a panel committee had earlier discussed the possibility of providing the leader with a salary for the first time, he felt that "instead of electing a provincial leader this year, we should use the money to hire another organizer." The motion was a direct affront to Jolliffe, who was well-liked by the vast majority of delegates, and as such did not receive the support of more than a dozen delegates. The Ginger Group then decided to present Temple as a candidate to contest the leadership, but perhaps unwilling to risk an embarrassing defeat so early in the elections, withdrew him at the last minute. When Jolliffe was finally acclaimed, for the tenth consecutive year, delegates gave him a five-minute standing ovation (some delegates, however, refused to stand).[26]

Perhaps sensing the restlessness of the delegates, Jolliffe delivered an acceptance speech that seemed to be aimed directly at the Ginger Group and other disgruntled CCFers. The party has many challenges ahead, he declared, but "it is impossible for any provincial leader to carry on without the full and wholehearted support of a very large number of people." In an obvious effort to heal the breach, he stressed the equal importance of both educational and organizational work in the party, but made it clear that too much attention to membership education was dangerous. "We would be making the greatest mistake we ever made," he said in a firm voice,

if we spent the next four or five years in small groups talking to each other and reading to each other, thinking our own thoughts and reading our own literature ... You may spend a pleasant evening and decide whether a paragraph should be changed in the Regina Manifesto, you may enjoy getting the better of someone you have known for twenty years in an argument, but you will do nothing for this movement unless you bring more people into the movement ... We must read more, we must meet more, we must think more, but we must do it in association with our fellow citizens ... because it is by their help and with their participation that we shall go forward.[27]

The message was clear: expand the movement by bringing in new members, and at the same time, try to make them into dedicated socialists. The Ginger Group, who had witnessed the decreasing attention given to political education over the past three years, with no increase in membership to compensate, must have been skeptical.

Then came the main event, the real test of strength for the Ginger Group. The administration's candidate, Ted Isley, would square off against the dissident's candidate, Bill Temple, for the position of party President. Although Temple was known in party circles as the "giant killer" (he had defeated Conservative party leader George Drew in 1948), the dissidents were worried that his strong views on temperance would cut into his support. These fears proved to be groundless. Temple delivered a strong plea for the convention's mandate which, judging from final vote count, appealed to many. "I am taking the stand," he told delegates, "that our party should be more concerned with economic reform than with mere tactics and strategy. In the caucus ... in the past three or four years we have tactic'd to death. I believe that we must gain the support of the broad mass of people in the province who are dedicated to a richer and fuller life." And this, he added, could only be achieved with a program that was both "progressive and militant."[28] When all the votes were counted, Isley had defeated Temple by a narrow 112 to 85 margin. It was an unmistakable sign that the Ginger Group was not simply another loud, but tiny, splinter group in a movement that prided itself on open and critical self-evaluation, but a rallying point for a large number of dissatisfied members.

Although the Ginger Group did not capture the main prize, it did elect two of its own, Bill Temple and True Davidson, to vice-president positions on the eighteen-person Executive, and approximately eight supporters to the much larger Provincial Council. Almost half of the Group's members, therefore, were elected to positions in which they could influence important decisions. But even this may understate the Ginger Group's support at the leadership level. It is likely that many leaders did not wish, for obvious reasons, to be associated with an organized faction such as the Ginger Group, but sympathized with its aims nonetheless; this was true of at least one other member of the Executive.[29] Evidence of even broader support was also apparent in the Executive's decision in August (at Temple's urging) to invite the controversial leader of the British Labour Party's left-wing faction, Aneurin Bevan, to speak under CCF auspices. Bevan, whose views were well known, had served as a model for many CCF dissidents in the early fifties. Fearing that Bevan would only fan the flames of internal dissent, therefore, several CCF leaders, as well as the National Office, strongly advised against the invitation.[30] The advice was ignored, but in the end Bevan declined the invitation, thereby putting the matter to rest. Clearly, support for the Ginger Group at the highest levels was not restricted to its official members.

One final manifestation of Ginger Group dissent occurred shortly after the convention and stemmed from the party's decision to pay Ted Jolliffe an annual salary for his services as party leader. After the 1951 election, in which Jolliffe lost his seat, the party decided – and Jolliffe concurred – that "there are no very strong reasons for having the provincial leader in the legislature." The National Office strongly disagreed with the decision, but the Ontario CCF would not back down. In a statement that clearly revealed the party's shifting emphasis away from indirect, caucus-based methods of organization toward more basic organization, Lazarus told Ingle that "we believe the effect of 4 or 5 weeks' work a year in the legislature on the Ontario public has been grossly over-estimated," and that "Ted can make a much more valuable contribution to the movement outside the legislature." But Jolliffe, lacking legislative remuneration, was without the means to carry on as party leader and was seriously thinking about returning to his private law practice, while doing party work on the side. To avoid losing Jolliffe's full-time services to the party, the Executive decided to ask the party for permission to investigate ways of providing him with a salary through a leadership fund of some sort. The convention approved the request and, in May, the Executive presented its proposals to Council for discussion. The leader would be provided with a salary, equal to that of the provincial secretary's, in return for his services as leader and for ten months of organizational work in the ridings. Financial contributions to the fund would be solicited from unions so that no cost would be incurred by the party. The leader would also be permitted to carry on his legal work, on a part-time basis, to supplement his income.[31]

While Jolliffe agreed to this arrangement, the question of a leadership fund created a wide split, along familiar lines, in the Provincial Council. Party loyalists supported the Executive and argued that the fund was necessary to allow Jolliffe to perform his numerous and vital leadership functions. "It is impossible," asserted Andrew Brewin, "for anyone to practise law and be political leader without getting into serious difficulties. The CCF has spent 10 years building up a provincial leader and this is the time to take advantage of it." The dissidents, led by leaders of the Ginger Group, opposed the fund. True Davidson and Avis McCurdy said it was demeaning for Jolliffe because, as the former explained, "it calls on the leader to make a personal sacrifice by becoming a paid member of the staff and I think this is unfair to him. It would mean a loss in prestige, because people like to think of a leader as being independent and successful." She also felt it represented a break with the party's tradition of voluntarism and self-sacrifice. "Others give much spare time to the party, sacrificing their own interests, and the leader should set an example. His duties could be carried on successfully in his spare time. At present, there is a greater need [of funds] for organization and education than for a well-publicized leader." Both she and McCurdy suggested, therefore, that the issue be postponed for a year or two. Several were quick to denounce this leader-as-martyr idea, which they felt was based on nostalgic recollections of J.S. Woodsworth. "The present ... provincial leader has made sacrifices and encountered serious difficulties," stressed Bill Grummett. "This is a matter for regret rather than pride, and the party should give more practical support to its leaders." Opposition was also based on the fact that even though the fund was to be administered by the CCF, it would be paid for by the unions, and therefore meant "control by that faction." Many felt, instead, that the money should come from individuals as well as unions. Some Ginger Group members even went so far as to suggest that the Executive had proposed the fund primarily to relieve Jolliffe of his recent financial difficulties. It was no secret within the party that Jolliffe had, over his many years of service to the movement, accumulated a substantial debt and owed a fair bit in income tax. The nasty rumours that had circulated at the convention, to the effect that the leader had not paid his taxes recently, were very much on the minds of the dissidents at the meeting. Bill Temple, who supported the idea of the fund in theory, suggested that Jolliffe return to his law practice to re-establish himself financially. These and other comments took on a distinctly anti-Jolliffe tone. Edith Fowke spoke about the rumours at the convention, saying: "The leader's job is to lead the group in the Legislature, which is no longer possible. There is not the same need for him to do other work, as statements to the press could be made by others." Another Councilor agreed. "I heard the leader was going to resign from the movement and there have been other rumours against him. The rumours are spreading. The York East [CCF] executive has raised the question of no confidence [in the leader], and it should be considered by the council."[32]

Finally, it was Jolliffe's turn to speak, and what followed was a tale that must have torn at the hearts of even his most determined opponents. It was the story of a man who had given up a life of comfortable prosperity as a successful labour lawyer in exchange for innumerable hours of criss-crossing the province, delivering speeches, attending committee meetings, giving interviews, and writing articles – all for the sake of the party and all at his own expense. Even during the years he was out of the legislature, between 1945 and 1948, and therefore not entitled to legislative pay, he had maintained a hectic and costly schedule of party work; and through it all, he had not once asked the party for remuneration. "The CCF has been my major interest in time and energy since 1934," he said, "and I have practiced law as a side-line. The result was that I have operated at a deficit and accumulated heavy obligations over a period of 18 years. I have done so consciously and without regret, because I felt it to be necessary, but I never expected that it would be used as propaganda against me by any comrades in my own party." He also put to rest rumours that he had failed to file tax returns. "I have done so in every year and always on time." But he made it clear that he could go no further into debt for the party and wanted to be reimbursed for all expenses he would henceforth incur as provincial leader. Directing his final words at his enemies in the party, he declared firmly that "no leader can expect unanimous support, and I do not. The convention, however, gave me a mandate to carry on and the mandate could only be implemented with the whole-hearted understanding and support of a great many people, which I believe I have a right to expect." The vote on the motion to establish a Provincial Leadership Fund was subsequently carried "with a substantial majority."[33]

While the Ginger Group was certainly the most serious threat to the CCF leadership in the months following the 1951 election debacle, it was not the only one. Many of the dissidents' concerns about bureaucratization and centralization were shared by the leaders of the Ontario Woodsworth Memorial Foundation, a socialist research and education centre composed primarily of CCFers. The Foundation was established in 1944 by a handful of CCF members and politically unaligned individuals who wished to erect a memorial to the ideals of J.S. Woodsworth. After soliciting donations for this purpose, they purchased a large, three-story brick house at 565 Jarvis Street in Toronto and agreed to provide the CCF Provincial Office with office space on the second floor of the building, for the then reasonable monthly rent of $150.

The Foundation was to remain independent from the party, however, and was not intended to be a CCF school in any formal sense. According to Bernard Loeb, former chair of the CCF's Finance Committee and the Foundation's first president, the party "insisted on the ... Foundation being an independent body ... They did not want to take the responsibility for the administration of the Foundation." And, in fact, they did all they could to disassociate themselves from the centre. All aspects of the Foundation were to be administered by a Board of Directors elected annually by the membership. The CCF was not even mentioned in the organization's charter, which described the Foundation as "an educational institution for the teaching of, and providing for courses and research in, the social sciences, economics, philosophy, and kindred subjects," in accordance with the ideas of J.S. Woodsworth.[34]

The Foundation's creators hoped that a formal non-partisan education centre would attract middle-class individuals with left-wing sympathies who were reluctant to join the CCF. They also foresaw a day when the Foundation would become primarily a labour college, working to heighten the political awareness of workers. The goal was to convert such persons to socialism, in the hope that they would join the CCF eventually, although it was widely understood that the Foundation would not take orders from the CCF or deliberately indoctrinate members with party propaganda. It was to be "an educational organization separate and distinct from, though sympathetic with, the CCF party."[35]

Admittedly, the line between CCF school and independent socialist education centre was a fine one. Many of the founders, and almost 75 percent of its members, belonged to the CCF. Moreover, the Foundation was administered by individuals who were either party members or who held to CCF principles. In effect, the Woodsworth Foundation *was* a CCF school, and was no doubt expected by its founders to play the same role the League for Social Reconstruction had played a few years earlier – that of a "brain trust" for the party.[36] But because the Foundation's charter constituted it as a completely autonomous body, with no formal connection to the CCF and with socialist (though not explicitly CCF) educational goals, the seeds of future controversy were planted at its conception.

Relations between the CCF and the Foundation were, indeed, strained from the very beginning, but mostly over financial matters. Because so many Foundation members belonged and contributed financially to the CCF, the centre received little in the way of financial contributions from its members and was constantly pressuring its largest tenant at 565 Jarvis to pay a higher rent. But under severe financial constraints of its own, the CCF invariably refused, often justifying its refusal with the claim that the Foundation was, after all, a CCF appendage. The issue of finances also created divisions among Foundation members, between those who disagreed with subsidizing the CCF through low rent and those who argued that the Board of Directors had simply been careless with the Foundation's money.[37]

Friction over money matters was compounded by disagreement over the purpose and usefulness of the Foundation. Certain members of the Board of Directors, particularly Frank Underhill, the Foundation's educational director and a vice-president from 1945 to 1949, insisted that the Foundation was an autonomous educational organization whose purpose was "not a propaganda job, but a constant seeking after the truth." The CCF faction on the Board, which happened to be in the minority, disagreed and repeatedly called for a clarification of the purpose of the Foundation; they believed, as Lewis recalls in his memoirs, that the Foundation was to "carry on educational work in support, but independent, of the party." This same group also accused the Board of Directors of having done a poor job of promoting research and education; financial mismanagement, it argued, had left little in the way of funding for these essential activities. The majority on the Board generally agreed that the education program was inadequate, but they blamed this on the CCF's low rent, which deprived the Foundation of the necessary funds. Suggested solutions from both sides therefore focused essentially on finances and ranged from getting rid of several full-time, paid officers, to raising the CCF's rent, to selling the house. But with many of these suggestions being no doubt perceived as personal attacks against one side or the other, no agreement was reached.[38]

The conflict came to a head at the Foundation's annual meeting on 27 February 1952. Even the CCF had recognized the significant increase during the Foundation's antagonism in the eight or so months prior to the meeting. In September 1951, the Foundation began issuing a monthly newsletter, written by Underhill, in which the CCF was strongly criticized, particularly its foreign policy. The first issue, in particular, aroused a good deal of anger within the party, especially with a provincial election just around the corner. "It is hard to believe that its incredibly bad timing was not deliberately planned to sabotage the chances of CCF candidates in the forth-coming provincial election," wrote one angry member. "Certainly I think Woodsworth Foundation leaves itself wide open to this charge."[39]

Underhill, who had become the leading spokesperson for the CCF's critics within the Foundation, supplemented the newsletter with a searing attack on the CCF in the February 1952 issue of *Canadian Forum*. Writing in the regular column entitled "What's Left," the party loyalist-turned-nemesis accused the CCF of being "too much dominated ... by bureaucrats on Jarvis St. and by politicians concentrated on considerations of expediency." This, he claimed, had resulted in a tendency to parrot old ideas at the expense of serious critical discussion, with the result that the party's philosophy and platform had become stale and unappealing. He argued:

Today the world situation has changed. It is no longer the deflation of depression that we have to deal with but the inflation of the welfare state, accentuated by the rearmament pressure of the Cold War. Capitalism has not failed on this continent to the degree that we thought it had failed for good in the 1930s. The CCF needs to think out both its basic philosophy and its practical program in relation to these changed conditions. To stand waiting with our mouths watering until that next depression brings the phraseology of the 1930s into fashion again and gives us another juicy chance is not a policy ... The socialism of the 1950s will at least have to put its emphasis upon rather different points.[40]

The only solution, concluded Underhill, was to maintain an independent centre for research and study, not unlike the Fabian Society in Britain, that could provide the CCF with new ideas.

The last straw for the CCF, however, came with the news that the Foundation was investigating the possibility of selling Woodsworth House, the party's headquarters, that it had no plans to accomodate the CCF in the future, and that it would introduce a motion to this effect at the 1952 Annual Meeting. A group of CCF leaders decided, informally, that they had had enough. In the three weeks preceding the meeting, they managed to sign up 69 new Foundation members and renew the memberships of 62 others – bringing the total membership of the Foundation to 336 – with a view to voting out the existing Board of Directors.[41] Aware of what the CCFers were planning, the Foundation's Board of Directors met at a special meeting two days before the Annual Meeting. There they overwhelmingly endorsed a motion "that this Board regrets the obvious campaign by certain CCF and trade-union officials to bring in, just before the annual meeting, a large number of new members who have not previously shown interest in any of the activities of the Foundation." Only one of the Board's fourteen directors voted against the motion.[42]

The Annual Meeting, on 27 February, began with the report of the president, Dr. H.N. Wilkinson. In it he expressed regret over the deteriorating relationship between the CCF and the Foundation, but said he was even sorrier that the CCF had chosen a "power drive" as the method to resolve the problem. Convinced that the party's actions were caused primarily by the Foundation's decision to sell Woodsworth House, he assured members that nothing would be done "without the fullest discussion," and that "the present Board have not, nor would not, think of 'kicking the CCF out on the street,' as has been suggested." He made no apologies, though, for the decision to sell the house; a decision, he noted, that was borne of sheer financial necessity. Nor did he or any other director apologize for the Foundation's newsletter. "No one," said Wilkinson, "least of all, I am sure, Professor Underhill, expected agreement by everyone with the views he expressed, but one thing Frank Underhill does do is to make us think." He concluded with a plea for the continued independence of the Foundation from partisan politics. "It is even more in the interests of the party," he declared, "that an independent group able to attract independent-minded people to a real study of social, economic, and cultural affairs should be in existence. In order to fulfil this role the Foundation must have real independence. It must never become merely a CCF front such as the Communist party might organize."[43]

Notwithstanding Wilkinson's comments, the CCF power play continued to unfold inexorably. No sooner had the membership approved the President's Report than David Lewis, former CCF national secretary and currently a member of the party's National Executive, presented a controversial amendment that called for three things: broader participation of "ordinary people" in the Foundation's activities, "research which will advance the idea of a co-operative commonwealth in Canada and can serve as ammunition to the socialist movement in its struggles," and the preservation of Woodsworth House as a home for the CCF. To achieve these goals, he recommended the establishment of a Labour College, the appointment of a knowledgable committee to formulate a "labour [education] program," and a pledge that Woodsworth House not be sold unless alternate accommodations for the Foundation and CCF were found, and then only with the CCF's consent. The amendment carried.[44]

The highlight of the meeting, and what the CCF hoped would be the *coup de grace*, was the election of officers and directors. Although Wilkinson was re-elected president by acclamation, two of the three remaining official posts were won by CCF partisans. As well, at least three of the six directors elected at the meeting were CCF "candidates." Therefore, although the coup was not entirely successful, in that the CCF did not end up controlling a majority of the board members, pro-CCF representation on the ruling body was strengthened substantially. This was clearly illustrated at the first meeting of the new board in March, at which a resolution condemning the tactics of the CCF at the Annual Meeting was defeated by one vote and CCF sympathizers secured the chairperson position of a number of key Foundation committees.[45]

During and after the Annual Meeting, opponents associated with the Foundation were highly critical of the CCF. They accused party leaders of trying to take control of the Foundation in order to convert it from an independent study centre into a vehicle for CCF propaganda, a view accepted by the media and even the CCF's National Office, and one that was largely valid. That the CCF had sought to gain control of the Foundation is without question. In the three weeks prior to the Annual Meeting, party leaders had persuaded a large number of individuals to join the Foundation or renew their memberships, hoping to facilitate passage of the Lewis amendment and to ensure election of CCF partisans to the new Board of Directors. Nor did the party deny this. After the meeting, Morden Lazarus informed Lorne Ingle at the National Office that "we do not control a majority on the Board, but hope that the enclosed resolution adopted by the annual meeting will keep the Foundation and the property intact until the next annual meeting when we hope to complete the job."[46]

Why the CCF wanted to control the Foundation, however, is not entirely clear. Because CCF records make little mention of the incident and because the comments of its partisans at the Annual Meeting were not recorded, we can only infer the CCF's motives – from the Lewis amendment, from the comments of the CCF's opponents, and from its official response to the accusations. These sources suggest several related motives. First, the CCF felt that the Foundation had neglected its responsibility to provide educational programs for unionists – and strong evidence of such neglect does exist – and had instead catered to middle-class professionals and intellectuals. That is, it wished to make the Foundation a Labour College, as originally envisioned by some of its founders. Second, the CCF believed that the Foundation had not fulfilled its obligation to serve as the party's own think-tank by producing socialist literature for CCF use. The Lewis amendment made this quite clear when it called upon the Foundation to produce "research which will advance the idea of a cooperative commonwealth in Canada and can serve as ammunition to the socialist movement in its struggles." At a later date, Lewis told a reporter that "the foundation ... has failed entirely to do any worthwhile educational and research work on social problems. The foundation has originally been established for educational and research work of the same kind as ... the Fabian Society in Great Britain. They have done none of it ... They published no literature except a couple of pamphlets on Woodsworth himself in eight years." The Directors of the Foundation conceded that they had not published much in the way of socialist literature, but attributed this to the inadequate financial resources.[47]

Another motive was the desire to restore the Foundation to a *pro-CCF* socialist research and study centre as opposed to a forum for constant criticism of CCF policies, which is what it appeared to have become by February 1952. At first, the CCF Executive was quick to deny that this was its purpose. It sent a letter to the Foundation informing the Directors that "we believe that there is value in a socialist education and research foundation not controlled by the CCF." But Andrew Brewin, who composed the party's official version of the affair several months later, admitted to readers of the *Canadian Forum* that the hostility of a few members of the Board of Directors toward the CCF "endangered the future usefulness of the Foundation. Although the Foundation could best carry out its educational functions independently of the CCF," he explained, "it could hardly do so effectively if it had alienated the sympathies of many loyal supporters of the CCF and had permitted hostility to develop into a complete separation or divorce." In other words, because the Foundation leaders had become increasingly critical of the party, and had thereby undermined the Foundation's traditional role as a pro-CCF socialist education centre, a purge was necessary. The CCF and its supporters in the Foundation, added Brewin, "were genuinely concerned that the Foundation should not be lost to the cause of promoting the socialist ideals of J.S. Woodsworth." At the same time, he reiterated the party's position that the CCF did not want to stifle free expression within the Foundation.[48]

Finally, and just as important, the CCF was worried that whatever ideological ties remained between itself and the Woodsworth Foundation would be completely severed by the Board of Directors' decision to sell Woodsworth House. "Such a course of action was deemed disastrous in the long run to the educational objectives of the Foundation," noted Brewin. What's more, the CCF was anxious that it would be without a home, and "to many loyal supporters of the Foundation and of the CCF, such a proposal seemed to be a breach of the implied trust created by the solicitation of funds [in 1944] on the basis that Woodsworth House was to be a centre for socialist activities, including those of the CCF."[49]

The initial criticism of the CCF's actions was relatively subdued compared with what was to follow. The strongest attack came in the form of another lengthy *Forum* article by Underhill, in which the author used the Woodsworth Foundation episode to present a broad and increasingly familiar critique of the CCF. The main reason for the CCF's recent decline, he argued, was its unswerving adherence to a set of outdated principles, a situation that he attributed to an absence of meaningful socialist research and study within the party. This was all the more reason, he explained, for the CCF to support an *independent* think-tank like the Woodsworth Foundation, for "it is groups of this kind who help keep socialist doctrine liberal rather than authoritarian, and the socialist approach to new problems experimental rather than dogmatic." That the CCF had become so doctrinaire, moreover, was due to "bad leadership". As Underhill put it:

The party machinery has fallen into the hands of a small clique who perpetuate themselves in party office regardless of the ups and downs in electoral results in the province. They have become adept in the art of managing party conventions and in using democratic forms to centralize power in their own control. They have almost abandoned the work of political education amongst the party membership, a work which is essential in any left party ... The CCF in Ontario has ceased for all practical purposes to be a missionary party concentrating on winning more and more converts, and it is slowly sinking into a sect whose leaders seem mainly interested in maintaining at all costs their own authority within the sect ... When the first moral fervour which has launched a new movement begins to cool, the bureaucrat and the organizers emerge and take over the management of affairs. Bureaucrats are very necessary functionaries ... but they are dangerous if there is not sufficient vitality in the rank-and-file membership to check their inherent drive for self-aggrandizement.[50]

Underhill believed that this fanatical drive for power and obedience, which eventually afflicts the leadership of all democratic organizations, was exacerbated by the growing influence on the CCF of a trade union leadership "intoxicated with power," because of its success during the 1930s and 1940s. The only solution was to restore the "vitality" of the rank and file, in part through the promotion of free and open discussion of party policy, such as that which had prevailed in the Woodsworth Memorial Foundation before certain CCF leaders decided to take control.[51]

In his version of the events surrounding the Foundation's Annual Meeting, Andrew Brewin responded directly to these general criticisms. He called the allegation that the CCF was controlled by a tyrannical, manipulative, self-seeking and self-perpetuating elite of leaders and paid officials, intent on suppressing dissent, "sheer nonsense." Not only was the CCF run by a "small paid staff" of "outstanding devotion, selflessness, ability and socialist vision," he asserted, but "with a few exceptions, the personnel of the provincial executive has constantly changed throughout the year."[52] Furthermore, he continued, "there has been absolutely no attempt to exclude newcomers or to stifle criticism or complete freedom of expression" within the movement. Nor did CCF leaders manipulate party conventions by presenting "slates" of preferred candidates, as was the practice in the Woodsworth Foundation. As for the party's narrow base of support and the charge of union domination, Brewin was emphatic: "The officers and executive of the CCF have long recognized that if the CCF is not to become a small sectarian group but an effective political party, it must secure the support ... of the basic economic groups in the country," including the unions. But he stressed that "at no time have the unions or any of its leaders made their support conditional upon any control or the adoption of any policy by the Ontario CCF. There has been absolutely no interference by the trade union movement." Brewin ended his rejoinder with a gesture of goodwill and cooperation. "From the administration side of the fence," he said, "let me say to Professor Underhill and his friends that they should forget fears and suspicions which are largely groundless. The socialist movement of Canada needs and appreciates their help and criticism and together we can contribute to the socialist commonwealth of the future."[53]

Relations between the CCF and the Woodsworth Foundation, however, did not improve. Shortly before the 1953 Annual Meeting, Edith Fowke reported that "the atmosphere at the last three board meetings has been so full of carefully disguised hostility that we have all come away from them feeling almost physically sick." Members of the new Board of Directors could not agree among themselves what the purpose of the Foundation should be: whether it should function as an independent study centre, emphasizing general education from a broadly socialist perspective and catering primarily to middle-class interests, or a Labour College, emphasizing CCF ideology and policy through programs developed specifically for the working class. As it became apparent that the latter function would prevail, and that steps were being taken to consolidate the CCF's power on the Board of Directors, including the termination of the Underhill newsletter, the trickle of resignations by old-guard directors following the 1952 Annual Meeting became a tidal wave.[54]

The event which triggered this mass exodus was the Foundation's Annual Meeting in March 1953, at which CCF partisans secured three of the four officer positions on the Board and at least four of the seven director posts, thereby taking control of the Foundation and "completing the job," as Lazarus had predicted. As in 1952, the CCF brought in a large number of new members shortly before the Annual Meeting, many of whom were trade unionists and their wives. This was facilitated by the recent introduction of a "corporate membership," which allowed unions to send a number of representatives to the meeting in return for an annual fee of ten dollars. Realizing what was in store for them, fifteen members of the Foundation, including all of the officers and most of the active Directors who had served since 1945, resigned *en masse* on the day of the Annual Meeting. In a widely publicized statement, drafted by Underhill and signed by all fifteen dissidents, they stated that they could no longer "cooperate with the new Board of Directors" because they disagreed with the new educational direction of the Foundation, which was to convert members into CCF socialists. The bulk of the statement, however, dealt with the CCF, and the central themes were the familiar ones of free expression versus party orthodoxy, and the need to attract the middle-class to the CCF. The dissidents argued that an infusion of middle-class members, in an atmosphere of free expression, would help fulfil the party's greatest need: an "objective re-examination of socialist ideas" with a view to liberalizing party doctrine. "We are all much more aware now than in the early 1930s of the dangerous trends towards the managerial society," they explained, "dangers which are not removed by the growth of a swollen state bureaucracy. The relation between socialism and freedom needs to be reassessed." In general, then, the statement was consistent with previous criticisms of the CCF by the Foundation's leadership; it represented the parting shot in the long-running battle between the two sides.[55]

It is at this point that the question of the broader significance of CCF dissent in the early fifties must be addressed. In other words, what did the Ginger Group and Woodsworth Foundation episodes really represent, in a broader thematic sense? To what extent, moreover, were these episodes simply two sides of the same coin? Although none of the major works on the CCF deals with these episodes in any detail or relates one to another, the standard interpretation of internal disagreements within the CCF movement across Canada in the early 1950s seems to be that they represented a struggle – between the pro-Communist "left" and the anti-Communist "right" wings of the movement – over the CCF's policy toward Communists at home and abroad. Observers point, for example, to the divisions created by the Ontario CCF's 1952 decision to have nothing to do with the newly formed Canadian Peace Congress or its peace petition, both believed to be Communist inspired.[56] Only Zakuta strays from this "Cold War" interpretation, arguing that the struggle, at least as far as the original Ginger Group is concerned, was part of the longer-term battle between CCF traditionalists (or "Old Guard") and CCF progressives (or "New Guard") over the very nature and purpose of the party.[57]

Neither of these interpretations, however, is entirely satisfactory. Although the Cold War interpretation is useful when applied to the foreign policy ideas of the original Ginger Group, it sheds little light on the concerns of the revived Ginger Group or the Woodsworth Foundation, both of which made few references to CCF foreign policy. The Zakuta thesis, although more helpful, even though it does not deal with the 1952 dissent movement specifically, also overstates the ideological dimension. Indeed, the internal struggles of the Ontario CCF in 1952 are more easily understood when viewed as closely related phenomena, based primarily on differences over party structure and organizational strategy and only secondarily over policy or ideology. Moreover, the language and concerns of both the revived Ginger Group and the Woodsworth Foundation, particularly the latter, suggest that CCF dissent in the early 1950s was influenced, to some extent, by the Cold War atmosphere of the period.

A quick review of the main concerns voiced by the 1952 Ginger Group and the Woodsworth Foundation leadership reveals several common features. Both groups believed that the CCF was becoming more bureaucratic and less democratic in structure – that for several reasons, especially the growing influence of the labour movement, power was becoming concentrated in the Executive; and that, to maintain their power, party leaders were suppressing dissent, replacing dedicated, independent volunteers with paid workers, and subordinating the open discussion of socialism to less inspirational organizational and fund-raising activities. The result was an increase in rank-and-file apathy and the overall decline of the CCF. In short, CCF dissidents in the early 1950s were mainly concerned with what they saw as the *structural* and *organizational* transformation of the CCF from a movement to a party, to use Young's terminology.

The convergence of views between the 1952 Ginger Group and the directors of the Woodsworth Foundation is hardly a coincidence. At least ten of the fourteen Foundation directors (1951–52) were also members of the Ginger Group and were, therefore, very much a lobby group of the Foundation, acting through the 25-member Ginger Group. So while the CCF leadership was attempting to gain control of the Woodsworth Foundation, the Foundation's leaders were trying to gain control of the CCF, through the instrument of the Ginger Group. Viewed in this light, members of the Foundation's Board of Directors were standing on shaky ground when they chose to criticize the CCF for conducting a power drive.

Nevertheless, if one accepts the notion that the dissidents were primarily motivated by nostalgic visions of an earlier era, a further question lurks. Why did the Ginger Group and Woodsworth Foundation leaders feel that these visions were suddenly in jeopardy by 1952? As argued, their perceptions were shaped, in part, by real developments within the CCF, such as the growing emphasis on organization and fund-raising at the expense of membership education. But it has also been shown that many of the dissidents' other beliefs were exaggerated or based on scanty evidence. This suggests that perhaps other, less tangible influences helped shape their perceptions (or rather, misperceptions). A clue as to what one such influence may have been is provided by a closer look at the themes and language CCF dissidents used to express their concerns.

Such an examination reveals that the comments of both the Ginger Group and the Woodsworth Foundation leaders were heavily ladened with terms and themes that, at the time, were being used by Western society to describe and derogate the totalitarian communist societies of Eastern Europe, and communism in general. The *Toronto Telegram* was not exaggerating when it observed, in April 1952, that "much of the daily news and the literature of three continents is concerned these days with Communism and Communists." The month before, in fact, the *Telegram* ran a series of nine front-page articles on the "Red Menace in Canada," by Allan Kent and Clem Shields. The articles described the main characteristics of Canada's Communist movement, such as its strict adherence to the party line, its intolerance of internal dissent, its creation of policy by a small "political committee," its widespread use (largely through infiltration) of "front groups" to indoctrinate unsuspecting Canadians, and its exploitation of apathy to spread Communist propaganda.[58] The Woodsworth Foundation leadership characterized the CCF leadership in much the same way. CCF dissidents, generally, expressed a fear of bureaucratization, dogmatism, indoctrination, centralization of power, and intolerance of dissent – in short, of totalitarianism in all its forms – and did so in terms which, at times, directly equated the CCF leadership with Communism. In reference to the CCF's attempted takeover of the Woodsworth Foundation in 1952, for example, Underhill noted that "the ... purge ... was carried out ... with an unscrupulous thoroughness that the Communists themselves could hardly have bettered."[59] The fifteen former Foundation officials wrote that the CCF leaders "have shown that they believe in free discussion in the same sense in which the Communists believe in democracy" and accused them of using "Communist techniques ... against their own political friends." A former Foundation president, Mark Cohen, wrote that the "back room boys" of the CCF had infiltrated the Foundation, Commie-style, and "when the meeting opened, the Storm Troopers were on hand in full force under the watchful eagle eyes of the local gauleiters." In his speech to the 1952 Annual Meeting, President Wilkinson, who was also a Ginger Group member, warned that "the Foundation must ... never become merely a CCF front such as the Communist Party might organize." And another Foundation officer and member of the Ginger Group, Art Haas, criticized the CCF's attempt to be "purely labour representatives" and to perpetuate the class struggle. "Surely the hydrogen bomb has taught us that society's fight now is not on the class warfare level," he stated, "but purely and simply between freedom and slavery. It means most of the old socialist clichés and marxian interpretations are as dead as the bow and arrow."[60] Clearly, while some of the dissident's perceptions were based on reality, many were rooted in the West's growing fear of Communist totalitarianism during the early 1950s, a fear heightened by the Korean war raging at the time.

This fear may also explain why the new Ginger Group abandoned the "Keep Left" approach of their predecessors and why the Woodsworth Foundation leaders, particularly Frank Underhill, demonstrated a near-fanatic desire to moderate CCF ideology – in other words, why the nostalgic impulses of the dissidents did not include a call for a return to pure socialism, as did those of the original Ginger Group. It is possible that the Cold War backlash against the Left and the growing concern over the threat of state intervention to personal freedom made the CCF dissidents more reticent about, or in the case of the Woodsworth Foundation, more uncomfortable with, CCF ideology, especially its centralist-statist prescriptions. Whereas the original Ginger Group encouraged the party to "Keep Left," its successor, speaking at a time when the Cold War was intensifying, simply wanted

CCF members to openly discuss (and perhaps revise?) CCF policy. To be sure, most members of the 1952 Ginger Group did not openly question the pillars of CCF socialism, for they could not easily break with their faith; but neither did they trumpet them. Those who did hark back to a more radical past – if one ever existed – were few in number.

The dissidents in the Woodsworth Foundation, whose stronger intellectual temperament made them more inclined to oppose dogmatism, went one step further and called for a revision of CCF ideology along more liberal-individualist lines. Recall that, in 1952, Frank Underhill told readers of the *Canadian Forum* that "it is no longer the deflation of depression that we have to deal with but the inflation of the welfare state," and that the CCF needed "to think out both its basic philosophy and its practical program" with this in mind. He also reminded readers that only critical study and discussion by independent groups could "keep socialist doctrine liberal rather than authoritarian, and the socialist approach to new problems experimental rather than dogmatic." Most of the Foundation's former directors, it will also be recalled, pointed to "the dangerous trends towards the managerial society, dangers which are not removed by the growth of a swollen state bureaucracy," and echoed Underhill's call for an "objective re-examination of socialist ideas." In short, given the context of the period as well as the many references to Communist tactics made by the leaders of the Woodsworth Foundation, this plea for ideological revision by CCF dissidents can also be interpreted as a manifestation of the Cold War.

It should be emphasized, however, that the possible effect on the CCF of something as intangible as the Cold War atmosphere must be considered in connection with circumstances within the party itself at the time. After all, the period immediately following the 1951 provincial election was one of intense turmoil for the CCF; morale was low and members continued to leave the party in droves. In response, the leadership adopted a course of action that emphasized fund-raising and poll committee organization – all of which, it hoped, would lead to organizational revival. But the strategy had serious and unforeseen repercussions. Prior to the 1951 election, a growing number of CCFers, some of whom were members of the original Ginger Group or the Woodsworth Foundation, had become concerned about the growing apathy within the party, a situation they felt was due largely to the decline in membership discussion and education. The election results simply confirmed their beliefs, heightened their discontent, and increased their desire for a return to an earlier, more movement-oriented approach. Thus, when the party administration proposed to intensify its fund-raising and membership recruitment activities for the coming year, activities which lay at the very heart of the growing internal dissatisfaction, the dissidents organized and took action. The result was a reciprocal drive for power. CCF dissidents, acting primarily through the Ginger Group, tried to capture control of the party, while CCF leaders sought to displace their critics in the Woodsworth Foundation. In the end, the administration prevailed, repelling the Ginger Group at the 1952 annual convention and asserting firm control over the Foundation by the following spring.

Nevertheless, as argued, the dissent movement's "reactionary" critique of the party leadership did not emerge entirely from endogenous factors. The language and themes of this critique clearly reveal the almost certain effect of prevailing international tensions. Even the CCF leadership could not escape the Cold War's influence. After the final purge of the Woodsworth Foundation, David Lewis told a reporter that the former Board of Directors had "run the foundation as a clique, as a little toy of its own special design ... They had always had themselves re-elected by some kind of self-perpetuating technique ... [and] are guilty of the most obvious Communist technique, that if they couldn't rule, they wanted to destroy."[61] It is wrong, therefore, to separate phenomena such as the Ginger Group and the Woodsworth Foundation struggles from one another or from the broader context of world events. Although the protagonists of these phenomena were motivated primarily by the determination to resist the transformation of the CCF into a traditional political party, in a structural-organizational sense, their perception of this transformation was shaped, in part, by the Cold War.

3 Reviving the Movement

The intraparty turbulence of the post-election period did not sidetrack the CCF's organizational plans for 1952. In fact, party leaders were as determined as ever to resuscitate the movement in time for the next provincial election. "Winning the government of Ontario still lies before us," the Provincial Council declared at the 1952 convention. "Whatever work we have done in the past, whatever progress we have made, whatever support we have won, we must double and treble our efforts."[1] This determination was strong enough to carry the CCF through the residual dissent, local apathy, and electoral set-backs of the next eighteen months, and to foster a number of innovative organizational techniques. What emerged, by the end of 1953, was a party with a new leader and a new, more sophisticated, organizational approach.

After the 1952 convention, the Provincial Office went about its business as planned. In May, the chair of the Organization Committee, Dudley Bristow, presented Council with a detailed organizing plan to supplement the more general one formulated earlier in the year. The plan divided the province into thirty-four "areas," each containing several ridings. Bryden and Young were responsible for visiting thirteen areas each; several Council members volunteered to cover the remaining eight. As well, the party secured the part-time services of seven volunteers to do summer organizing, largely in eastern and north-central Ontario. The purpose of the plan remained the same as before: to encourage ridings to expand their membership, preferably through the poll committee structure, so that by June 1953 total membership would be restored to at least the 1948 level of 8,700. The plan also placed special emphasis on the nomination of candidates for the next federal election, since candidates were seen as the most likely persons to initiate the desired organizational structure, in order to get themselves elected.[2]

The party's continued determination to expand the movement in this way, however, provoked resistance from one of the more recalcitrant dissidents on the Council. At the May Council meeting, Avis McCurdy complained that the "emphasis on membership is misplaced" and that "too much effort is being expended by members in working in the membership drives." She then shocked a good many colleagues by suggesting that "for one year at least, we should limit the program of increasing our membership and concentrate on building a hard core of members which we could depend on. This core should concentrate on sympathetic contacts in each riding and convert them into socialist-thinking persons before they joined the movement." As for the rest, that is, the non-active, apathetic members of the CCF, McCurdy felt they should be ignored for the moment and that no effort should be made to retain them as party members.

But most Council members rejected this suggestion outright, fearing that it would mean the disappearance of the CCF. As one Councillor put it, "Either you have a mass movement or you have not. The core is important and does exist at present in the movement, but we cannot afford to give up the basis of a mass movement. To do so, even temporarily for a year or two, would be political suicide for the CCF ... It has taken us years to build mass support for the CCF and it would be folly to carry out the policy suggested by Mrs. McCurdy and abandon that support now." The director of the province's USA members, Larry Sefton, agreed. "I do not believe in having a small select group of informed socialists without mass support as we know what the fate of these ... groups has been," he stated. "We must continue to build our movement on a mass support basis in order to function as a political party and not a socialist debating society."[3]

Simply put, the issue was whether the CCF should try to convert people to socialist ideology *before* or *after* recruiting them as party members. The debate was resolved when several Council members proposed that membership education and recruitment could occur simultaneously, during canvassing: "We must take socialist education to the doors of our people," explained Fred Young. "The contact with our members while canvassing for renewals is invaluable and may be the only one; [and] for that reason membership drives are important."

Ken Bryden added that "the real test as to whether an educational job has been done is if you can persuade someone to become a member. A person does not have to be an expert on socialist theory to become a good working CCF member." The compromise that emerged – "that this committee go on record as being in favour of the largest possible membership and along with it a vigorous educational program of socialist principles" – was recorded in the motion and approved by Council. For the time being, and apart from some minor sniping in the months ahead, the dissidents were appeased; the CCF could pursue its organizational goals with the blessing of most members.[4]

Nor were the Provincial Office's plans distracted to any great extent by two federal by-elections held several weeks later in the ridings of Waterloo North and Ontario. In past years, the CCF had eagerly contested by-elections because it was able to concentrate its limited financial and human resources in one or two ridings, thereby off-setting, to some degree, the superior resources of the two major parties. And as a result, it had done reasonably well. Between September 1938 and May 1952, the CCF participated in fifteen federal and provincial by-elections in Ontario. It won two of these, finished second in four, and came a close third in five; in only four of the fifteen by-elections did it finish a distant third. But in May 1952, with the party's membership and morale at their lowest point in years, the Provincial Office was reluctant to divert its valuable organizing staff to the current slate of by-election contests and decided, therefore, to let the ridings fend for themselves. The decision was made easier by the knowledge that the CCF had held both ridings in the past; that both contained major industrial centres with many unionists; and that, in each riding, local PACs were assisting the CCF organization. Nevertheless, the CCF ran a poor third in both contests, with a lower popular vote than in the 1949 federal election.[5]

Instead, the CCF continued to place its hopes in the efforts of its full-time organizing staff. In July, this staff was expanded to three when the United Steelworkers of America offered to hire two "staff representatives" to act strictly as political organizers for the CCF. Fred Young was hired to do full-time work in southern Ontario, while C.C. "Doc" Ames was taken on to cover the dozen or so large ridings in the North. Ames, a one-time first-aid worker in the Kirkland Lake gold mines and later the town's pharmacist, was also a veteran CCFer and, at the time Donald MacDonald convinced him to become a provincial organizer, one of the party's vice-presidents.[6] By far the most colourful CCF personality in this period, Ames was also one of the best liked; in the years to come, he would attack his duties with a sharp tongue and a volatile passion. With such organizational talent suddenly at its disposal, the CCF was perhaps justified in expecting gains.

Progress, however, was excruciatingly slow. Although Young and Ames managed to bring in about 500 new members by year's end and revive activity in a number of ridings that had previously been dormant, the situation remained bleak. Membership levels rose in Toronto and the far North, but fell everywhere else. Levels in eastern Ontario were so low that the party had to regularly waive its constitutional rules regarding nominating conventions, permitting riding associations to leave membership lists open until the night of their convention to ensure that sufficient members would be present. Overall, concluded Bristow in October, "the present ... picture in regard to membership and organization is not at all satisfactory. The general picture is one of the organizers working hard to maintain the membership at its present level." By December, CCF membership rested at 7,300 – an increase of only 500 over 1951, and well short of the goal of 8,700 set by the Provincial Council in May.[7]

The root of the problem was a familiar one – local apathy. Most CCF riding associations and party members outside Toronto and parts of the North were not willing to build the party on their own initiative, despite repeated exhortations from party leaders. Based on reports from the provincial organizers, the Organization Committee concluded that in "more than half of the ridings outside Toronto and District," membership levels were either stagnant or falling because of "the reluctance of our local people ... to tackle the job of building an effective organization." The widespread indifference stemmed in large part from the discouragement veteran CCFers quite naturally felt after years of defeat – a phenomenon that the party leadership referred to as feeling "browned off." Local activists often told CCF leaders that they would only resume working for the party "if and when some results are apparent."[8] This approach, of course, simply bred the familiar vicious circle into which the movement had been drawn.

Some party members, however, continued to blame the Provincial Office for the situation, and their criticisms were proof that the debate between the "educate first, sign up later" voluntarists and the "sign up first, educate later (or simultaneously)" bureaucrats had not died with the Ginger Group in the spring. In the November issue of the CCF News, one CCFer argued that instead of hiring additional organizers to sign up more members, the leadership should be stimulating existing members into becoming dedicated, self-sacrificing volunteer workers who would educate voters in the principles and policies of socialism. "A strong organization is not denoted by the number of organizers it can put in the field or the number of members it can obtain, but by the number of active, volunteer workers within its ranks ... What we need are not more members, but more active members."[9]

The Provincial Office was not about to discard its main strategy of using paid organizers to expand membership, but it certainly agreed that more of the burden for organizing the party had to be assumed by the local level. The poll committee plan was, in fact, the first move in this direction; with the exception of York South and Temiskaming ridings, however, it had not been adopted. Another suggestion that emerged in 1952 was to hold a number of regional conferences at which members from several ridings, as well as labour and farm representatives if possible, would learn about organizing techniques and get to know one another better. The Executive hoped that this would help revive local interest and eventually result in the establishment of self-financing regional CCF committees, each with its own organizer. In the fall of 1952, CCF organizers helped arrange several such conferences across the province, and although no regional committees emerged from the meetings, they did revive interest and may have accounted, in part, for the unusually high number of new members who joined the party in November.[10]

The next major project aimed at reviving the movement was the province-wide Spring Membership Drive of 1953. Resembling the National Expansion Drive of a few years back, it replaced the "CCF Week" concept introduced in 1952 and marked the beginning of a CCF tradition. The Provincial Office divided the province into nine areas and gave each area, as well as each of the eight or nine ridings within an area, a target quota of new and renewing members. To encourage competition, the Provincial Office offered monetary prizes to the three ridings with the best results. Canvassers, equipped with membership cards and party leaflets, were encouraged to contact ten new people each, including local CCL union officers and stewards (the "10 Contact" plan).

Party leaders had several reasons to feel confident that such an undertaking would succeed. First, the annual membership drive of the Toronto and District CCF had shown that an intensive canvass of many ridings could produce good results. Second, as the chair of the Organization Committee observed in the new year, "We are definitely in the strongest organizational position of all time to stage an effective membership drive across the province ... [since] we will have four full-time organizers working throughout the drive." In the end, the CCF's first Spring Membership Drive was fairly successful. An impressive 80 percent of the aggregate quota was achieved, and the party fell only 200 members short of its goal of 8,700, a figure it would surpass by 300 in June.[11]

The efforts of the CCF to revive the movement were not directed at CCF members alone. The party, in close conjunction with the OFL-PAC, also focused its sights on the union rank and file, hoping to increase labour's support for the party; in particular, it hoped to re-establish the sort of grass-roots cooperation between union and CCF members witnessed during the 1951 election campaign, when joint union-CCF committees and consultation between riding executives and local union leaders were regular features in many urban-industrial areas of the province. The object now, according to CCF leaders, was to maintain the same degree of cooperation *between* elections, for without more regular and formal ties between workers and CCFers at the local level, the union leadership's support for the CCF would never rub off on the average worker.[12]

The thinking was the same at OFL headquarters in Toronto, but with a preference for year-round political action in general, as opposed to simply cooperating with the party at the local level. "The job PAC must do now," Henry Weisbach told the OFL Executive following the election, "is to lay the ground work for further [political] activities. We must make our people realize that PAC cannot operate just six weeks before an election and be forgotten the rest of the time." He recommended, therefore, that an "extensive education campaign" be carried out among OFL members to teach them the importance of political action. Some OFL officials questioned the usefulness of continuing the PAC, in light of the election results. But most members of the Executive agreed to continue PAC "and intensify our efforts in this regard." If the election had shown anything, they reasoned, it was that most union members still had to be persuaded that their legislative interests could only be protected by voting for, and assisting, the CCF on a year-round basis. The Executive's decision was endorsed by the OFL's annual convention in February, at which delegates also affirmed their traditional support for the CCF as labour's political arm and passed a motion authorizing the establishment of a permanent PAC fund, paid for by a *voluntary* per capita tax on the locals.[13]

These two objectives, increasing the political awareness of ordinary union members and forging closer links between CCF and OFL members, resulted in several joint CCF-PAC projects. In January and February, 1952, the PAC and the Toronto CCF held a series of weekly talks and discussion groups for unionists at Woodsworth House on the subject of socialism. And in March of that year, the PAC and the CCF's Trade Union Committee, the party's counterpart to the PAC, sponsored an educational conference in Toronto, at which approximately forty AFL and CCL union leaders from Hamilton and Oshawa discussed ways to attract workers into the CCF. It was hoped that local union leaders would use the information they gleaned on these occasions to establish PACs in their own unions and persuade members to support the CCF in some way.[14]

To advance the cause of closer labour-CCF relations, the CCF revamped its Trade Union Committee (TUC). In May, it gave AFL and CCL unions affiliated with the CCF direct representation on the Committee and, with the assistance of these labour representatives, pledged to set up similar joint committees in various cities. In addition, the TUC sought to develop a political education program that would result in an influx of individual union members into CCF riding associations, or the formation of CCF clubs ("industrial committees") within the unions themselves.[15]

In essence, the new TUC was similar to the joint CCF-PAC committee established for the 1951 election. Its main task was to bring labour and CCF representatives together in the urban centres so that more formal cooperation could be established, in the form of local TUCs. One such meeting resulted in the establishment of the Toronto CCF-Labour Council, which in turn organized gatherings of CCFers and local unionists in Toronto ridings. But apart from this, and a bit of informal consultation between CCF and union leaders in a few ridings, no other joint committees appear to have been established at the local level.[16] The reasons are unclear. Members of the TUC may have simply lacked the time to do the necessary organizing work at the riding level. As the TUC reported in October 1952, "Most of the Committee's members were busy with their own union and CCF activities, and the question of staff was a problem." The TUC's objectives may have been hindered, as well, by internal disagreement over the methods to be used to effect greater political action among rank-and-file unionists. Some Committee members, for example, supported the idea of establishing "industrial committees" to publicize the CCF in each plant; others felt that more emphasis should be placed on organizing within the union locals. As well, one member suggested that key union leaders in each riding get more involved in the work of CCF riding associations, although this was opposed by those who felt that "we must stick to organizing in the trade union field ... and leave the straight CCF organizing job to the CCF riding associations." In the end, the only point of agreement was that union leaders would "educate" workers at the plant level, using CCF literature.[17]

But perhaps the most plausible explanation for the failure of the TUC to achieve its goals was the strong undercurrent of anti-labour sentiment within many CCF riding associations in this period, and the mutual antagonism of CCFers and unionists in general. Members of the Ginger Group in the winter of 1951–52 had made no secret of their antipathy toward organized labour, particularly its allegedly anti-democratic, power-hungry leaders. Many CCFers were therefore reluctant to cooperate too closely with labour on a permanent basis, if at all. As a result, CCF leaders held out little hope that riding associations would take the initiative in approaching the unions. "I have a feeling," MacDonald confessed to Lazarus in early 1952, "that we cannot leave the initiative so completely with them [the riding associations], namely, that they invite the PAC leaders." He suggested, instead, that local PAC leaders be pressured by the provincial PAC to make the first move. The TUC nevertheless did send letters to riding associations, encouraging them to contact labour leaders and to establish TUCs of their own; the nature of the response was illustrated by one Committee member's proposal that the CCF amend its constitution to *force* ridings to set up TUCs, an idea that was quickly rejected.[18]

Sensing that its efforts on behalf of the CCF were not appreciated and that rank-and-file CCFers wanted little to do with organized labour, labour leaders and their followers felt hurt and frustrated. "What good can it do," Weisbach asked the CCL's secretary-treasurer, Donald MacDonald, "if we go out and induce our members to join the CCF, and work and vote for the CCF, when on the other hand the CCF refuses to give recognition to the trade union movement" by way of a greater voice in party affairs, a demand which CCFers viewed as labour's attempt to dominate the party. The Ginger Group's comments, in particular, had done a great deal to sour relations between the OFL and CCF. Its statements, asserted Weisbach, "certainly left a very bad taste in many ways" and had even spurred demands among labour for an independent labour party. At the local level, labour reciprocated the suspicion and hostility of certain party members by either refusing to get involved with the CCF or, when they did, excluding non-union CCFers from constituency meetings and activities. This, in turn, merely confirmed and exacerbated suspicions that labour was trying to "dominate" the party, making CCFers even more reluctant to work with the labour movement. It is also quite possible that apart from the resentment they encountered in certain quarters of the CCF, union leaders and rank-and-file members refused to cooperate with, or assist, the CCF in any way because they were as apathetic as regular party members, particularly after the demoralizing defeat of 1951.[19]

Some leaders openly pleaded with party members to reconsider their attitude toward organized labour, but to no avail.[20] The powerful anti-labour sentiment within the CCF persisted; when combined with the backlash from labour and the inability of provincial labour and CCF leaders on the TUC to overcome this fundamental problem, it guaranteed that the TUC would fall far short of its more ambitious goals. Except for the formation of the Toronto TUC and its efforts to sign up factory workers during the CCF's 1952 spring membership drive, closer and more permanent CCF-labour relations along the lines of the 1951 election campaign did not emerge. OFL and CCF leaders simply continued on in much the same way as before, urging local unions to revive or establish PACs, encouraging workers to join the CCF or contribute money to PAC on a regular basis, and educating them politically through courses and conferences.[21] The lack of local or even regional TUCs meant that the long-awaited bond between grass-roots unionists and CCFers remained elusive and that CCF-labour cooperation remained a top-level experience.

Even the federal election campaign in the summer of 1953 did not alter the picture of CCF-labour relations dramatically. Shortly after the election was announced, PAC representatives began visiting union locals to set up PACs where necessary and instruct union leaders to "clear the decks for political action." As in the recent past, political action at the local level meant inviting CCF personalities to speak to workers, assigning staff members to promote the CCF within the unions, paying for almost all of the CCF's publicity, and finding union members willing to run for election as CCF candidates.[22] But the degree of CCF-labour cooperation in the campaign does not seem to have equalled that of the 1951 campaign. No CCF-PAC election committee was established (the OFL and CCF formed separate election committees), and evidence of local cooperation by way of joint committees is lacking. Certainly the CCF's Provincial Office encouraged riding executives to contact local PACs to discuss election planning, but as the party's former president, Miller Stewart, observed during the campaign, "We have a great deal to learn about effective cooperation with these committees – and, it must be admitted, many of these committees are somewhat at a loss as to how they can work with us." The PAC also tried to foster cooperation, but its efforts to arrange meetings between union locals and CCFers were hampered by the fact that with so many of their members on vacation, many local union offices had shut down for the summer.[23]

Notwithstanding the absence of extensive CCF-labour cooperation, CCF leaders instructed candidates and election workers to do whatever they could to attract the workingman's vote. "The federal election of August 10, 1953, will be the CCF's greatest labour election and will call for our first real labour party campaign," declared Miller Stewart in the CCF *News*. "The voters who can win this election for the CCF carry lunch pails and the way for us to win is to run a lunch pail campaign." Consequently, CCF candidates and party literature emphasized such things as health care, taxes, and housing, issues of particular interest to workers. In addition, party spokespersons repeatedly told workers that the federal government had purposely called a summer election in order to "disenfranchise industrial voters," many of whom would be on vacation when election day arrived. They insisted, as well, that only by electing their own representatives to Parliament could labour be assured of getting a fair deal from government. All of these were manifestations of the pro-labour slant of the CCF's campaign.[24]

With the assistance of the PAC, the emphasis on "labour" issues, and some encouraging reports from organizers and campaign managers across the province, the CCF was confident of a real breakthrough. But as in 1951, it was to be deeply disappointed. Although the CCF elected twenty-three M.P.s across the country, ten more than the previous election, only one – Joe Noseworthy of York South – was elected from Ontario; elsewhere in the province the party ran a poor third. In addition, the CCF's popular vote in Ontario dropped – from the 15.2 percent of the 1949 election, to 11.1 percent.[25]

If nothing else, the results of the 1953 election *did* reinforce the CCF's belief that poll committee organization was the key to rebuilding the movement. In the one riding the CCF won in 1953, York South, a form of poll organization had been put in place well in advance of the election and soon became the blueprint for other ridings. During the election campaign, CCFers in York South had managed to enlist, through house meetings and telephone canvassing, a virtual army of volunteer workers, nearly 700 in all, most of whom were not yet members of the party. These workers were assigned specific tasks on a poll-by-poll basis, such as distributing leaflets and contacting other potential volunteers, and were the determining factor in the CCF's victory. After the election, therefore, the Organization Committee unveiled a "Program of Action" for the coming nine months, patterned on York South's organization. Ridings were urged to contact people who had helped out during the election and to get them involved as quickly as possible in specific aspects, "no matter how limited," of CCF organizing work. This should be done one poll at a time, through house meetings, with a view to setting up permanent committees of party workers in each poll. At the meetings, workers would be made more aware of the CCF's program and various canvassing techniques in order to increase their self-confidence. By building up its corps of workers in this way, the CCF hoped to be in a better position to expand the movement and, more important, to have at its disposal an army of workers who could drum up support for the party during election campaigns.[26]

It should be noted that the primary goal of this latest organizational plan was not simply to obtain a *larger* membership, which is what the CCF chose to emphasize for the twenty or so months following the 1951 election, mostly for financial reasons. It was to create a more *active* membership, working through poll committees. By late 1953, with membership levels once again at their 1949 level and with a significant improvement in its finances, the CCF could approach the question of organization more calmly and rationally, with less of the anxiety engendered by years of falling membership and the 1951 election results. This more relaxed disposition, plus the apparent success of York South's organizing techniques during the federal election, resulted in a more refined organizational strategy, with an emphasis on getting more people involved with party work on a long-term basis through the poll committee structure. The Organization Committee spent most of the fall urging riding associations to implement the plan and arranging conferences to teach local leaders about poll organization.[27]

The new organizational plan was also significant because it represented a further, if unintentional, concession to those within the CCF who had been calling for a less centralized, less bureaucratic organization, one in which leaders placed more emphasis on teaching a small core of members about socialism than on adding new members. The more refined plan, with its focus on poll committees and active members, appeared to respond directly to many of the dissidents' basic concerns. Admittedly, socialist education remained at a low level in this period, but the dissidents must have considered the more decentralized organizational thrust a partial victory nonetheless.[28]

It was perhaps appropriate that at the moment the CCF reached a small turning point in its organizational impetus, it also found itself looking for a new leader. Ted Jolliffe, at forty-four already a veteran of the political scene, had decided to call it quits. A Rhodes scholar, journalist, and former member of the British Labour Party, he had joined the CCF in the early 1930s as a provincial organizer and, after several unsuccessful attempts to gain election to Parliament, was persuaded, in 1942, to become the Ontario party's first leader. Known for his keen debating skills and his deep concern for the workers and farmers of the province, Jolliffe left a lasting impression on his colleagues. When outside the legislature, he worked tirelessly for the CCF cause, stumping the province to deliver speeches, assisting local riding associations, and serving on numerous party committees. But by 1953, after almost twenty years of service to the party, he was physically and financially spent. As well, the legal firm he had established with David Lewis and John Osler to help the labour movement in its struggles was in growing need of his undivided attention. Therefore, in July he privately informed the Executive of his decision to resign, a decision not made public until shortly after the federal election.[29]

Jolliffe's resignation had two immediate consequences. First, it ensured that no future CCF leader would be forced to endure the sort of financial deprivation he himself had suffered in his eleven years as leader. The Provincial Leadership Fund, which the party established in May 1952 to alleviate this problem, did not grow as expected. As of September 1953, the labour movement had made only one contribution to the fund, amounting to $3,500, part of which was used to pay for Jolliffe's expenses as an organizer over the previous twelve months. No salary, however, was ever paid to Jolliffe. Shortly after Jolliffe's resignation, therefore, the Provincial Council decided that, from then on, the party would provide its leader with an annual salary of $6,000, plus expenses, from its general revenues.[30]

The other consequence was the calling of a special convention for late November to choose Jolliffe's successor. It took place at the College Street Legion Hall in Toronto and aroused a great degree of interest within the party; close to 400 delegates attended, from almost every riding in Ontario, an unusual occurrence as far as CCF conventions were concerned. They met in an atmosphere that was jovial and friendly, from the dinner banquet held to pay tribute to the departing leader, right through to the election itself. The main contestants were Fred Young, Donald MacDonald, and Andrew Brewin. Brewin, a well-known civil liberties lawyer in Toronto who had served as a party officer for many years and would eventually be elected to Parliament, and MacDonald, a former teacher and journalist with several years service at the National Office in various capacities, were considered the "establishment" candidates. Young, on the other hand, was the favourite of the grass roots, and his last-minute decision to contest the leadership was largely a response to pressure from the ridings to run as the "anti-establishment" candidate. In an extremely close race, in which the early favourite, Brewin, was forced to drop out after the first ballot because of an unexpectedly strong showing by Young, MacDonald came from behind on the second ballot to edge out Young by only seven votes. The contest was a civil one, for the most part, although there were some momentary hard feelings in the Brewin and Young camps, stemming from the belief that MacDonald's forces had brought in some last-minute trade union support to eke out the victory. But these feelings were soon set aside, and in a show of unity the delegates closed ranks to endorse MacDonald as the unanimous choice of the convention.[31]

After all was said and done and the bitterness of defeat had receded, the delegates probably felt quite good about the leadership race. They had, after all, been offered a choice of three very capable contenders. And in Donald Cameron MacDonald, the thirty-nine-year-old father of three, they were certain they had picked a leader who could bring the party closer to power. Indeed, MacDonald was well suited for the position. Raised on a farm in Ormstown, near Montreal, he had a natural affinity with the farming community. His work in the 1930s as a teacher, journalist, and overseas lecturer helped fine-tune his oratorical skills, and his years of service in the federal government's Wartime Information Board during the war enhanced his knowledge of government. While in Ottawa, MacDonald came into contact with CCF leaders who, recognizing his abilities, quickly found a place for him in the party after the war. In 1946, he became the president of the Ottawa CCF Club, a member of the Ontario CCF Provincial Council, and the national education secretary.[32]

It was his work as national organizer and treasurer in the early 1950s, however, that made MacDonald a household name in the Ontario CCF. His duties surrounding the National Expansion Drive, in particular, took him across the province several times and imbued him with an understanding of the Ontario scene few CCFers could claim to possess. His influence on the Ontario party was felt even more directly, thanks to his specific and well-reasoned proposals for expanding the movement through poll committee organization. Not surprisingly, therefore, he accepted his new position easily and with confidence. He would start campaigning immediately, he told CCFers in his acceptance speech, and would visit every riding to rejuvenate the party in time for the next provincial election. Within one year, he promised, the Ontario CCF would have rebuilt its organization completely, so that "when the next election rolls around, the Frost government will receive the opposition it has always needed ... As far as we're concerned, the 1954 election has already started. We must start now and plan for the biggest battle this province has ever known."[33]

The resignation of Ted Jolliffe and the accession of Donald MacDonald were the latest in a series of events that marked the CCF's road to organizational recovery following the 1951 election. Despite the initial storm of dissent, and the subsequent drizzle of protest, party leaders were determined to shake CCF riding associations out of their complacency and to steer the party toward an earlier organizational high mark: a membership level equal to that of the late 1940s. And assisted by a larger organizing staff, as well as some innovative organizing techniques, such as the regional conferences and spring membership drive, the CCF was able to achieve its objective by the summer of 1953.

The situation among the labouring rank and file, however, was less promising. Except in Toronto and parts of the North, neither CCF, nor OFL-PAC leaders were able to extend the sort of cooperation achieved on the restructured Trade Union Committee down to the grass-roots where it counted most. The CCF's poor showing in Ontario in the 1953 federal election was, in part, testimony to this failure. The election also indicated to the CCF that a large membership in itself did not guarantee electoral success and that a new, more refined organizational approach was necessary. As a result, party leaders revised their organizational strategy to include greater emphasis on creating more active, dedicated members, operating through the poll committee structure. This seemingly more sophisticated approach, combined with the presence of a confident and capable new leader at the helm, rendered the CCF's prospects for the near future brighter than they had been for some time.

4 One Step Forward ...

The next step in the CCF's plan of organizational revival was spelled out quite clearly in the August 1953 "Program of Action." "Our next major test in Ontario," declared the Organization Committee, "will be a provincial general election which will undoubtedly be held within the next 18 months. Our task between now and then is to strengthen our organization so that we will enter the election campaign as an effective fighting force." The Provincial Office took on this task with single-minded determination, confident that the rebuilding process begun in 1952 would culminate in electoral gains. But this was not to be. The revival peaked in the spring of 1954, with the introduction of a "new" official CCF program, and was followed by an unexpected decline in membership and the well-publicized expulsion of Communists from the party. These blows were too much for the CCF, particularly in the still unfavourable political climate of the mid-fifties. Therefore, despite some impressive assistance from organized labour and the reality of a government plagued by scandal, the long-awaited electoral test of 1955 gave the CCF little to celebrate. The latest phase of rebuilding the CCF could only be deemed a failure.

That phase nevertheless began on a promising note. According to Donald MacDonald, who, as promised, began touring the province shortly after his victory in November 1953, the enthusiasm and optimism witnessed at the leadership convention carried over into the new year. From January to March, the new leader visited most of the

ridings in northern Ontario, where he addressed numerous party functions and spoke regularly on radio. His tireless efforts did much to
renew enthusiasm within party ranks, and upon his return he was
pleased to report on "the revival of spirit in our own movement. In
many places there has been an encouraging change in outlook ... In
many places, local organization is being revitalized, with newcomers
stepping up to share the work with experienced old-timers. Most of
the job lies ahead as yet, but there appears to be a new spirit and a
will to tackle it."[1]

Although MacDonald's comments were intended in part to rally the
troops, they cannot be dismissed as simply rhetoric, for in some ways
they represented an accurate depiction of the party's condition at the
time. Since the spring of 1952, the CCF had experienced a process of
organizational and spiritual renewal, albeit gradual and uneven, which
manifested itself in several ways: membership levels were restored to
respectable levels, internal dissent was muted, and a new leader had
been chosen at a lively and well-attended convention. Although much
remained to be done, the party was more united and more confident
of its prospects by the spring of 1954 than it had been in years.

Contributing to, and reflecting the renewed spirit was the CCF's
adoption of a new official program. The decision to revise the existing
program, the first such revision since 1948, was made by the party
Executive in early 1953 and was based on the desire to provide the
party with a "dynamic provincial election program" for the next campaign. The preliminary draft, entitled "Looking to the Future," was
composed by the CCF Research Committee in the fall and presented
to Council in January 1954. In February and March, the CCF Membership Education Committee conducted seven regional conferences to
give party members a chance to discuss the draft and submit recommendations, before Council presented it to the annual convention in
May for final approval.

CCFers grasped this opportunity enthusiastically. Attendance at the
conferences was high, participation was good, and the number of recommended revisions amounted to almost twice the size of the program
itself, thus forcing Council to "substantially alter" the original draft in
time for the convention; the program was published the following year.
Looking back, MacDonald believes that the whole process "played a
fairly important role. In the disillusionment and general collapse of
things ... after 1951, it was for people who were interested in the
movement and what it stood for – a recreation, a revitalization of what
the party stood for."[2] If the CCF had indeed become an authoritarian,
anti-educational political party by the 1950s, as many inside and outside the party claimed, it was certainly not evident on this occasion.

Nor is it apparent, from the new program, that the CCF had become less socialist. Although the program was largely a result of the desire to renew the movement, neither its components, nor the philosophy that bred and unified them differed very much from the party's 1948 policy statement, *First Term Program*. In the latter document, the CCF's democratic socialist philosophy was stated clearly and succinctly at the outset: "The Cooperative Commonwealth Federation is a democratic movement which believes that people are more important than profits. It stands for economic planning and social ownership to develop our natural resources for the good of *all* the people." The ultimate goal, in short, was to establish a "cooperative commonwealth," where cooperation replaced competition and wealth was distributed more equitably.

The remainder of the document explains how·a CCF government in Ontario would advance this ideal during its first term. The primary method would be extensive government intervention in the economy and in other areas of everyday life, either through regulation or outright ownership. The CCF promised, for example, to establish "a planning board to direct the development of natural resources and advise on public ownership in the fields of mining, petroleum, food processing, farm implements, the liquor industry, and building materials," and to nationalize highway bus transportation. In addition, it would develop new power sources, lower electricity rates, and provide consumers with electrical appliances "at cost."

In the area of social services, the CCF's proposals were much more extensive. For low-income tenants, the CCF promised to build a large number of housing units and to regulate rental charges. To aid the sick, it would introduce a hospital insurance scheme, establish health centres in rural areas, and provide free treatment for certain serious diseases. Moreover, health care would be provided free of charge to the elderly, the disabled, and single mothers, all of whom would receive higher social security benefit payments as well. Wage earners (including civil servants) were offered "collective bargaining and union security," a forty-hour work week, two weeks paid vacation, 100 percent workmen's compensation coverage, equal pay for equal work, and higher minimum wages. Rural inhabitants would receive better roads as well as legislation to give farmers greater control over the marketing of their products. To preserve the natural environment, moreover, a CCF administration would introduce soil conservation and reforestation projects and would impose tighter control over Crown lands. Other promises included larger grants to municipalities, "municipal distribution of milk, bread, and fuel," low-cost public automobile insurance, larger educational grants, lower university fees, more scholarships, more temperance education, a Bill of Rights, and a Department of Cooperatives to provide cooperatives with loans and technical services.

In *Looking to the Future*, the CCF demonstrated the same concern for the principles of cooperation and planning as in *First Term Program*.[3] As such, it maintained its promises regarding public ownership with only slight alterations; telephone companies and grain storage facilities were added to the list of potential targets, while companies in the food-processing industry were omitted. Moreover, the CCF's pledge that "where an industry is subject to unreasonable monopoly control, pilot plants will be established to induce competition and force prices to reasonable levels" suggested that the party was just as committed to public ownership and "central planning" in 1955 as it was in 1948.

Nor did it water down its commitment to the other form of "social ownership," namely, cooperative enterprise. "We are convinced that the individual realizes his greatest well-being and best develops his own special talents in an atmosphere of cooperation," states the opening section of the program. "We believe that both federal and provincial government should strive, within their appropriate spheres, to create a society in which such cooperation is the guiding principle." Therefore, where the party decided that nationalization was inappropriate in a particular industry, such as food processing, it encouraged the establishment of producer and consumer cooperatives instead.

In fact, the only significant change in the political-economic section of the new program was the stronger emphasis on public participation in the planning, regulation, and ownership processes of government. "A conscious effort will be made," promised the CCF, "to encourage direct participation of as many citizens as possible through regular consultation with farm organizations, trade unions, cooperative societies, consumer organizations and representative business groups." One can perhaps attribute this new emphasis to the growing fear of centralized state bureaucracies, a fear prevalent among some party members and among many voters during the tense Cold War years of the 1950s.[4]

Most of the changes in the 1955 statement, however, are found in the section on social matters and involve either the *extension* of existing CCF policies, such as the introduction of comprehensive medical insurance once a hospital insurance scheme was in place, "free education and social services" for the elderly, higher mothers' allowance payments, and the establishment of a Human Rights Commission, or the *addition* of new policies. Among the latter is the commitment to abolish university fees, expand correctional services, humanize the penal system, reduce pollution, subsidize the arts and recreation, and reduce waste and corruption in public administration.

The CCF's 1955 program, therefore, was almost identical in philosophy and policy to the previous program. *Looking to the Future* simply updated the 1948 statement slightly to suit the province's new concerns and, perhaps for that reason, aroused little controversy within party circles. Some criticized the party's failure to advocate *further* nationalization simply because such a position was increasingly unpopular. Others, perhaps seized by the anti-Communist mentality, deplored what they perceived to be the party's "over-emphasis on government paternalism" at the expense of "that active, participating democracy which determines to build a new social structure [primarily through cooperatives], come hell or high water." Such criticisms were rare, however, and their thrust simply confirmed the lack of significant change in the CCF's ideology and program since 1948.[5]

Rewriting its official program was only one of the organizational moves the party made to prepare for the next provincial election. Party leaders were continuing to encourage and direct basic organizational expansion. In April, the CCF held its annual Spring Membership Drive, along more or less the same lines as the previous year. The province was divided into ten areas, each containing a number of ridings, and membership targets were set for each area and riding. Unfortunately, the results, too, were similar. With the exception of two or three northern ridings, commented the Drive's chairperson afterwards, "we could not conscientiously claim that our membership situation was satisfactory as yet." Even with the moderate success of the Drive, in fact, party membership fell by several hundred between July 1953 and July 1954.[6]

To reverse this discouraging trend in what had appeared to be a pattern of overall revival, the CCF reverted once again to its most basic organizational strategy: that of encouraging members to sign up as many new members as possible. The confident optimism which, less than twelve months earlier, had generated an emphasis on sophisticated poll organization and active members was replaced by an anxious determination to simply lengthen the membership lists. In fact, the CCF declared war on falling membership. Now headed by Marjorie Pinney, a long-time CCF activist from Halton county who was known for her straight-talking, no-nonsense approach, the Organization Committee adopted a new plan whereby it hoped to double party membership within two years. Called the "CCF Brigade," its object was to persuade an army of 200 party members to openly pledge themselves to sign up 50 new members over a two-year period.

"Everyone who joins the Brigade," Pinney declared to readers of the CCF *News*, "will automatically become No. 1 Heroes of the Ontario CCF," and "suitable awards" would be made to those who fulfilled their pledge.[7]

On the surface, the Brigade gimmick seems to have been directed at the rank and file. In fact, recalls Pinney, it was directed at the "party brass" on the Council and Executive. A strong advocate of organizing from the top, Pinney seems to have headed up a less discernable third faction in the CCF, one which fell in behind Fred Young during the 1953 leadership race and which was continually pushing the party to hire more organizers. If the "educator-voluntarists" were one organizational pole in the party, Pinney and the other "organizers" – people like Macdonald, Bryden, and Young – were the other. The majority of the CCF's leaders and regular members fell somewhere in between. With the Brigade scheme, Pinney hoped to spur the leadership into doing more in the way of signing up members and setting an example for the rank-and-file. With undiminished passion, she recalls that

the thing which used to make me mad was that we had people – and Eamon Park [Steelworker, former PAC Director and CCF M.P.P.] was one of them, and there were others – that didn't sign up a single member in their entire life! ... [Park] thought that just because he was a union guy and willing to play a role in the party that that was enough ... To me that's a form of lip service ... I was trying to challenge them: do you want a nice debating society, or do you want a political party? If you want a political party, then you can't pick and choose what you want to do. Everyone must ... take their share. So the Brigade was designed to put all these people on the spot. What I said to them was, "You can't expect Joe Blow out there in the boonies to go out and knock on doors or sign up people if we don't set the example."

Pinney designed a pledge form for this purpose "and practically shamed them into signing it." With a chuckle she adds, "I had it set up so that Eamon Park had to be the first one to sign!" In addition, Pinney asked members of her committee to contact Council members personally and encourage them to sign the pledge. The Brigade concept would only be extended to "the general membership," she told them, "after all the possibilities of the present plan [to enlist the leadership] had been exhausted."[8]

There is no doubt that Pinney was a thorn in the leadership's side, and she frequently vented her frustration and impatience through the pages of the CCF *News*, in a column appropriately entitled "Needles from Pinney." "The reluctance [to join the CCF] is not on the part of those whom we approach to become members," she told her readers in 1954, "but rather it is in those of us who hesitate to go out and do the kind of work that must be done ... We have to quit playing around with it [i.e., the party], stop thinking of it as a hobby or as something to do when we have nothing else on tap. We will not do this job if so many continue to put their church work, service clubs, union meetings and social life ahead of the CCF. We should be thinking in terms of the CCF every day of our lives."[9] The hard-sell approach of Pinney and her committee clearly had an effect. By December, over ninety persons had enlisted with the CCF Brigade, half of them members of the Provincial Council. Unfortunately, the 500 new members that this contingent had managed to sign up since June were offset by "the failure of ridings to keep [membership] renewals up-to-date"; by the end of the year, total membership had fallen to less than 8,000.[10] Like the Spring Membership Drive, therefore, the Brigade concept was only partially successful.

The attempts to expand membership were accompanied by efforts to raise money and prepare riding associations for the next election. The Organization Committee conducted a finance drive among members in Toronto in January and February, 1955, while the new provincial secretary, Ken Bryden, and the provincial organizers, Ames and Young, encouraged riding executives to assemble teams of election workers, choose enumerators, set up poll committees, and, most important of all, nominate candidates; once nominated, candidates received copies of MacDonald's speeches, CCF press releases, party literature, and instructions on election organizing. At the same time, a number of well-attended educational conferences were held across Ontario to prepare party workers for the campaign.[11]

It was at this point, however, several months before the June 1955 provincial election, that the final curtain was falling on a long-playing drama – one which threatened to undermine all that the party had done since the summer of 1953 to ready itself for the election. In early April, newspapers across the country announced that the Ontario CCF had recently expelled fourteen Communists from its ranks, a move upheld by the party's annual convention that month. Although party leaders had done everything possible to keep the expulsions a private, internal matter, to avoid the inevitable (and lethal) accusations from party detractors that the CCF was a party riddled with Communists, media people at the convention had somehow slipped unnoticed into the private session during which the expulsions were being discussed. For a party on the road to recovery, the revelations could not have come at a more inopportune moment.

This was certainly not the first time that Communists had created problems for the CCF. Throughout its brief history, the party had been plagued by elements on the extreme Left; these alternately sought to cooperate with it in a "united front," or to destroy it either by infiltrating its ranks and converting its members or by endorsing it publicly (the "kiss of death" scenario).[12] Invariably, the Communists were rebuffed, for the CCF made it a strict rule to have no dealings whatsoever with revolutionary socialist movements. Any other policy would have been politically suicidal, given Ontario's basically conservative political culture. Nevertheless, the Communists' repeated efforts to warm up to, sabotage, or infiltrate the CCF left a lasting image in the minds of Ontario voters that the party was tinged with communism, an image that was reinforced periodically by the CCF's enemies and that the party did its best to dispel, notwithstanding its limited resources.[13]

The latest encounter with the Communists actually began in April 1952 when a Trotskyist organization, known as the Workers Revolutionary Party (WRP), led by Ross Dowson, publicly announced that it was disbanding so that it could continue its struggle to win the hearts and souls of Canadian workers through the more popular CCF. The CCF Executive responded by asking the provincial secretary, Ken Bryden, to "hold up any applications from this group subject to the advice of this Executive." The first test came six months later when Dowson's brother, Murray, applied for membership. Relying on the party's constitution, which restricted membership in the CCF to "persons who have agreed to subscribe to the principles and policies of the CCF," the Executive decided that ex-Communists would be granted membership only if they renounced their former beliefs. Since this did not appear to be the case with Murray Dowson, the application was rejected.[14] One year later, a similar application from Ross Dowson was rejected on the same grounds.

Despite the CCF's best efforts to block infiltration, CCF leaders were certain that some of the less prominent members of the WRP had slipped through the net. They could take no action, however, because "concrete proof was not available" – that is, until August 1954. At that time, the CCF discovered that the WRP had not disbanded after all, but had simply gone underground to improve its chances of infiltrating the CCF; members had continued to meet clandestinely at the party's headquarters in a Labour bookstore on Elm Street in Toronto. In late 1953, however, a serious rift developed within the WRP which, by the following April, left the party divided into two factions. Fortunately for the CCF, a disaffected member of one of the factions, Leslie Dawson, decided to turn informer. In August 1954, he gave the CCF solid evidence, in the form of minute books and membership lists, that he and fourteen other members of the WRP had infiltrated the CCF and were currently members; four of the fifteen even held key positions within the CCF party. In Dawson's own testimony to the Executive, he admitted that "the formal dissolvement [sic] of the RWP some two years ago was only a smoke screen for other purposes. The Trotskyist party has maintained its character, membership and structure up to the present ... In Canada all Trotskyists ... are within the CCF. It is their aim to eventually disrupt and split with sufficient forces to build a revolutionary party centered around themselves. They are at present undermining the membership of the CCF by fomenting disputes."[15]

After a two-month investigation by a subcommittee of the CCF Executive, the results of which confirmed Dawson's revelations, the Executive prepared charges against the fifteen CCF members in question. The accused, all of whom were young CCF members from the Toronto area, were charged which violating Article III, Section 4, of the party's constitution, which stated that any CCF member who was at the same time a member of "another political party, or any organization ancillary thereto," would lose his/her membership in the CCF. Although they were given the opportunity to appear before the next Council meeting, in late October, to give their side of the story, only nine of the accused availed themselves of this opportunity. Two pleaded guilty to the charge, while another, who objected to the nature of the proceedings, dismissed himself. The remainder pleaded "innocent" and were subsequently tried.[16]

The hearings were conducted much like a regular criminal trial. Representatives of the CCF and the accused presented evidence and cross-examined each other's witnesses; after each case had been heard, the Council rendered its verdict. To prove that the accused were members of the WRP, the CCF relied primarily on the testimony of their star witness, Leslie Dawson, and, in all but two cases, on corroborative written and oral evidence. Faced with this nearly conclusive evidence, the accused could do little but question its validity. The only other defence, usually presented by representatives from the defendant's riding association, was that the accused had been "useful members of their riding association and had not shown any overt disruptive tendencies." But Council members viewed this as irrelevant. After all, they reasoned, "It was inherent in the nature of the [Communist] conspiracy ... that members of the Fourth International should seek to achieve positions of confidence and responsibility in the CCF by their activity in their riding associations and by carefully concealing their connection or sympathy with the Trotskyist party." Dawson had admitted as much to the Executive.[17]

Although proper constitutional procedure had been followed, with each of the accused having a fair chance to present his or her case, most Councillors were in no mood to be lenient. The penalty for dual membership prescribed by the constitution was expulsion, and they were determined to carry out this provision to the letter. Yet without questioning the Council's verdict, many Councillors objected to the severity of the punishment. In cases where there had been "mitigating circumstances," such as the "unsettled mental and emotional condition" of the accused or their willingness to renounce their Trotskyist beliefs, many Council members recommended more lenient sentences, such as temporary expulsion. After a lengthy deliberation, however, six of the accused were found "guilty" and expelled indefinitely; one was found "not guilty" due to insufficient evidence; and two cases were referred back to the Executive for further investigation. Those who had not bothered to appear before Council, with the exception of a repentent Dawson, were also expelled indefinitely.[18]

Unfortunately for the CCF, the expulsion episode did not end there. Eight of those expelled from the party took the fateful step of appealing the Council's decision to the annual convention in early April, 1955. Four of the eight, who had chosen not to appear before Council in late 1954, were not permitted to speak to the convention, and their expulsions were sustained. The four remaining appellants were tried in the same fashion as before. In their defence, they argued that Trotskyism was simply a variation of democratic socialism and that the CCF leadership was trying to suppress legitimate dissent. "The Ontario CCF may not wish to adopt what might be called Trotskyist interpretations or some other interpretations of socialist policy," they declared in a statement presented to the convention, "but are you not … being asked to ban, to outlaw Trotskyism, or what is alleged to be Trotskyism, from the movement? Isn't this the dreaded virus of THOUGHT CONTROL being planted in our movement?" But since the issue was whether the accused held dual membership, delegates became very impatient with such evasive arguments. "Answer yes or no!" they shouted. "Do you belong to a second party?" The accused would not respond directly. Interpreting this "as an admission of guilt," delegates "overwhelmingly rejected their appeals."[19]

The extreme measures taken against the fourteen "CCFers" between October 1954 and April 1955 were severe enough to have been potentially divisive. After all, members did not take such actions lightly and without some remorse; in the May issue of the CCF News, one member commented that "every CCFer deeply regretted having to hear appeals of four whose cards had been cancelled due to membership in another party." The CCF was fortunate, therefore, to have emerged from the experience with its unity intact – a sign that members were satisfied that proper and democratic constitutional procedures had been followed throughout, and further evidence that the party's so-called "left-wing" was indeed an insignificant force in the fifties, notwithstanding the conventional wisdom.

Nevertheless, the expulsions were not entirely without repercussion. From the start, the CCF had tried to keep the expulsions a party secret. Riding executives were told to restrict information on the hearings to CCF members only, and the appeals to the convention were held in closed session, with those in attendance sworn to secrecy. Although the CCF would later claim that these measures were taken to protect the right of the accused to a fair trial, it is difficult to see how the publicity could have affected anything but the CCF's chances in the upcoming election. Despite these efforts at secrecy, several reporters disguised as delegates managed to attend the closed session at the convention. Reports of the expulsions were subsequently carried prominently in the Toronto dailies, including the *Globe and Mail*.[20]

For the most part, media coverage of the event was fair. Despite the proximity of the provincial election, columnists and editors resisted the temptation of using the episode to score political points. Nevertheless, it is safe to speculate that the publicity only served to reinforce in the public's mind the age-old association between the CCF and the Communists. It was unlikely that the average reader of the *Toronto Star*, for example, understood the fine distinction made by that paper's editor when he pointed out the divergent methods advocated by the CCF and Communists to achieve what he called a "similarity of aims." But if the media refrained from deliberately linking the CCF with the Communists, some politicians did not. In Ottawa, Finance Minister Walter Harris evoked a flurry of angry denials from CCF leader M.J. Coldwell when he lambasted the party's so-called Trotskyist affiliations. Yet what was the average Ontario voter to think when amid these denials could be heard the embarrassing remarks of CCF M.P. Colin Cameron, who unabashedly criticized the Ontario CCF's actions?[21] And this only ten months after another prominent CCF leader from British Columbia, Rod Young, had captured headlines with his boast that he would be proud to be called a Communist and that he knew of a least fifty party members who were former Communists. Perhaps Ontario voters were thinking along the same lines as Ontario Liberal leader Farquhar Oliver, who told fellow Liberals in Toronto that "this party, which harbours pinks and Reds, has been disturbed recently by the numbers of pinks and Reds that have moved into its ranks. They got 15 of them during the expulsions, but no one knows how many they missed." Or perhaps they nodded knowingly when Gladstone Murray's anti-Communist information sheet, "Outlook," told them that, "as the Ontario Election campaign develops it becomes apparent that the CCF and the Communists [i.e. LPP] are getting together ... The Trotskyites found refuge in the CCF until recently when they were publicly exposed and expelled. This eviction is now bearing fruit. The LPP has responded with growing affection for our Socialists ... All citizens of Ontario who wish to protect the freedom and growing prosperity of the Province should consider it a duty of primary importance to vote against the latest left-wing conspiracy."[22]

The impact of the expulsions on the party's support was assuredly negative. A Gallup Poll released two weeks after the revelations indicates that support for the two major parties had fallen significantly since the 1951 election, but that this widespread disillusionment had not translated into greater support for the CCF. In fact, the CCF's support remained where it had been before the 1951 election, at around 12 percent, while the "undecided" vote grew to a phenomenal 35 percent, indicating that voters felt uncomfortable with the CCF as an alternative to the Liberals or Conservatives.[23]

As far as the CCF was concerned, however, the expulsions were simply an annoying and regrettable sideshow; the main focus continued to be the upcoming provincial election. This is not surprising, since much of the party's time and energy over the past eighteen months had been directed at improving its prospects in the contest: it had chosen a leader who, it felt, could bring it closer to power and, without making any fundamental changes, had revised its program to stimulate party members and make the CCF more attractive to voters. In addition, it had taken measures to expand its membership, raise money, and galvanize riding associations into action.

Of course, these election-oriented activities were not unusual. The CCF was, after all, a political party, and so behaved in ways intended to improve its electoral prospects. What *was* perhaps unusual was the singleness of purpose reflected in the various activities of the party during this period. Almost everything it did between September 1953 and June 1955 was shaped in some way by the provincial election. Even by-elections, which in the past had been valued as important prizes, were increasingly viewed in terms of how they would affect the party's chances in the next general election. In 1952, when the Provincial Office decided to devote fewer resources to the by-elections of that year, it did so for the potential long-term gains. The same disposition explains the party's decision to contest most of the federal and provincial by-elections of 1953 and 1954. Although the party finished a distant third in all but one of the seven by-elections it fought during these two years, the CCF's decision to participate was motivated in large part by the potential long-run benefits.[24] "These are not ridings that have been strong CCF territory in the past," declared the Finance Committee with regard to the 1954 by-elections, "and no one is expecting any miracles ... Nevertheless, in all the ridings affected, real opportunities for building the CCF are now presenting themselves ... We can lay real foundations in these six ridings [i.e., create a base of supporters and workers]. Thus we will be that much further ahead when the provincial election comes along."[25]

Complementing this methodical and far-sighted organizational strategy were two promising developments. The first was the continuing strong support from the OFL-PAC following the 1953 federal election. In conjunction with the CCF's TUC, the PAC continued to organize political education conferences for union leaders and to set up PACs or "informal CCF units" in unions "that had no previous connection with political education and action"; it also provided the CCF with candidates, workers, and money for the various by-elections. Preparations for the 1955 provincial election, specifically, began shortly after the OFL's annual meeting in February of that year, at which delegates reaffirmed their support for the CCF and OFL leaders promised to "leave no stone unturned to bring about the election of a CCF government." Subsequently, the PAC asked labour councils and union locals to provide it with staff for the campaign and to establish or reactivate local PACs "to work closely with CCF constituency organizations." Local PACs were given a handbook listing the things they could do to help the CCF, such as raising money, bringing union members into the party, providing enumerators and canvassers, and inviting CCF candidates to speak to plant workers. In addition, the PAC spent $16,000 on newspaper and radio advertising and prepared several leaflets on the CCF for distribution among workers; this publicity resulted in a large influx of union members as campaign workers and CCF candidates, even larger than in 1951 according to both CCF and OFL leaders. The PAC itself provided four full-time organizers to do "political work" for the CCF from early March through to the election. These organizational efforts were combined with repeated pleas from OFL leaders to union members to get out and vote and, more importantly, to vote for the CCF.[26]

The second auspicious development for the CCF was the emergence of a made-to-order issue that became the central theme of the 1955 campaign, remaining in the forefront of Ontario politics for several years to come. That issue was political morality, and it emerged a year earlier in connection with an episode known as the "Highways Scandal." In early 1954, four minor officials in the Highways Department of the Ontario government were found guilty of "irregularities" in the letting of contracts; they were sent to prison, while several construction firms, which had received undeservedly lucrative contracts from the Department, were given fines. In addition, the deputy minister of Highways was transferred to another department and the minister, George Doucett, resigned. But the matter did not end here. Both the Liberal and CCF parties believed that this was just the tip of the iceberg – that the problem of corruption went beyond simply one department and that additional ministers and civil servants were also involved. Furthermore, argued the CCF, the government had not dealt with the root of the problem: the method of party financing. Politicians and civil servants were abusing the public trust and misusing public monies in large part because of the substantial political contributions they received from companies doing business with the government. The CCF therefore demanded that a Royal Commission be established to investigate the highways scandal, particularly the issue of political contributions from road contractors.[27]

Despite some initial hesitation, based on Donald MacDonald's concern that sufficient evidence was lacking, the CCF decided to make the most of the related issues of political contributions, corruption in office, and government extravagance in the time remaining before the next election. Speaking to the OFL's annual convention in February 1954, MacDonald asserted that "the scandal that has emerged in government administration in government departments" was causing a "ground swell" of discontent among Ontario voters. "Quite apart from this highway scandal," he continued, "the present government has built up over the past eighteen months, out of the embarrassing surplus that Premier Frost has had in the last years, a fifty-three million dollar so-called highway reserve fund ... to confuse the issues to get the working people thinking that the Frost Government is a very generous government."[28] One month later, the CCF caucus accused the Select Committee which the government had established to investigate the recent scandal of trying to cover up the affair and demanded the establishment of a Royal Commission. Delegates to the party's annual convention in May passed two resolutions on the subject, one echoing the call for a Royal Commission, the other asking the people of Ontario to "throw out the Frost government" in the next election.

After eight months of relative silence on the issue, the CCF issued a press release in February of 1955 in which it criticized the government's pre-election public works spending, calling it "the type of spending that has the greatest potential in providing election patronage" and in "fill[ing] the campaign chests of the Tory party." Party leaders continued to make similar comments at open meetings and party gatherings in the months that followed. In the legislature, meanwhile, the party's lone M.P.P.S, Bill Grummett and Tommy Thomas, began turning the heat up on Frost's cabinet as soon as the second session of the legislature convened in February. Referring to the transfer of the deputy minister of highways to another department, the normally unaggressive, congenial Thomas demanded an explanation: "Why was he transferred to another position? What was the reason? These are the questions the people of Ontario are asking. Did he know too much? What was the reason?" Needling of this sort led to several acrimonious exchanges on the floor and made for the stormiest session the legislature had seen in years.[29]

Not surprisingly, the issue of government morality became a central theme during the spring election campaign, especially after the news that the Tory party brass had refused to endorse the nomination of Renfrew South M.P.P., James Dempsey, for failing to report campaign donations he had received from a timber operator during the 1951 election. The CCF jumped on the "Dempsey Affair" as proof that the entire Frost administration was rotten to the core. "Revelations of political contributions in South Renfrew," MacDonald told a gathering of unionists in London, "is just further evidence that the basis of financing the old parties is a source of corruption of our public life." He then called upon the government to outlaw contributions from firms doing work for the government, for limitations on election spending, and for a more open accounting of the sources of party funding. CCF candidates, meanwhile, repeatedly compared the Frost government with Quebec's Union Nationale, accusing the Tories of using its "Highway Reserve Fund" as a slush fund to buy votes. A CCF government, promised one candidate, would "put a stop to the rotten political patronage system of government today."[30]

Although the CCF hammered away at the morality issue during the campaign, it took great care not to implicate Leslie Frost in the alleged wrongdoings of his government. After all, the premier was still very popular and his character was seen as unimpeachable. Donald MacDonald recalls that political corruption "was a difficult topic to deal with because Frost was a man of towering political stature and unquestioned personal integrity." As a result, the CCF was forced to take the position that behind the innocent Leslie Frost was a rotten Tory political machine that was "using and abusing more and more of the government departments and public administration for its own political purposes." The Liberals, who were equally vigilant in their attacks on Tory corruption during the campaign, wisely adopted a similar approach.[31]

The constant attacks from the CCF and Liberal parties put the Conservatives on the defensive for much of the campaign. Tory candidates spent a good deal of time responding to the numerous charges of corruption and inefficiency and very little time trumpeting their government's accomplishments or laying out future plans. Nor did their responses do much to deflate the accusations. Attorney-General Dana Porter, admitting that his government had made mistakes, offered one of the more ironic explanations. "We are just as human and have as many failings as anybody else in this country," he told supporters at a nomination meeting in Toronto-Woodbine, "but we have played fair."[32]

Either way, Ontario voters were unmoved. Times were good and the average Ontarian had few complaints. Many voters no doubt concurred wholeheartedly with the premier's typically optimistic declaration that "we are living in a great, dynamic province, a province in which the horizons have been lifted." And on June 9th, they returned his Conservative party to Queen's Park with a substantial majority. In a victory almost as daunting as their 1951 triumph, the Tories carried eighty-three of ninety-eight seats and 48 percent of the popular vote. In Toronto and the Yorks, they swept nineteen of the twenty seats available, including the lone Communist seat held by veteran M.P.P. Joe Salsberg. The ineffectiveness of the opposition's attacks on the government's integrity was clearly illustrated with the re-election of all but one Tory cabinet minister, including George Doucett, the former highways minister; James Dempsey was also returned.[33]

Needless to say, neither the Liberals nor the CCF could boast of such accomplishments. Led by Farquhar Oliver, a veteran of the legislature and an eloquent speaker, but someone who lacked the energy, enthusiasm, and broad knowledge of the issues required of a party leader, the Liberals captured only ten seats, three more than in 1951. The CCF, with their new leader at the helm, increased its representation by only one seat, to a total of three.[34] More foreboding was the fact that the Liberals made inroads into traditional CCF territory in Toronto and the Yorks, the only bright spot being the election of Donald MacDonald in York South.

The results must have been a severe blow to the CCF, the usual effusions of "moral victory" aside. Despite the four-year long effort to revive the movement, and notwithstanding the support of the labour movement and the apparently opportune emphasis on political corruption during the campaign, its gains were minimal; it actually received a smaller percentage of the popular vote (2.5 percentage points less) than in 1951. The reasons are many. First, the Liberals decided not to contest several ridings that the CCF was expected to win, thus ensuring a united "anti-CCF" vote and a Tory victory in these ridings. As a result, the CCF's widely respected veteran House Leader, Bill Grummett, was defeated in Cochrane South, and the party's popular northern organizer, Doc Ames, went down to defeat in Temiskaming. Second, the CCF's expulsion of Communist infiltrators eight weeks before voting day and the occasional instance of red-baiting during the campaign probably frightened away a number of potential supporters and might even account for the significant drop in CCF support in greater Toronto – a traditional party stronghold, but also the place where the Communist infiltration had occurred. What was worse, the party was unable to repair its damaged image because a shortage of campaign funds had resulted in a sharp reduction in CCF publicity and advertising.[35] Third, the CCF was again hurt by the fact that organized labour did not vote for it, when it voted at all. Most of the urban-industrial ridings were captured by the Tories, in part because the CCF could not get its labour supporters to the polls; voter turnout in these ridings was below average, particularly in Toronto, Hamilton, and Ottawa.[36] Although more workers assisted the CCF than during the 1951 election, Henry Weisbach observed, "It's very obvious we didn't have the necessary organization to get the labour vote to the polls." One "disgusted [CCF] housewife" wrote that "on election afternoon I telephoned all the homes on one voters' list where the husbands' jobs suggested trade union affiliation, and suggested they get out and vote ... Over half of those I telephoned did not even realize it was election day." Political apathy among traditional CCF supporters had once again left its mark.[37]

The main reasons for the CCF's poor performance, however, were the familiar and closely related problems of political climate and organization. A popular premier, a booming economy, and an ongoing Cold War were not circumstances likely to enhance the popularity of an avowedly socialist political party in 1955, especially one that many voters probably perceived as being ridden with Communists. In this context, accusations of government immorality did not go far. It was no doubt with a strong sense of frustration that poet and former LSR leader, Frank Scott, told a gathering of the party faithful in late 1956 that "we seem to be in danger of losing our sense of values in the tremendous material boom. Governments in Quebec and British Columbia have this year been re-elected by an apathetic public after scandals that would have brought governments down into complete disaster half a century ago." Frost's biographer summarizes the problem even more completely when he writes that "it was an unenviable task to conduct an opposition in prosperous times, especially against a chief target so impervious, so adept at turning aside their thrusts, calming agitation and fostering the impression that, on the whole, the universe was unfolding as it should."[38]

The unfavourable climate, in turn, made it difficult for the CCF to attract and keep new members. Consequently, it lacked the number of active supporters necessary to make a significant impact on voters. In the twelve months before the election, the CCF had added only 553 members to its ranks. Had membership grown by only half as much as party leaders expected when they introduced the Brigade concept in 1954, the CCF would have had the funds and the workers required to make a greater impact on the electorate – through canvassing, publicity, and overall visibility – and to get their supporters to the polls. "Our basic weakness continues to be lack of effective organization at the riding level," concluded the Executive in post-election analysis. "Although the general political climate was unfavourable, it nevertheless should have been possible, with effective election organization, to have won 10 to 15 ridings ... With only one or two exceptions at best, there were no ridings in the province where we had the machinery to get out the CCF vote on an informed, selective basis."[39]

But knowing the reasons for its poor performance probably did little to ease the disappointment leaders and members no doubt felt at the time. From a party point of view, the CCF was still a viable organization, thanks to the determined efforts of its top leaders. This was no small achievement under the circumstances. But from an electoral point of view, years of careful preparation and attention to basic organization had clearly not paid off. In the fall of 1953, when it appeared that the CCF's revival was well underway, party leaders had decided to focus almost entirely on laying the groundwork for the 1955 election. They directed the formulation of a new official program, devised ways to strengthen party membership and finances, participated in numerous by-elections, helped CCF riding associations prepare for the provincial election, purged the party of its harmful communist elements, and cultivated a potentially lucrative election issue. But a sudden decline in membership, combined with the untimely revelations of Communist infiltration and expulsion, did much to undermine these efforts. The party had taken one step forward, and two steps back. It was time for the movement to take stock.

5 The Winds of Change

The results of the 1955 election were disappointing, but the resiliency of the party was not diminished. Party leaders, in their never-ending quest for organizational buoyancy, were certain where the party's salvation lay. "Organization is [still] our No. 1 problem," affirmed the Executive in its post-election assessment, "and ... our major efforts in the coming year should be directed toward building the kind of organization that can win [individual] ridings."[1] For the next two years, therefore, the Provincial Office concentrated its limited resources in certain key ridings. The results, as measured in part by the gains of the 1957 federal election, were encouraging, but were set against a bleak background of rapidly declining membership, mounting financial pressures, and growing concern for the future of the movement among CCFers across the country. Largely in response to this concern, party leaders at the national level initiated a process of renewal that would have significant implications for the future of the CCF in Ontario.

The election defeat of June 1955 brought in its wake the usual introspection. In general, party leaders were convinced that, despite the unfavourable "political climate," a substantial vein of CCF support existed and was just waiting to be tapped, if only the riding associations could create the necessary organizational capacity. Most agreed, therefore, that the first step was to help the ridings integrate as many of the recent campaign workers as possible into the CCF on a full-time basis, instead of allowing them to slip away as in the past. The CCF Executive instructed the Organization Committee to find "one or more persons in each riding who will give leadership in developing organization, and working through these people," especially former CCF candidates, to "aim at developing the basic kind of organization required to win elections." The Membership Education Committee was told to work closely with the Organization Committee, "particularly in training personnel to give local leadership in developing organization."[2]

Of course, this strategy of getting local leaders and members to take more responsibility for building the party between elections was not new. It had been pursued in one form or another for many years and, according to party leaders, remained the key to successful expansion. This time, however, the leadership had reason to believe it would work. There were signs that the recent election had not left the rank and file demoralized or bitter, in marked contrast to the apathy, shock, and dissension that followed the 1951 contest. In fact, the election seemed to have inspired the troops to greater efforts. "The punch [of the defeat] didn't knock us out," insisted one member, "it just made us mad. Many new candidates of high calibre, whose community service had precluded much organizational work in the CCF itself prior to election time, received a rude shock. Now they know what needs to be done." Post-election enthusiasm was also based on the election of Donald MacDonald to the legislature and on the infusion of new, young election workers, many of them trade unionists, who were "without the discouragement of having fought previous losing battles." Provincial organizers reported that CCFers across the province were holding meetings, organizing dances, forming CCF clubs, signing up new members, and pledging to devote more time to the party. In addition, many CCF candidates expressed a willingness to run again and to help build up organization in the interim. In short, declared the CCF News, members were "rarin' to go!"[3] From these optimistic reports the Executive concluded that "there appears to be little if any discouragement among CCF workers. On the contrary, workers in many ridings are eager to get started on preparations for the next election ... It is important that we should take advantage of this situation ... New workers should be integrated into our organization ... [and] trained in doing effective election work."[4] Perhaps the CCF could at last restore its organization to what it was during the party's heyday of the mid-to-late forties.

But party leaders were still faced with a familiar dilemma. In carrying out their latest program, should they concentrate their limited resources entirely in the most promising areas or should they continue the policy of trying to gain a foothold in every riding? The question had arisen several years earlier, in 1952, when several members of the Organization Committee argued successfully that organizers should not waste their time in less promising regions, such as eastern Ontario, but should instead be assigned to stronger ridings in the larger cities of southwestern Ontario. This approach did not last, however, and the issue resurfaced in 1955. "The [Organization] Committee is giving insufficient attention to the need for concentrating our limited resources in the ridings where they will do the most good," argued Andrew Brewin before Council. "If necessary, we should be quite ruthless in applying this principle of concentration." But not everyone agreed. "We cannot desert the ridings that do not have any immediate prospect of electoral success," replied Spencer Cheshire. "If we neglect them in favour of a few good ridings, our organization in most of the province will fall apart." Some also felt that such an eventuality would be particularly dangerous "in view of the probable tactics of Social Credit in the next few years ... Experience in other provinces has shown that Social Credit strength can mushroom in a phenomenal manner in situations where there is a political vacuum."[5]

To solve the dilemma, the Executive devised a compromise strategy known as "concentration." Organizers would concentrate initially on the more promising ridings so that enough time would be left before the next election to organize the less promising ones. This meant, in effect, paying more attention to urban-industrial ridings in southern Ontario and in the North, where the party had traditionally done well, but which were more volatile because of their heterogeneous socio-economic make-up.[6] But before this, the Organization Committee would try to capitalize on the post-election enthusiasm by personally contacting as many recent CCF candidates and election workers as possible, throughout the province, in order to recruit them as chief organizers and help them devise "detailed zone and poll organization" plans for their ridings. The chief organizers would then be trained for their responsibilities through a series of regional education conferences in the fall. Subsequently, the Organization Committee staff would be free to concentrate all its resources on "a selected group of ridings that are considered to have the best prospects of electoral success." Time permitting, the Committee would then help the weaker ridings. The "concentration" plan was, in effect, the amalgamation of years of experience with different organizational approaches and it coloured almost every aspect of the party's efforts during the next two years.[7]

Throughout the summer and fall of 1955, the Organization Committee, led by the indefatigable "Marj" Pinney and assisted by the party's full-time organizers, Ames and Young, worked diligently to lay the groundwork for poll organization in a number of ridings. Local leaders were contacted, plans were drawn up, and follow-up meetings were held. Before long, Pinney was speaking of a "new interest in organization" at all levels, and with some justification. By November, between twenty and thirty ridings had already established, or were in the process of establishing, the poll committee structure. In addition, the Provincial Office organized, often with the cooperation of local riding executives, eight regional education conferences. Emphasizing poll organization techniques for local organizers, the conferences were described as "successful" and "spirited."[8]

But these apparent advances were deceiving, for in the one area where it counted most, that of party membership, the results were disappointing. The post-election enthusiasm that facilitated the Organization Committee's drive to extend poll organization into a greater number of ridings than ever before did not translate into an overall increase in members. In fact, between October 1954 and October 1955, total membership fell by 200. The immediate reason was clear enough. Although the CCF Brigade had brought in over 1,600 new members between June 1954 and June 1955, that same period witnessed the departure of at least 1,100 existing members, a sign that the riding associations had permitted many memberships to lapse. "A more systematic and determined effort on [membership] renewals is required," Pinney told the Council shortly after these figures were compiled, for "much of the work of the pledge campaign is serving only to plug the gaps in the regular membership work."[9] A problem first detected in the fall of 1954 had suddenly snowballed.

In addition to promoting poll organization, therefore, the Organization Committee began stressing the importance of membership renewals. In January 1956, Pinney told members that the CCF Brigade had brought in over 2,000 new members and asked how many were "backing up this terrific work by seeing to it that renewals are picked up in your riding." A handful of ridings were "right on top of their renewals and steadily increasing their membership," she said, "but too many of us are falling down on the job." The annual spring membership drive helped raise membership levels by about 600 members over October 1955; by September 1956, however, they had fallen quite dramatically, to a level *below* that of the previous October. In fact, between October 1955 and September 1956, the party lost over 900 members, all from ridings outside Toronto; between June and October, 1956, alone, nearly 1,500 members left the party.[10]

It was normal for the party to lose some members during the summer months, when in the ebb of the spring membership drive members were either too tired or too busy to continue organizing. But the absolute decline in membership over the previous year began to worry party leaders. "This is a matter for real concern," a solemn

Pinney told the Council in September, "since it indicates that there is a genuine decline in membership and not merely a seasonal fluctuation." She blamed the problem on the ongoing failure of the riding associations to renew lapsed memberships. "Not enough effort is going into this," she berated members. "It is one of the prime responsibilities of the riding associations, and it is being neglected by too many." Verbal reprimands were accompanied by urgent letters to riding association presidents, but to no avail. "There was a significant response from only a handful of ridings," a dejected Pinney told the Executive in November. "Still another letter will be sent out but we are frankly worried about the situation. A very large number of lapsed memberships are still outstanding, yet there is little doubt that most of them could be picked up if the ridings would take some action." With no improvement in the situation by December, however, Pinney admitted to Council that "we are at a loss to know what to do ... We seem to be up against a stone wall in our attempt to get any activity in all but a few of the local areas."[11] It would not be a particularly joyous New Year for the CCF leadership.

Why were CCF members permitted to slip away in such large numbers? And why had the influx of new members not offset these losses, as it had in the past? Regrettably, the answer is not clear. Many top leaders, including Pinney and Bryden, who along with Donald Mac-Donald were the organizational gurus of the party, believed that members were placing too much emphasis on educational functions instead of trying to find new members and renew old memberships. In one of her now-familiar tirades, Pinney lashed out at members, and particularly the leadership:

For too long, we have tried everything else and refused to face up to the hard facts of political life – that we are a political party and must organize as one ... We've been suspicious of the very word organization; thinking it is some soulless monster that will rob us of that which sets us apart from other political parties. An organization is nothing more than a sane, sensible mobilization of our human resources to work towards a common goal.

To be a political party, we must ... accept as our goal the election of sufficient CCF members to form the government. That seems obvious, but to many it is a side issue. They feel our goal is to educate, to influence, to create programs, etc. All that must be done in achieving our goal, but should not be substituted for it. Discussions of policy and program are important and necessary. But if we are content to stop there we become a relatively small group of well-informed people without any real impact on society.[12]

It would be difficult to find a more cogent or forceful elucidation of the CCF's organizational thrust in the 1950s and early 1960s than this.

As an explanation of the latest decline in CCF membership, however, it was not entirely convincing, for there were few indications in this period that a sizeable faction within the party disagreed with the emphasis on basic organization. That is, the educate-organize debate that had erupted after the 1951 election did not re-emerge in the aftermath of the 1955 contest. Rather, it appears that most CCFers concurred with Pinney's view of the party's main function as a political party, a fact borne out to some extent by the large corps of election workers recently attracted to the CCF, and by the impressive growth of zone and poll structures during the summer and fall of 1955.[13]

More plausible reasons for the overall decline in membership lie elsewhere. In part, it may be attributed to the delayed return of rank-and-file apathy, which was not unusual between elections and which may have been intensified by the growing realization that despite years of hard work and optimism, the party was really no further ahead. This would certainly account for the slower rate at which the Brigade was attracting new members after June 1955 and the higher rate at which memberships were being allowed to expire.[14] As well, the stress on recruiting *new* members which lay at the heart of both the Brigade and poll organization concepts may well have distracted CCFers from the equally crucial task of renewing existing memberships.[15] On a more mundane level, it is possible that the growing inactivity of party members was partly due to the novelty of television in the mid-fifties. In February, 1956, Ames reported that many CCFers in northern Ontario preferred watching television to canvassing. "T.V. is a real problem that we must face," he told the Provincial Office. "People resent interruption when they are looking at it. My suggestion is to call them by phone beforehand or use a good T.V. program to get them to a house and then have a chat about organization." Fred Young encountered the same problem: "I remember ... a week I spent in London working with the local people ... and this is when television was just new. People resented being interrupted when they were watching television. And this is when it first hit me hard that this thing was a new factor in our whole membership thing ... also at election time."[16] This is not to suggest that Milton Berle and Lucille Ball were single-handedly destroying the dream of the cooperative commonwealth, but they certainly did not help.

If the causes of the absolute decline in members were unclear, the short-term results were not. The drop from a relatively impressive membership of 9,300 at the time of the 1955 election to a dismal membership of 6,800 by September 1956 – a 27 percent decrease in just fifteen months – meant that responsibility for organizing the movement would fall even further to an already overburdened Provincial

Office.[17] It also meant a significant reduction in revenues from *regular* membership dues, putting a strain on party finances and making the Provincial Office's task even more difficult. When faced with a similar decline in membership and revenues after the 1951 election, the party was saved by the Steelworkers union, who agreed to pay the salaries and expenses of two full-time organizers. This time the CCF was not as fortunate.

From 1954 to 1956, the party's financial situation worsened. The money which the Provincial Office received annually from donations, membership fees, and union contributions remained almost constant in this period, while certain unavoidable expenditures, such as rent, Provincial Office salaries, office expenses, and especially the cost of producing the CCF *News* continued to rise along with all other general operating costs. In addition, for the first time in its history, the CCF was paying its leader an annual salary, plus expenses. To avoid running a continual net deficit, therefore, the CCF was repeatedly forced to make draconian cuts to the salary and expenses of the Provincial Leader and part-time organizers. Any weakening of the Provincial Office's strength in this way was bound to reverberate throughout the movement.[18]

The party began to experience serious financial difficulties in 1954. Faced with a projected year-end deficit of over $2,000, the Provincial Office was forced to take "emergency measures" to balance its budget. It cut its part-time organizing staff, reduced the CCF *News* from twelve to eight pages, and made a plea to twenty or thirty individuals for an "emergency contribution of approximately $50." Matters improved slightly in 1955, despite the election and the decline in regular membership dues thereafter, primarily because membership levels had increased steadily until June and because election spending was cut to such an extent that the party actually emerged with a surplus on its election account. The party was thus able to avoid a repeat of the drastic cost-cutting measures of the previous winter and finished the year with a "modest surplus" of $1,000. In 1956, the party narrowly averted another potentially serious financial crisis, stemming from the massive haemorrhage of members between June and October, by further reductions in Provincial Office expenses and by the timely increase in contributions from unions, 500 Club members, and Sustaining Members.[19]

Besides hampering the CCF's organizational efforts, the shortage of funds also placed subtle strains on party unity. It led, first of all, to a tug of war between the Provincial Office and the ridings over the scarce available funds. During the 1955 election campaign, for example, CCF riding associations were required to remit 20 percent of any money they raised to the Provincial Office to assist the latter with its own campaign efforts. But the provincial secretary, Ken Bryden, accused the ridings of not paying their fair share and of not cooperating with the Provincial Office in general. "It is quite clear that the aggregate payments on quota were far less than 20 percent of the total amount spent by the ridings in the campaign," he told the Council in June. "Moreover, although all ridings had been asked shortly before the election to estimate the amount they would likely be able to pay on quota, very few had done so, with the result that it had been impossible to budget intelligently at the provincial level ... Some ridings fail to take seriously the idea of contributing anything beyond their own local requirements [and] ... have been very slow even in paying their literature accounts."[20] Council responded by authorizing the Provincial Office to apply any rebates it owed to a riding (from membership dues, for example) against the amount owed by the riding to the Provincial Office.

The financial crisis also gave rise to a lengthy re-evaluation of the party's official organ, the CCF News, and in the process created some minor internal disagreements. Because a certain portion of the regular membership fee was used to finance the cost of producing the News, the steady decline in CCF members in this period, combined with rising production costs, placed the party's official organ in serious financial difficulty. To give the paper a stronger financial footing, the Executive decided that production costs should be paid out of general party revenues and that more advertising revenue should be sought. When this solution proved only temporary, the CCF considered cutting the size of the News in half, from eight pages to four, a suggestion that provoked a long and lively discussion within the Council between those who saw the move as "psychologically bad" for members, "at a time ... when we should be expanding," and those who argued that unless membership fees were increased, which no one really wanted, the party had no alternative. The Executive ultimately decided not to change the paper's size, and, instead, to try harder to increase the flow of advertising revenue.[21] Nevertheless, the debate symbolized the subtle tensions created by the need for more money.

Perhaps the most important thing to note from the financial crises and internal tensions of this period, however, is the extent to which they illustrated the interdependence and fragility of the party's organization. During the discussion over the CCF News, Donald MacDonald correctly noted (although it was probably not considered very helpful at the time) that "the crux of the problem is the membership situation" and that "if we had 10,000 members or more, there would be no serious difficulty in financing [the] CCF News."[22] The rapid decline in members was, indeed, *the* basic problem, for it reduced the vital supply of money and workers needed by the Provincial Office to sustain and expand the party. This, in turn, led to cuts in staff; to an unhealthy internal competition over diminishing funds; and to pressure on the party's key educational and unifying instrument, the CCF News – all of which made it even less likely that the party could reverse its organizational decline.

As disturbing as it was, however, the resumption of the Ontario CCF's decline in the wake of the 1955 provincial election defeat – and yet another unsuccessful by-election campaign in the fall – was merely symptomatic of the movement's stagnation across Canada. The CCF's fall in national popularity in 1955 from 13 to 10 percent and the lack of any signs of recovery prompted CCF leaders at the national level to respond.[23] "We have all been concerned with the failure of our movement to advance more rapidly in the last few years," commented the National Council in November 1955, "[and] it seems to us that this situation imposes a duty on the National Council and on the leadership in each of the provinces to give some careful thought and study to the reasons underlying it. It may well be that the answer lies not only in our purely organizational handicaps but in the basic approach of our movement to the people of Canada and to our program."[24] In response to a request from the National Council, the Ontario CCF Executive discussed the matter at length in late 1956 and early 1957. Its proposals fell fairly evenly into two broad and complementary categories. Spokespersons for the first category tended to favour what had become the standard prescription in the Ontario party: more intensive basic organization at the local level, led by party leaders. Spokespersons for the second category, however, believed that the CCF had to make changes to both its basic program and structure, by bringing the former up to date and by broadening the latter to include greater participation by labour and farm organizations.[25] In the end, the Executive submitted both of these suggestions to the federal party.

Based on these ideas, and those of the other provincial sections, the national CCF chose the second option: to make changes in its structure, program, and philosophy. In terms of structure, the CCF agreed to "do a much more intensive, scientific and sustained job of building its organization," and to "recognize the importance of securing, as was the original objective of the CCF in the 1930s, a far more broadly based people's movement among the workers and farmers of this country." In its program, it would stop predicting economic recession and ("while retaining its basic goals") would "make its appeal more pragmatic, more empirical, more geared to the issues of the day," by demanding, for example, more social security programs, greater economic and social equality, increased aid to foreign countries, and an end to foreign domination of the Canadian economy. Philosophically, it would replace its very first statement of basic principles, the Regina Manifesto, with a new statement, one which would "define more clearly the extent and place of social ownership in its program," while emphasizing the moral and ethical goals of democratic socialism. In short, through a more up-to-date program and philosophy, as well as a more intensive organizational effort, the CCF set out to fashion the sort of broadly based party it had intended to create when it was formed almost a quarter-century before.[26]

The first step in this transformation took place at the CCF's national convention in Winnipeg in early August, where the National Council presented delegates with a new statement of principles known as the Winnipeg Declaration. This five-page document, since seen as a watershed in the party's development, was approved by the convention with very little fanfare or controversy. According to J.B. McGeachy of the *Financial Post*, the entire affair "was very orderly, well-conducted, serious without being excessively solemn. There were no parades, no noisemakers, no brass bands, no brawls, nothing unseemly about the proceedings." He added that delegates were given ample opportunity to debate the new statement and that party leaders made no attempt to impose their views on the convention, an observation with which most media personnel concurred.[27]

But support for the Declaration was by no means unanimous. A group of about twelve to fifteen CCFers, led by Robert Kenzie and Spencer Cheshire, both of the Ontario CCF, firmly believed that the new statement represented a watering down of the key socialist principle of public ownership; they attempted several times, therefore, to introduce a resolution reaffirming the party's commitment to nationalization. The leadership, however, considered the resolution out-of-order. Its very existence implied that the Declaration had somehow backtracked on this commitment, which people like National Chairman David Lewis and George Grube, who argued against the resolution, were not willing to concede. "This is a 'when did you stop beating your wife type resolution,'" declared Lewis. "It's not needed." Most of the delegates evidently agreed, for when the resolution was finally introduced, with the debate limited to two speakers, one for and one against, all but thirteen of the delegates endorsed a motion to table the resolution, thereby ending debate before it began. Nevertheless, Kenzie, Cheshire, and other members of the Ontario CCF would continue to attack the Declaration, and its apparent betrayal of socialist principles, in the months ahead. Some grumbling would also be heard about the insufficient time given to delegates to review the draft of the Declaration.[28]

Generally speaking, though, the Winnipeg Declaration proved to be a temporary godsend for the Ontario CCF: it provided new hope at a time when membership numbers were tumbling and pressures mounting on finances and party unity. It was "just what we need to get the CCF moving again in Ontario," declared a jubilant Peg Stewart, the party's president. Hoping to use the interest surrounding the Declaration to revive the party, the Provincial Office organized eight large regional educational conferences, in the fall and winter of 1956–57, where members discussed both the Declaration and the new federal election program issued in January. For the most part, these gatherings were successful, with several party sources reporting high attendance and "lively and fruitful" discussion.[29]

Another indication of the renewed interest in party policy created by the Declaration and the federal election program was the sudden increase in demand from CCF riding associations for party literature. The Provincial Office had occasionally complained that the ridings paid too little attention to promoting literature and discussion among members. In part, the low interest in membership education was due to the CCF's inability to produce attractive, concise literature dealing specifically with Canadian problems from a socialist perspective; a more important reason, though, was the persistent apathy of members. One of the main factors responsible for reversing this situation, apart from the availability of many good new pamphlets by 1955–56, was the renewed interest in the CCF's program and philosophy sparked by the events of the Winnipeg convention. Sales of party literature to the ridings suddenly rose substantially in 1956, with an even greater increase in 1957.[30]

Curiously, however, the revival in spirit and interest among party members in the months following the 1956 federal convention did not translate into any significant organizational renewal – whether in the form of more CCF clubs, more members, or more money.[31] Indeed, this continued stagnation was clearly evident in the results of the Provincial Office's efforts to prepare the party for the next federal election, expected sometime in 1957. The Organization Committee turned its attention to election matters in early 1956, hoping to get about sixty candidates nominated well in advance of the election so that ridings could begin preparing for the campaign. But party organizers encountered great difficulty simply finding candidates. Some ridings, not believing in the efficacy of early nominations, refused to heed the pleas of the organizers, frustrating the latter no end. Other ridings simply lacked qualified persons willing to toss their hat into the ring. In many northern ridings, for example, capable CCFers were busy with other things, such as their own businesses or union work. In some cases, union leaders in the North were prevented from running for the CCF by factions within their local opposed to political action. Another problem was disillusionment: some local CCF executives, pessimistic about the CCF's chances, did little to prepare for the election. Finally, some riding associations were weakened by the recurring reluctance of older workers to accept the help of new, younger workers. The end result was that only fifteen candidates had been nominated by December.[32]

The slow pace of election preparations created an even more serious problem. It jeopardized the CCF's new policy of "concentration," by which the party's limited human and financial resources were to be concentrated – first, in the most promising ridings, and only later in the weaker areas, where token candidates would be nominated. According to the Organization Committee, approximately thirty-three ridings were in the former category and about twenty-seven in the latter. But because so few candidates had been nominated in the stronger ridings by the end of 1956, the Organization Committee could not yet afford to divert its staff to the weaker areas. For the sake of appearances, however, the party wished to make at least a token showing in the latter. Torn between these two imperatives, and determined to abide by its policy of concentration, the Executive decided to assign the Provincial Organizers to the stronger ridings and to ask Council members to take responsibility for the twenty-seven or so ridings "where the candidate problem is difficult."[33]

This makeshift solution seems to have worked. By the time the June 1957 federal election rolled around, the Provincial Office had reached its goal of sixty candidates and, with the help of two additional temporary organizers and several Councillors, had managed to set up the necessary election machinery in most of the province's eighty-five federal ridings. Its efforts were undoubtedly facilitated by the usual pre-election fever and the spring membership drive, both of which spurred members to action and added 900 potential election workers to the party's ranks. Additional assistance came from the OFL, whose PAC contributed $14,000 toward the campaign and whose local unions donated party workers and endorsed CCF candidates.[34]

In view of the weakened condition of the Ontario CCF by 1957, the movement's declining popularity across Canada, and the sluggish response of many ridings to the election campaign, party leaders were not entirely unjustified in feeling pleased with the election results. In Ontario, the party increased its popular support from 11 to 12 percent, and gained two additional seats, for a record high of three. Given that it ran five fewer candidates than in the 1953 federal election, in order to concentrate on the more promising ridings, the CCF also took satisfaction from the fact that it was able to save the deposits of twice as many candidates as before and poll over 20 percent of the vote in close to one-third of the ridings. To some extent, these gains were based on the growing public disaffection with the Liberals, who lost nineteen seats and four cabinet ministers in the province. In fact, the Liberals suffered several of their worst defeats at the hands of the CCF. In Port Arthur, the CCF's Douglas Fisher defeated St. Laurent's right-hand man and "Minister of Everything," C.D. Howe, and in Temiskaming, thanks to a vigourous campaign by Doc Ames and candidate Arnold Peters, the CCF upset the Liberal's only female M.P., Ann Shipley. The CCF's third seat went to the likeable fire fighter from Timmins, Murdo Martin.[35]

Party leaders attributed most of the gains to their policy of concentration. They did not tire of pointing out that all three CCF victories were achieved in ridings where members had worked hard over the past year or so, with the help Doc Ames and the Provincial Office, to increase membership and prepare for the election; and that by June 1957, these ridings boasted the largest membership in the province. "We have reason to be pleased with the election results in Ontario," Pinney told her colleagues on the Executive. "The moral of the election is that we have to win individual ridings ... The results reflect the policy of concentration which we decided on a year or two ago – insofar as we were able to carry it out with our limited resources." Even the former leader of the Ginger Group was inclined to agree. "We cannot emphasize too strongly the importance of riding work," said Bill Temple. "If we are going to win more seats in the future, it will only be by building up riding organizations which can take advantage of swings in opinion." How the times had changed![36]

The CCF's gains may be attributed to one other factor as well: the performance of the provincial leader. Although Donald MacDonald's precise impact on the party and the public is, naturally, difficult to measure, it can be argued that, at the very least, he attracted new members to the CCF, inspired existing ones to greater effort, and gave the CCF a higher public profile. From the minute he assumed the position of leader in late 1953, MacDonald was determined to make himself seen and heard on the political scene. Before and after his election to the legislature in June 1955, he undertook extensive tours of the province at least once each year, speaking at various party, labour, and farmer gatherings and making numerous appearances on radio and television. "His activities have resulted in outstanding publicity in both press and radio throughout the province," reported the Provincial Council in 1954, and "he [has] stimulated renewed enthusiasm for the CCF." This was particulary true in northern Ontario, where MacDonald spent much of his time when he wasn't in the legislature and where, incidentally, the CCF made its greatest gains in the 1957 election. In a widely reprinted newspaper article in December 1955, columnist Don O'Hearn documented the leader's high visibility across the province:

The CCF ... is a very lively party ... This stems primarily from the activities of one man: leader Donald MacDonald ... The fact is that for a one-man show, Mr. MacDonald is carrying out a mammoth task. He is organizer, leader and publicity man rolled into one. And he is doing such a good job that in each category he is doing better than the whole Liberal organization. The buildings see a lot of Mr. MacDonald. The province sees a lot of him. And the press hears a lot from him. He is always on the go, and he usually has a statement ready on any issue of importance. The impression inevitably is left that the CCF is an active party, and this is going to win it votes.[37]

The CCF leader was equally vigilant inside the legislature, notwithstanding the crushing burden of his legislative duties.[38] Aided by his relatively subdued colleagues, Reg Gisborn and Tommy Thomas, he vigorously pursued the government on many of the issues CCFers had talked about for years, including health insurance, hospitals, social programs, affordable housing, agricultural marketing schemes, corporation taxes, unemployment, wages, grants to municipalities, and conservation. So strong and so persistent were his attacks on the Tory government that he soon earned his party the reputation as the only real opposition in the legislature, a perception the leader did much to cultivate. "I operated on the assumption that the CCF was the only real opposition, and that the government had to be attacked on all fronts," he recalls in his memoirs. "Major speeches in the Throne Debate, or response to the budget, invariably ran up to three hours. If the Legislature had ceased to be the political forum it should be, that was restored by the stronger CCF presence."[39]

The government's response was often harsh and abusive. One CCF member who was visiting the legislature during the 1955–56 session was disgusted to find that "while Donald MacDonald was speaking he was constantly interrupted and heckled by the Conservative members.

When he started to speak of the plight of the farmers, one member shouted, 'A cow makes as much noise as you and gives milk too ...' Personal insults such as 'it was a lucky thing for the school children when you decided to go into politics' [a reference to MacDonald's days as a school teacher in Quebec] were quietly rebuked by the Speaker."[40] This intolerance was understandable given MacDonald's skill at exposing and making the most of sensitive issues, the highways scandal of 1954 being a case in point. It is possible, as well, that the Tories had become so accustomed to a small and relatively silent opposition after 1951 that the sudden appearance of a vociferous CCF caucus came as a rather rude shock. "One had the impression," observed MacDonald, "that any challenge to their rule was considered to be out of order. Those who feel they rule by divine right tend to regard opposition as a form of heresy." But MacDonald took it all in stride. If the Tories were hitting back so hard, he reasoned, he must be doing something right. Specifically, he took satisfaction in the belief that his vigilance had made the various government departments more alert and responsive to the needs of the population.[41] Moreover, MacDonald's continual needling of the Frost administration, and the anger he provoked as a result, clearly belie the claim put forth by at least one partisan observer that Frost's government received more sniping from the large and sometimes restless Tory caucus of the 1950s than from either of the two opposition parties.[42]

But if the Tories did not care much for MacDonald's efforts, party members did. All indications are that CCFers were more than pleased with MacDonald's performance and that he did much to boost their morale. "We are all very proud of the job that you are doing," Ames told MacDonald in early 1956. "[It] appears to be giving some of our people more heart for the task ahead." These sentiments were echoed by True Davidson, editor of the CCF News, who later that year wrote that "Don's wit, courage, perseverance and human sympathy have endeared him to every CCFer, and many resolutions [at the 1956 convention] were worded as commendations of this or that stand he had taken on some moot question." In addition, the vicious attacks MacDonald and his caucus were forced to endure probably stiffened the resolve of party members to fight back. In April 1956, the CCF News informed its readers that "Donald MacDonald and his small group in the Legislature have been working incredibly long hours, [and] they have been taking unbelievable abuse from the Tory Benches. The rest of us MUST DO OUR PART too and do it to the utmost of our time and ability."[43]

Clearly, then, the CCF's ebullient new leader had made an impression. Because of his example, party members were more highly motivated to work for the CCF and, at the very least, the public was more aware of the party's presence. This, together with several other factors, contributed to the increase in *new* members and to the CCF's respectable showing in the federal election. Nevertheless, MacDonald's impact was not strong enough to reverse the party's overall decline in this period. From June 1955 to June 1957, the failure of local riding associations to renew lapsed memberships resulted in a net loss of almost 1,400 members.[44] This put heavy strains on party finances, which in turn led to retrenchment measures and subtle pressures on party unity. The CCF's new policy of concentration, although it may have helped win more seats in the 1957 federal election, was no more successful than MacDonald in offsetting the general decline. At the national level of the movement, however, the winds of change were blowing, a result, in part, of the Ontario CCF's decline. The Winnipeg Declaration marked the first step in the federal party's long-term plan to revive the movement. Over the next five years, these winds would accelerate into a virtual tornado of activity, tearing across the movement and sucking up each provincial section on its way to the creation of a new party.

6 Origins of the New Party

The Winnipeg Declaration was only the first step in the CCF's effort to attract a wider following and revitalize the movement. The next step, as planned, was to change the party's structure by giving it a stronger basis in economic organizations, primarily the trade unions. The desire for a more organic relationship with organized labour was inspired, in part, by the formation of the CLC in April 1956 and, more important, by the labour movement's growing sympathy for political action in the late fifties. From 1956 to 1958, national CCF leaders worked closely and quietly with labour leaders sympathetic to a new relationship, and by April of the latter year they were on the verge of launching a new, more broadly based party.

For the Ontario CCF, however, it was business as usual. After the election of a minority Conservative government in Ottawa in June 1957, preparations were immediately begun for the next federal election. By March 1958, the party was once again ready to face the voters. The interim was marked by the usual efforts to find candidates and election volunteers, raise money, and sign up new members. But more so than in the past, these efforts were animated by a strong belief among party leaders that the CCF's fortunes were on the rise. As a result, the CCF had insufficient time and perhaps too little interest to ponder the momentous changes taking place at the national level. Although the Ontario CCF would eventually play a key role in the development of the new party being planned by its federal counterpart, the summer of 1957 found party leaders brimming with hope about the immediate future and eager to pursue conventional organizational methods of political recovery.

Party leaders in Ontario were quite optimistic after the 1957 federal election for two reasons. First, although the CCF's gains had been modest, they were seen as a vindication of the concentration policy adopted several years earlier and as a sign of things to come should the policy be continued. Second, and more important, the election results were viewed alongside what many CCF leaders believed was the beginning of the end for the seemingly omnipotent Liberals. The fall of the Liberals from power in Ottawa, attributable in large measure to the loss of nineteen seats in Ontario, was seen as a golden opportunity for the CCF to once and for all replace the Liberals as Canada's truly "progressive" party. "The Liberals are reeling," proclaimed an enthusiastic Marj Pinney, in her post-election rallying call to members. "Let's make sure we administer the knockout blow next time. Then we shall see a truer political alignment in Canada. The forces of big business and reaction will line up with the Conservatives, as always, and the forces of progress and humanity on the side of the CCF."[1] The provincial secretary, Ken Bryden, echoed the sentiment. "The once mighty Liberal machine is shaken and demoralized," he declared. "The Conservatives will undoubtedly make a strong bid on it from the one side [and] ... if we pile in on it from the other side, we can conceivably destroy altogether that big behemoth that has so long occupied the centre of the road."[2]

But to become a major party the CCF believed it had to first shake its *image* as a minor party, while retaining its image as a progressive, "people's" party. As Bryden explained to his colleagues on the Provincial Council, the party's perpetual third-place finishes were primarily due to the swing nature of Canadian national politics, otherwise known as the "wasted vote" phenomenon. That is, people did not vote for the CCF in greater numbers because they were determined to defeat the government, which meant voting for the party perceived as having the best chance of replacing it, namely the number two party. During such large swings in voter support, he concluded, the CCF inevitably got left out in the cold.[3] The Council agreed with Bryden's solution: to continue to concentrate on winning the most promising ridings, thereby increasing the CCF's legislative representation and further enhancing the perception among voters that the CCF was a viable alternative to the governing party. Only then would the CCF become the main beneficiary of the anti-government vote. Councillors also agreed that continued adherence to the policy of concentration had to be combined with renewed efforts to portray the CCF as a genuinely progressive party, thereby undercutting recent attempts by the Liberal and Conservative parties to don the cloak of progressivism.[4]

Along with the party's optimistic view of the future and self-assured confidence in its organizational strategy was the feeling that the Diefenbaker government's minority status would almost certainly bring Canadians to the polls again, within a year. Preparations for the next federal election, therefore, began immediately. Staff from the Provincial Office and Organization Committee spent the summer of 1957 touring the province encouraging CCF riding executives to choose candidates, assemble teams of election workers, and establish poll committees. Even the weaker ridings received attention, this despite the CCF's commitment to concentrate on the stronger ridings first. Fred Young, for example, was sent to do some "preliminary work in a few ridings in which we did not have candidates last time," while Donald MacDonald did "considerable work in Eastern Ontario." In addition, a young Stephen Lewis was hired as a summer organizer to work in the Niagara Peninsula region, where his efforts did much to revive membership and organization in the area.[5] The results of the summer organizing, according to CCF leaders, were encouraging. "The morale of our movement is now higher than it has been in recent years," an exuberant Finance Committee chairperson told fellow Council members in August. Bryden, who had visited many of the party's more promising ridings in southern and northern Ontario, was equally sanguine. He reported that "most of the riding associations were in good spirits and ready to go again" and that "a good many ridings have already started to get ready for the next election."[6]

But the optimism was short-lived. Summer organizing was followed by a fall membership drive, in place of the usual fall educational conferences or election workshops, the results of which did not confirm the earlier reports of "renewed interest" and overall revival. Nor did the CCF come close to the 2,000 new members it had hoped would join as a result of the drive. A large influx of new members did occur in several northern and southwestern ridings, but these gains were offset by dramatic declines in other ridings within these regions, and in several eastern ridings as well. After the drive, the party's total membership stood at just under 8,100, a net post-election gain of only 130. Although the party could boast over 1,000 members more than the previous November, the total was still well below the June 1955 figure of 9,300. The limited vitality of the party was further reflected in the slow pace at which riding associations were nominating candidates. Notwithstanding the constant entreaties of the Organization Committee, only thirteen ridings had chosen candidates by year's end.[7]

But this situation was no different from previous periods of electoral preparation, and as soon as rumours of an election announcement became widespread, CCFers intensified their efforts. The result was a dramatic change in the membership and candidate picture come the New Year. By election day, March 31st, total membership stood at over 9,100, a remarkable increase of over 1,000 members since the fall membership drive. The onset of election fever also led to an appreciable rise in the number of CCF candidates. Sixty-three carried the CCF banner on election day, three more than in the previous election. Greater local effort was matched by a more frenzied pace at the provincial level. The Provincial Office hired additional organizers and office staff for the campaign, and the CCF Election Committee, which had begun meeting regularly after the election was announced in early February, spent most of its time producing election leaflets on CCF candidates, distributing election literature for the National Office, preparing newspaper and radio advertising, and helping to plan speaking tours for federal party leaders, including a large rally for federal leader M.J. Coldwell at Massey Hall in early March. Additional publicity and encouragement were provided by the provincial leader and provincial secretary, both of whom attended nominating conventions for CCF candidates and spoke on what the federal party felt were the important issues of the campaign: unemployment, Parliamentary rights, falling agricultural prices, and foreign control of Canadian resources.[8]

In fact, only a few minor problems marred what was otherwise a well-run campaign. Party leaders were perturbed, for example, when the media quoted Coldwell as saying that the CCF was setting its sights on Official Opposition status. This provoked an angry letter from Ellen Camnitzer, caucus secretary and a member of the Executive, to the national secretary, Carl Hamilton: "I AM GOOD AND MAD ... Since when do we concede elections in the middle of a campaign? Surely while we fight elections, we fight them to win, not to run 2nd, 3rd, or 4th place – wherever we may end up. It is bad enough that MJ [Coldwell] hasn't learned yet that one doesn't make election predictions ... This kind of thing has a devastating effect on our candidates and organizers. Let's not make any predictions in future. Let's just fight it to win and cheer madly if we do make the Official Opposition."[9] The complaint was a touch ironic in view of the fact that Donald MacDonald made similar statements during the campaign and CCF candidates in Ontario spoke often of replacing the Liberals as Canada's Official Opposition.[10]

The Provincial Office also complained that it was once again having a hard time persuading the ridings to contribute 20 percent of their election funds to the provincial campaign. "The situation with regard to riding contributions is quite unsatisfactory," asserted the Election Committee. "Several ridings which are known to be spending large sums of money on their local campaigns have contributed little or nothing to the provincial campaign." Nevertheless, the CCF entered the 1958 contest in fairly good financial shape. After the lean years of the mid-fifties, Provincial Office revenues began to recover by 1957, due in large part to the success of the finance drive held each January in Toronto and other large cities, and to cuts in spending during the 1957 election, both of which allowed the party to increase the salaries of its full-time staff as well as the expense allowances of Council and Executive members.[11]

The CCF's financial position going into the campaign was further strengthened by the substantial assistance it once again received from the labour movement. The OFL-PAC wasted no time in mobilizing its election machinery for action. Only days after the election was announced, it sent three full-time staff members into the field to raise money among OFL affiliates. Their efforts, combined with larger contributions from the headquarters of several international unions and the funds raised during the year through regular per capita payments to PAC, resulted in a 40 percent increase in election revenues over the 1957 campaign. The PAC used the money to produce 250,000 election leaflets on unemployment, purchase pro-CCF advertisements in a dozen urban dailies, and once again pay for all CCF newspaper advertising. The PAC also financed the campaigns of the record high number of labour candidates running for the CCF – forty in all – and paid the deposits of several non-union CCF candidates in northern Ontario. Financial assistance was even more extensive at the local level. Labour's contribution was not restricted to purely financial matters, however. In addition to providing CCF candidates, the PAC provided and paid for ten organizers who were to drum up support for the party in urban areas across the province; several of these organizers were staff members on loan from the CLC. As well, two PAC representatives attended all CCF Election Committee meetings to help coordinate election activities between workers and party members.[12]

It is not surprising, therefore, that the CCF was confident of its chances in the election. The significant rise in membership in the twelve or so weeks preceding the election and the substantial assistance of the labour movement meant that the party was able to conduct a campaign at least as intense as the year before. Moreover, the declining popularity of the Liberal party continued to fuel hopes that the CCF would replace the latter as Canada's other major party. CCF leaders across the country repeatedly predicted during the campaign that Canada's "government party" would at last disappear and that a "genuine" two-party system would emerge, with the CCF on the left and the Tories on the right.[13]

It would be too hasty to conclude, however, that the CCF's rosy predictions were classic examples of political grandstanding or the usual campaign rhetoric aimed at rallying the troops. Instead, the CCF may have purposely adopted this cocky posture to escape the wasted vote problem, and hence minor party status. That is, by convincing the public that the Liberals were on their death bed and thus unlikely to form the next government or opposition, the CCF may have hoped that those wishing to vote against the government would switch their vote to a stronger contender, namely the CCF. Unfortunately, no evidence exists to suggest that this was a deliberate campaign strategy. A more plausible explanation is that party leaders actually believed what they were saying – that is, that the Liberals were, indeed, on the way out. It will be recalled, for example, that many party officials privately made such predictions shortly after the 1957 election. Nor would their hopes have been diminished either by the fact that many prominent Liberals refused to run again in 1958 or by the recent opinion polls indicating significant support for the Tories in the long-time Liberal bastion of Quebec.[14]

Assuming, then, that the CCF's optimism was largely genuine, it nevertheless flew in the face of a more grim reality. Polls showed that ever since the 1957 election, the CCF's popularity had remained steady at about 9 percent, while the Tories had climbed to about 57 percent, largely at the expense of the faltering Liberals. In short, voters were not switching from the Liberals to the CCF, but to the Tories. In addition, despite the resurgence in CCF membership and the strong assistance of the labour movement, few experts in the media gave the CCF much of a chance. But none of this seemed to bother party leaders. "Notwithstanding the pollsters and the pundits," Ken Bryden told supporters at a candidate's rally in Algoma East, "the CCF has more volunteer workers, more money, and more confidence in the current campaign than in any in my memory. The pollsters have been wrong before and I am certain they are wrong this time."[15]

They were not. Canadians awoke on the first morning of April to find that they had given John Diefenbaker's Tories the largest majority government in the country's history and that the opposition parties had been virtually annihilated.[16] In the face of the Conservative landslide, the CCF managed to hang on to only eight seats and 9.5 percent of the popular vote. Even worse, the party lost several well-respected parliamentarians, including Coldwell, Knowles, and Alistair Stewart. In Ontario, the CCF narrowly recaptured its three northern seats, but with a popular vote 1.5 percent lower than in 1957. In Toronto and the Yorks, where the CCF usually did well and where it had concentrated much of its effort during the campaign, the CCF vote fell by 8,800 and the party ran third in 16 of the 18 ridings. The *Globe's* labour specialist, Wilfred List, was moved to point out the painful irony that "a significant feature of the election in the Toronto area was the decline of CCF strength at a time when organized labour in Ontario had waged an active campaign in support of the Socialist party."[17] Overall, the Conservative's massive triumph had set the national CCF's parliamentary representation back nearly twenty years. Far from becoming Canada's newest major party, the CCF was virtually eliminated from the federal political arena.

The significance of the 1958 federal election for the CCF went far beyond the decimation of its parliamentary representation. More important, the unequivocal verdict delivered by the electorate on that gloomy day in late March gave further impetus to the process of renewal that had begun approximately two years before, in January 1956, when the National Office decided to solicit suggestions from its provincial sections on ways to revive the movement. One of the main recommendations it received at that time, and which it would eventually adopt, was that the party broaden its base of support by modernizing its program and seeking closer ties to other progressive groups, especially labour. The Winnipeg Declaration in August of that year was the first step in this direction. At the same time, a few top party leaders began a series of low-key discussions with the newly formed Canadian Labour Congress, hoping to forge a closer relationship with the labour movement.

This quest to broaden the movement's organizational base was nothing new, however. The party was, after all, founded as a partnership of farmer, labour, and socialist groups forged in the flames of Depression-era discontent.[18] Moreover, as a democratic socialist party in an increasingly urban-industrial society, its leaders came to realize that the CCF's future success hinged on attracting the support of organized labour in particular. CCF parties, therefore, made provision in their constitutions for the affiliation of "economic and cultural organizations": in return for modest affiliation dues, members of trade unions or other organizations could become affiliated members and receive a limited voice in party affairs. But support of any kind from organized labour was slow in coming. A sometimes strong tradition of non-partisanship within Canada's main labour body, the Trades and Labour Congress (TLC), as well as the anti-CCF influence of Communists therein, prevented closer relations with organized labour in the early years, despite determined efforts by such influential socialists as the party's national secretary, David Lewis, to secure affiliations or, at least, declarations of support. CCF leaders nevertheless did establish strong contacts with key union leaders, many of whom became active CCF supporters within their unions.[19]

It was only with the formation and explosive growth of the Canadian Congress of Labour (CCL) in the early 1940s, led by A.R. Mosher, that things began to change. Unlike their more conservative brethren in the TLC, members of the CCL were more sympathetic to partisan political action and at their 1943 convention passed a resolution endorsing the CCF as their "political arm." This action was not taken, however, without a good deal of hesitancy and heated debate, for many in the CCL were fearful of the divisiveness of political action and its effect on the Congress's relations with governments.[20] Nevertheless, a Political Action Committee was established the following year, charged with the task of educating members in political matters, assisting the CCF during election campaigns, and encouraging local unions to affiliate with or endorse the party.

But the aversion to political action in some quarters, combined with the presence of Communists in key CCL unions, meant that few unions or locals responded positively to the PAC. The general opposition to direct affiliation, for example, was clearly reflected in President Mosher's reassurance to delegates at the 1944 convention that "no congress union ... is under any compulsion to become affiliated with the CCF, so far as the Congress is concerned." For the next three years, the PAC was largely inactive. In 1947, PAC chairperson, Larry Sefton, informed the CCF that "since the endorsation [sic] of the CCF party as the political arm of the CCL, there has been no organized plan put into effect to give real meaning to the endorsation and bring [the CCF] into power." Closer ties were further hindered by the strong undercurrent of anti-labour sentiment in the CCF, especially among the left-wing "old guard" who feared that large-scale affiliation would allow labour to "dominate" the CCF and dilute its principles. Closer ties were also impeded by CCF constitutional requirements, which gave a voice in riding association business to large affiliated unions, but not to smaller ones.[21]

Efforts by the PAC to deliver the trade union vote and bring workers and CCFers together, half-hearted though they may have been, coincided with similar efforts by the CCF. Between 1941 and 1946, CCF organizations at the national, provincial, and local level had established "trade union committees" (TUCs) to serve essentially the same function as the PAC, but with a stronger emphasis on ridding the CCL of Communists. In Ontario, the provincial TUC tried to establish local TUCS in each riding or small groups of pro-CCF workers ("industrial units") within unionized plants, as lobby groups of sorts, to persuade other workers to join the party as individual members, support affiliations, donate money to the party, or at least vote CCF. It also organized regular union-CCF conferences, at which mutual concerns were discussed and the foundation for future political cooperation laid. Using these methods, the TUC was able to secure a few endorsements, contributions, and affiliations; but for the most part, it was no more successful than the PAC in bringing labour and CCFers together at the local level.[22]

Nevertheless, consultation between CCF and CCL leaders continued throughout the forties and these ties began to solidify as talks became more regular and leaders were invited to attend one another's meetings. All this was accompanied by substantial electoral assistance from the CCL and its provincial federations. In 1948, the OFL established its own PAC to assist the CCF in the provincial election of that year. The OFL-PAC solicited money from local unions and labour councils, most of which went to pay for CCF campaign advertising, and assigned staff members to do election work on behalf of the party. Horowitz describes the campaign as, "the first and last unqualified success of CCL political action in Canada. Twenty-one CCF candidates were elected to the legislature, the great majority of them in industrial constituencies in which the OFL-PAC had concentrated its efforts."[23] Similar assistance was extended by the CCL when it revived its PAC for the federal election of 1949. As a result, the CCF was able to hold its own in many urban ridings, despite the large number of seats lost. Apart from such informal consultation and *ad hoc* electoral cooperation, however, the CCF and CCL were unable to establish a more permanent working relationship. In 1947 the two organizations did establish a liaison committee to coordinate political activities, but it remained inactive. The committee was revived briefly in 1950, but once again "achieved little." Only the lump-sum financial contributions of the United Auto Workers and Steelworkers unions to the joint committee – a much-needed source of income for the CCF – made the project worthwhile.[24]

By the early 1950s, the prospect of closer and more formal cooperation became even more remote as relations between CCL and CCF leaders at all levels deteriorated. In May 1952, the CCL-PAC's secretary, Henry Weisbach, told CCF national secretary, Lorne Ingle, that "a recent trip across Canada had disclosed certain difficulties in CCF-PAC relations, as well as misunderstandings which should be straightened out." The main cause was the growing fear among many older CCFers that labour was becoming too influential within the party – that it wanted to "take over" the party, according to Ingle. This coincided with the growing belief within labour circles that the CCF was content to accept the PAC's electoral assistance without giving it any voice in party affairs. These conflicting perceptions, neither of which was entirely accurate, arose largely from the fact that the CCF and CCL disagreed on the exact role labour should play *vis-à-vis* the party. The CCF felt that labour should consult and cooperate with the party regularly and continue to extend financial assistance through PAC, but without receiving the rights of individual or affiliated members with respect to nominating candidates, sending delegates to party conventions, or holding office in the party. The CCL, on the other hand, wanted a greater voice in the party, but without binding itself to the CCF through formal cooperation, consultation, or even affiliation. The CCL argued that union members who contributed to PAC should be given a voice in party affairs, a demand that many in the CCF viewed as an attempt to "dominate" the party from the outside. That labour simply wanted a larger say in return for the generous electoral assistance it regularly extended to the CCF, without necessarily dominating the party, was not completely understood or accepted by the CCF. In the same way, the CCL may not have understood that the CCF did not want to exclude labour from the party, but simply wanted it to become a more integral part before granting it a greater voice. The perpetually poor communication between the two sides after 1948 did little to lessen the misunderstanding and suspicion. "Poor co-ordination, fears of labour 'domination' on the one hand, and resentment at the CCF's 'exclusion' of labour on the other," Horowitz concludes, "were the main problems in PAC-CCF relations from 1948–1952."[25]

Relations between the Ontario CCF and the OFL followed a similar pattern. The two sides worked together – or more accurately, side by side – during elections, but were unable to establish formal cooperation between elections, particularly at the grass roots. Generally speaking, union leaders were either too busy establishing new locals to assist the CCF or were understandably reluctant to disrupt newly established locals by raising the divisive issue of political action. Even among some of the older international unions, such as the United Auto Workers (UAW), recalls a former CCL-PAC director, "There was a lot of antagonism to the whole concept of political action because ... their union had been ripped [apart] on a couple of occasions" in the United States.[26] Moreover, where union leaders were supportive, their sometimes overzealous efforts to promote the party often created a backlash of resentment from the membership. This was particularly true in northern Ontario, where a bitter and protracted battle took place in

the late forties and early fifties, between CCF and Communist supporters over the political allegiance of the working class. Realizing that the
party's success depended heavily on winning over organized labour,
the former worked hard to rid the CCL of its Communist influences,
eventually winning this battle (the Communists were removed from
key union posts and the unions they controlled were expelled from the
Congress), but often at the high cost of alienating the average worker,
who became disillusioned with politics altogether.[27] Thus the OFL was
forced to attract support for the CCF using more indirect methods,
such as the PAC. But this, unfortunately, did little to foster the impression among workers that the CCF was *their* party.[28] This feeling was
reinforced by the persistent undercurrent of anti-labour sentiment
within the CCF, which found clear expression through the Ginger
Group and which subsided only slightly in subsequent years. Old-
timers, in particular, feared that labour would try to dominate the
party and dilute its ideology if given the opportunity. Snobbery was
also a factor. According to Fred Young, "You had that [anti-labour
feeling] from a lot of people ... A lot of middle-class people ... felt
that we didn't need these [union] people: they're dirty, messy, they
don't talk the way we talk, they swear." Murray Cotterill, the USA's
public relations director (and former CCL-PAC director), noticed a similar middle-class, intellectual bias. "There was an atmosphere that
would be very difficult to pinpoint, ... in the academic community and
elsewhere," he recalls, "that unions were the great unwashed, and
[that] they couldn't possibly be ... useful to the party because their
members hadn't gone to school." In the early years of the CCF, at
least, politically minded unionists reciprocated this cavalier attitude.
The constituency associations were viewed as middle-class bastions
full of utopian, armchair ideologues possessing scant awareness of the
blue-collar worker's basic needs.[29] This perception no doubt persisted.
All factors considered, then, it is hardly surprising that attempts by
PAC and TUC to foster full-time local cooperation between CCFers and
unionists were half-hearted and unsuccessful. In general, the CCF-
labour relationship in Ontario could best be described as one of limited cooperation *during* elections, in the form of "parallel campaigns,"
and very limited cooperation *between* elections, particularly at the
local level. But it was the sort of "arm's-length" relationship that
neither side seems to have minded very much.

Nevertheless, throughout the 1950s, both the PAC and the TUC continued their efforts (primarily through political education conferences)
to secure affiliations to, or at least increase support for, the CCF among
union members. But even these limited goals were not reached. Neither
side could persuade the working rank and file to commit themselves

to the party, either formally or at election time. Between 1945 and 1956, the number of union members affiliated to the Ontario CCF actually fell, from 12,500 to 5,500, and almost all of those who did affiliate belonged to the railroad, steel, or packinghouse unions in Toronto and Hamilton.[30] Nor did labour vote for the CCF in large numbers, as one election after another saw the urban-industrial ridings go to either the Liberals or the Conservatives. In this context, the OFL's annual endorsement of the CCF appears to have been little more than a half-hearted ritual, soon forgotten or thwarted once the delegates returned to their locals.

The inability of PAC and TUC to persuade organized labour to join the CCF as regular or affiliated members, or even to vote for the party, was a result of many of the same factors hindering joint cooperation and consultation – namely, disillusionment, resentment, and preoccupation with union affairs. But it was also due, in part, to the changing emphasis of the PAC after the 1951 election disaster. In spite of all the talk by the new OFL-PAC director, Henry Weisbach, about intensifying political education efforts among the rank and file, the PAC seems to have reduced its activities after 1951, largely because Weisbach was also the Executive Secretary of the CCL's PAC, which frequently took him away from his work in Ontario.[31] Fred Young, who spent a good deal of time trying to secure union affiliations, recalls that local PACs in this period were "generally ... pretty inactive" – that "they didn't count for much in those days, and they weren't being pushed from the top by the leadership, not until later." Moreover, the PAC began emphasizing political action in the *municipal* field, in a non-partisan capacity, rather than pro-CCF activities in provincial and federal politics, because, as Weisbach told the CCL Executive in 1953, "We feel that it is important for Labour to gain experience in municipal affairs" as a stepping stone to provincial and federal politics. This new emphasis meant, of course, that local PACs also diverted time and resources away from pro-CCF political education and action toward municipal politics, and may partially explain the perpetually low level of rank-and-file labour support for the CCF during the first half of the 1950s.[32]

By the mid-fifties, however, dramatic developments in the attitudes and structure of the labour movement offered new hope to the proponents of a stronger, more meaningful labour-CCF relationship. The first change was the increasing sympathy for political action among the rank and file of the traditionally non-partisan TLC, particularly within its largest affiliate, the Ontario Provincial Federation of Labour (OPFL). Beginning in the early 1950s, the demand for political action at OPFL conventions grew louder each year. In 1954, a resolution calling for direct affiliation with the CCF was narrowly defeated after several prominent CCF unionists spoke against it. Doug Hamilton, the OPFL's secretary-treasurer, persuaded most delegates that "it would not be in the best interests of either the Federation or the CCF Party to attempt outright affiliation at this time as it might tend to divide rather than solidify the labour group."[33] Although some CCF unionists supported the resolution, the convention's decision to reject it was probably a wise one given the potential explosiveness of the issue. Nevertheless, the significant support garnered for the proposal was indicative of the dramatic changes taking place within the TLC.

Over the next two years craft union support for the CCF and for political action in general continued to grow. At the 1956 OPFL convention, a resolution calling upon the Federation to simply endorse the CCF was narrowly defeated on a tie vote of 133 to 133. Speaking in favour of the motion, Doug Hamilton echoed the sentiments of many delegates when he warned that "until the trade union movement puts the same energy into the political field as in the economic field, we are doomed to failure. We are not going to get the things we need and want. We don't have to affiliate with a political party but we must support one."[34] The same division, between those wishing to support the CCF and those wishing to take political action without tying themselves to any one party, was equally apparent at other levels of the Congress. At the 1954 convention of the Ontario Federation of Printing Trades, for example, a resolution urging "full support for election to office of CCF candidates" was adopted by one vote. Those opposed to the motion agreed that political action of some sort was necessary, though not in association with any one party. The growing grass-roots support for political action was also expressed at the highest level of the movement when the 1954 TLC convention established the TLC's first political education department (PED) and elected Claude Jodoin, an advocate of political action and a secret CCF sympathizer seeking closer relations with the CCF, as its new president.[35] All of this augured well for the CCF, and party leaders monitored the situation closely.

The second significant development was the merger of the CCL and TLC into the Canadian Labour Congress (CLC) in April 1956. When the merger was announced in 1955, the proponents of pro-CCF political action realized that the growing CCF support in the TLC, combined with existing support in the CCL, would give CCF sympathizers an easy majority in the new Congress. The merger, therefore, was viewed as a golden opportunity to swing the entire labour movement behind the party. But for some, it conjured up even grander visions. The ongoing decline of the CCF across Canada and the party's poor performance in the recent Ontario election led a number of influential CCF and CCL leaders, including David Lewis, Stanley Knowles, Charlie Millard, Henry Weisbach, and Claude Jodoin to suggest that a united labour movement was not simply an omen of stronger labour "support" for the CCF, but could actually be the first step toward a more organic relationship between labour and the CCF, through either a restructured CCF or perhaps a new party. According to Horowitz, this idea of a new political alignment, containing a large wing of labour and other organizations affiliated directly to the party and taking an active interest in its affairs, was first discussed seriously at a meeting of the Ontario CCF's TUC in December 1955. It was also endorsed by the National Council during its soul-searching sessions the following month and by a TUC conference of CCL and CCF leaders in London, Ontario, in February 1956.[36]

As much as CCF and CCL leaders favoured some sort of new alignment, however, they felt it would be unwise to advance the idea at the CLC's merger convention. Partisan political action was still a sensitive subject within some TLC affiliates and neither the CCL nor the CCF wished to jeopardize the merger by forcing the issue. Instead, they sought merely to establish the foundations of the alignment at the convention, in the hope that after a few years the Congress would take a more partisan stand along the lines they envisioned. As such, they formulated a political action policy which, as one observer noted, "steered a middle course between the political neutrality of the TLC and the open endorsement of the CCF Party by the CCL." The policy, which received near-unanimous consent from the delegates, consisted of two resolutions. The first acknowledged the CCF's efforts on behalf of labour, but left CLC affiliates free to pursue the political action policy of their choice; members were simply encouraged to "take the utmost interest in political affairs." The resolution also established a Political Education Committee (PEC) to devise and implement non-partisan political education programs and assist affiliates with their chosen political activities. The second resolution was slightly bolder. In a plea for the formation of a broad political coalition of "humanitarian" forces, it called upon the PEC to approach non-CLC unions, farm groups, cooperatives, and the CCF "or other political parties pledged to support the [CLC's] legislative programme" with a view to achieving "co-ordination of action in the legislative and political field." In short, although the CLC's political action policy did not tie the new Congress to the CCF, it did commit it to take partisan action in the future, with the CCF as a major partner. It is no wonder that the policy was often described, at the time, as "political neutrality in favour of the CCF."[37]

Over the next two years, CCFers inside and outside the CLC worked to implement the political action policy of the Congress. They secured the rapid establishment of the PEC, chaired by a CCFer, consisting primarily of party members, and propagating an education program that was unmistakably, though not explicitly, pro-CCF. This was followed by a series of high-level talks beginning in early 1957 between "a few key figures" in the CCF and CLC regarding the party's future relationship with the labour movement. During this time, CLC leaders became increasingly convinced that the CCF should be transformed into a new party, with a strong affiliated union wing and solid ties to other groups, especially farmers. In February 1958, the CLC's Executive Council decided to present a resolution to this effect at the upcoming annual convention. At the same time, CCF leaders grew less enthusiastic about such a realignment. The party's promising gains in the 1957 federal election had reduced the urgency of finding a dramatic solution to the CCF decline, and by 1958 party leaders were no longer sure that a new party was necessary or even desirable.[38]

Most CCF reservations about the new party, however, were quickly swept aside by the Diefenbaker landslide of March 1958, after which key labour and CCF leaders agreed to present a "new party" resolution to the CLC's national convention in late April. The now famous resolution, calling for the democratic creation of a broadly based party by several groups and authorizing the CLC Executive to enter into talks toward that end, was read to the delegates by Eamon Park, chair of the CLC's PEC:

The time has come for a fundamental re-alignment of political forces in Canada. There is a need for a broadly based people's movement, which embraces the CCF, the labour movement, farm organizations, professional people and other liberally minded persons interested in basic social reform and reconstruction through our parliamentary system of government ...

... In participating in and initiating the creation of a new political movement, Labour emphasizes that not only is there no wish to dominate such a development, but there is the fullest desire for the broadest possible participation of all individuals and groups genuinely interested in basic democratic social reform and the democratic planning necessary to such reform ...

... This Convention, therefore, instructs the Executive Council to give urgent and immediate attention to this matter by initiating discussions with the CCF, interested farm organizations and other like-minded individuals and groups, to formulate a constitution and program to the next convention of the Congress for action.[39]

Although the resolution "came as a complete surprise to the vast majority of convention delegates," who were not expecting such a dramatic political action policy so soon, it received near-unanimous approval and marked the official launching of the New Party.[40]

Many observers argued at the time, and it is still widely believed, that the disastrous setback for the CCF in the 1958 federal election underlay the decision to create a new party. This misconception should be laid to rest, however, for it is quite clear that CCF and labour leaders began formally laying the plans for a new political instrument of some sort as early as 1955 and that members of both organizations were aware of the possibility. The New Party concept was "not a sudden idea," as Stanley Knowles pointed out at the time, but "a culmination" of years of top-level discussions aimed at forging a stronger labour-CCF relationship. In fact, the devastating losses incurred by the CCF in the election could have easily destroyed the new party. Although the defeat removed many reservations CCF leaders may have had about the new party, it made them worry, ironically, about whether or not the CLC leadership was still committed to the idea. Perhaps the latter might not wish to tie their flag to a party that could no longer serve as a formidable force in Parliament on labour's behalf? At an impromptu meeting with CLC leaders shortly after the election, therefore, David Lewis offered to release the CLC from its commitment to the New Party project. Fortunately for the CCF, CLC President Claude Jodoin was still very enthusiastic about proceeding with the plan and the other key CLC leaders fell in behind him. In this respect, the New Party was launched in spite of the 1958 election, not because of it. The election defeat did not give rise to the new party idea, nor did it necessarily guarantee its unveiling in April 1958. The only certainty, as Horowitz states, is that "the *final, definite* decision to proceed with the new party resolution was not made until after the election."[41]

Shortly after the CLC convention, the CCF and CLC Executives agreed to establish a Joint National Committee (JNC) for the purpose of discussing the development of a new party. Both the New Party idea and the JNC were strongly endorsed, in a lengthy resolution, by the CCF's national convention in July. In its entirety, the resolution emphasized the need for a broadly based movement of the Left, with the ultimate goal of establishing a society based on the principles of democratic socialism. It authorized the CCF to enter into talks with the CLC and other interested groups, and stipulated that any proposed constitution for the New Party should first be circulated among party members for full discussion.[42]

If the two years following the birth of the CLC were marked by the persistent efforts of CCF and CLC leaders at the national level to advance the concept of a new political alignment, they were in distinct contrast to the activities and concerns of the CCF in Ontario during the same period. With few exceptions, party records and statements in the post-merger period strongly suggest that CCFers in the province were preoccupied with more mundane matters of organization, fundraising, and elections, and that CCF leaders were certain the party's decline could be reversed through the proven organizing strategy of "concentration." Except for the recommendations forwarded by the Provincial Council to its federal counterpart in January 1956, upon the latter's request, and the occasional call for closer ties with labour, the idea of broadening the party was not officially discussed or promoted by the Ontario party. Nor is there any indication that Ontario CCF leaders were privy to the secret discussions taking place between labour and the CCF at the national level in these years.[43]

Relations between labour and the CCF also remained the same during the period 1956 to 1958, despite a startling 300 percent increase in the number of affiliated members resulting from the affiliation of an Auto Workers local in Toronto and a Steelworkers local in Hamilton (the number resumed its decline thereafter).[44] The PAC and TUC simply continued to urge unionists and CCFers to seek closer ties. In September 1956, for example, the TUC issued a statement echoing what was becoming a familiar refrain: "There should be a much closer relation [sic] between Riding organization and trade unions. Political Action Committees should be invited to cooperate with riding organizations. If there are no PAC's then it would be wise to set up a CCF trade union committee ... We should [also] encourage affiliation from locals to the CCF."[45] But as always, these admonitions seemed to have gone largely unheeded. In 1957, the Provincial Council was still urging greater cooperation between riding associations and unions, and at the 1958 convention it observed that "no particular effort has been made to persuade trade unions to take advantage of the affiliation clauses in our constitution." Even the union leadership seemed less enthusiastic about keeping close ties with the CCF in these years. As Bill Sefton told his brother Larry in 1959, "Few if any of the top brass of the Unions have made [an] appearance at National conventions of the CCF and certainly this is true of Ontario."[46]

Apart from the usual reasons – union leaders fearful of splitting their locals along political lines, rank and file resentment at having the CCF "shoved down their throats," the feeling among labour unionists that the CCF just wasn't "their party," and the reluctance of some

CCFers to associate with groups that they feared could dominate the party and dilute its socialism – a few new obstacles to labour-CCF cooperation appeared in these years. One was the growing international image of unions as corrupt and violent, a view based to some extent on the violence surrounding labour relations in Ontario in the early 1950s, but mostly on the more recent revelations of racketeering in certain American-based unions.[47] Consequently, parties identified with organized labour, however loosely, suffered from guilt by association, which naturally made some CCFers more wary of even closer ties. In Kenora-Rainy River, for example, a CCF riding leader refused to hold a joint nominating convention, at which union and CCF representatives in the riding would together choose a candidate for the 1958 federal election, because of the bad publicity this might attract. Another problem was the tendency of CCF spokespersons and organizers to overemphasize the general CCF program when speaking with workers, rather than the pro-labour content of the program; the result was a feeling among many unionists that the CCF did not really represent the working class and that it was simply trying to indoctrinate them.[48] Thus, the persistent suspicion and resentment on both sides kept labour-CCF cooperation to a minimum in the post-merger period.

At the same time, ironically, support among organized labour in Ontario for partisan political action was growing. At its 1956 convention, the OFL once again endorsed the CCF as its political arm and encouraged the soon-to-be established CLC to do the same. The OFL-PAC, meanwhile, suddenly found itself overburdened with requests from local PACs for assistance. "The demands on this Department in Ontario have been growing steadily since May 1956," wrote Weisbach to the CLC's secretary-treasurer, and "it is at times almost impossible to look after all the demands."[49] The desire for political action within the OPFL increased as well. By the late fifties, rising unemployment, growing industrial automation, and recent efforts by employers to impose restrictions on unions, including the "indiscriminate use of immigrant labour by employers to undermine the whole fabric of the trade union movement," were compelling more and more craft unionists to seek political solutions to their problems.[50] Speaking at a CLC-sponsored political education conference in March 1958, OFL President Cleve Kidd noted that "a number of unions which have not previously taken up active interest in politics are now showing a desire to participate." And in a special *Globe and Mail* series on labour and politics that same month, James Senter observed that "during the past year many of the politically neutral craft unions have become just as interested as the industrial groups" in political action. Their politicization was reflected in the proliferation of PECs within such traditionally non-partisan crafts as carpentry, plumbing, garment-making, and steam-fitting, as well as in efforts to revise craft union constitutions to permit political activities.[51]

The trend toward partisan political action gained momentum in March 1957 when unionists from across Ontario met in Toronto to witness the merging of the OFL-CCL and OPFL-TLC into the Ontario Federation of Labour (OFL), an organization encompassing almost half the membership of its parent body. Unlike the CLC's founding convention, however, OFL delegates enthusiastically declared their support for a resolution endorsing the CCF, urging "all affiliated unions, and their members that are free to do so, as well as labour councils, to give all possible support to the CCF and its candidates in the forthcoming ... election." A second resolution, closely resembling that passed at the CLC's merger convention, established a PAC to implement the OFL's political action program and "arrange meetings with representatives of farm organizations and the CCF in Ontario, to explore the possibility of co-ordinated action in the legislative and political fields within the province."[52]

More significantly, many delegates expressed a desire to go beyond simple endorsement of the CCF. In fact, mere endorsement was seen by some as problematic insofar as it could provide an excuse, as it had in the past, for labour to do nothing, thus leaving the real political action up to the CCF activists. This approach benefited the CCF, because the latter received financial and electoral assistance from labour without having to surrender control over the party, but it left labour with little influence over party policy and other matters. Instead, what was needed was a party – either a new party or a revamped CCF – in which labour dominated, much like the British Labour Party with its large affiliated union wing. The only delegate to oppose the resolution endorsing the CCF, for example, told the convention that "we cannot delegate our whole political responsibility to a party without having control over party policy." This sentiment was no doubt shared by many who supported the pro-CCF resolution. "Labour wants a labour party," declared one such individual. "The CCF is controlled by professional workers and lawyers."[53] Murray Cotterill, in his typically flexible approach to political action, the ultimate aim of which was to create or capture a party for labour, also warned that simple endorsement of the CCF was "dangerous" – that it must be accompanied by the creation of a political instrument, such as the PAC, which labour could call its own:

Some of the people who claim that endorsation [sic] of a party alone means that we get ourselves tied to that party, have a great deal of truth in what they say. If the resolution ... is all we do, we are making a bad mistake. Any endorsation of any group must be temporary and must be conditional ... It is not enough to just merely pass resolutions of endorsation. By establishing a [political action] department ... we will be able to get all of the unions to participate in our political programme; not only those unions which have supported a political party in the past, but those unions which have not because the important thing to remember is that *whatever we do it must be labour's political programme.*"[54]

That most delegates agreed with these addenda to the endorsement resolution was apparent in their instruction to the Federation's secretary-treasurer, Doug Hamilton, that he begin consulting with socialist parties around the world on how to make unionists a more integral part of a political party. Overall, the new OFL evinced a clear desire to take political action through a *new* instrument of some sort and, if possible, to do so in conjunction with other progressive groups.[55]

Notwithstanding the unequivocally partisan sentiment of its founding convention, the OFL was slow to implement its political action program. Immediately after the convention it set up a temporary "PAC Committee," directed by Weisbach, to help the CCF prepare for the upcoming federal election. The election, plus the fact that the Federation was also busy finding new office space, establishing new records management procedures, getting supplies, hiring staff, and integrating new affiliates, meant that the OFL could not set up a full-time Political Action Department until September and thus only appointed a director for the department, Lloyd Fell, in November. At about the same time, the CCF's TUC decided to approach the OFL "to see if the time is now ripe to take action on the resolution passed at the founding convention ... instructing the Executive to explore the possibility of joint action in the political and legislative field by trade unions, farm groups, and the CCF." Certainly, the TUC was eager that talks toward this end begin, in part out of concern that the OFL's enthusiasm for political action might possibly take an independent direction, even though the significant number of CCF supporters in the Federation made this unlikely.[56] But discussions along these lines could not have gone very far, as preparations for the 1958 federal election moved into high gear several months later.

The results of that election, however, thrust the issue of the new party into the foreground and, in effect, set the respective agendas of the OFL-PAC and Ontario CCF for the next three years. The OFL greeted the decision by the national conventions of the CLC and CCF to build a new party with enthusiasm. A special PAC meeting in late May noted that "the reception of the [CLC's New Party] resolution in the labour movement has been good" and "delegates have been reporting to their locals in favourable terms." This was confirmed at the OFL's second annual convention, in October, at which delegates unanimously endorsed the resolution and passed another urging all labour councils and affiliated unions to intensify their political education efforts. Furthermore, the OFL Executive was instructed to meet with the CCF, farm groups, and liberal-minded individuals or groups to plan the formation of the New Party.[57]

The Ontario CCF, in contrast, greeted the New Party resolution with reserved optimism, surprise, and, in a few cases, outright opposition. The PAC noted privately that "there is more questioning [of the resolution] in CCF ranks, where the membership was less prepared for a new remedy to what was becoming a chronic ailment – failure to win elections." As a result, perhaps, the Provincial Council's endorsement of the New Party at the 1958 provincial convention was anything but stirring. The New Party, it declared, would mean "the achievement in the foreseeable future of the original objective of the CCF, namely, to join together in a single political force our great labour, farm and cooperative movements as well as professional people and other individuals who adhere to the basic socialist philosophy of humanity first."[58] Nor was the convention's endorsement any more inspiring: "Be it resolved that this Convention wholeheartedly endorse the recent move of the CLC and CCF National Convention to move hand in hand with like-minded progressive organizations towards the formation of a broadly based Canadian people's party."[59] And while the CCF talked about reaching out to other groups and creating a broadly based party, the Provincial Council made sure to emphasize the equal importance of maintaining the CCF's organizational strength, since "the only political organizational facilities which will be available to the New Party when it comes into being will be those provided by the CCF. An active and flourishing CCF organization will therefore be of great importance to it."[60] In short, it appears that the CCF was somewhat stoic about the New Party initiative and was certainly as eager to preserve its own organizational integrity as it was to build a new party, a disposition that was bound to create tension and contradiction somewhere along the way.

The Ontario CCF's lukewarm reception to the New Party idea was, to some extent, predictable. Although some of its leaders had recommended to the National Council, in early 1956, the creation of a broader alignment, the party did not formally discuss the subject thereafter, and party leaders did not participate in the all-important negotiations that culminated in the New Party resolution of 1958. Moreover, the history of CCF-labour relations in the province would not have created much enthusiasm within the party for such an experiment. Indeed, despite the CCL's habitual endorsement of the CCF and a sudden increase in affiliated members by the mid-fifties, the efforts to bring workers and CCFers closer together were unsuccessful. The two sides usually saw each other only at election time. Mutual suspicion and other preoccupations kept the them apart the rest of the time.

Instead, the New Party concept was almost exclusively the initiative of key CCF and CCL (and CLC) leaders at the national level and was inspired by their particular concerns. By the mid-fifties, the declining fortunes of the national CCF coincided with the growing desire of a united labour movement to improve its lot through direct political action. The result was a cautious, yet determined plan by CCF sympathizers to commit organized labour to participation in the creation of a new, broadly based political party that could satisfy the needs of both labour and CCF. With both the CCF and CLC unanimously behind the project by 1958, the stage was set for the long process of political education, organization, and fund-raising that lay ahead.

7 Building the New Party

The process of building the New Party is one of the most fascinating aspects of the Ontario CCF's history, primarily because things were not always as they seemed. On the surface it appears that the OFL and CCF simply used a succession of methods to create a new, broadly based movement of the Left – from the large political education conferences of 1958–59, aimed at soliciting input from unionists and CCFers concerning the shape the New Party should take; to the establishment of New Party Clubs in 1960–61, which sought to bring farmers and other "liberal-minded" individuals into the process. From this emerges the distinct impression, reinforced by the fulsome rhetoric of its promoters, that the New Party project in Ontario was a sincere attempt to create a broadly based, left-wing "people's" movement, incorporating labour, farmers, and the liberal-minded. And to some extent it was.

But more important, the New Party was a well-intentioned experiment adapted by the Ontario CCF to serve its own particular organizational needs. The party's lukewarm response to the New Party idea and unwavering determination to preserve its existing organization practically guaranteed that this would be the case. Therefore, rather than try to integrate the liberal-minded into the movement on an equal basis, in accordance with the letter and spirit of the 1958 resolutions, the CCF simply paid lip service to this ideal, focusing instead on strengthening its own movement. Acting through a joint committee of OFL and CCF representatives known as the Ontario Committee for the New Party, the CCF pursued this strategy relentlessly. It included the liberal-minded in the New Party movement only insofar as that action promised to fill gaps in CCF organization or helped uphold the *image* of a broadly based movement of equal partners. This pragmatic approach, which manifested itself time and time again in the period 1958–61, is the dominant theme of the New Party movement in Ontario.

Immediately after the 1958 CLC convention, CCF and OFL leaders began a series of "informal discussions" on ways to implement the New Party resolution. They agreed that the past sporadic cooperation between labour and the CCF had to be replaced with "a formal relationship," one which could eventually be extended "to farm and other groups within the province." But first, as instructed by the New Party resolution, they agreed that the rank and file in each movement, as well as the liberal-minded set, were to be given an opportunity to discuss the project; by the fall, therefore, the CCF and the OFL-PAC had made tentative plans for organizing regional political education forums on the subject of the New Party. From October 1958 to May 1959, somewhere between twenty-two and twenty-six conferences were held, eight of them in Metro Toronto.[1] Although the conferences were officially joint projects, it is clear from the various announcements and conference reports that most were sponsored by local labour bodies and attended primarily by labour representatives. Perhaps the largest of these conferences was held in Hamilton in February 1959, under the auspices of the CLC's PEC. Described as the CLC's "first venture into the field of Labour education" on a provincial basis, it was attended by 600 delegates from local unions and labour councils throughout Ontario. Only in Toronto could one find a veritable trinity of representatives – CCF, labour, and liberal-minded – attending the New Party conferences.[2]

The conferences were usually two days long, with the New Party often just one of the items on the agenda. Because raising the political awareness of those in attendance was usually the main objective, other topics included public relations, the economy, and foreign affairs. A conference began with a panel discussion by guest speakers representing labour, the CCF, or other liberal-minded groups, followed by a question and answer period. Delegates then split up into small "buzz groups" to discuss the problems associated with forming a new party. In the first few months, discussion almost invariably relied on the widely distributed booklet *A New Political Party for Canada*, issued by the JNC in 1958 as a sort of outline and reference manual for New Party discussions at all levels. The booklet asked the reader for suggestions as to the nature of the New Party's program and how the party should be structured. The groups would then report back to the conference and their suggestions would be collated by the conference sponsor and sent to the JNC for its consideration. The booklet's authors were careful to emphasize that "the members of CLC unions, the CCF and other organizations should play a full part in working out the programme and constitution of the proposed new party," and that no rigid conclusions should be arrived at by the study groups so that future suggestions from other groups could be received with an open mind.[3] The emphasis on broad, democratic participation at this first stage of the New Party development was unmistakable.

The exact response of conference delegates to the New Party concept is difficult to measure, but the large number and significant size of the forums revealed a widespread and growing interest in the New Party, primarily among organized labour. The CCF News, while describing most of the gatherings as "highly successful," often used the terms "consensus" and "unanimity" to describe delegate response. Morden Lazarus, the PAC director and a key figure in organizing the conferences, remarked that "these new party conferences are one of the most useful educational projects the PAC has ever undertaken," and described the response from rank-and-file unionists as "encouraging." Many conference chairmen also spoke of the forums as effective, with fair to good participation by those in attendance.[4]

The forums came to a temporary halt in May 1959, however, so that the CCF and OFL could concentrate on the upcoming provincial election. Nevertheless, the new cooperative spirit between labour and the CCF that the forums and the whole New Party development symbolized carried over into the election campaign. In January, an election committee consisting of six members from the PAC and CCF had been set up to plan the campaign and coordinate the political activities of CCFers and unionists to prevent any duplication of effort or expenditure. Although joint election committees were not new, this particular body cooperated and pooled its human and financial resources to a larger extent than in previous campaigns. As Lazarus observed after the election, "The CCF and the OFL ... campaigns were virtually combined into one this time"; as a result, PAC and CCF leaders were able to conduct a more efficient campaign than ever before. As well, the PAC once again paid for a substantial portion of the party's election expenses.[5]

Another reason for the high degree of cooperation during the election was labour's determination to create a stronger base for the New

Party by increasing the CCF's legislative representation. Many politically conscious labour leaders associated with the PAC viewed the 1959 election as crucial to the success of the New Party. Bill Sefton, the sometimes mercurial chair of the Toronto and District Labour Council's PEC, was especially worried that the Liberals would make a comeback and remain the alternative to the Tories. "It is urgent and important," he told Bill Dodge, a CLC vice-president, "that we do in fact become the alternative to the Liberals in the ... election." Sefton considered the election one "that could be the making or the breaking of the 'New Party.'" His determination was no doubt a factor in the Labour Council's decision to hire (with some assistance from the Toronto and District CCF Council) a dozen organizers for the campaign who would do political organization in the Toronto area and provide financial assistance to many CCF candidates. The PAC, too, was concerned that the CCF do well and saw the New Party political forums of 1958–59 not only as a necessary step in building the New Party, but also as a way of stimulating labour political action during the election.[6]

The CCF, on the other hand, did not equate CCF success in the election with the potential success of the New Party to anywhere near the same extent. In fact, judging from the nature of its campaign utterances and publicity, the CCF may have tried to disassociate itself from the New Party. This was not its original intention, however, for the Provincial Council initially planned to use the New Party idea to get votes for the CCF. That is, it would try to convince voters that a vote for the latter was actually a vote for the former. But for reasons that were never made explicit, the CCF did not mention the New Party at all during the campaign. Certainly it wished to do well, since a larger legislative contingent would allow it to enter the New Party with strength and make the latter a credible alternative to the Liberals; party leaders probably reasoned, however, that if the CCF was too closely equated with the New Party in the public's mind, the New Party would likely suffer the same fate electorally as had the CCF. The CCF's goal, as later developments would reveal, was to create at least the *image* of a new party and not simply a rehashed version of the CCF. As a result, the CCF did not try to make the 1959 election a test of the New Party idea and, therefore, was not as concerned as some labour leaders that the New Party project stand or fall with the results of the contest.

This reasoning may also explain why the CCF – and in particular, Donald MacDonald – chose to focus its campaign publicity, instead, on a theme that it had returned to time and time again since 1954: government scandal. The main issue this time around was natural gas.

In the 1958 legislative session, MacDonald, who by this time was known as "Mac the Knife" among Tory backbenchers, had questioned Premier Frost about the July 1957 resignation of Mines Minister, Phillip Kelly. He suggested that his resignation was related to Kelly's 20-percent financial interest in Northern Ontario Natural Gas (NONG), a firm that was receiving substantial financial assistance from the provincial government to construct a pipeline across northern Ontario, and whose stockholders had profited lucratively from some rather questionable transactions prior to public issuance of the stock. Although Frost denied the accusation, it was common knowledge around Queen's Park that Kelly had been forced to resign because of his NONG involvement. Subsequent newspaper revelations that Frost's Minister of Public Works, Bill Griesinger, had also purchased NONG shares led to a second cabinet resignation. At the same time, it was revealed that even the leader of the Liberal Party, John Wintermeyer, was implicated in the affair. Wintermeyer had purchased NONG stock on a tip from Kelly and had therefore known of Kelly's own conflict of interest. MacDonald charged that Wintermeyer's involvement had effectively silenced the Liberal leader, forcing him to abdicate his responsibility as leader of the Official Opposition. The issue reached a fever pitch in February 1959 after the release of the government's internal investigation of the scandal, which revealed massive stock profiteering by NONG directors and several high-ranking Tory party officials, and after Kelly's insinuation that still more M.P.P.s were involved. There was also evidence, introduced by MacDonald in March, that Frost knew full well of his ministers' involvements in NONG long before the media's revelations forced their resignations. When the smoke finally cleared, three cabinet ministers had resigned over the scandal and a number of other public figures had had their reputations badly tarnished, including the premier himself.[7]

MacDonald, who during the campaign did more handshaking, speaking, and touring (over 4,500 miles in his own car) than any other leader, and who in many ways *was* the CCF campaign, made the most of these developments. At almost every stop, he criticized Wintermeyer's involvement in, and silence during, the scandal, reminding voters that this was but another example of Tory immorality; he also demanded an independent judicial investigation of the affair and challenged both Wintermeyer and Frost to a debate on NONG. For the first half of the month-long campaign, the premier displayed his usual low-key, humble, friendly "tea-party" style, focusing on his government's strong record in economic matters and promising only more of the same. But MacDonald's continual barrage of accusations eventually pushed Frost beyond his limit and, in an unusual departure from equanimity, he lashed out at the CCF leader. Donald MacDonald, he told an audience of Tory supporters in Galt in late May, "is a reckless, glib, ridiculous, absurd man with no logic and a disregard for truth calculated to hurt and destroy the great historic parties in Ontario ... That [his attention to scandal] is a disregard of the responsibilities we all have to the high conceptions and principles of public life ... means nothing to him. It is intended to destroy the confidence of the people in the political life of our province and its standards and its honour."[8]

Notwithstanding the series of confirmed improprieties that had beset the Frost administration since the Highway Scandal, and which the CCF had done much to uncover and publicize, the irony of the premier's comments was obviously lost in the hot, humid weather of the 1959 campaign. On 11 June Ontario voters returned the Conservative government with a somewhat reduced, though still comfortable majority, and doubled the Liberal representation at Queen's Park. The final distribution of seats and popular vote was: Conservatives seventy-one (46.2%), Liberals twenty-two (36.6%), and CCF five (16.7%). MacDonald, Gisborn, and Thomas each recaptured their ridings and were joined by two newcomers: Ken Bryden from Toronto-Woodbine, who won by a slim 267 votes over his Tory opponent; and Norm Davison from Hamilton East. The CCF increased its popular vote by only .2 percent over 1955, compared with an almost 4 percent increase for the Liberals. Moreover, its strength continued to be concentrated in the Far North and in the large urban centres of south-western Ontario, where the Liberals had made impressive gains.[9]

Despite the NONG scandal and the closer cooperation of the PAC and CCF, especially in Toronto, the party was once again dealt a severe blow by Ontario voters. And once again the causes are partially identifiable. It seems that politically minded local labour leaders were still too busy with their day-to-day union business to give anything more than lip service to political action. Several months before the election Bill Sefton told the CLC's vice-president, Bill Dodge, that "the absence of real organization at the riding level where elections are fought and won, is now, has been, and will continue to be the real problem ... The result has been that most of our campaigns, despite all the good work that has been done, get bogged down. This is true of the Steel-workers even though we are supposed to be in the van[guard], and ... I am positive it is true of other unions as well."[10] The part-time organizers hired by the PEC and CCF in Toronto had been valuable, to be sure. In most of the industrial ridings the CCF won over 22 percent of the vote, and as much as 50 percent in some ridings. But, as Sefton noted, to establish the organization needed to capture more of the labour vote would require permanent "political" organizers, provided and paid for by labour, who would cooperate with the new party in each riding. Without this basic organization in place, the labour vote would not be secured, and "the 'New Party' will be still born."[11]

The absence of strong political action at the local union level was matched by the continuing weakness of party organization at the constituency level. Ken Bryden, who was elected in Toronto-Woodbine on the basis of a strong local organization, told members that the low profile of the party in many ridings left the impression that the CCF was not a serious contender, which in turn fostered the "wasted vote" mentality and ensured that the CCF would finish third even though support for the government fell.[12] It is also possible that MacDonald's constant harping on government immorality, although certainly vindicated by subsequent investigations and convictions, as well as his unfortunate tendency to question the integrity of specific individuals on the basis of circumstantial evidence alone, may have offended the prudish sensibilities of Ontario voters and gradually eroded the party's credibility.[13] Certainly scandals had figured prominently in the defeat of past governments, particularly when combined with examples of inept adminstration, and this is an aspect of the province's political culture that the CCF may have been trying to exploit. But by 1959, many voters probably felt as exasperated with the CCF's mud-slinging tactics as did, for example, the *Globe*'s admittedly partisan editor, who during the campaign declared that "the CCF may at one time have had some nuisance value in the Province's political life [but] today ... is all nuisance and no value."[14] Out of such a concern had come pleas from several top party officials urging MacDonald to tone down his emphasis on the scandal side of the NONG issue. Doc Ames, in his usual unequivocal manner, asked MacDonald in the summer of 1958 to "completely drop the scandal aspects of the pipeline and stress the positive." "Let's not be too damn self-righteous!" he continued. "I am sure the public are thinking as they did with the Jolliffe Gestapo charges [in the 1945 election] – they are fed up and think we are muck-raking."[15] Notwithstanding these criticisms, the drop in Tory support – at a time when economic conditions were improving slightly; when the St. Lawrence Seaway, hospital insurance, and cheap natural gas from Alberta were popular government accomplishments; and when Frost's cabinet boasted a number of new, young faces – strongly suggests that the numerous revelations of scandal, which MacDonald did much to publicize, may indeed have had an impact on voters. Unfortunately, it was the Liberals, not the CCF, who reaped the benefits.

The election results confirmed the belief of CCF and OFL leaders that the CCF proper was going no where and that for the New Party to avoid a similar fate the rank and file of both movements had to become more active, preferably working side-by-side, in building the new political instrument. It was clear, too, that the regional conferences had not been as effective as expected in stimulating widespread discussion, political action, or CCF-labour cooperation at the local level of both movements, in part because of the high cost and numerous difficulties associated with attracting persons to the large regional conferences. Indeed, only 200 of the OFL's 2,000 locals had sent delegates to the various conferences in 1958–59, forcing Lazarus to conclude that "the major job of reaching the majority of the locals in this province has only begun."[16]

Consequently, the CCF and OFL-PAC decided after the election to place responsibility for political education with local leaders and to encourage union and party members to establish regular ties with one another as well as other liberal-minded groups. In October, the CCF Membership Education Committee encouraged riding associations and clubs to discuss the New Party and to "join with labour councils to plan New Party Conferences in their area." That same month the Provincial Council asked delegates at the CCF's annual convention to begin consulting with local unions and other interested groups to establish the basis for a broadly based New Party constituency association. This was followed by a large number of CCF riding association conferences on the New Party, from which numerous suggestions on structure and program emerged.[17]

Efforts by the CCF to create stronger grass-roots interest in the New Party were reciprocated by the OFL-PAC. A number of weekend institutes and workshops were held throughout the winter of 1959–60 to familiarize union representatives with the New Party. In addition, Morden Lazarus received approval for a program intended to obtain public endorsement of the New Party from individual locals, who, after having thoroughly discussed such things as the Party's constitution and program, would be encouraged by the PAC to sign a "Statement of Support"(SOS). The SOS program, it was hoped, would stimulate more extensive discussion about the New Party, create some favourable publicity, and provide an indication of the extent of union support. In general, then, the CCF and PAC placed "less emphasis" on regional political forums than it had before the election.[18]

While the CCF and PAC encouraged closer ties between workers and CCFers and more discussion of the New Party, efforts were also underway to incorporate the so-called liberal-minded into the movement. Since 1958, the sponsoring bodies of the New Party had made sure to emphasize that they were seeking a broadly based movement that included farmers and other liberal-minded individuals. Labour was especially concerned that this be the case, so that it would not be accused of dominating the New Party. But the CCF was equally concerned, and one of the strongest proponents of broadening the base of the movement was Donald MacDonald, who, in July 1959, declared that "the New Party must be something more than a marriage of the CCF and those sections of the trade union movement which have determined to take direct political action if it is to fulfill the vision which inspired the historic resolutions [of 1958]." Consequently, he urged the National Committee for the New Party (NCNP, formerly the Joint National Committee [JNC]) to create a new instrument through which organizationally unattached persons – that is, those not belonging to a union or the CCF – could become involved in building the New Party. In November came the announcement that the NCNP had created such an instrument, known as the "New Party Club."[19]

The New Party Club program was directed by R.D. ("Des") Sparham, under the authority of the NCNP; it had at its disposal the services of Lyal Tait and Fred Young, both of whom were assigned to work as full-time Club organizers in the rural areas of southern and southwestern Ontario. In its *Guide for the Establishment of New Party Clubs*, the NCNP defined a Club as "a group of people who support the movement to form a new national party which will unite all democratic Canadians of the political left," and stipulated that anyone was eligible to join, provided they were not already members of the CCF or a union. Clubs could be established in neighbourhoods or by specific "interest" or occupational groups. To be recognized as legitimate, however, a Club had to have at least six members and each member had to contribute one dollar per year to the NCNP. Once approved by the NCNP, the Club was eligible for representation at the founding convention and received various publications to keep its members informed of New Party developments. Clubs also had "the right to ... share in the study, discussion, and promotion of the new party project." They were provided with copies of a preliminary New Party constitution and program, drafted by the NCNP in 1959, and encouraged to submit their views directly to the Committee. The New Party Club concept was aptly described as "an expression of interest at a cost of one dollar," with membership expiring at the time of the founding convention. Thereafter, Club members who wished to join the New Party as full-fledged members would have to pay full fees.[20]

Ostensibly, the New Party Club idea was a tactic devised to allow non-unionists and those reluctant to join the CCF to play a role in the New Party development, thereby fulfilling the 1958 promise of broad participation. But the Ontario CCF had a very different use for the Clubs. In reality, they were to be simply one facet of a brilliantly pragmatic organizing strategy, aimed at plugging holes in the party's organization across the province. This strategy was unveiled for the first time in October 1959 at a meeting of the Organization Committee. Party leaders decided that New Party Clubs should only be established in the thirty or so federal ridings in which the CCF had little or no organization, and that in other areas priority should be given to maintaining and expanding CCF riding associations. "Where there is already a greater or lesser degree of organization," stated the Committee, "the first responsibility of this committee is to ensure that the CCF organizations in those areas become as effective as possible." In those areas where the CCF was weak, however, "it may be desirable to encourage the ridings to branch out into such fields as the establishment of new party clubs ... There is little point at this stage in trying to set up CCF organizations in areas where such do not now exist. Most of these areas are rural, and ... Lyal Tait has now been taken on by the NCNP as a rural organizer in Ontario. His principal job will be to get new party clubs functioning wherever possible."[21] Consequently, organizers were instructed "to take into account the circumstances of each individual riding they are dealing with and [to] use good judgement as to the kind of projects they encourage each riding to undertake."[22]

The strategy was purely pragmatic. In areas where party organization was strong, New Party Clubs were seen as redundant, and perhaps even risky, insofar as riding leaders and members might neglect their own organization in trying to form Clubs or, even worse, might decide to leave the riding associations for the Clubs. Party leaders realized that full individual membership in the New Party, through a CCF riding association, was far better than the *possibility* of future membership through a New Party Club, notwithstanding all the public rhetoric about creating a broadly based party. In areas where the CCF was weak, however, the New Party Club was an ideal way of attracting to the New Party those liberal-minded persons who did not belong to a union and who were reluctant to join the CCF. In short, the New Party Club was simply a device used to supplement existing CCF organization. MacDonald stated this clearly when he told the Organization Committee's chairperson, Marj Pinney, that "in the long run, New Party Clubs are going to be merely a 'gimmick' for broadening the base of the existing CCF organization so that when the New Party is formed, the two will be welded into one organization."[23] Clearly, party leaders were not willing to create a broadly based "people's" movement of workers, CCFers, and liberal-minded individuals if it meant endangering the organizational base they had struggled so hard to maintain and expand over the years.

Some CCF members, however, had reservations about the strategy; they advocated, instead, the promotion of New Party Clubs alongside, or even in place of, existing riding associations. Donald MacDonald felt that, even in the stronger ridings, "The New Party Club might prove an effective means of expanding the organization base among those who have not or will not join the CCF, but who are interested in the New Party." Doc Ames agreed, and his work as a CCF/New Party organizer in northern Ontario indicates that he strayed somewhat from the organizational strategy laid down by the Organization Committee. Moreover, both Macdonald and Ames seem to have had the support of Des Sparham and the NCNP. For example, shortly after getting wind of the Ontario CCF's strategy, Sparham's secretary, Audrey Kari, told Ames, "I am very glad ... you have taken the view that there is nothing incompatible in promoting ... the local CCF Club and seeking to establish a New Party Club at the same time."[24] What people like Mac-Donald and Ames failed to realize, however, was that their more ambitious, "broadening out" strategy ran the risk of weakening the existing CCF organization – that is, the regular, dues-paying membership – by diverting the resources of the Provincial Office and local riding associations toward the interim organizational vehicles, the New Party Clubs. Perhaps because of this ambivalence, the results of the Provincial Office's strategy were mixed. By 1961, in the thirty or so ridings in which CCF organization was "poor" or "non-existent," the CCF succeeded in establishing one or more New Party Clubs in approximately half of them. But in five of these weak ridings, and eight or nine of the stronger ones (in which CCF organization was "fair" or "good"), New Party Clubs seem to have been established at the expense of a decline in CCF members in the riding.[25]

The Ontario CCF's selective organization of the liberal-minded set began in rural areas, among farmers, where the CCF had had trouble attracting support in the past. Efforts to establish closer ties with the rural sector and improve relations between farmers and urban labourers were not new. Party leaders had always retained the hope that the farmer-labour cooperation that characterized the post-World War One alliance of the United Farmers of Ontario (UFO) and the Independent Labour Party, or the ephemeral union of the early thirties, could be revived. In the latter instance, Ontario farmers were repelled mainly by the communistic elements within the labour section of the nascent CCF. According to Agnes Macphail, Canada's first female M.P. and later a member of the Ontario CCF caucus who did much to attract the UFO into the CCF in the first place, the farmers were "badly shaken" by the experience of that period. "They believed in the CCF platform ... but the very shadow of communism contaminated the whole movement for them." Party leaders had this tragic episode in mind years later when deciding what to do about Trotskyist infiltration into the party in 1953. "In the early days of the CCF in Ontario," David Archer told the Provincial Council, "the Stalinist communists got into our organization and the effect of their disruptive activities has been that the farm organizations have been alienated from our movement and we have never had any significant farm support since then."[26]

Following the abandonment of the federated structure in 1934 and the departure of the UFO shortly thereafter, Macphail had left the CCF in disgust and did not rejoin the movement until the early forties, when she once again began recruiting farmers into the party. Her efforts led to the formation of an "impressive" CCF Farm Committee, with its own organizer and research committee. But this advance, too, was short-lived. When the UFO merged with the Federation of Agriculture in 1943 to form the strictly non-partisan Federation of Agriculture of Ontario (FAO), relations with the CCF worsened. "The organized farmers of Ontario ... entered a political cloister," recalled Macphail. "Direct communications became difficult, and without communication there is small likelihood of persuasion."[27]

During the 1950s, the CCF did what it could to recover farmer support. The party's revived Farm Committee, a mere shadow of its predecessor and consisting of about a dozen representatives from the CCF and various agricultural organizations, spent much of its time and money, as it said, trying to "make contacts with key people in organized agriculture, as well as with leaders in the Co-op movement." It arranged meetings with the leaders of the FAO, the province's largest farm body, as well as with the heads of numerous commodity producer groups. Farm Committee members also attended the annual conventions of these organizations and frequently approached their leaders for consultation. Whenever the Committee found prominent farm leaders sympathetic to the party, it would arrange and publicize meetings at which these individuals could speak to other farmers about common problems. Three or four meetings were held annually, and the hope was that these farmers would follow their leaders in supporting or joining the CCF. The Committee also played a leading role in developing CCF farm policy, preparing party literature for farmers, organizing its contacts into CCF clubs, supplying CCF speakers for farm meetings, finding farmer candidates, and advertising the CCF's farm policy in rural newspapers; similar actions were taken by CCF constituency associations in predominantly rural areas.[28]

These efforts were supplemented admirably by the party's legislative caucus and, in particular, Donald MacDonald. Having grown up on a farm, MacDonald had a natural affinity for rural Ontario, which he demonstrated by regularly attending and addressing meetings and conventions of the FAO, the left-leaning Ontario Farm Union (OFU), and the numerous commodity groups. "Down through the years," he recalls in his memoirs, "I am confident that no other member of the legislature visited more farms and attended more farm meetings, with the possible exception of the Minister himself." Moreover, as the party's agricultural critic, MacDonald fought vigorously for the farmers' interests inside the legislature. Despite jeers from opponents, who quickly labelled him the "asphalt farmer" because of his urban, middle-class status, he was forever pressing the Frost government to bolster farm income with price supports, improve marketing legislation, and nationalize the industries that farmers depended on for implements and supplies.[29]

Despite these efforts, however, farmer support for the CCF grew very slowly after the war. One problem was the party's deteriorating financial position after 1949, which resulted in a shortage of rural organizers. In 1952, the Farm Committee lamented "the complete lack of organization or party machine in the rural areas or, as far as that goes, even in most of the urban areas outside of Toronto ... There are no established contacts between the CCF and the rural population except a few isolated members."[30] The party's 1955 decision to concentrate its resources on the most promising ridings merely exacerbated the situation.

A more serious problem was the farmer's long-standing suspicion of organized labour, whose interests were seen as coincident with big business and thus directly contrary to those of the farmer. "The farmer who is working long hours, seven days a week, trying to produce to the limit of his capacity," observed a member of the Farm Committee in 1952, "has no patience for the continued demands of labour for higher wages for less work." Quite simply, farmers viewed organized labour as an isolated, selfish, interest group, enjoying high wages and a short work week, with little concern about agricultural producers. As ties between labour and the CCF increased in the forties and fifties, the CCF became even less attractive to farmers, who also resented the influence labour seemed to wield over the CCF in what was supposed to be a "cooperative commonwealth of farmer, labour, and other groups." To some extent these feelings were mutual, as workers resented the independence and property of farmers, as well as the prosperity they seemed to enjoy as a result of ever-rising food prices. Over the years, both CCF and OFL leaders tried to remove these misconceptions. At annual Farmer-Labour conferences or in speeches to farm meetings they stressed that both "producing classes" were victims of the same monopolistic, profit-hungry manufacturers and processors, and that only by taking concerted political action could they hope to resolve their common grievances.[31] But the mutual resentment remained.

The main obstacle to closer ties between the CCF and farmers, however, was the lingering, yet strong suspicion that the party was too radical, perhaps even communist. According to the Farm Committee, many farmers shared the same christian, cooperative ideals as the CCF, but feared that a CCF victory could result in "complete state control of the economic, cultural, and eventually political system – in one word, communism." Even those who did not hold this view were unwilling to risk social ostracism by proclaiming their support for the party. "A large number of Ontario farmers hold ... CCF ideas," noted the Committee, "but if so told, retract immediately." The communistic image was perpetuated, in part, by the urban media, but most of the information farmers received on the CCF came from rabid anti-communist organizations such as the Canadian Intelligence Service, the Anti-Communist League, and the Social Credit party, all of which placed anti-CCF advertisements in rural newspapers on a regular basis. "The farmer has been indoctrinated with the idea that socialism means totalitarianism," reported the Farm Committee in 1954, and "quite a few ... believe that the CCF stands for materialism and is antireligious." That same year the Committee complained to the National Office that representatives of these anti-communist organizations were hurting the CCF cause among farmers in Grey County. One individual in particular, it reported, "is working hard here in Grey County and really stirring up the people." Although the party did its best to counter the propaganda, the "dangerous radical" image persisted.[32]

To some extent, the weak support among farmers was also a reflection of the good economic times for farmers in the 1940s and early 1950s; thus when conditions began to change thereafter, so did the attitudes of the agricultural community. After 1951, commodity prices fell and production costs rose, lowering farm income and forcing many farmers to supplement their livelihood with other work. Anxiety over economic conditions in the midst of nationwide prosperity was mixed with growing frustration over the provincial government's failure to respond to the farmers' concerns. By 1955, then, farmers were in open revolt against the government's farm policy and the high cost of agricultural implements.[33]

As a result, support among farmers for political action grew and CCF leaders became cautiously optimistic. In November 1953, the Farm Committee's chairperson boasted that although "farmers ... are [still] further away from political action than their [union] cousins in towns and cities ... conditions among farmers are more auspicious for the CCF than they have been for some years." CCF and OFL hopes were further buoyed by the continued growth of the more militant OFU; the influx of young, "progressive" leaders into official positions in the FAO; and the larger crowds that CCF speakers were drawing at farm meetings and Farmer-Labour conferences by the mid-fifties. These developments, coinciding with the dramatic developments in the labour movement, encouraged the belief that it was only a matter of time before a truly broad-based party of the Left would emerge across Canada.[34]

The party's sense of a breakthrough among farmers was no doubt reinforced by the fact that rural discontent peaked just as the New Party movement was getting underway. Tired of the ongoing decline in farm income by 1957, several commodity groups took matters into their own hands and began setting up new cooperative marketing systems that effectively undermined the power of large processors and packers to set commodity prices. When the Hog Producers Association established such a system in 1958, against the opposition of the influential meat packers, the Frost government introduced Bill 86, giving its own Farm Products Marketing Board the power to restrict the freedom of all producer marketing boards. Viewing this as a direct threat to the principle of producer-controlled marketing schemes, Ontario farmers loudly opposed the measure. Meanwhile, their strongest ally in the legislature, Donald MacDonald, introduced a bill to rescind Bill 86, while the CCF worked hard to mobilize farmer protest through press releases, direct mailings, and speeches.

The result was a growth in farmer support for the party, or so it seemed. Many farm leaders spoke in favour of MacDonald's bill, including members of the traditionally hostile FAO, while some even called for farmers to actively support the party. As well, consultation between the OFU and the CCF caucus increased as the legislature debated and studied the measure. Farmer discontent reached a fever pitch with the passage of Bill 86 in the spring of 1960, and with Premier Frost's threat to replace producer-elected marketing boards with a government-appointed agency.[35] By the time the CCF began building the New Party, therefore, its leaders had reason to believe that farmers would join the movement through the New Party Clubs.

But events would prove otherwise. Although quite a few Clubs were established in predominantly rural areas, strictly farmer Clubs were few in number – a scarcity suggested by Lyal Tait in his report to the Provincial Office in 1960 that he had encountered "great difficulty in persuading farmers to actually organize New Party Clubs"; and confirmed by the low number of genuine farm "delegates" at the Ontario New Party's founding convention in 1961.[36] Although the reasons for this situation vary, the main ones can be seen in the events surrounding the only New Party farm forum of any significance held during this period, at the Woodsworth Memorial Foundation in Toronto in April 1960. In trying to drum up interest in the forum, the CCF had been careful to emphasize that the meeting was *not* organized by the CCF. In the invitations sent out to key farm leaders, for example, it avoided using CCF letterhead, a sign that the farmers' ingrained antipathy toward the CCF had not waned. Moreover, because Tait had apparently encountered much anti-labour sentiment during his travels in rural Ontario, he recommended to the CCF's provincial secretary, Peg Stewart, that someone be present at the forum "to explain the labour role, and try to break down some of the prejudice and suspicion which has so successfully kept farmers and industrial workers apart." At a farmer-labour conference in 1959, the OFU's president, Gordon Hill, confirmed that the image of labour among farmers was still unfavourable. "There is a very vicious anti-Labour campaign going on," he regretfully told delegates, "and I am very much disturbed with the success it is having in some farm quarters. I am even disturbed by the success it has had on some of our Farm Union people." In the end, only forty farm leaders participated in the forum.[37]

Apart from the ongoing suspicion of the CCF and organized labour, other factors precluded the participation of farmers in the New Party development. First, the CCF's high-profile opposition to Bill 86 did not result in any noticeable increase in farmer support for political action, in large part because the CCF's publicity may not have filtered down to the grass roots. "The Provincial Leader has been doing a good job in getting the true facts across," observed the Farm Committee shortly before Bill 86 was introduced, but "much of what he says does not appear in the papers which farmers read most [often]." Second, the farm sector itself was internally divided and thus difficult to mobilize. Sam Bowman, the OFU's provincial secretary, informed delegates at the April 1960 farm forum that "there are many conflicts, not only ... between Labour and farmer, but conflicts between farmers with different products and different interests." He later told Peg Stewart that "there never has been a time when farmers were at such logger heads as they are now, and never has the entire agriculture scene been in such a state of turmoil." Donald MacDonald, who spent a disproportionate amount of time trying to attract farmer support for the New Party, also noticed the existence of deep divisions within the farming community, divisions that farm leaders themselves felt would only be exacerbated if their organizations come out in support of the New Party. Geography, too, was a problem. While some farmers were sympathetic to the New Party idea, their very "scattering" across the province, in isolated pockets, made the job of organizing them into clubs difficult, particularly since the CCF's Farm Committee was virtually defunct and the NCNP lacked the funds to hire more personnel. Any remaining hopes for a breakthrough in rural Ontario during the first phase of the New Party development were probably extinguished when, in October 1960, the OFU reaffirmed its traditionally neutral political position by refusing to endorse the New Party.[38]

The New Party had an equally difficult time attracting support from non-Anglo-Saxon ethnic groups, or "New Canadians" as they were called. With the tremendous influx of European refugees and immigrants into the province after the war, the ethnic factor added a new element to the urban political scene, but one to which the CCF was slow in responding. The party made few attempts in the early postwar period to mobilize the newcomers, no doubt being more concerned with simply retaining its existing membership. As such, the initiative to organize New Canadians was left to local riding associations, several of which established CCF ethnic clubs, such as the Polish and Lithuanian clubs set up by the Hamilton East CCF in the early fifties. Certainly, the CCF welcomed with open arms those who had belonged to socialist organizations in their home country and who, upon arrival, wished to get involved with the CCF. But armed with some introductory literature from the Provincial Office and the names of a few local CCF contacts, such persons were expected to find their own way to the nearest riding association or club. Apart from this minimal guidance, the Provincial Office encouraged ridings to nominate ethnic candidates in areas of high ethnic concentration, placed election advertisements in the ethnic press, and sponsored the occasional talk by prominent European socialist leaders. There was, in other words, no formal effort by the provincial CCF to organize the ethnic community as a distinct section of the party, such as the "language federations" organized by the Communist Party in its early years, for example. In 1951, there were only four ethnic CCF clubs – three Lithuanian and one German – although according to the Provincial Council, "many individual members from various language groups hold cards in our riding associations."[39]

One of the biggest obstacles to organizing the ethnic community, apart from language, was the fact that many of the recent arrivals were Catholic refugees from Communist bloc countries who brought with them an intense hatred of communism and socialism. Such groups were easily led to believe, mostly by supporters of the two old parties, that the CCF was communistic.[40] CCF efforts to counter this by denouncing communism, educating New Canadians in the meaning of CCF socialism, and speaking out for their rights and interests were largely ineffective. Indeed, many newcomers remained highly suspicious of the CCF. On the other hand, some rejected the CCF for not being *more* socialist, and would have been more likely to support the LPP. In short, traditional ideological battle lines between communist and anti-communist tended to reassert themselves in the ethnic communities, leaving few democratic socialists among them; this was particularly true in the Ukrainian community, one of the largest ethnic groups in Ontario. The number of potential CCFers was further restricted by a federal immigration policy that deliberately weeded out left-wing "subversive" applicants.[41] Another problem was the antagonism, whether justified or not, which many rank-and-file unionists felt towards New Canadians, whom they accused of depressing wages, serving as strikebreakers, and intensifying the competition for jobs. This meant that riding associations with a high concentration of unionists were not likely to seek out ethnic members or to form ethnic clubs, and that CCF leaders would not want to antagonize existing and potential labour support by doing the same, at least in a big way. Finally, the fact that invitations to ethnic community functions were usually only extended to M.P.P.s, of which the CCF had few, meant that CCF leaders had few opportunities to establish contacts among New Canadian groups or push the CCF message. All factors considered, it is easy to understand why the CCF's earliest efforts to organize New Canadians were restrained and unsuccessful.[42]

This began to change somewhat by the mid-fifties. In 1955, the CCF set up an Ethnic Council, "to develop a closer contact between the CCF and ethnic groups, to convey information about the CCF to ethnic groups and to convey information about the ethnic groups to the CCF." Chaired by Dr. Frank Ancevich, a Lithuanian law professor forced to leave his country because of his socialist beliefs, and consisting of representatives from each major ethnic group, the Council's specific duties included preparing foreign-language leaflets on CCF policy, finding prominent ethnic community leaders willing to run as CCF candidates, arranging meetings between CCF leaders and ethnic groups, and establishing contacts in the ethnic community. These activities did not produce more ethnic CCF clubs, but they did reduce suspicion and gave the party a higher profile among New Canadians by the time the New Party movement began.[43]

Information on the role of ethnic groups in the New Party is, unfortunately, very sketchy. It is clear, though, that few ethnic groups formed New Party Clubs. One reason for this was the shortage of organizers assigned to this task, as a result of the party's preference for constituency rather than Club organizing. Another was the fear that ethnic Clubs could become a prime target for Communist infiltration. As a result, ethnic organizing was left to members of the Ethnic Council, who likely lacked the time and money to do a proper job. In 1960, Bill Sefton observed that there were over half a million New Canadians in Toronto, "amongst whom very little organizational work has been done of a lasting nature." That same year, Ancevich complained that New Canadians were being neglected in the New Party development. He told the OFL's annual convention that "so far as I know, there is only one ethnic group that has organized a New Party Committee" [i.e., Club], and strongly urged that "New Canadians ... not be neglected in this drive." In general, most of the NCNP and OCNP's efforts to mobilize ethnics took the form of publicity, and nothing more.[44] That few New Canadians took the initiative in forming their own Clubs could have been due to the close association between the New Party and the unions, unions which in the past had shown little sympathy toward the plight of New Canadians. As a result, no more than half a dozen ethnic New Party Clubs seem to have been established, and those primarily in Toronto and Hamilton, by the time the Ontario NDP was founded in October 1961.[45]

Although the CCF was more successful organizing the urban liberal-minded than the New Canadians in the initial phase, here, too, it encountered difficulties. Des Sparham, who did much of the early Club organizing himself, reported in March 1960 that "there is a scattering of groups across the northern and central parts of the province" but that "the real heartland is Toronto," where Clubs were springing up among high school teachers, doctors, professors, insurance agents, engineers, ethnic groups, and women. Only about a dozen recognized Clubs were established in the first four months of the program, but by May 1960 the number had tripled. The rapid growth, combined with a scarcity of Club organizers (Sparham had moved on to other provinces), led to a situation that the NCNP's provincial equivalent, the Ontario Committee for the New Party (OCNP), described as "chaotic" and "confused."[46] The OCNP's secretary, Peg Stewart, summed up the problem as follows: "We are ... looking seriously for an organizer to work in Ontario and carry on where Des Sparham began the work among New Party members. The situation is acute as the groups which have been set up lack direction and leadership, and we are really at a loss when individuals ask for a group to join."[47] The result, according to Sparham, was that "the New Party movement has no way of getting into touch with these thousands of farmers, co-operators, professional people and the like who are sympathetic to the democratic left." Indeed, by January 1961, only three bona fide New Party Clubs existed in Toronto. The OCNP's lack of information about the actual number of Clubs was compounded by the fact that because the media and many employers were generally unsympathetic to the New Party idea, many middle-class individuals were reluctant to either publicize their involvement with a Club or assume a prominent position therein, for fear of experiencing repercussions in their daily lives – such as the loss of their jobs.[48] Nor did the Ontario CCF help its own cause much with its strategy of selectively promoting New Party Clubs. By focusing their efforts on CCF riding associations, party leaders practically guaranteed that Club growth would, to some extent, outrun the desire or capacity of organizers to control it.

In spite of these obstacles, Sparham managed to set up an *ad hoc* New Party Co-ordinating Committee (NPCC), consisting of seven Club representatives from the Toronto area, which began meeting in June 1960 to discuss New Party issues, coordinate Club activity, organize Club forums, and constitute itself on a formal and broader basis in order to qualify for representation on the OCNP and at the founding convention. This "group of seven," which met informally at Sparham's home, represented a variety of Clubs consisting of insurance agents, social workers, engineers, medical technicians, doctors, and nurses. Reports from each representative on the status of their Club indicated that while several were expanding rapidly, most were having trouble attracting members from their respective professions. Different work schedules and places of residence made it difficult for members of certain professions to meet at one time and in one place, while some groups found that their colleagues were "extremely reluctant to make political commitments."[49]

Deliberations of the NPCC focused primarily on the status of the Clubs in the New Party movement, but members also spent a good deal of time planning a New Party conference for the liberal-minded to be held in Toronto in October 1960. By far the largest and most highly publicized meeting of the liberal-minded contingent, it was attended by approximately sixty delegates, most of whom belonged to New Party Clubs and had no previous connection with either the CCF or the labour movement; a wide variety of middle-class professionals were represented. As with other New Party conferences, delegates were addressed by keynote and guest speakers, divided into discussion groups, and asked to present reports and pass resolutions. Unlike other conferences, however, this gathering expressed deep concern over the proposed structure of the New Party. "They showed real anxiety to be considered a contributing group," noted the CCF Executive, "and were very much afraid of being swamped by CCF and trade union members at the [founding] convention." This fear was embodied in a resolution calling for equal representation of the liberal-minded faction on the NCNP. The OCNP had, in fact, anticipated this concern. When considering the matter of guest speakers for the conference, for example, it made sure to select only high-profile individuals not connected with the party. It chose Dr Charles Godfrey as chair and Professor Walter Young as keynote speaker because, as Donald MacDonald told the Provincial Council, "neither of these men has been identified in any way with the CCF in the past, and indeed both are examples of people who have not yet committed themselves but [who] are sufficiently interested to appear in public in connection with the New Party."[50]

The sudden growth of New Party Clubs in the spring of 1960, the formation of the NPCC, and the large gathering of the liberal-minded in Toronto suggest, therefore, that many white-collar professionals were interested in the New Party. But the CCF's (and OCNP's) strategy of selectively promoting New Party Clubs and using them primarily to portray the *appearance* of a broadly based party indicates that New Party promoters in Ontario were not committed to fully mobilizing this largely spontaneous support. This, in turn, explains the rather haphazard evolution of the Clubs in 1959–60; it also explains the care taken by the OCNP to create the appearance of a truly tripartite, "people's party," as seen in the arrangements for the farmer and urban professional conferences.

The OCNP's pragmatic use of New Party Clubs had one further consequence: it created a serious division between the CCF and certain labour leaders on the OCNP. According to NCNP policy, New Party Clubs were intended solely for persons who were neither union, nor CCF members. But when the OCNP discussed the policy in December 1959, the question arose as to what should be done in the not uncommon situation in which union members were barred from participating in the New Party development because of constitutional barriers within their union. The policy agreed upon at the meeting was unequivocal: "New Party Clubs are not appropriate for either union members or CCF members – the Clubs should be the medium of participation for people outside the two original founding bodies ... If union members wish to join new party clubs, they should do so entirely outside their unions, in company with other people, and should not form a group within their union which might be in opposition to the majority and therefore a cause of dissension."[51] Clearly, the OCNP wished to avoid a split in the labour movement along political lines, for this would damage the chances of forming a broadly based party incorporating the greater part of unionized labour. More important, the presence of labour-dominated New Party Clubs would foster the impression that labour was trying to dominate the New Party, therefore destroying the image of a broadly based party of equal partners. The Ontario CCF Executive, especially Ken Bryden, was emphatic about this policy, particularly the rule that New Party Clubs not be formed by unionists under any circumstances.[52]

It seems, however, that the policy was not followed and that Clubs were formed consisting primarily of CCFers or union members. In September 1960, therefore, the CCF was forced to reiterate the OCNP's position. "It is recognized that in many cases the club is, in fact, organized by CCF members or by trade union members," stated the Executive, "but *the bulk of membership must come from other categories.*" The main opponent of this policy was Bill Sefton, chairperson of the Toronto and District Labour Council's PEC, who felt that New Party Clubs should not be restricted to non-CCF and non-union members since in many areas former CCFers who did not wish to rejoin the party, as well as union members facing constitutional barriers, preferred to form New Party Clubs. Although the CCF representatives on the OCNP relented on the first point, agreeing that it was acceptable for former CCF members to set up Clubs and constitute the majority therein, they would not soften their position on the issue of labour-dominated Clubs. They insisted that union members should not be permitted to form the majority within a Club, even where constitutional barriers existed or where the majority of union members refused to sign the SOS. OFL President David Archer sided with the CCF. To permit unionists in New Party Clubs, he argued, "would mean an opportunity for a lot of very unfavourable publicity," insofar as labour might be accused of trying to dominate the New Party by gaining double representation at the founding convention, through the Clubs as well as their own unions.[53]

In this controversy, Sefton's proposal was very democratic, insofar as it supported the establishment of Clubs by union members who were forbidden from engaging in political activity within their organizations.

The OCNP's approach, however, was purely pragmatic. Most CCF and OFL leaders felt that the *image* of the New Party as a new, broadly based party, in which no one group had the upper hand, would be undermined if the public felt that New Party Clubs were merely fronts for unionists seeking dual representation at the founding convention. This would raise the spectre of Big Labour, which could frighten potential New Party members from the liberal-minded category and also raise anxieties within the CCF. Therefore, to preserve the New Party image, the OCNP insisted that the majority of Club members not be unionists. Not until March 1961, when the OCNP discovered that the SOS campaign had made only slow progress in the craft unions and felt confident that the tripartite image was fairly secure, were unionists permitted to form labour-dominated Clubs outside their unions, and then only under certain conditions.[54] The OCNP had, nevertheless, sacrificed short-run participation of union members in the New Party movement to preserve an image which, it hoped, would attract the liberal-minded set and create a broadly based party in the long run.

Another example of the OCNP's pragmatic organizing approach to the New Party, particularly its overriding concern with image, was the evolution of the OCNP itself. Most of the New Party activities outlined thus far came under the general supervision of this committee. The idea of setting up what was, in effect, the provincial counterpart to the NCNP was first broached by Ken Bryden in the summer of 1959; and by late October, a joint committee was in place, consisting of seven members from each organization and possessing the power to make additions if desired. In general, the OCNP mandate was twofold: first, the organization was to symbolize the mutual cooperation and coming together of the three main sections, called for in the 1958 CCF/CLC resolutions, by inviting the liberal-minded to participate as equal partners on the Committee; and second, it was to be responsible for conducting a single, integrated campaign for the New Party in Ontario.

But once again, the CCF's single-minded concern for its organizational vitality prevailed and neither of the OCNP's idealistic objectives was achieved. Initially, the OCNP intended to make itself into a veritable tripartite committee, by inviting New Party Club representatives to participate. "The Provincial Committee is most anxious to involve people outside the two founding bodies in its work," Stewart wrote to the NCNP in February 1960, "and is now considering some specific additions." Moreover, the Committee would choose these additions from among the liberal-minded on the basis of their usefulness to the Committee's work, "rather than deciding on classifications and then seeking someone to fill them."[55] Consequently, Lyal Tait was invited to join the OCNP because many felt that the experience he had gained while trying to organize farmers would be valuable as a guide to the Committee's future activities in this area.

By the spring of 1960, however, it was clear that the OCNP had no intention of adding a large number of "useful" liberal-minded persons. Instead, it began selecting a token number of such representatives based on the prestige and image they would impart to the OCNP. In an invitation to Sam Bowman, the well-known farm leader, the OCNP stated that it had "decided to invite a few people who are not specifically associated with either the CCF or the labour movement to join the Committee, with the idea of getting different points of view, and, frankly, in some cases adding prestige. For the latter reason we are making it plain that new members will be announced to the press, so that anyone who would be embarrassed by having his participation known ... should be warned in advance."[56] The new approach was confirmed when the OCNP met in May 1960 to discuss "the type of Committee desirable – a large, impressive committee, or a small, working committee." It decided that "the two ideas might be combined, having the working part composed as it is now, of people already involved in the CCF or labour or both; and the impressive part composed of people of prestige whose main contribution would be their names on a letterhead."[57] OCNP members were therefore asked to inform the Committee's table officers – Lazarus, Stewart, and Weisbach – of any prestigious candidates who might be persuaded to join the Committee.

When the OCNP eventually realized it had strayed from its original objective, it decided to shorten its list of prominent individuals to be contacted. Nevertheless, the Committee remained very selective in its choice of new members. When in June 1960 the leader of the *ad hoc* New Party Club Co-ordinating Committee, Bev Robinson, requested representation for New Party Clubs, he was told that this was impossible. The OCNP, Peg Stewart informed him, "is a more or less arbitrarily appointed committee representing provincial organizations, but with power to add, as distinguished from liability to be added to." When Des Sparham encouraged the OCNP to accept the NPCC's request, Stewart replied that to do this would set a bad precedent, insofar as acceptance "reverses what we had in mind – which was to pluck off prestige people and add them as we wish."[58] As a result, by the end of the year only two persons from the so-called liberal-minded category sat on the OCNP.

In January 1961, the OCNP's federal counterpart, the NCNP, announced the addition of six liberal-minded persons to the Committee, thereby placing the liberal-minded on an equal footing with labour and CCF at the national level. The OCNP, however, continued to drag its feet. That same month it invited one other person, Dr David Summers, to join its ranks. Summers was chosen for his visibility and broad appeal as opposed to his qualifications *per se*. Not long after joining the Committee, however, Summers was complaining that the CCF and OFL representatives "have more rights and responsibilities granted to them" than the New Party Club representatives. Not until late July, the month of the national founding convention, were the liberal-minded finally given equal representation on the OCNP, and then only after Donald MacDonald "brought to the attention of the Committee the fact that the CCF and OFL are well represented ... but [that] the New Party Club persons are not." A subcommittee pursued the matter and five members were soon added, representing New Party Clubs, farmers, and ethnic groups. To attain maximum publicity on this occasion the OCNP issued a press release informing the public of its long overdue action.[59]

The Committee cited two reasons for its tardiness in appointing non-CCF, non-unionist members. First, it explained that "there are difficulties in having people elected [to the OCNP] from New Party groups because of the lack of organization and genuine representation" of these groups. In addition, the OCNP felt that liberal-minded persons "might be uncomfortable on the Committee as it is at present, as there is so much routine business." To some extent, these were legitimate reasons, although at the time they were given there were more than thirty-six recognized New Party Clubs across Ontario from which representatives could have been selected, including the NPCC. Moreover, far from feeling "uncomfortable" at the prospect, the liberal-minded individuals evinced a strong desire to play an equal and meaningful role in the New Party process. A more truthful reason lay in the OCNP's overriding concern with image, combined with the belief of many CCFers that the liberal-minded had not really paid their dues and were therefore not entitled to an equal role in building the New Party.[60]

The conduct of the OCNP betrayed the idealism of the New Party resolutions in one other way and, again, the CCF's overriding concern with its own basic organization played a key role. Contrary to its original objective and to the public image of a unified, cooperative effort by the OFL and CCF in building a new political instrument, the OCNP failed to create an integrated New Party organizing campaign in which both sides pooled resources and contributed equally to *all* areas of New Party organization, under the final authority of the OCNP. What developed, instead, were two separate, almost autonomous and often conflicting, campaigns. The OFL-PAC continued to organize primarily among unions, urging them to set up PACs and sign the SOS, while the CCF continued to pursue its strategy of focusing on its own organization first, and on strictly New Party organization second.

The success of the OFL's New Party campaign between 1958 and 1960 is difficult to evaluate, as the evidence tends to indicate both progress and stagnation. The PAC approached a number of labour councils and locals across southern Ontario and encouraged them to sign the SOS. In the twelve-month period following the introduction of the SOS program in November 1959, 260 locals, representing slightly less than half of all OFL union members, did just that. In addition, the OFL's annual conventions of 1959 and 1960 unanimously endorsed the continued cooperation of labour with the CCF and other liberal-minded persons in the establishment of a new party. In 1960, delegates also passed a resolution supporting the New Party Founding Fund (NPFF) drive to raise $250,000 from the unions for the New Party. Labour's interest in the New Party was further demonstrated by good attendance at New Party conferences and a high demand for New Party pamphlets published by the PAC in 1959.[61]

But the signs of stagnation were far more plentiful. Most former TLC unions, for example, were reluctant to sign the SOS. Although CCF and OFL leaders were convinced that the tide was turning in these unions, as constitutional barriers to political action were slowly removed, only two craft unions – the Ontario Council of Carpenters and local 46 of the Plumbers and Pipefitters Union – had publicly endorsed the New Party by August 1960. Another discouraging sign was the slow rise in the number of union members affiliating with the CCF in this period. After a 20-percent rise in affiliated members in 1958, as a result of the affiliation of one United Packinghouse local in Toronto, total membership declined steadily thereafter to a net gain of only 8 percent by the end of 1960.[62] This suggested that the labour movement's desire for direct political action (as opposed to simply political education) had not increased significantly, despite the extensive New Party conference program. In fact, the PAC concluded that the conferences were of limited value, because they did not teach workers how to go about actually organizing a political party. They "put a great deal of emphasis on the constitution and program of the new party," it told the OFL Executive in March 1959, "but very little on concrete problems that will face the new party just as they faced the 'old' one." It finished by warning that "we must not become so obsessed with the importance of statements of principles that we fail to appreciate the extreme importance of organization. We must avoid, to put it bluntly, the old pitfall of *political action by convention resolution.*"[63] Apart from this, the PAC found that because labour councils were either prohibited by their constitutions from taking political action or felt that potential members would be repelled by a union that was too involved in politics, "most of the [political] committees" established by labour councils were political *education* committees, not *action* committees; only sixty union locals had either by June 1960. Consequently, several delegates attending the OFL's 1959 and 1960 conventions criticized their colleagues for simply paying lip service to political action through a few pious resolutions "and letting it go at that."[64]

There were other signs of stagnation as well. In September 1960, Lazarus reported that a "vast amount of work" remained to be done among the unions, even among the steel locals that had been subjected to political education for many years. This was confirmed by the CCF *News*, which was critical of the poor quality of discussion concerning the New Party at the OFL's 1960 convention. "There is too much belabouring of the obvious," wrote the editor, "too much flag waving and sloganeering. More incisive questioning of the New Party's tentative program and constitutional makeup would be in order."[65] Further confirmation came from certain union staff representatives, who felt that the New Party idea was not catching on in labour circles. "I am seriously worried," Ames told Lazarus, "about the cynical attitude I have run into with some very fine politically conscious staff reps, who feel that we are going nowhere fast in this whole New Party development ... They do not feel that we are breaking any new ground and that the interest generally among our union membership in the New Party is very weak."[66]

Some union leaders blamed the problem on a lack of direction and financing from the top. In December 1958, Bill Sefton complained to the CLC's vice-president, Bill Dodge, that he and other staff representatives had received little information on the New Party and, as a result, did not know how to promote it. The Steelworkers' union also complained, saying that the OFL "has not been using enough of the PAC funds in regard to the new party program."[67] All of this seemed to indicate that although enthusiasm for the New Party remained strong at the highest levels of the labour movement, support for the New Party among the rank and file was growing much slower than expected. It also indicated that the PAC was restricting itself to organizing support for the New Party among its own constituents.

The CCF, too, concentrated on maintaining and expanding its own membership, at the expense of other components of the New Party movement. During the 1960 spring membership drive, party leaders emphasized how important it was that the CCF increase its membership and be well represented at the founding convention in 1961. They were secretly worried that if membership levels were not maintained the CCF could be swamped by labour at the convention. Thus the Executive expressed regret at the "recurring problem of ridings which wish to sign up New Party Club members rather than CCF-New Party members" and reiterated that "New Party Clubs should be an extension rather than a substitute for CCF activity."[68]

It is clear, therefore, that contrary to the OCNP objectives as well as the spirit of the New Party, the CCF and OFL carried out two separate New Party campaigns under the aegis of the OCNP. Even financially, labour and CCF activities were kept distinct, as PAC funds were channelled solely into trade union organizing. The almost total lack of cooperation drove one member of the CCF Provincial Council to express his deep disappointment with the Committee's progress and left him wondering when it would start to operate as a "real" committee. The OCNP did not even *meet* very regularly, according to Peg Stewart, "the day-to-day activities being carried on by Henry Weisbach ..., Morden Lazarus, ... and myself."[69]

In June 1960, ostensibly to remedy the OCNP's dual administration of New Party organizing, the CCF Executive presented the OCNP with a part-time organizer plan, whereby both the CCF and the OFL-PAC would be obliged to contribute organizers who would work for the New Party in *all* areas – unions, ridings, and Clubs – and who would come directly under the authority of the OCNP. In reality, the plan was a veiled attempt by the CCF to supplement its own organizing efforts, which to that point had been disappointing. The summer membership drive in 1959 resulted in "some increase" in total membership, according to the Organization Committee, but "the increase ... had probably not been as great as we had hoped." The spring membership drive the following year was also "considerably less successful than anticipated," and reports from party organizers revealed that prospects for the CCF in certain areas, especially northern Ontario, were very grim – a result, it was believed, of too few CCF organizers. Finally, almost 2,000 CCF memberships had been permitted to lapse in the first six months of 1960 alone. Overall, between July 1959 and July 1960, the party lost between 2,500 to 3,000 members – a good many to New Party Clubs, no doubt. The CCF hoped that the part-time organizer plan, therefore, would help restore CCF membership to its former level, or at least prevent further deterioration.[70]

Ironically, the plan only widened the division within the OCNP. Disagreements arose over who was to have final jurisdiction over the organizers and how the money provided by the OFL-PAC for the plan would be spent. Lazarus felt that the money should be used strictly for part-time organizers working within unions, under the authority of the OFL-PAC, and that full-time OCNP organizers, such as Ames, should assist labour councils in getting union locals to sign the SOS. In addition, part-time organizers "would help the local PAC committees to carry out an effective PAC program and tie the unions in with the [CCF] constituency organization." The CCF, of course, opposed Lazarus's proposal. It wanted the money to be used to hire a full-time New Party organizer or several part-timers to work primarily in New Party Clubs and CCF riding associations, under the OCNP's auspices. When Lazarus refused to grant the money for this purpose, the battle lines were drawn. Believing that Lazarus's plan would simply perpetuate the organizational division that had plagued the OCNP to that point, the CCF insisted that the OCNP "act as an integrated body in all respects, financial and organizational, rather than as two separate groups meeting together in a limited field." Stewart was especially adamant that the organizers be placed under the OCNP's authority and that they be "directed into CCF or New Party work according to the logical needs of the area concerned."[71] In a letter to Ames asking him not to participate in Lazarus's plan, she revealed the deepening division within the OCNP:

We had another session about the OCNP at the [CCF] Executive meeting on Tuesday. Marj Pinney has stated she will resign if we turn over our organizing staff to the OFL-PAC ... I must ask you to be very careful. This is not simply a matter of prestige. If you become involved in the part-time organizer plan under the OFL-PAC, it is a complete departure from the idea of your work as a CCF organizer ... It seems to me that the part-time organizer plan now being promoted by Morden [Lazarus] is definitely work primarily among unions ... I do not need to waste your time or mine in expressing how contrary this is to what the Ontario Committee expressed itself as having in mind.[72]

The letter also demonstrated how strongly the CCF felt about pursuing its primary goal of strengthening its own constituency associations. The CCF feared, with some justification, that any plan under the auspices of the PAC would entail organizational work exclusively within unions. Under the OCNP, however, organizers could be directed to work within riding associations and, if necessary, New Party Clubs. When Lazarus continued to reject the CCF's part-time organizer plan, which seems to have had the support of most OCNP members, the whole New Party development in Ontario neared the brink of collapse. "I know how eager you are to get ... rolling," Stewart told Ames, "but you're going to find yourself right in the middle of the embattled forces if the CCF gets mad enough – as it is fixing to do – to tell its organizers to have nothing whatever to do with PAC work – that would mean this part-time organizer scheme, schools, and all the rest ... We may eventually move towards a meeting between the CCF executive and the OFL executive in an effort to keep the Ontario Committee from blowing up."[73] A compromise was finally reached in September 1960. The part-time organizers (nine in all) would work primarily in the riding associations and New Party Clubs, under the OCNP's authority, but part of their duties would include pushing the SOS in unions.

Nevertheless, the basic organizational division in the OCNP continued. The PAC continued to divorce itself from all non-union activity, making sure that most of the OCNP's part-time organizers worked in the unions – organizing New Party conferences, getting locals to sign the SOS, raising money, and urging labour council PACs to support the New Party. It appears that only one of the part-time organizers performed duties relating to constituency associations and New Party Clubs. In January 1961, the CCF Provincial Council calmly observed that "the work of these organizers has been mainly in the trade union field, and will probably continue to be so." Some CCFers, however, were not pleased. Referring to Lazarus, Ames informed the CCF Provincial Office that "it would appear ... he is going to keep the unnecessary separation of PAC and New Party until July 31st, 1961 [date of New Party founding convention]. Our relationship has not improved ... and there seems to be nothing we can do about it." In an attempt to alter the situation, the OCNP's subcommittee on organization recommended that union staff members "who are specifically interested in New Party work" be asked to help set up New Party Clubs. But by this point it was too late: the part-time organizers' terms had elapsed and no renewals were made.[74]

The OCNP, therefore, failed to live up to its original goals. When it was first established, its members hoped to create a broadly based and unified central committee, through which the resources of the OFL, CCF, and liberal-minded would be shared and applied equally to all three sections of the movement. By the time of the founding convention, it reasoned, all three sections of the movement would be sufficiently developed to enable them to come together as equal partners in the New Party. What occurred, instead, was a race between the PAC and CCF to strengthen their respective organizations before the time came to join hands under one roof. The competition came close to destroying the OCNP and the whole New Party project in Ontario, as both sides tried to divert the OCNP's resources for their own purposes. The main casualties in this organizational competition, however, were the liberal-minded. The PAC's focus on unions and the CCF's concentration on constituency associations left little time or personnel for New Party Club work. The OCNP chose, instead, to cultivate the *perception* that a broadly based "new" party was being built by the selective inclusion in the process of a few high-profile token individuals from the liberal-minded arena, and by the adoption of several essentially undemocratic policies, such as the restrictions on unionists and former CCFers in New Party Clubs.

One final illustration of the OCNP's pragmatic approach to the New Party and its selective inclusion of the liberal-minded was its policy on local "co-ordinating committees." In December 1960, the OCNP supplied constituency associations with a *Guide to the Establishment of New Party Co-ordinating Committees*, in which ridings were encouraged to establish committees with representatives from labour, the CCF, and the liberal-minded arena, along the same lines as the OCNP. But the policy of encouraging broad participation was tempered by the stipulation that "ridings which have strong and efficient CCF organizations should concentrate on keeping them as they are, enlarging membership in the CCF, and moving into the New Party as of right. *The co-ordinating committees are not necessary in these ridings.*"[75] In other words, strong CCF associations were discouraged from setting up co-ordinating committees. Although this policy seems curious, it actually flowed logically from the OCNP's strategy of promoting either New Party Clubs or CCF riding associations depending on local circumstances. In fact, the OCNP could adopt no other policy, given its strategy of ignoring New Party Club organizing in areas where the CCF was well established. Any attempt to set up a tripartite coordinating committee in such areas would have been nearly impossible; and to set up a bipartite committee, containing only unionists and CCFers, would have exposed the party's pragmatic strategy of selective New Party organizing, thereby belying the New Party's broadly based image. The OCNP was not prepared to do either. In fact, the OCNP was so emphatic that only tripartite committees be established that it often refused to recognize those that were not. Instead, only in multiple constituency areas, such as Toronto, Hamilton, London, and Oshawa, where all three sections of the New Party movement were highly developed, did the OCNP recommend the establishment of coordinating committees. This advanced the desired image of the New Party, while at the same time allowing the CCF to maintain its organizational strength in key areas. Except in multiconstituency areas, therefore, constituencies were deprived of that trinity of sections so loudly heralded by the CCF and OFL from day one.[76]

This shrewd policy was put to good use even before it became official OCNP policy. On 31 October 1960, in the Peterborough federal by-election, a thirty-one-year-old high-school teacher named Walter Pitman ran under the New Party banner and scored a stunning upset victory over his Conservative and Liberal opponents, becoming the first New Party representative in the House of Commons. The "Peterborough

Miracle," as it was dubbed, attracted some very favourable publicity and created a surge of interest in the New Party that would express itself in an explosion of New Party Clubs in 1961. It also led to predictions that the New Party could easily become the next Official Opposition or even form the government of Canada. "The election of Mr. Walter Pitman," declared Montreal's *Le Devoir*, "is by far the most important event in terms of its long-range consequences"; it added, "The reversal of a Conservative majority of 11,000 in a riding that is traditionally Tory and the decline of the Liberals in the same constituency has given Mr. Diefenbaker and Mr. Lester Pearson something to think about." In fact, when the 13,887 votes polled by Pitman were combined with those received by the New Party candidate who ran a strong third in the Niagara Falls by-election that same day, the New Party had polled more votes than the combined totals of each of the two other parties.[77]

One of the key reasons for the New Party's success in Peterborough was the perception of the New Party as a vibrant, broadly based movement, a perception that the New Party planners did much to foster, and worked hard to preserve, after the victory. Preparations for the Peterborough campaign began in June 1960 when Donald MacDonald visited the riding and persuaded Pitman to offer himself for nomination as the New Party candidate. Though MacDonald harboured no illusions about the party's chances of winning the seat, he felt it would be useful to set up a New Party Co-ordinating Committee consisting of the CCF, labour, and liberal-minded. But MacDonald was motivated by something other than the desire to establish a truly representative Committee on which all three groups would participate equally. Instead, he believed such a Committee would help the New Party's image. "I've been wondering about the possibility of a New Party Club being used as the framework to bring together a selected group of newcomers," he told Peg Stewart, "so that they could be given formal representation on the overall committee, and in the process, ... could be reduced in influence and numbers in the bigger group."[78] The liberal-minded, in other words, would have only token representation on the Committee, but would give the New Party the desired image of being broadly based. The Peterborough campaign was therefore yet another example of the OCNP's strategy of excluding the liberal-minded from the New Party development, except where it served to fill in organizational gaps or uphold a certain image.

The Pitman victory also marked the end of the first phase of the New Party movement in Ontario, for by the end of 1960 much of the groundwork for the party had been laid. Regional conferences in the winter of 1958–59 had stimulated a high degree of discussion among labour leaders, as had the PAC's SOS campaign at the local level. Efforts had also been made to mobilize farmer support, but in both cases, results were not as good as expected. Local unions, perhaps lacking sufficient information on the New Party, continued to pay only lip service to political action, while most farmers, despite their increasing militancy, continued to harbour suspicions toward CCFers and unionists. On the other hand, support among the urban liberal-minded sector grew fairly quickly. The introduction of the New Party Club program gave middle-class professionals the opportunity to participate in the movement, resulting in the rapid emergence, often spontaneously and haphazardly, of numerous Clubs in cities across the province – a phenomenon that New Party promoters were neither able, nor willing to control.

But behind the facade of the CCF, labour, and liberal-minded working together as equals to build a new political party was the reality of a tightly controlled and sometimes acrimonious process, dominated by CCF and PAC leaders determined to strengthen their respective organizations in time for the founding conventions and, in the CCF's case, willing to integrate the liberal-minded only insofar as was necessary to supplement party organization and sustain the image of a broadly based, "new" party. The OCNP's policies regarding New Party Clubs and co-ordinating committees, as well as the conflict between the PAC and CCF over part-time organizers, are ample testimony to this pragmatic organizing strategy. As the New Party movement entered its final phase, all eyes turned to the founding conventions.

8 Consolidating the Grand Illusion

As the New Party entered the final stage of its development, the attention of Ontario CCF and OFL leaders turned toward the founding conventions in 1961, slated for the national party in late July and for Ontario in early October. With this new focus came what seemed to be a dramatic change in organizing strategy. Unlike the first phase, during which the OCNP focused almost all its resources on union and constituency organization, the final phase found the OCNP making an official commitment to devote as much time to the liberal-minded as it had to the other two players in the New Party movement; the need to ensure that the so-called broadly based character of the New Party was a salient feature of the founding conventions required such a commitment. But in the end, old habits died hard, for despite a remarkable surge in liberal-minded interest in the New Party in 1961, the CCF and OFL paid little attention to New Party Clubs and continued to worry primarily about their own constituents. To achieve at least the necessary semblance of broad, tripartite support at the highly publicized founding convention, therefore, the OCNP reversed its policy on New Party Clubs in unions, kept the liberal-minded segregated from riding associations until well after October, granted farmers an undeservedly high profile at the convention, and, in general, did whatever was necessary to present the proper image at the convention itself. In short, the pragmatic organization strategy of the first phase persisted, and the founding of the Ontario NDP became a triumph of image over reality.

In March 1961, the OCNP's subcommittee on organization formulated new plans for New Party organizing. These specified that the short-term objectives leading up to the founding conventions were to have strong representation at the conventions from constituency associations, labour unions, and New Party Clubs – to "assure the continuance in strength of the CCF"; and "to try to get at least one delegate ... from every riding, however weak." The goal, in short, was to secure strong representation from all three sections and from all regions of the province, while making sure that CCF's organization did not suffer. This necessarily required a more equal distribution of the OCNP's resources than during the first phase, when the OCNP had given priority to riding associations and labour unions. The OCNP, Peg Stewart informed the Metropolitain Toronto committee for the New Party (MTCNP), "is definitely moving into the field of general organization." Up to the end of May, its organizers would help prepare unions and riding associations for the founding conventions; thereafter, they were to assist New Party Clubs.[1]

In trade union circles, meanwhile, the OFL-PAC continued to concentrate primarily on the SOS and on raising money for the New Party Founding Fund, with modest results. Although union contributions to the fund increased rapidly after March, especially from Ontario, the bulk of the contributions came from unions that had traditionally supported the CCF – the Steelworkers, Packinghouse Workers, and Automobile Workers. Results from the SOS drive were also deceiving. From October 1960 to August 1961, the number of locals that had signed the SOS increased from 260 to 370, although the total number of union members involved still only represented approximately half of the Federation's membership. As well, union affiliations to the CCF continued to fall, by almost 2,000 members in 1960 alone. Organizational efforts among unionized workers were further circumscribed by the termination, in June, of the OCNP's part-time organizer scheme, which the PAC later described as "reasonably successful."[2]

Greater strides were made in CCF organization. In April and May, the OCNP conducted a vigourous New Party "founding member" drive to increase CCF membership and therefore send a large CCF contingent to the founding convention. Prospective members were told that membership in the CCF would revert automatically to New Party membership once the New Party officially came into being. According to the Organization Committee, the results of the drive were satisfactory, as over 1,000 founding members were signed up. "One of the most encouraging signs," remarked chairperson Marj Pinney, "was the number of new members we picked up."[3]

The most noticeable increase in support for the New Party, however, occurred in the New Party Club section of the movement. It will be recalled that the growth of Clubs in Ontario in 1959–60 was impressive, but somewhat chaotic, largely because of the low priority they were accorded by the OCNP. Despite this, the number of Clubs continued to grow and by 1961 were proliferating at an unmanageable rate, as voters became increasingly dissatisfied with the federal Conservatives and increasingly anxious about rising unemployment. In February, 49 Clubs were officially recognized in Ontario, but by September the total had grown to 155 – a 300 percent increase in eight months, much of it in northern and southwestern Ontario, especially Toronto. The only area of major growth in eastern Ontario was in Cornwall, where practically overnight the largest New Party Club in the country, with close to 350 members, was established.[4]

But the rapid growth in New Party Clubs created problems. The growth was so sudden and unexpected that the NCNP was unable, first of all, to handle all the work involved in processing the many applications for recognition and requests for literature that flooded Sparham's office from OCNP organizers, Club presidents, and individuals eager to start their own Clubs. To cope with the deluge, in February the NCNP turned over all administrative responsibility for the Clubs in Ontario to the OCNP. But the time lag involved in the transfer of responsibility, combined with the continued growth in New Party Clubs and the ongoing shortage of Club organizers, only added to the backlog of applications and requests for information. This, in turn, hampered the growth of New Party Clubs. Under the OCNP's supervision, but with little or no assistance from OCNP organizers, the Clubs continued to proliferate. By September, 1961, there were approximately 6,000 New Party Club members in the province, a remarkable figure considering that the CCF's membership at the time was not much larger than this and that most of the growth was spontaneous. Moreover, this figure did not include the many Clubs of which the OCNP was not even aware – Clubs that had sprung up overnight but not bothered to seek official recognition. Had the OCNP actively promoted the Club section and been prepared to deal with the sudden rise in interest among the liberal-minded, it is safe to say that the latter would have outnumbered CCFers in the New Party movement.[5]

The rapid growth of Clubs also made it difficult for the NCNP and OCNP to prevent the influx of undesirable left-wing elements into the New Party. Stewart informed Sparham in June that "we are experiencing a sustained, energetic, and organized campaign to admit to the New Party through New Party Clubs (particularly Youth groups) and trade unions the highly undesirable Trotskyists and Communists.

These people have advertised that they are going to have good representation at the [founding] convention and it is obvious that they are not fooling."[6] Past experience had, of course, made the Ontario CCF alert to the tactics of such undesirables, and the OCNP was equally determined to prevent any association whatsoever in the public mind between the New Party and the Communists. In the first few months of phase one, therefore, Sparham's office informed the OCNP of the Clubs and individuals to which the NCNP had recently extended recognition, so that "undesirables" could be detected. But this arrangement soon proved unsatisfactory, particularly as Sparham did not always keep the OCNP up to date on new Clubs and members. Stewart, the OCNP's secretary, subsequently insisted that all correspondence respecting New Party Clubs be channelled through the OCNP *before* Sparham's office extended recognition and sent Club information. By June 1960, she was vetting lists of prospective Clubs and members to identify known Communists or members of other political parties. In fact, fear of infiltration was one reason for the Ontario CCF's lukewarm reception of the New Party Club concept when it was introduced in late 1959. It was also one of the main reasons for the NCNP's decision to give the OCNP complete adminstration over the Clubs in early 1961: the OCNP insisted that in order to block infiltration it required more authority to scrutinize applications for recognition.[7] The tighter reign acquired by the OCNP over the development of New Party Clubs in phase two of the movement, therefore, reduced (but did not eliminate) the growing threat of infiltration that coincided with the rapid growth of the Clubs.

Despite these minor irritations, the swift and largely spontaneous growth of liberal-minded support for the New Party helped the party to achieve the somewhat contradictory goals outlined in its "new" organizational strategy: substantial representation from all three sections of the movement at the founding conventions; and the maintenance of CCF strength. Despite its decision in March 1961 to concentrate equally on all three sections of the New Party movement, the OCNP still had only a limited number of organizers at its disposal and seemed reluctant to assign them to New Party Club organizing. The ongoing chaos in the Club section and the fact that OCNP organizers were assigned to Club organizing in June – but only after they had completed their work in unions and riding associations – attested to the OCNP's priorities. In other words, New Party leaders were unwilling to completely abandon the original strategy of promoting the CCF first, and New Party Clubs second, particularly in areas with strong CCF riding associations. In January, Donald MacDonald told a farmer in Janetville, Ontario, who wished to organize New Party

Clubs, that such Clubs should not be too numerous since they were drawing regular party members away from the once-sizeable riding association. "While it is inevitable that some CCF members will become involved in New Party Clubs and, therefore, let their CCF membership drop," he said, "we must not permit this possibility to become too widespread. Otherwise, the CCF will reach the Founding Convention with much less influence than the Ontario section is entitled to ... In the past 18 months our membership across the province has dropped from approximately 10,000 to 7,500 ... We must build New Party Clubs, but we must not let the CCF waste away."[8] The OCNP was even more direct. In August it sent a memorandum to all riding associations, coordinating committees, and New Party Clubs in which it encouraged the subscription of as many CCF members as possible, to ensure a strong organizational base for the New Party. Only where the limits of CCF organization had been reached did the OCNP sanction the establishment of New Party Clubs. Therefore, despite the OCNP's need to secure significant representation of the liberal-minded at the founding conventions – which it knew was necessary to sustain the New Party image – the organization of New Party Clubs continued to take a back seat to CCF and union organization.[9]

Again, what allowed the New Party architects to resolve this apparent organizational dilemma – that of trying to secure broad representation at the founding conventions without channelling resources into organizing the liberal-minded – was the rapid and largely spontaneous growth of the Club movement in 1961. With a minimum of commitment and effort, the OCNP would eventually mobilize this last-minute surge in liberal-minded support for the New Party and guarantee that a fairly large delegation of Club representatives was sent to the founding conventions. But the OCNP, who could not foresee these developments in early 1961 and feared that the liberal-minded group would be well outnumbered at the conventions, therefore decided to do whatever was necessary to create at least the *impression*, at the conventions, that the New Party was an equal partnership of all three sections.

The first sign of the OCNP's determination to sustain the proper image right through to the founding conventions was its unofficial acceptance of New Party Clubs in unions. This sensitive issue was revived in March 1961 when the OFL-PAC recommended to the OCNP Executive that union members whose organizations were barred from taking political action be allowed to form New Party Clubs within the unions themselves; they could then participate in the New Party development and obtain representation at the founding conventions. The Executive – Weisbach, Lazarus, and Stewart – concurred with the suggestion and presented it to the full Committee for approval. The OCNP, after recognizing that such Clubs had unavoidably emerged, reiterated its traditional policy that "the organization of New Party Clubs within unions is not desirable," and that "union members can join New Party Clubs, preferably along with other people." Nevertheless, the OCNP's tacit acceptance of *existing* Clubs within unions indicates that while it still disapproved, it was willing to turn a blind eye to the matter, the implication being that no action would be taken should other such Clubs appear.[10]

The OCNP was initially opposed to union-based Clubs, or to Clubs outside unions in which union or CCF members constituted a majority, because such developments could have led, in the first instance, to accusations of labour domination, and, in the second, to accusations that the New Party was the CCF in new garb. This would have damaged the New Party's new, broadly based image. But as the founding conventions approached, the OCNP obviously felt that the need to portray the right image at the upcoming founding conventions (by securing a large contingent of New Party Club delegates, no matter their composition) outweighed any possible damage to that image which could result from revelations that Clubs were being formed in unions or by CCFers exclusively. With the impressive growth of New Party Clubs in 1961, moreover, the OCNP was almost certainly less worried that the New Party would be accused of labour domination. Consequently, it tacitly accepted the fact that a large number of New Party Clubs, primarily in northern Ontario, had been formed within unions or were comprised almost entirely of union members.[11]

That the portrayal of a broadly based image at the founding conventions was a leading consideration among New Party planners by 1961 was further demonstrated by the way in which the liberal-minded were themselves presented at the conventions. The day before the national convention, for example, the NCNP established a National Council of New Party Clubs from among the fifty New Party Club delegates. The Council was given the same status as the CCF's National Council and the CLC's National Executive Council, insofar as all of its members were granted delegate status – or in this case, since members were already delegates, the Council was entitled to approximately twenty-five *extra* delegates. The purpose of the Council, essentially, was to increase the visibility and representation of the New Party Club section. As Sparham noted, "This National Council ... has mainly symbolic significance. Its life will be at an end after the Founding Convention." Moreover, because the allotment of twenty-five extra delegates to the New Party Club section through the last-minute creation of the Council was not justified by an actual increase in New Party Club members across Canada, the liberal-minded were deliberately overrepresented at the national founding convention. This aberration from normal democratic procedure was allowed so as to illustrate, publicly, that the third section of the New Party was on an equal footing with the CCF and CLC. A similar New Party Club Council was established in Ontario in August, again for its symbolic value, and was entitled to the same number of delegates as the Provincial Council and the OFL Executive Council. Unlike the National Club Council, however, members were chosen specifically by New Party Clubs, in addition to regular delegates, and not from among existing Club delegates to the convention.[12]

Nevertheless, the OCNP was just as determined as its national counterpart to ensure the appearance of a strong liberal-minded representation at the founding convention. In April and May, it passed motions stating that all New Party Clubs in Ontario recognized before 16 July 1961 would still be recognized as distinct Clubs *after* the national convention; thus they could obtain separate representation at the provincial convention. Moreover, new Clubs could still be formed from 7 August to September 1961, in order to gain representation, on condition that members be full NDP members. The OCNP also recommended that a resolution be submitted to the founding convention "authorizing existing New Party Clubs to [remain distinct and] participate in the setting up of constituency organization[s]," up to 31 January 1962, at which time all Clubs would dissolve. In short, although the Clubs would be integrated into the New Party sooner or later, since Club members would be full members of the NDP, the OCNP would allow Club members to remain distinct from the other two participating sections up to, and including, the period immediately following the provincial founding convention. The OCNP explained that this policy of segregation was adopted to protect the liberal-minded sector from being swamped by CCFers and unionists in the new NDP riding associations when the time came to elect delegates to the convention. Of course, it was equally concerned with maintaining the image of the New Party as a coalition of all three sections, by ensuring that the liberal-minded were well represented, as a distinct delegation, at the convention.[13]

The OCNP's desire that the liberal-minded segment appear to be well-represented at the founding of the New Party also shaped its approach to farmers in 1961. Lyal Tait, who remained the main organizer in rural areas, was still having problems organizing groups of farmers into New Party Clubs, "though as individuals," he told the

OCNP in January, "they are very interested." Donald MacDonald, who toured the province during the winter and spring and who largely assumed Tait's role as rural organizer in the summer, discovered essentially the same thing; he, however, was confident that farmers could be persuaded to play a prominent role in the New Party project. In particular, he was determined that the rural sector should be well represented at the founding convention. MacDonald spent six weeks during the summer touring the back concessions of eastern Ontario – a distance of 2,600 miles – and, like Tait, found a number of individual farmers receptive to the New Party. He told local party organizers to place special "emphasis on the particular value of any New Party Club or organization sending a farmer if available, no matter how rank-and-file a type he may be." Even though the potential support among farmers for the New Party was low, MacDonald wished to find as many farm delegates as possible for the founding convention, for he "was persuaded that the public image would be important."[14]

In addition to securing farmer representation at the founding convention, MacDonald worked indefatigably to establish a "Farm Committee" from among the forty or fifty most prominent farmer delegates, whom the OCNP had agreed to accredit as delegates in the same way that the NCNP had given additional representation to liberal-minded individuals through the New Party Club Council. But like the Club Council, the Farm Committee was intended primarily as a show-piece for public consumption, and a deceptive one at that, for although the members of the Committee were *accredited* delegates, they were not *veritable* delegates. As MacDonald explained to the Ontario Committee for the New Democratic Party (OCNDP, formerly the OCNP), the Farm Committee had no organizational backing, since no farm organizations had officially endorsed the New Party.[15] In other words, the Committee members joined strictly as individuals, and despite their elevated status within their own organizations, did not speak for a larger constituency. Although it would appear, therefore, that the farm sector was well represented at the convention, this, too, was largely illusory. In short, the OCNP's pragmatic strategy of placing CCF and union organization ahead of New Party Club organization, while at the same time manufacturing the perception that the New Party was broadly based, continued into the final phase of the New Party development.

In addition to the arduous task of designing and implementing such a complex strategy, OFL and CCF leaders had to contend with a leading threat to that strategy: attacks on the New Party, or particular aspects of it, from the media and from within the CCF. A hostile press was, of course, nothing new to the CCF. The party had been subject to bouts of anti-socialist propaganda throughout much of its history and was accustomed to being on the defensive. In fact, the dramatic changes initiated by the national CCF in its program and structure after 1955 were largely a grandiose attempt to shed the unfavourable image created, to a large extent, by that propaganda. Nevertheless, the press were about as receptive to the New Party as they had been to the CCF, and as the founding date approached, so did the tendency of columnists and editors to criticize the New Party or present it in a negative light. A good deal of publicity, for example, was given to the division between the party's left and right wings during the race for the leadership of the proposed New Party between Hazen Argue, CCF national leader, and Tommy Douglas, the popular CCF premier from Saskatchewan. Argue was depicted as the spokesperson for the party's doctrinaire-socialist wing, while Douglas was portrayed as the machine-backed, moderate reformer. The unusually widespread and prominent coverage of the split gave the impression that the New Party was badly divided. In some cases, it also left the impression that labour would dominate the New Party. Accusing the CLC of giving unfair advantage to Douglas in his leadership bid, for example, the *Toronto Telegram* concluded that "the New Party will be a merger of the CCF and the labour movement, with the Canadian Labour Congress expected to play the dominant role." In fact, the press almost always referred to the New Party as a wedding between the CCF and labour, with the latter "pulling the main strings"; it usually asserted that because labour would be financing the New Party quite heavily, it would also be calling the shots. Such talk, of course, worried CCF leaders at all levels, because of the traditional antipathy toward labour in some quarters of the party and the fear of Big Labour generally.[16]

Another frequent media criticism concerned the way in which the New Party planned to collect membership dues from affiliated members. The method proposed was one whereby those union members whose organizations affiliated themselves with the New Party but who themselves did not wish to contribute to the party could, upon request, opt out of paying affiliation dues (i.e., "contract out"). Many newspapers, however, charged that this was a violation of the unionist's right to a secret ballot, and one that exploited workers too apathetic or intimidated to opt out. Even the province's attorney-general criticized the "contracting out" scheme, saying it involved an element of "extortion." Moreover, several commentators insisted that such "undemocratic" methods would alienate rank-and-file labour support for the New Party and eagerly pointed to the refusal of many craft unions to endorse the New Party as proof. To further discourage labour support, some journalists argued that political action would significantly reduce the labour movement's political influence, and that the New Party's proposed program was vague, unrealistic, authoritarian, and anachronistic; they often accused the New Party of being the CCF in "disguise."[17]

Without evaluating the accuracy of the media's observations, it is clear that the tone of many of their statements suggested a great deal of "whistling in the dark." In some cases, there was even unconcealed fear that, with the financial backing of the labour movement, the New Party might displace the old line parties, as well as the vested interests they favoured. Whatever their motivation, and despite the New Party's efforts to turn back the various charges levelled against it, one can safely say that the large amount of adverse publicity hurt the image that the CCF and OFL had worked so hard to create. Probably, too, it meant less support for the New Party than might otherwise have been the case.

The New Party was plagued, too, by some rather imprudent criticism from within its own ranks, criticism that the media were only too eager to publicize. The most vociferous critic was Douglas Fisher, CCF M.P. from Port Arthur, who along with several other CCF members from northern Ontario, including the president of the Temiskaming CCF, Arnold Peters, first expressed his reservations publicly in October 1959 at the Ontario CCF's annual convention. Quite simply, Fisher opposed the closer cooperation with the trade union movement that the New Party project entailed. He argued that because labour had always been politically apathetic, except at election time, it would not contribute much to the New Party on a day-to-day basis, and that a closer association with unions would only give the New Party a bad image;[18] he also accused the labour movement of having few intellectuals or capable leaders in its ranks. In short, Fisher predicted that the New Party would fail.[19]

Apart from his antipathy toward unions, Fisher expressed a strong dislike of the "party brass," and in particular, David Lewis. He argued that Lewis, along with "his henchman, Stanley Knowles," had masterminded the entire New Party scheme from its inception and had succeeded in brainwashing the CCF rank and file into supporting it.[20] By September 1960, in one of his last public attacks on the New Party, Fisher revelled in what he considered to be the fulfillment of his earlier prediction. In a *Canadian Forum* article entitled "The Last CCF Roundup," he remarked: "After 28 months of effort and agitation, the only solid gain for the New Party has been the CCF. Farm organizations have openly rejected the cause. Those amorphous characters, the liberally-minded, may be ready to go but not a single prominent Canadian who might fit such a category has declared himself. The reaction of organized labour has ranged from enthusiasm to hostility."[21] These pessimistic statements, coming as they did from an insider, probably did little to inspire the uncommitted citizen to jump on the New Party bandwagon; as a result, CCF leaders were frequently forced to respond to Fisher's criticisms in order to counter the widespread publicity he received.

While Fisher's criticisms of the New Party were inspired by his sincere reservations concerning the project, it should be noted that his opposition was related to other factors as well. First, Fisher was a member of the small CCF federal caucus, led by Hazen Argue, that had survived the Conservative landslide of March 1958. Because many in this ensemble were newcomers to Parliament, bereft of the guidance of experienced CCF parliamentarians, they lacked the discipline and intellectual rigour of earlier caucuses. This, in turn, made them obstreperous and troublesome and, therefore, more inclined to openly criticize initiatives emanating from party headquarters. Furthermore, they felt neglected by the party hierarchy, who were concentrating more on the New Party in this period. So bitter were they about this perceived neglect that they almost refused to let Walter Pitman, the first (and last) New Party M.P. elected, sit with the CCF caucus. Relations between the caucus and the CCF Executive, Pitman recalls, were "very strained. ... [The caucus] wanted to remain CCF. They had no interest in this new party at all. They weren't in the least anxious to see all this new crowd [i.e. the liberal-minded] sort of clamouring around, all the amateurs getting into the game."[22] Although Pitman eventually helped smooth relations between the two sides, the hard feelings remained and contributed to Hazen Argue's damaging defection to the Liberals in 1962. To some extent, therefore, Fisher's attacks on the New Party were a product of his experience in Parliament.

Second, Fisher was in many ways simply the spokesperson for the initial opposition of many northern CCFers toward the New Party. This opposition was based on a deep-rooted resentment of organized labour in that region, as well as the traditional suspicion of northerners, fed by the geographic isolation of the region, that the party was controlled by southern Ontario, particularly Toronto. In Peters' riding of Temiskaming, a CCF stronghold, the feeling against the New Party was so strong that the constituency association threatened to run an independent CCF candidate in the 1959 provincial election if the New Party project went ahead. Indeed, during the September 1960 provincial by-elections, its candidate deliberately ran under the CCF banner instead of the New Party label so as "to underplay the closer association with the trade union movement which the New Party represents," according to the Provincial Office. In Fisher's riding of Port Arthur, the local CCF voted in December 1959 not to support the New Party until the rank and file had an opportunity to vote on the whole issue at the next national CCF convention (the provincial CCF convention had already endorsed the New Party movement). According to Donald MacDonald, who attended the meeting, this attitude was based on a "pretty deep-seated distrust of unions" among the predominantly middle-class members in the riding and on their resentment of labour's sporadic support for political action in the past. CCF resentment against organized labour and the whole New Party idea was equally strong in the Timmins CCF. In addition, according to the CCF M.P. for the riding, Murdo Martin, CCFers were "lukewarm to the new party idea" because they had elected M.P.s and M.P.P.s for many years as a result of their persistent organizing efforts and felt that hard work, and nothing else, was the answer to the party's problems. After all, they argued, the north had elected the CCF's only Ontario M.P.s. The need for a new party was therefore not as apparent in Timmins and in other regions of northern Ontario, where the party had traditionally done well, as it was elsewhere.[23]

But the main reason for the opposition of some key northern leaders and their supporters seems to have been their ignorance of the OCNP's pragmatic organizing strategy. That strategy, which put a premium on CCF constituency organization and called for New Party Clubs *only* where the CCF had little chance of gaining a foothold, was founded on the assumption that the CCF must not only be well represented at the founding convention but also hold a commanding position within the New Party. Thus, New Party planners were as wary of New Party Clubs and the spectre of union domination as were the dissidents. Had Fisher and his peers been better informed about the CCF's plan and general mode of thinking *vis-à-vis* the New Party, they would have known this. Unfortunately, there was a serious lack of communication between members of the Provincial Office in Toronto and CCF leaders from northern Ontario. According to Ken Bryden, who twenty-five years later still fumes at the mention of Fisher's name, Fisher rarely attended annual conventions or NCNP meetings: "I remember at our [1959] convention that Doug Fisher comes out of a clear blue sky with a great statement against the whole [New Party idea] ... He had been on the NCNP and hadn't attended one meeting. He just appears at this convention, the only time he'd ever been at one, [and] of course got headlines all over the country for it."[24] Moreover, the CCF was well aware that lack of communication was the main problem. Peg Stewart noted that the misunderstanding and friction between northern M.P.s and the top leadership could not be resolved because the former did not attend National Council meetings on a regular basis. "If they all attended regularly," she said, "we would not get into the kind of mess we did over the New Party – nor about other things which go on, and the Caucus seems unaware of."[25] The poor communication with respect to the OCNP's organizational strategy is perfectly illustrated in a letter from Ames to Stewart following a meeting of the Temiskaming CCF Executive in March 1960. "The meeting went well until I gave my report," wrote Ames, "and then Arnold [Peters] teed off on the idea of a CCF organizer going around organizing New Party Clubs. He felt that it was a plot of the Ontario Executive until I finally got through to him that you and the executive were as worried about [setting up New Party Clubs] as he was. What did he suggest we do in the areas where we had a political vacuum? He did not have an answer, as one would expect."[26] To improve relations with this troublesome group, the OCNP eventually invited Fisher to become a member of the Committee – an invitation he declined. Nevertheless, the OCNP was able to "communicate" with Fisher and the Port Arthur CCF at some point along the way, for by March 1961 Fisher was helping to set up New Party Clubs in his riding and by July his association had established a tripartite co-ordinating committee.[27]

Much of the credit for the new attitude in northern Ontario toward the New Party belongs to the CCF/OCNP's hard-working northern organizer, Doc Ames, who did a fine job assuring anxious CCFers that they were free to establish either CCF clubs or New Party Clubs, depending on what appealed to the people of the riding. This "satisfie[d] them that we [were] not attempting to destroy the CCF," Ames informed the Provincial Office, but that the OCNP was simply trying to extend the party's organization any way it could.[28] Another reason for the turn around in northern Ontario may have been the disappointing defeat of the Temiskaming CCF, under the CCF label, in a September 1960 by-election. The Provincial Office later called the decision to reject the New Party label "a mistake" because it "ruled out ... any effort to exploit the greater potential support among disillusioned Old Party supporters."[29] In general, therefore, the internal dissent over the New Party in Ontario more or less disappeared as the dissenters became aware of the pragmatic approach of the Provincial Office to the New Party.

In view of the OCNP's efforts to bring Fisher and the other northern dissidents on side, it is ironic that, in the final analysis, members of both sides shared many of the same concerns. The OCNP was undoubtedly sympathetic, for example, to the dissidents' concern that labour would not be willing to play an active role in the New Party. After all, the OCNP almost disintegrated over this very issue. At the time of the part-time organizer crisis, when the PAC refused to finance or provide organizers to work strictly on political organizing, Ames remarked that "Morden [Lazarus] may not know it but he is playing right into the hands of fellows like Peters and Fisher who have maintained all along that this situation would arise."[30] The OCNP was equally aware of the negative effect that closer relations with labour could have on the broadly based image of the New Party, as seen in the Committee's policy on New Party Clubs in unions and its numerous pronouncements that the New Party would not be dominated by any one group.

Where the OCNP and the dissidents parted company was over the dangerous tendency of the latter to voice these reservations in public, where the media were quick to use it against the New Party movement. In a veiled appeal to all internal critics, the NCNP warned party members in May 1960 that "the Canadian press will be quick to play up the slightest criticisms [of the New Party], and a party, if it is to appeal to the electorate effectively, must be united. Our job must be to fight the Tories and Liberals, not ourselves. Devices or vehicles allowing for the full play of democracy *within the New Party* must be found, bearing in mind the need to present a solid front to the voters."[31] Past experience made CCF leaders keenly aware of the need to avoid airing dirty laundry in public, so as to leave the impression that the party was united and hence capable of governing. What was more, and this bore even more directly on the New Party's chances for success, the anti-labour remarks of Fisher and others fed existing fears among the general public that unions, controlled by American racketeers, would dominate the New Party. This, in turn, undermined the OCNP's efforts to create in the public's mind the image of a democratic, broadly based New Party.

The second major incident of dissent within the CCF took place shortly before the founding convention and it, too, focused on the relationship between labour and the New Party. It was also one of the most instructive examples of the CCF's pragmatic approach to the New Party development and the unflagging concern with basic organizational expansion that underlay that approach. The incident involved the question of affiliated members (i.e., unions) and the basis upon which they should be allowed, by the terms of the Ontario New Party's constitution, to participate in local nominating conventions of the New Party. To deal with this and other constitutional questions, OFL President David Archer was placed in the unenviable position of having to put together a preliminary draft of the constitution based on the suggestions submitted by constituency associations, New Party Clubs, and members of the OCNP; the draft would then be presented to the provincial founding convention for approval. His Constitutional

Sub-committee presented the first draft to the OCNP's table officers in June 1960 for their thoughts. The relevant clause read as follows: "Affiliated organizations shall participate in the activities of the constituency associations on the basis to be decided by the constituency association and the affiliated organizations." The decision, in short, would be left to the constituency association. But in July 1961, when the draft was presented to the full Committee, the OCNP decided that members of affiliated organizations should be given *full* voting rights at nominating conventions (on an equal basis with individual members) and instructed Archer to make the appropriate revisions. It was at this point that the CCF members of the OCNP, led by Donald Mac-Donald, began to voice their misgivings about the proposal and decided to submit their own proposal to Archer's subcommittee.[32] Speaking on behalf of the majority of the CCF Executive, MacDonald wrote to Archer suggesting the following amendments. It is worth citing portions of MacDonald's letter at length, for it is an excellent summary of the CCF's fundamental motives in the whole New Party project. MacDonald spoke of his misgivings:

At the OCNP meeting last Wednesday I had some misgivings regarding the proposal that members of an affiliated organization should be granted equal voting powers with full individual members of the party at constituency nominating conventions ... Only after the meeting was over, did I consider the matter fully, and discuss it with others ... and my misgivings grew the more I thought about it ...

My initial worry regarding the proposal ... stemmed from the fact that this is a reversal of what has generally been understood in the whole promotion of the New Party since [1959].

MacDonald argued that affiliated organizations should receive only *delegate* representation at nominating conventions:

It had never been understood that every affiliate member would have full voting rights in the choice of candidates ... In short, the decision which we accepted at the OCNP is not only a very fundamental one, but at variance with the accepted view of a great many key persons in the whole New Party development. My guess is that the overwhelming majority in the CCF support the view that affiliated members should be given voting rights at nominating conventions only when they have taken out full membership in the Party, and that at least a significant minority in the trade union movement do likewise.

MacDonald then proceeded to give the main reasons for his position. Equal status for affiliated members at nominating conventions, he said, would take all the steam out of any campaign to persuade affiliate members to become full individual members, and assume all their rights and obligations in the party ... not just choice of candidate, but the day-to-day organizational work, policy resolutions, choice of riding delegates to conventions, etc ... It is all too easy now for the average citizen, be he trade unionist or not, to shun the time and work involved in political action at the local level; but grant the affiliate member full voting rights in choice of candidate without becoming a full member, and the incentive to take out full membership will be sharply reduced. The New Party will be in exactly the same position as the CCF has been for over twenty years in Cape Breton – with thousands of affiliated members believing they are full members of the party, turning up only at nominations after elections have been called, with the result that the Party has no basic organization with which to win elections.

The second major reason, MacDonald argued, was that

the granting of full voting rights ... will destroy the image of a broadly-based party, involving all sectors of the community at the riding level. It will bolster the fears of those within the party that it is dominated by labour, and it will give our opponents convincing evidence with which to clobber us from the outside. Certainly the task of those of us, on both the trade union and CCF side, to counter in the public mind the fear of Labour domination will be infinitely more difficult.

In my own riding [York South], for example, ... a hotly contested nominating convention would open the door to thousands of affiliated members being organized into attendance – so that the [CCF members] ... would be swamped by persons who had never taken an active role at the riding level, and who would likely never turn out again until the next nominating convention ... I shudder to think of how completely that kind of situation would be made to order for our opponents.[33]

Essentially, MacDonald emphasized the two main goals of the CCF in the New Party project: to increase individual membership, so as to provide the New Party with a strong base of dedicated workers with which to attract new members and sell the party to the voters; and to present to the public the image of a broadly based party in which no one group dominates.

At the OCNP meeting of 12 July 1961, however, the Committee decided to reject the CCF Executive's proposal as outlined by Mac-Donald. Moreover, within a week, several members of the CCF Executive had changed their minds and endorsed the OCNP's position, leaving the Executive more or less evenly split on the issue. Nevertheless, Stewart wrote to Archer urging him to make certain amendments that would exclude the provision of full voting rights in the constitution.

"We have considered [the CCF's] ... objections," a besieged Archer replied impatiently, "and made changes. Simply because we [the sub-committee on constitution] do not concede to every demand surely can't hold up the constitution forever or have review after review until we do what they desire ... I have neither the time, the desire, nor the necessary stenographic help to continue in this manner. Frankly, I think it is a hell of a way to run a railroad."[34] A compromise of sorts was finally reached in mid-August when the OCNDP passed a motion providing that "the section 10(c) dealing with the eligibility of affili-ated members to vote at nominating conventions should not be part of the constitution," which required a two-thirds majority vote to amend. The compromise was to present the founding convention with a resolution, containing the following key phrase: "This convention therefore decides that members of affiliated organizations are entitled to attend and vote at nominating conventions providing their names are registered with the constituency secretary 15 days prior to the date of the nominating convention."[35] In other words, although affiliated members would receive full voting rights, despite the strong objections from certain CCF leaders, these rights would not be entrenched in the NDP's constitution. The OCNDP subsequently proposed several addi-tional resolutions that called for wider participation of affiliated mem-bers in everyday constituency affairs; and these, too, became part of the resolution.[36]

The climax to the more than three years of political education, organizing, promotion, and planning for the New Party came during the week of 31 July 1961 at the old Coliseum in Ottawa. Billed as the largest and liveliest political gathering ever held in Canadian history, with over 2,200 delegates in attendance, the founding conven-tion of the federal NDP displayed a mood of spontaneity and celebration noticeably absent from the conventions of the old-line parties. The profusion of banners, flags, buttons, hats, and music, all in full view of the national media, was also in marked contrast to CCF conventions, known as they were for their steadfast avoidance of hoopla and the solemn study and presentation of resolutions. Not that serious debate was eschewed on this occasion. "What really flabber-gasted journalists," recalls Ken Bryden, "was that for every [policy] session the hall was packed, right from the opening bell until adjournment time ... These people were all right there, all the time, fighting about everything under the sun."[37] During the five days of what another observer described as "hectic debate and heady emo-tionalism," delegate excitement reached a fever pitch over the Douglas-

Argue leadership race, while heated exchanges took place over the New Party program and official name. Overall, the founding convention was a resounding success. "For once," writes Desmond Morton, "the Canadian Left had appeared in the major leagues – confident, strong, efficient, yet retaining the idealism and the basic democracy which had given it its distinction."[38]

The Ontario NDP's founding convention in Niagara Falls in October was more subdued, but no less exciting. "The meeting had none of the suspense or drama of the Ottawa Convention," noted the party's official organ. "There was no leadership race to quicken the pulse; there were few surprises and floor revolts; there was little of the colour and song that won the national convention superlatives in the daily press. And yet, by God it was never dull."[39] Although intended to be a "noses-to-the-grindstone, no-nonsense convention," focused on the important tasks of electing officers and approving the constitution, the convention nevertheless provided delegates with much to get worked up about. One reason for the excitement was the widespread feeling that the New Party was on the verge of an electoral breakthrough. A recent Gallup poll showed a 4 percent increase in support for the NDP since January, and delegates went into a frenzy after hearing that Premier Frost would soon be resigning. Donald MacDonald, whom delegates unanimously elected as the Ontario NDP's first leader, agitated the convention further with a rousing speech calling upon members to build the New Party into a contender in time for the next federal election. "Let us go forth as political missionaries," he shouted, "seek out friends and neighbours – yes, even strangers, and talk to them about the new party ... [for] only if each one of us ... does his part, will this broadly-based movement be built in the limited time at our disposal." He finished with a ringing declaration that "we have launched here a political force that will sweep the province like a mighty Niagara Falls."[40]

Excitement also centred on the sometimes heated discussions over resolutions. After a bitter half-hour debate between left-wing pacifists and moderate multilateralists, for example, delegates overwhelmingly endorsed the National Convention's recent decision to oppose nuclear arms in Canada and support Canada's continued participation in NATO.[41] The most acrimonious debate, not surprisingly, took place in response to the OCNDP's resolution on the rights of affiliated members in constituency associations. In its final form the resolution declared that

members of affiliated organizations are entitled to attend and vote at constituency meetings and nominating conventions provided their names are registered with the convention secretary ... for at least thirty days ... Where a constituency convention is called on a delegate basis, affiliated organizations will be governed by the basis of representation established by the constituency by-laws.[42]

The only other restriction was that affiliated members could not vote in the election of constituency delegates to provincial or national conventions, since this was normally done through the affiliated organization itself. Those in favour of the proposal argued that it would encourage affiliated members to participate in the activities of the riding associations, with the chance that full membership would follow. Those against argued that allowing full participation for affiliated members would, in fact, dissuade the latter from becoming full members and, furthermore, could lead to the "packing" of nominating conventions by unions and to the perception that labour was dominating the party. In the end, the resolution was passed by a narrow margin.[43] That it was passed at all, given the inherent risks, was no doubt a manifestation of the optimism that prevailed on this occasion.

Another salient feature of the convention was its broad-based appearance, which was anything but fortuitous. Preparations for the event had begun in late 1960. The following spring, the OCNP established an Arrangements Committee to issue the Convention Call (rules for prospective delegates), distribute convention literature, mail out credentials, and make other arrangements. In line with its overall strategy, the OCNP was anxious that the convention be clearly seen as representative of all three sections. Originally, for example, it had arranged for only Tommy Douglas and the Ontario NDP's leader-elect to speak to the delegates; but when Donald MacDonald suggested that the tripartite image of the new party could be enhanced by inviting prominent speakers from each section, the agenda was revised accordingly.[44] In addition, the CCF suggested that the OCNDP "reconsider the basis of representation at the founding convention, with a view to widening it in order to get as large attendance as possible." The CCF felt that the qualifications for representation of riding associations and New Party Clubs, in particular, were "unduly restrictive" and so proposed a new formula. Its proposal, which favoured riding associations, New Party Clubs, and unions, in that order, was approved by a slim margin and the Convention Call was amended to reflect the change. The final distribution of delegates at the founding convention was unions 519, CCF 265, and New Party Clubs 155.[45]

The tripartite nature of the convention was also evident in the election of several liberal-minded and labour representatives to the NDP's Executive Committee. Although the top positions of leader, president, and secretary-treasurer were won by former CCFers, the vice-presidents consisted of a teacher, a farmer, a physician, and two union representatives; the remainder of the Executive boasted several farmers, professors, teachers, doctors, and unionists. Thus could the *Toronto Star*'s Pat McNenly conclude that "the new image of the New Party is reflected in ... the larger-than-ever group of doctors, lawyers and other 'intellectuals' attending the Left Wing gathering." Even the relatively small group of farmers at the convention drew attention, especially during the lengthy and vigourous discussion that took place over the NDP's tentative farm program.[46] "One of the outstanding things about the founding convention," MacDonald recalls with obvious satisfaction, "was the surprise of the convention as a whole [with the farmers]. They thought farmers were being dragged in with a few token people. But when the farm debate came up, they were not only vocal, but they were obviously top-flight people. And ... one of the most inspirational moments in the convention was the uplift in the [delegates] as a whole when they suddenly realized, by God, the farmers were with us – they're on the team!"[47] Clearly, then, the New Party planners in Ontario were highly successful in portraying the founding convention as an exciting, democratic experiment, encompassing a broad spectrum of the province's progressive elements.

The founding convention was the culmination of many years of planning and effort aimed at broadening the base of the CCF into something resembling what the movement's founders had envisioned in the thirties. In this sense, it was a climax of sorts. But the events of 1961 and, in particular, the persistence of the CCF's pragmatic strategy, belie the notion that something "new" was created. Despite its commitment to mobilize the liberal-minded contingent in time for the founding convention and the fact that many members of the white-collar middle-class showed a keen interest in the project, the OCNP continued to focus primarily on riding associations and unions, instead of New Party Clubs. To fill the void in time for the founding convention, where the new party would be unveiled to the public, New Party leaders resorted once again to image-making: union-based New Party Clubs were tolerated to increase so-called liberal-minded representation at the convention; Clubs were kept separate from riding associations until 1962; a Farm Committee was established to give farmers a prominent place at the convention; and convention arrangements were geared to creating just the right image. What unknowing observers witnessed in October 1961, therefore, was not the birth of a new, broadly based "people's" party, but the appearance of one. NDP leaders no doubt saw the founding convention as a starting point, as the first step toward a true people's party. Once assured that the CCF's organization was securely entrenched in the New Party, that all which they had worked for since the 1930s was safe, party leaders could then try to capitalize on the "new party" image they had created and hope that somewhere down the road a more broad based movement would emerge. In the words of the CCF *News*: "When the bunting is down and the lights out; when the placards are packed and the coliseum cleared of convention debris; when the last resolution is passed and the last speech an echo in a lonely hall – the fight for a new party will not have ended. It will barely have begun."[48] Not many could have detected the painful truth in these few, highly prophetic lines.

9 Conspiring Events

This train pulled into Ottawa one bright and shiny day,
When she steamed into the station, I could hear the people say,
It's that brand new party special from the mountain and the plain,
We're going to ride to victory on that brand new party train.[1]

Spirits in the Ontario NDP ran high after the two founding conventions in 1961. After years of preparation, everything seemed to have come together nicely. Millions of people across Canada had witnessed the lively and dramatic birth of the federal party on nationwide television, followed a few months later by an equally successful provincial convention. The invincible Leslie Frost had recently resigned. Polls showed the party's popularity on the rise; and the image of a broadly based party of the Left had been so carefully crafted that many NDPers no doubt viewed their party as a serious contender for office. The future looked bright, indeed, for this political infant.

But as was so often the case with the CCF, high expectations were quickly and forcefully destroyed. The period from November 1961 to September 1963 was a terrible one for the NDP; it seemed that events were conspiring maliciously against the party at every turn. Some of the problems were familiar ones – inadequate finances, stagnant membership, poor image – but many were unexpected and seemingly beyond the party's control: the rapid succession of elections, four in less than two years including the five by-elections in January 1962; the well-publicized defection of Hazen Argue and several prominent party leaders in Ontario; growing tension between labour and non-labour members, and between the Provincial Office and the ridings; intensive attacks from both Communists and capitalists; and growing doubts within the party about its viability as a separate entity. By the fall of 1963, the intoxicating spirit of '61 was no where to be found. The new party train had never left the station.

The Ontario NDP had had barely enough time to savour the euphoria of a successful launching before the long and arduous string of electoral contests began. The first was a series of five provincial by-elections in early January 1962. Party leaders considered them to be extremely important. As the first real test of the "new party," they would indicate what sort of electoral success the NDP could expect in the near future; they would also "establish the political climate" for the upcoming federal and provincial elections, noted the provincial leader. As such, the NDP concentrated the bulk of its human and financial resources, which were severely weakened after years of New Party organizing, into what everyone was calling the "little general election." Regular and part-time organizers were sent into Kenora, Brant, Eglinton, and Renfrew South, and veteran organizer Marj Pinney was hired to work in the Beaches; a minimum of $1,000 dollars was provided to each riding.[2]

Despite all this, the party's efforts went unrewarded. It finished last in four of the five ridings, although it came a very close second in the Beaches. Contrast this with the Liberals, who captured three of the five seats (taking one away from the Tories) and increased their popular vote over 1959 by an impressive 7 percent; or the Tories who, although they had 11 percent shaved off their popular vote, hung on, albeit barely, to the remaining two ridings. The NDP had not expected to do well in either Brant or Renfrew South, since both were rural ridings that the CCF had either never contested before or had run only token candidates in and therefore lacked basic organization; the party took solace, however, from the fact that most of the increase in its popular vote came from these ridings. The most disappointing result, then, was in the Beaches, where the party lost by less than 200 votes after having put on a strong campaign. Pinney had been called in especially to give organizational assistance; Ken Bryden, M.P.P. from nearby Greenwood-Woodbine and himself a top-notch organizer, was the campaign manager; and Stan Bullock, a very capable and hard-working, if somewhat colourless, individual, who was well known in the riding as a community activist and trade unionist and had been campaigning for several years, was the NDP candidate. By the time election day rolled around, the team of Pinney, Bryden, and Bullock had in place an extensive zone and poll organization, consisting of more than 300 volunteer workers. On top of all this, the opposing candidates were newcomers. A victory in the Beaches would have changed the entire tone of the by-election results, remarked Donald MacDonald afterwards. Instead, the results suggested a resounding rejection of the "new party."[3]

The reasons for the NDP's poor showing were, as always, varied. On the one hand, the party had little time to prepare for the contests, since they occurred at a time when many NDP riding associations, as opposed to the New Party tripartite committees, were still being formed. Most of the ridings had to scramble to nominate candidates and to set up some sort of campaign machinery at the last minute. As well, the Liberals benefited substantially from the sensationalist revelations on organized crime in Ontario which their leader, John Wintermeyer, had recently exposed in the legislature. Their assertion that the NDP was dominated by labour, that the Tories were dominated by Big Business, and that only the Liberals represented the "little guy" was also effective. As a result, the anti-government vote went primarily to the Liberals, a trend that worried NDP leaders, who were banking on the "new party" to supplant the Liberals as the alternative to the Tories.[4] Another key factor, it seems, was the Communist party's favourite tactic of trying to sabotage the NDP's chances by publicly endorsing the party. The "kiss of death" was particularly effective in Eglington and the Beaches, where the Communists placed pro-NDP advertisements in the *Globe and Mail*, distributed leaflets of a similar nature, and made telephone calls announcing their Communist affiliation and urging voters to support the NDP candidate. The problem of Communist sabotage, MacDonald reported to Council afterwards, was "appearing with new emphasis." On top of these problems was the bitterly cold weather, which according to Pinney kept many party supporters and workers inside on voting day, and the anti-union bias of many voters, at least in the Beaches.[5]

One other factor was the lethargy that seems to have infected the NDP generally in the months following its birth. Given the tremendous effort invested in launching the NDP and the emotional high of the founding conventions, it was perhaps inevitable that many party activists would be too physically and mentally drained to convert the excitement surrounding the "new party" in 1961 into organizational expansion. Some party leaders warned against the natural tendency for complacency to set in. "The Founding Convention ... both here in Ottawa and in Niagara Falls ... surprised and, I think, overwhelmed us by its success," wrote federal President Michael Oliver. "But the response to the New Democratic party ... will not last long by itself. The public forgets easily ... [and] in the coming months, we must build on that enthusiasm, exploit it, make it work for us."[6] This advice, though, apparently went unheeded. Marj Pinney recalls the frustration and sense of lost opportunity she felt in the immediate post-founding period in Ontario:

It was a magnificent [national] convention ... and we were so excited. I came back really rejuvenated, gung ho, ready to go. And I can remember it so well:

absolutely nothing happened for months. I mean nothing! It was like we never had the convention. It was like nothing had changed ... You kind of were waiting for something to happen that never happened ... Those of us who were the movers and shakers in the party were expecting an influx from elsewhere ... and didn't expect we were going to have to pick up the load and do the same damn things we'd been doing for the last twelve years ... I think we really captured the imagination of the people. We had the most marvelous opportunity and we just pissed it away. We've never recovered that ground.[7]

Ken Bryden's recollections of the post-founding period are strikingly similar. "The minute the convention was over," he states, "everything just collapsed. Everybody was completely worn out. [Russell] Bell and [Doug] Hamilton went off on holidays to Vermont. There was absolutely no follow up. And looking back I can see now that we should have been planning for after the convention. ... It was a great tragedy because I think an opportunity was missed. We could have gone forward, because certainly there was a tremendous amount of excitement."[8] In short, a general feeling of complacency may have weakened organizing efforts at all levels of the party leading up to the January by-elections.

But the NDP had little time to dwell on the results of its first electoral test. A federal election was clearly about to be announced and all efforts had to be focused on this next challenge. There was much to be done. As mentioned, many of the local tripartite committees were in the process of being transformed into bona fide riding associations; moreover, no candidates could be nominated or election campaigns mapped out until founding conventions were held to elect NDP riding executives and area councils. For the most part, this process went smoothly, if slowly. Naturally, the Provincial Office did what it could to move things along at a brisk pace. The secretary-treasurer, Peg Stewart, reminded New Party Clubs, for example, that they "must now become full members of the NDP, or take steps to affiliate their groups, as provided in the Constitution." She emphasized that New Party clubs could remain in existence, especially "where this is desirable organizationally," (i.e., where no other NDP organization existed), but that Club members still had to be full, or affiliated, members of the NDP. The Provincial Office also insisted that while speed was of the essence, with the 1 March deadline for establishing constituency associations, local founding conventions had to be "broadly based", with representation from affiliated unions as well as former (and existing) New Party Club members. Ridings that did not follow these democratic procedures – and there were a few – were refused recognition.[9]

Apart from these urgings and admonitions, however, not much seems to have been done by the Provincial Office (or the ridings) to integrate New Party Club members into the NDP, or to provide assistance once they did join. The riding of Stormont is a case in point. At one time, it boasted the largest New Party Club in the country, with over 300 members, and was known across the country as the showpiece of the New Party; party leaders naturally had high hopes for the riding. But by the spring of 1962, the Stormont NDP had only seventy-three members, almost all of whom lacked any political experience, and whose organizational impotence was aggravated by what the Provincial Office called serious "personality clashes." Faced with a divided, demoralized and confused riding association, however, the Provincial Office could offer little but verbal encouragement, a response that typified the NDP's approach to the liberal-minded in general after the founding convention.[10]

In addition to ensuring that the basic party structure was in place at the local level, the NDP set out to strengthen its membership base. Despite the wide publicity created by the founding conventions and the slight surge in the New Party's popularity in 1961, the formation of the NDP had not resulted in any immediate influx of regular members; the prevalence of post-foundation apathy and exhaustion as well as the relative neglect of the liberal-minded certainly contributed to this situation. While it is true that approximately 5,000 people joined the Ontario NDP between October 1961 and January 1962, this figure is deceiving. No doubt it included many of the 3,600 CCFers who, between 1959 and 1961, had let their membership expire, while they either joined New Party Clubs or awaited the birth of the NDP before "re-joining" the party as full members. When the number of members who belonged to the CCF in mid-1959 is compared with the number who belonged to the NDP in January 1962 (10,000 or so in both cases), it is clear that in the short run the New Party project did not produce a larger regular membership. Hence the Provincial Office could not count on a huge, enthusiastic corps of new members to do the organizational work needed at the local level before the next election, such as finding candidates, setting up a campaign headquarters, recruiting volunteer workers, preparing posters, and raising funds. The problem was compounded by the fact that while the provincial organizers had devoted all of their time to the by-elections, many ridings had simply stagnated.[11] In early 1962, therefore, the NDP expanded its full-time provincial organizing staff from two to six and decided to concentrate on the seven most promising areas of the province. In addition, the Provincial Office approached area councils and affiliated unions in these areas with the suggestion that they contribute to a special Organizing Fund that would underwrite organizers for work in that area alone. As a result, Bob Mackenzie was hired as an organizer in the Hamilton area. Despite these steps, however, the still unsettled state of affairs at the riding level and the late start at the provincial level augured badly for the NDP's first federal election in June.

The other major preoccupation of the NDP after its founding convention was fund-raising. Funds were desperately needed to pay off the large debt incurred during the recent by-elections and to finance the larger organizing staff. More important, money was needed for the impending federal election. In February and March, therefore, the Ontario NDP cooperated with its federal counterpart in a "Victory Drive" aimed at raising the ambitious sum of $300,000 in Ontario. Stephen Lewis, the federal coordinator of the drive, was assisted in Ontario by the provincial coordinator, Phil Carberry. They travelled from one area council to the next, setting up fund-raising committees and, for the first time, organizing special teams of fund-raisers to collect money from liberal-minded, middle-class professionals and small businessmen. But the drive was a flop. It was slow in getting started, since many ridings were still setting up shop. Moreover, once it did get rolling, it was interrupted by the announcement of a June election. As a result, the NDP raised only $41,000, and by mid-March, according to Fred Young, its financial situation was "pretty desperate."[12]

The party's financial burdens prior to the 1962 election were eased somewhat by two developments. The first was the fact that the federal party assumed responsibility for expenses which, in the past, had been incurred by the provincial parties, namely television advertising and election leaflets. The second was the assistance of the labour movement. Although the unions were not asked to contribute to the Victory Drive, the NDP solicited funds during the election campaign from labour councils and affiliated unions. For the first time, this appeal was made directly to the unions, rather than to the OFL's Political Education Committee (PEC);[13] it was done "to involve the locals directly in the New Democratic campaign," thereby reinforcing the idea that the NDP was *their* party. "The response was good," reported the Council, "though many locals preferred to support the candidate in their own constituencies directly." The PEC also did its share, spending approximately $7,000 on leaflets, posters, advertisements, and NDP candidates. Meanwhile PECs in Hamilton and Toronto supplemented this with about $4,000 worth of their own advertising and candidate contributions.[14]

As a result, the NDP was able to put on a respectable campaign. Out of eighty-five Ontario ridings, it managed to field eighty-one candidates, the highest proportion ever for the party. It also gave assistance to its candidates in the form of leaflets, television and radio advertising, and cash. Nor was individual effort lacking. While the perpetually active Donald MacDonald delivered speeches throughout Ontario, Tommy Douglas was making three exhausting tours of the province (he was forced to cancel his last few appearances due to illness). Candidates and leaders alike stressed such key party planks as full employment, a national health plan, portable and contributory pensions, affordable housing, fair labour standards, regional disparity, and foreign investment. The campaign culminated in June with a series of automobile processions through the streets of Toronto, followed by a large rally for the national leader at the O'Keefe Centre in Toronto.

But as the by-elections had foretold some six months earlier, the results were disillusioning. Across the country, the NDP captured only 13.5 percent of the vote and nineteen seats. Even the Social Credit party did better. In Ontario, the party's popular vote was only slightly higher, at 16 percent, yet this generated three new seats, thereby doubling the NDP's representation from the province. Fisher, Martin, and Peters regained their seats in the North, where an impressive 25 percent of the electorate had voted NDP; David Lewis finally won the riding of York South, after several attempts; Andrew Brewin, the veteran CCFer whose campaign team and organization were second to none, captured Greenwood; and Reid Scott, a one-time CCF M.P.P. in the forties and later a Toronto alderman, triumphed in Danforth. These were seen as considerable gains, although the narrow defeat of Walter Pitman in Peterborough, the spiritual home of the New Party, took some of the gloss off the feeling of progress.[15]

It is not hard to see why the party's gains were modest. Many riding associations had had insufficient time to prepare for the campaign so soon after the founding conventions; as well, they had received little help from the Provincial Office until after the by-elections and federal finance drive. Local campaigns were further hindered by the inexperience of many new campaign workers, primarily from the unions, who knew little about canvassing, poll organization, and the like. But at least some unionists had actually made an effort. The overwhelming majority of them, however, as in the CCF years, did not even *vote* NDP, this despite the growing number of affiliated unions.[16] The NDP's lack of preparedness and its inability to attract the labour vote, therefore, must be counted as factors in the party's poor showing.

Another, more important factor was the persistence of the Communist smear campaign, emanating from Communist, business, and political circles. Shortly after the federal election was announced, the Communist party (i.e., LPP) publicly declared that it would be supporting the NDP in all ridings save those in which it fielded its own candidates. As a result, Communist party members frequently voiced their support for NDP candidates on the hustings, in newspaper advertisements, and in election leaflets; this campaign was especially intense in the urban-industrial ridings of Toronto and Windsor. Despite the suggestion from some riding associations to simply ignore the Communists, the NDP leaders, who were as sensitive to this problem as the CCF had been, made every effort to disassociate the party from Communism. Party leaders and candidates openly repudiated Communist party endorsements; they asked the media to print such repudiations alongside any Communist Party declarations of support and to refuse "malicious" Communist advertising. The NDP even tried taking legal action to stop the Communist's distribution of pro-NDP leaflets. In early June, several NDP candidates in Toronto filed a suit under Section 62 of the Elections Act, charging that the leaflets constituted a violation of the Act insofar as the latter forbade the expenditure of funds on candidates except through, or with the approval of, the candidate's official business agent. The charges were eventually dropped, however, because the NDP was unable to prove to the Justice of the Peace that the Communists had actually paid a printer to produce the leaflets. Lastly, the party refrained from referring to itself by the initials "NDP" because of the resemblance to the Communist party's initials, "LPP"; too many recent immigrants had lived in fear of communist or fascist parties in their home countries or understood the initials to mean "New Displaced Person," a derogatory term.[17]

In the months leading up to the election, the need to repudiate Communist support at every turn was further heightened by the presence of a well-organized, well-financed, anti-socialist propaganda campaign called "Operation Freedom," conducted by the Canadian Chamber of Commerce.[18] The roots of the campaign were complex. They lay in the fear of higher taxes and reduced personal freedom that the Chamber believed would follow from an enlarged Welfare State, or "socialism" as it called the latter, and in the belief that should a socialist party come to power, communism was sure to follow. Although the Chamber made few direct references to the NDP in its propaganda, it is clear from the timing of the campaign and the oblique references to the "socialist political threat" that the campaign was primarily directed against the NDP.[19] The president of the Chamber summed up the thinking behind "Operation Freedom" at the Chamber's annual meeting in October 1961. "It is high time that we realized," declared William Kirkpatrick, "that the next election may very well be fought on the very vital theme of Socialism versus Free Enterprise, and Socialism is but a step away from Communism. It is time, therefore, that we realized this situation and personally take some active part [in politics] no matter what party we support, if we care to push our wagon out of the mire of the Welfare State."[20]

Notwithstanding the negligible political threat posed by the NDP according to the polls (from January to September 1961 its popularity increased only 4 percent), its recent birth nevertheless aroused the Chamber's fear that a socialist party – one boasting a program of extended social legislation and government "planning," heavily financed by dues from affiliated unions, and led by the magnetic Tommy Douglas – could potentially wield much influence in Ottawa. This perceived threat was even greater given what one political analyst called the "acute state of fluidity and ferment" that marked national politics during this period. A November 1961 Gallup Poll indicated that the undecided vote was a record high 28 percent, suggesting that "the Canadian electorate was in a state of hapless confusion."[21] In short, the Chamber felt that a minority government with the NDP holding the balance of power after the next election was a distinct possibility, and it responded accordingly. Anti-socialist literature was sent to every local chamber of commerce and board of trade for distribution through the media, businesses, and community organizations, including schools. The literature emphasized protecting Canada's so-called free enterprise system, as the only guarantor of personal freedom, against the threat of socialism and communism. Negative media reaction, however, forced the Chamber to officially withdraw the campaign a month before the federal election; unofficially, though, "Operation Freedom" continued unabated at the local level.

Conservative and Social Credit party spokespersons also employed the anti-socialist, anti-communist line during the 1962 election campaign, but for more blatantly partisan purposes. Tory candidates sometimes referred to certain NDP candidates as "Communist sympathizers" and to the CCF government in Saskatchewan as an "Iron Curtain" state. Such accusations were heard more frequently in strongly anti-Communist ethnic ridings. At a March 1962 rally in Toronto, for example, federal Justice Minister Davie Fulton warned recent immigrants of the dangers of Communist tyranny through mind control, while Pierre Sevigny, the associate minister of National Defence, told voters in Montreal-St. Denis that "the Liberals are more leftist than the NDP" and that they would have to choose "between free enterprise and the slavery of socialism which has destroyed every country it [has] entered." The Social Credit party, led by Robert

Thompson, Canada's answer to arch-conservative American Senator Barry Goldwater, was even more vitriolic in its attacks, warning that government taxation had reduced Canadians to the status of "half slaves," and attacking socialism as "the road to Communism."[22]

The 1962 federal election campaign therefore witnessed a strong current of anti-socialist, anti-communist propaganda directed primarily against the NDP. Coupled with the Communist Party's public endorsement of the party, this was sure to hurt it at the polls – not by repelling its existing supporters, who were accustomed to these sorts of attacks and who knew better, but by reducing its *potential* support. Of this, the NDP had no doubts. In her letter to the riding associations warning them to repudiate Communist Party support in no uncertain terms, Peg Stewart warned that "this unwelcome 'support' can be used by the group etc. behind 'Operation Freedom' and [by] the Social Credit people who are doing their vicious best to tie us up with Communism."[23] The Communist smear campaign, therefore, was almost certainly another factor in the limited success of the NDP in the 1962 federal election.

But perhaps the most important factor was the well-publicized defection of NDP House Leader and former leadership hopeful, Hazen Argue, to the Liberals in late February, amid charges that the NDP was dominated by labour. On 18 February, he announced to the media that "the NDP has now become the tool of a small labour clique and is effectively under their domination and control."[24] No other charge could have been more devastating to the party, given the great deal of time and money expended by CCF and labour leaders over the previous four years as they tried to create the image of a broad-based and democratically run party, with no single dominating group. The possibility of these efforts bearing fruit in the June election – although, admittedly, there were few signs of such success – was destroyed by Hazen Argue in a matter of minutes. Notwithstanding the assurances of party leaders, Canadians suspected, and the media never ceased to remind them, that the labour movement was, in fact, calling the shots in the NDP in return for financial contributions. "Mr. Argue has thus confirmed," wrote the *Globe's* editor, with a sense of vindication, "that the NDP has not the interests of all Canadians at heart, but is the voice of one class, labour-dominated and dedicated to a policy of greater power to the labour unions." This belief had been circulating inside and outside CCF circles since the 1940s, and was strengthened by the wedding of the CCF and CLC in 1961. To many voters, the Argue defection simply confirmed their suspicions.[25]

Nonetheless, Argue's seemingly villainous actions must have boiled the blood of many a dedicated NDPer in Ontario, or at the very least caused significant consternation. There were, however, few outward signs of this. Instead, party leaders adopted a low-key, pitying response, in the hope that this would foster the impression that Argue's defection arose from a puerile feeling of "sour grapes" at having lost the leadership race to Tommy Douglas the year before; hot denials, in contrast, might have suggested to some that Argue had struck a chord of truth. Nevertheless, the Provincial Office moved swiftly to control the damage caused by the affair. The day after Argue's speech in Parliament, it asked all federal candidates in Ontario to immediately issue statements expressing support for the national leader as well as for the structure and financing of the party. At the same time, party officers issued a press release that declared, in restrained fashion, that "as elected officers, we have had no experience to suggest that the Party is controlled by any labour clique," and that Mr. Argue's defection "is prompted not by the reason which he now advances but because of inability to accept unmistakable and conclusive defeat [at the founding convention]."[26]

Among its own members, the leadership adopted much the same low-key approach, combined with reasoned rebuttals and a show of determination. The party's official organ, *The New Democrat*, emphasized that the twenty-eight-person Provincial Executive contained only eight trade unionists, that the proportion was similar at the federal level, and that the unions' financial support was insufficient to allow the party to bypass finance drives, such as the Victory Drive. Meanwhile, Provincial President George Cadbury assured members that "there is no sign that the steady growth of the New Democratic Party is being hindered by this irresponsible defection." He argued that Argue's actions had, instead, helped create an *esprit de corps* among a betrayed rank and file.[27] Party leaders then crossed their fingers and hoped.

It is safe to say that the impact of the Argue defection was decidedly negative, although the extent of the damage is unclear. It almost certainly hurt the NDP's chances in the federal election four months later. Polls show a decline in the federal NDP's popularity from 12 percent to 9 percent between January and May, rising to 14 percent on election day. Indeed, without that decline prior to June, the NDP's final vote might well have been 3 or 4 percent higher. In Ontario, the party's popular support remained unchanged at about 16 percent over that same period;[28] the defection, however, probably displaced votes that might otherwise have gone to the party. After all, accusations of labour domination were kept in the public eye right up until voting day, and NDP candidates were continually hounded by reporters and opposing candidates who wanted to know whether the party was in fact dominated by labour. It is also possible that Ontario voters went to the polls with recollections of the charges made in January by Ontario Energy Resources Minister, Bob Macaulay, against Donald MacDonald. Macaulay charged the NDP leader with conflict of interest for accepting supplemental pay from the party, part of which came indirectly from trade union contributions. The implication was clear, but MacDonald called the charge "the prize red herring of the year." He explained that supplemental pay came from the party's general revenues and that the leaders of the old parties had always accepted such pay from wealthy corporate benefactors. It is unlikely, however, that this explanation persuaded many voters, for the *appearance* of conflict of interest was undeniable. In short, the cumulative effect of the various occasions on which the NDP was publicly accused of being controlled by unions in the six or so months before the election, apart from all the other factors working against the party, was bound to persuade the many undecided voters *not* to vote NDP on 18 June.[29]

As for the impact of the Argue defection on the Ontario NDP proper, although it may have been in some measure beneficial, it was on balance detrimental. To begin with, it did not cause an immediate exodus of members from the NDP. Nor does it appear that members let their memberships lapse in the long term or that potential members were deterred, for the records indicate that total party membership increased at an impressive rate in the ten months after the defection – from 10,000 in January to 14,000 by December. Considering the normal lag in organizing activity after elections, these figures are all the more impressive. They suggest a strong effort in many ridings to expand the party – a result, in part, of the *esprit de corps* of which Cadbury spoke and which organizers' reports coming into the Provincial Office confirmed.[30]

On the other hand, Argue's actions did cause uncertainty and confusion in some ridings, probably more so in areas where support for the New Party movement had been tentative. Provincial organizer Gerry Clarke reported that many ridings in the London region, for instance, were not buying the "petulant child" explanation presented by the Provincial Office and were demanding to know whether Argue's accusations were correct; party leaders came across similar questions in other ridings. In some cases, party activists simply left their riding associations without officially resigning. Moreover, at least two prominent resignations in 1962 can be linked to the Argue affair. The first began with a letter to the editor of the *New Democrat* in April from the NDP's federal candidate in Eglington, David Gauthier, a philosophy lecturer at the University of Toronto, in which the writer clearly sympathized with Argue. While he felt that Argue's criticisms of the NDP were "exaggerated and even distorted," Gauthier insisted that this "should not blind us to the very real faults in our party," especially the fact that the NDP was paying too much attention to labour, as it had in the formation of the New Party. "The belated and haphazard attempt to establish New Party clubs," stated Gauthier, "confirms the claim that disproportionate organizational attention was given to labour." Eight months later, Gauthier resigned from the party, arguing that the NDP's emphasis on economic "planning" would lead to excessive bureaucratization and that the party should unite with left-leaning Liberals to create a two-party system. In his response to the resignation, NDP President George Cadbury referred to Gauthier as a "political experimentalist" whom the party did not regret losing. But this response led, in turn, to the resignation in January of Eamonn Martin, the party's provincial candidate in Eglington riding, and Gauthier's mentor. Martin echoed Gauthier's sentiments and accused the NDP of being rude and ungrateful toward Gauthier. Both resignations were well publicized. Clearly, the Argue defection had had an internal impact on the party.[31]

It is certain, as well, that the accusations of labour domination stemming from, and to some extent preceding, the Argue incident did not help win more farmers to the NDP. Most Ontario farmers were highly resentful and suspicious of organized labour; their feelings, which went back to the early years of the CCF, would only have been intensified by the defection of the NDP's major farm spokesperson from Saskatchewan – who warned farmers to avoid the NDP "like the plague."[32] The Argue defection was on the agenda of most, if not all of the NDP's farm policy conferences in the spring of 1962, forcing party leaders to respond to Argue's charges. Admittedly, the NDP was doing very little organizing in rural areas after the founding convention, because of a shortage of knowledgable organizers and the concentration of resources in more promising areas, and therefore had little to lose. But any chance that farmers might have supported the party in the near future was likely extinguished by the whole affair.

The most serious repercussion of the Argue defection, however, related to the NDP's relations with organized labour. Simply put, the growing belief that labour was dominating the NDP made unionists reluctant to play a prominent role in the party. One suspects that this low-key approach was adopted partially because Argue's accusations hurt, although the desire not to lend substance to his charges no doubt predominated. Witness what happened when the NDP invited the OFL in March to form a joint committee "to discuss mutual problems," as the CCF and OFL had often done prior to elections: members of the Federation's Executive refused, saying they preferred informal consultations. "To establish a formal committee that met regularly and discussed problems of the party," they said, "in the light of the Argue accusations, could be wrongly interpreted." It could lead to accusations that "there is a group over and above the Executive of the New Democratic party making or influencing decisions that should be theirs alone." Similarly, when the NDP asked OFL President David Archer to act as co-chairperson at the party's first convention, the Federation's Executive stated that "the political interests of the NDP would be better served if Brother Archer was not co-chairman."[33] The message was clear. Organized labour would have to watch its step as far as political action was concerned because every move it made was being measured against the theories of Argue and his lot.

But the last thing the NDP wanted, of course, was for labour to play a lesser role in the party. The NDP had been formed largely in the hope that union members would play an active role at the riding level, first as affiliated members, then as full members. Such participation would strengthen the party's organization substantially, which would likely mean more seats on election day. By declining to be seen in public with the NDP, OFL leaders were not sending out a very encouraging message to rank-and-file unionists, who were expected to "get involved" in the constituency associations. The lower political profile of labour leaders would also have important symbolic consequences, as far as making workers feel that perhaps the NDP was not "their" party after all. Either way, the NDP would suffer. It would be seen as a party controlled by organized labour, but from which it would, in fact, be receiving less support. This is exactly what transpired, and herein lay the cruel irony of the Argue incident as far as the NDP was concerned.

After the Ontario NDP's founding convention, the OFL had concentrated on getting local unions and labour councils to affiliate to the party. The process involved holding a vote and, if more than 50 percent of the members approved of affiliation, deducting 5 cents per member per month for the NDP, excluding those members who "contracted out." This would replace the traditional per capita payments to PAC, which were phased out by January 1962. The OFL hoped that affiliated members would then take advantage of the NDP's constitutional provision that allowed them to participate fully in riding activities, except for the election of delegates to party conventions. With any luck, the unionist would eventually take out full membership and assist in the creation of a strong riding organization. In short, the OFL viewed affiliations as "a basic underpinning ... on which the organizational superstructure can be built," and which would, in the meantime, help finance the party.[34]

The OFL aimed for an affiliated membership of 200,000 by October 1962. Although this was an ambitious goal, given that only 40,000 had affiliated by December 1961, the OFL seemed determined to reach its objective. At its annual convention in November 1962, it passed a resolution calling on the Federation to "urge its affiliates to support and affiliate with the New Democratic Party." The bulk of this task was left to PEC Director Morden Lazarus, whose committee regularly sent information to locals and labour councils outlining the importance of affiliation and the procedure involved; the PEC also arranged workshops at OFL seminars and conferences to discuss the issue as well as other forms of political action. The rapid increase in affiliations in the first six months of 1962 was due largely to these efforts. By July, close to 130,000 union members, representing just under 400 locals, mostly Steelworkers and Autoworkers, were affiliated to the NDP. The Argue incident had clearly not had much affect here.[35]

But, thereafter, the number of affiliations slowed dramatically. By November, the number had levelled off to approximately 133,000, well short of the goal. That more affiliations were not secured beyond this level was due primarily to constitutional restrictions on political action within certain unions, particularly the building trades. Although some international unions had removed such restrictions on their Canadian locals, many had not. Locals in such unions were often eager to affiliate to the NDP, but were reluctant to defy their constitutions or pressure the international parent body for amendments. Some pro-NDP locals may also have been sensitive to the commonly heard criticism that the "contracting out" provision was undemocratic.[36] Nevertheless, the number of unionists affiliated to the NDP by the end of 1962 compared quite favourably with the earlier CCF figure of only 17,600 affiliated members, exactly two years earlier. Clearly, the financial base of the party was substantially strengthened as a result of the new emphasis on affiliations.[37]

The record with respect to the number of affiliated members becoming full members of the party or participating in riding activities, however, was much less favourable. Although no figures are available on this matter, the evidence that such instances were a rare phenomena is close to overwhelming. Reports came in from all over Ontario suggesting a high degree of political inactivity at all levels of the labour movement. In December 1961, several months before the Argue defection, the New Democrat noted that "trade unionists who could make a real contribution to parliament [by running as NDP candidates] are holding back because they don't want to encourage the myth that labour is dominating the New Democratic Party." In March 1962, the PEC reported that while affiliations were progressing well, "the number of individual members is well behind the objective." In October,

Ames told MacDonald that "the record of ... unions in the north, as in the south is, in the main, very poor. We are getting neither affiliations or involvement." He also expressed his concerns to the new provincial secretary, Jim Bury, who was also a staff representative for the Packinghouse Workers. "We have not had any significant union participation or involvement in the riding election organization," he wrote in November, "and there is no immediate indication that we will." This was true of not just the rank-and-file members, but also of "our trade union staff, business agents, heads of many of our unions, etc." In December, the PEC of the Toronto Labour Council informed Bury that "we have been most concerned about the lack of participation of the affiliated union membership at the riding level ... Many of the affiliated members are not aware of their rights as provided in the constitution of the Ontario New Democratic Party to attend and vote at constituency meetings and nominating conventions." Granted some unionists did lend a hand during the 1962 federal election – canvassing, distributing pamphlets, driving supporters to the polls, and so on – but no more than they had in the CCF years, and perhaps less. The 1962 election was a real "eye opener," commented one delegate at the OFL's annual convention. "We found out that we didn't actually have the machine that was needed. In some areas, in fact, we had a broken down machine." And in what was likely typical of many unions, the head of a carpenters' local in northern Ontario observed that "interest and participation in political action [during the election] by the membership ... [was] found to be very disappointing and ... promoted by the so-called 'few.'" To the extent that such inactivity existed from the founding convention onwards – and the evidence strongly suggests this – Argue's charge that labour was controlling the party seems all the more ironic. "If anything," said Doug Fisher shortly after Argue's defection, "there is a vacuum in leadership because labour people are hanging back."[38]

As usual, there is no simple explanation for all of this. The problem seems to have been one of ignorance (in the literal sense), logistics, and above all a lack of will. The Toronto Labour Council's belief that affiliated members were "not aware of their rights" was surely correct in some cases. After all, the PEC spent most of its time and energy encouraging affiliations, but seems to have said little to local PECs about the rights associated with affiliation. Even at the various education conferences arranged by the PEC in 1962, the topic of riding participation ranked second to that of affiliations. Pinney contends that while certain NDP activists worked hard to convert affiliated members into full members, "you weren't getting the same push from the labour side to use their organizers to get people to sign up in the party," largely because "labour was just being typically labour – they did their own [union] job first, as you would expect."[39]

Logistically, the PEC and NDP had difficulty coordinating the process of integrating affiliated members into riding associations. At first, the Provincial Office told ridings to contact affiliated unions to find out which unionists would be willing to sign a "participation form," expressing a desire to participate in riding activities. But by early 1962, because certain Hamilton ridings were the only ones using this prescribed procedure, the Provincial Office tried a new tack: to the riding associations it sent lists of affiliated unions, with the names of the officers; to the union it sent the names of the riding association officers. The hope was that one side would contact the other and that affiliated members would either request, or be invited, to participate in the association's activities. But this did not seem to work either. As the Provincial Council reported at the 1962 convention, "Both the ridings and the unions in many cases were not too sure which of them should take the first steps to make this a reality"; the problem was compounded in multi-constituency areas, where affiliated members were often spread out over several ridings. The party expected the affiliated unions to sort out which of its members belonged to which riding, and then forward this information to each riding association or to the Provincial Office, which would then forward the information to the riding. According to the Provincial Council, however, "This has not been sufficient to get the project rolling in the way its sponsors had hoped"; it concluded that "bringing so large a number of our supporters into active political work has not been easy." Even if the riding association managed to obtain a list of affiliated members, it had to contact each member to determine who was interested in getting involved with the association. In the end, most ridings figured it was hardly worth the trouble and simply gave up. This problem was eased somewhat by the "registration" system, which the NDP adopted in December 1962, whereby affiliated unions were asked to distribute registration cards on which their members could express a desire to participate in the riding association. The cards were then given to the riding leaders, whose time spent on the telephone would then be reduced substantially. But no evidence exists to suggest that cooperation between affiliated members and regular members increased as a result of the new procedure.[40]

In addition to problems of communication and coordination, perhaps the major obstacle to NDP-labour cooperation at all levels after the founding convention was the feeling of unease that some party members seemed to harbour toward labour. Because this feeling surfaced publicly on numerous occasions, most blatantly during the

Argue affair, the effect was to make unionists feel unwelcome in the party, as they already had for many years in the CCF. A few examples will suffice. It is likely, first of all, that many ridings had a hard time accepting the right of affiliated members to participate in party activities as though they were full members. Such reservations were expressed by CCF leaders during the New Party's formation, and the resolution authorizing this practice was only narrowly passed at the founding convention after a bitter debate. But the reservations did not disappear. Shortly after the founding convention, two NDP riding associations in Toronto complained to the Provincial Executive that neither affiliated members nor New Party Club members should be allowed to attend their local founding conventions. They reasoned that the constitution did not specifically grant these members the right to attend, and more important, according to the president of the Spadina riding association, George Grube, "It may cause some resentment, and again give occasion for our enemies to raise the cry of union domination." The Provincial Office replied that the constitution should not be interpreted so literally during this transitional phase, when attempts were still ongoing to get affiliated and New Party Club members to sign up as full members; they added that it was more important to have a broadly based founding convention as a means of encouraging this eventuality. But only one of the ridings abided by this advice.[41] In insisting on the strict letter of the constitution, these ridings were to a great extent expressing the latent fear that affiliated members could, without sufficient warning, swamp riding association conventions during important votes.

The charges made by Argue in February would certainly have intensified this fear of labour domination. So would the media reports surrounding a nominating convention in the Toronto riding of Broadview, in March. In this instance, the successful candidate was the business agent for the Labourers' Union, Gerry Gallagher, who defeated the riding president for the nomination, apparently by marshalling the last-minute support of many affiliated members. The president claimed that he had never before met Gallagher, that his opponent's campaign had been shrouded in secrecy, and that "it's the promotion of this man Gallagher that bothers me most of all." Regardless of the accuracy of the story, the spectre of union domination that it raised simply added to existing suspicions among NDPers; and for many voters, it simply confirmed the charges levelled by Argue a few weeks earlier. Clearly, the Provincial Office was aware of these fears, for when it decided to introduce the registration card system to encourage affiliated member participation, it emphasized that "caution ... [must] be shown that we do not flood the ridings with names of trade unionists who have signed registration cards." In other words, the fear of union domination accounted in large part for the lack of NDP-labour cooperation at the local level.[42]

Relations between the co-founders of the NDP were further strained by criticism from some NDPers that labour was not doing enough for the party, at least not enough to offset the negative publicity that the closer tie with labour was attracting. An article in the November issue of the *New Democrat*, for example, criticized the activities of labour in the 1962 federal election. This provoked a sharp response from Morden Lazarus, who felt that it was not only insulting to union supporters of the party but, as he told the provincial secretary, also "does considerable damage and ... break[s] down confidence of ... union members on [sic] [the] relationship with the party." And in a veiled threat to end the "contracting out" method of affiliation, which the article criticized, Lazarus said that "any time the party wants it, I'd be surprised if the unions wouldn't accept it, except it would undermine [the] financial base of the new party." The NDP's response was obsequiously apologetic, but the damage had been done.[43]

Prior to this, the *New Democrat* had printed an even more insulting article written by the party's recent candidate in York Centre, Val Scott, whose maverick tendencies and penchant for public controversy would manifest themselves again and again in the years to follow. In the article, Scott presented his candid thoughts on why the NDP had done so poorly in the federal election. He listed several reasons, but in particular he pointed a finger at affiliated members. "There has been no organized attempt east of B.C. to turn the affiliated members into regular members and integrate them ... into our riding associations (in spite of promises, speeches and resolutions at conventions)," he wrote. "Instead we seem to have a lot of nameless nickel-a-month individuals who apparently can't even be counted on to vote for us, much less work for us." He concluded that because affiliated membership provided the perfect excuse for the unionist to do nothing more for the party, it should be abolished. Although these comments were directed primarily at the *concept* of affiliated membership, and not the affiliated members themselves, it is easy to see how Scott's comments would have served to polarize rather than build bridges.[44] In addition, the article provoked a major response from party members, all of whom seemed to concur with Scott's analysis and prescriptions. One reader stated outright that the middle class would not support a party that is "primarily labour-oriented. The white collar and professional people see the NDP as a labour-dominated party – which it is." Another reader agreed and suggested that the NDP disband so that its members could join the Liberals. "History may yet reveal," concluded the writer, "that Hazen Argue was not the fool a lot of people seem to think he was."[45] Once again Lazarus lashed out defensively against such criticisms, and at a Provincial Council meeting in August, defended the efforts of organized labour. "The Trade Union movement has made an enormous contribution across the country in assisting the formation of our party and in helping with election funds," he asserted. "We should recognize the work which has been done, and not allow ourselves to be critical and impatient in regard to that which remains to be done."[46] In short, the affiliated members' low level of participation in the party was based very much on feelings of unease and ill will harboured by party members toward labour, feelings which the Argue defection and the electoral setbacks of 1962 merely intensified.

The growing tensions between labour and the party peaked at the NDP's first annual convention in Toronto in early October. For the most part it was a fairly dull affair; that is, until the third and final day, when the chairperson, George Grube, nearly lost control of the delegates "during four or five heated skirmishes with the floor." Some of these battles centred on the party's new program, but one in particular focused on a resolution presented by the St. Paul's NDP that called for the strike weapon to be replaced by a form of compulsory arbitration. Although the top officers of the OFL had previously expressed approval of such a motion, labour delegates denounced it vigorously from the convention floor. Some were also upset by the fact that the resolution was presented without any recommendation for support or rejection by the Provincial Council, which seemed to suggest concurrence at the highest level. Although divisions along labour-party lines emerged on other issues, the anti-strike resolution was the main bone of contention. Commenting on the convention afterwards, one labour leader strongly suggested to Donald MacDonald that "some attention ought to be given to bringing together the sentiments and principles ... of understanding between labour and non-labour members of our party. I noticed at the Convention that there was quite a bit of misunderstanding ... between [sic] the aims of labour by the non-labour delegates. I have noticed this prior to the Convention as well."[47] The editor of the New Democrat, John Brewin, issued a similar report on the gathering. "The atmosphere governing the relations between the trade union movement and the party," he urged, "must be improved to the point the two work together smoothly and effectively."[48] Even the irrepressibly optimistic Donald MacDonald criticized these internal divisions, particularly the talk in some quarters about a merger with the Liberals. At a Council meeting in December, he stated: "We have problems within our own movement. At the present time there is much soul-searching going on in the party ...

[But] we must remember that we are a party made up of socialists, trade unionists, and liberal-minded, and it is about time that we became less superficial ... All these groups are necessary for the building [of] an effective Democratic Peoples Party. Any further discussion on the question of the proposed merger with the Liberals is not in the best interest of the New Democratic Party."[49] Much of the bitterness evident at the NDP's first convention was no doubt a product of the tension that had been building for some time between labour and non-labour sections of the party.

The NDP's first convention was notable for one other event: the declaration of its new official program, entitled *A New and Democratic Program for Ontario*. The development of the program had begun in January 1962, when a policy committee was established to arrange for research to be done, by individuals from various fields of expertise, on resolutions presented at the founding convention. The Executive, deciding to gear the new program to the "consumer," instructed the policy committee to focus on such issues as medicare, full employment, minimum wages, and education – issues it felt would likely go over well in the next election. In its final form, the new program amounted to an excessively long thirty-eight pages, divided into three sections. The first section, aimed at "consumers," promised a government bureau to prevent monopolistic pricing policies and other corporate abuses; encouragement of cooperatives; universal, contributory public medicare and pension plans; no-fault, low-cost public automobile insurance; extended sickness and accident benefits; enhancement of Ontario's cultural and recreational opportunities; and "town and country" planning, including urban redevelopment, low-cost public housing, and better transportation facilities. The second section promised "citizens" greater educational opportunities; improvements in secondary school education; a more equitable level of educational standards across the province; "honest and effective government" through ethics guidelines, more open election financing, and legislative reform; a constitutional Bill of Rights; a provincial ombudsman; faster judicial proceedings; improvements in the correctional and welfare systems; and larger, better financed regional governments. In the final section, "the people" were offered "genuine democratic, economic and social planning"; public investment where necessary; assistance to particular industries; regional economic equality; proper resource management; higher farm income through cooperatives and lower production costs; jobs for all workers through government planning; less government interference in labour-management relations; higher minimum labour standards; less wasteful government spending, again through planning; and higher taxes on large incomes and profits.[50]

As intended, the central theme of the 1962 program was the individual consumer and citizen, as opposed to particular economic groups, such as farmers or workers. The only sense of class or group conflict even remotely implied by the program was that between consumers and monopolists; generally speaking, the emphasis was very much on individual well-being. Another theme was the more equitable distribution of social services for all people and regions, and making such services flexible enough to meet a variety of needs. One cannot help but notice, as well, the party's emphasis on improving and extending *existing* programs and institutions – in other words, the belief that an NDP government could "do it better." The recurrence of phrases such as "the program ... will be speeded up," and the NDP "will continue to expand ...," reflects the fact that by the early 1960s the Conservatives, as well as the Liberals, had adopted a number of policies formerly advocated by the NDP or CCF alone.

In content, however, the 1962 program was quite similar to the CCF's 1958 program, *Challenge for Ontario*. Only a few of the issues had not been previously covered, such as judicial and legislative reform, for instance. In terms of underlying principles, the similarities were also strong. Neither presented a separate section on general principles, but reading between the lines one sees the notion that people's needs should be placed before all else, especially profits, and that economic growth should be geared to satisfying those needs. In general, the 1962 program was simply more detailed: twice the length of its predecessor, its phraseology and organization placed more emphasis on the consumer than it did on specific groups such as farmers or workers.[51]

The two documents' only noticeable – some might say substantial – difference was the differing emphasis placed on the role of government in each. In *Challenge for Ontario*, the CCF's economic program (subtitled "planning for progress") constituted the *first* of three sections and included a separate section on "public enterprise." In *A New and Democratic Program for Ontario*, the economic program (subtitled "Wealth for Our People") constituted the *last* of three sections and had no separate section on public enterprise. Since the core of the CCF's program had always been its economic proposals, particularly the notion of government "planning" (which the 1958 document called the "keynote" of its program), the change in emphasis by 1962 is perhaps noteworthy. The two programs' different proposals for public ownership is evidence of further change. In 1958, the CCF declared that the "extension of public ownership will be an integral part of CCF economic planning" and promised to nationalize natural gas distribution, telephone communication, bus transportation, and brewers' warehouses and retail stores. In 1962, it vaguely promised to "step up its own programs for investment" in essential areas where private investors refused to invest; it also pledged to use "public investment" (which was more innocuous sounding than public ownership) in natural gas distribution, and in the facilities used for processing, storing, and distributing farm products. In general, although the commitment to a strong government presence of some sort is similar in both programs, by 1962 the use of nationalization as an instrument to achieve broader social goals had been replaced with "regulation." Although subtle, this difference does suggest a move away from traditional socialist prescriptions. And indeed, during the 1963 provincial election campaign, little mention was made of planning or public ownership.

It was this perceived change in emphasis that created the most turbulence at the 1962 annual convention. A small group of young party members vociferously opposed the subordination of aggressive economic policies to what they called crass, materialistic consumer issues "worthy of the other parties." "Let's not compromise our basic principles to win cheaply a victory at the polls," declared one of the purists. The continual barrage of "loud and emotional harangues" from this group eventually got the better of M.P.P. Ken Bryden, who was heard to shout, "All day they've been running to the microphone to show what hairy-chested, virile Socialists they are, but they really know nothing about socialism."[52] Once tempers had cooled, however, the new program was easily approved by the majority of delegates.

The central division at the party's first convention, however, was between unionists and non-unionists. Perhaps it was in response to this split that the party Executive established a joint OFL-NDP committee in November, to "work out ways and means to encourage affiliated local membership into active New Democratic Party membership." But the method eventually adopted to achieve this objective, or at least to make union members more supportive of the NDP, originated not in such high-level consultations, but in growing pressure from the grass roots of the labour movement. In August, OFL President David Archer told CLC President Claude Jodoin that he was not only "receiving complaints from the PAC about the lack of money for the NDP and to a lesser extent the lack of union participation," but also was being criticized by labour councils and unions "for what they consider the lack of leadership on the part of the Congress and the Federation in the 'Medicare' fight." To "kill these two criticisms with one stone," the OFL decided to establish a Medicare Fund. Raising money for the Fund would, it hoped, get rank-and-file unionists active in politics, if not the NDP directly. Furthermore, the funds raised would be used to publicize medicare, and, presumably, would increase support for the NDP as well. "In this way," concluded Archer, "local unions and individuals who have been yelling about the inactivity of the CLC and OFL will be forced to put up or shut up and the PAC enthusiasts will have all the activity they desire." The NDP was receptive to this idea. Ames told Lazarus that many pro-NDP labour councils had been reluctant to discuss affiliation to the party for fear of causing internal divisions. But by using the medicare issue as an "in," he argued, "we will create a political discussion without antagonism." The OFL's medicare campaign began officially in February 1963, and, before long, local labour councils were being encouraged to sponsor medicare meetings in their areas.[53]

At about the same time, the NDP began a medicare campaign of its own, the object being to capitalize on the growing public support for medicare in time for the next provincial election. In particular, the NDP wanted to get a jump on the Liberals, who had recently become supporters of medicare (and other NDP policies) and who threatened to steal the party's thunder on the issue. The NDP also hoped that a detailed exposition of its medicare policy would help distinguish it from that of the Liberal party, thereby quelling some of the talk in its own ranks about merging with, or voting for, the Liberals in the future.

But the whole issue of compulsory, government-run health insurance was not easily dealt with. The Saskatchewan CCF government's promise to introduce medicare the year before had been responsible for the defeat of all the province's NDP candidates in the June federal election, including a stunned Tommy Douglas, and sparked a province-wide doctors' strike the following month. For three tense weeks in July, all eyes were on Saskatchewan, especially NDP eyes, for the credibility and image of the NDP as a movement depended on how well the Saskatchewan government handled the crisis and countered the charges of tyranny coming at it from all directions. The Ontario NDP did its part by recruiting Ontario doctors to work in Saskatchewan during the strike, sending Stephen Lewis and John Brewin to help with publicity, and mailing open telegrams from "prominent" groups and individuals who supported medicare to the Saskatchewan College of Surgeons and Physicians.

Above all, the Ontario NDP wished to avoid a similar debate on medicare in Ontario, with all its potential for bad publicity. "The manner in which this Executive deals with this issue in the next few months," stated one party leader, "is of the utmost importance with respect to the future success of our Party in Ontario"; it was particularly important that an "orderly campaign" on medicare be conducted. As a result, a special Medicare Committee was established in August to formulate a comprehensive scheme, based on expert advice, for presentation to the 1962 convention for approval; until then, the party kept a tight reign on any statements regarding medicare. After the convention, the publicity campaign went into full swing: a medicare leaflet was issued, party leaders spoke frequently on the subject, and bumper stickers and medicare stamps associating medicare with the NDP kept the issue a prominent one until the election.[54]

In addition to its own medicare campaign, the labour movement was expected to assist the party more directly through financial contributions to the NDP's Organizing Fund, alluded to above. Early in 1962, party leaders devised what was called a "regional organizer plan." This involved soliciting money from local labour councils and NDP area councils in electorally promising areas for the hiring of area organizers. A similar scheme hatched in the bleak days of the mid-fifties had failed to arouse any interest, but by 1962 local apathy was less of a factor and the need for concentrating organizers in key ridings more widely understood. Thus, early in the year, the party was able to hire Bob Mackenzie in Hamilton and Gordon Brigden in Toronto, mainly from PEC contributions in those cities; some area councils even established their own organizing funds, again primarily from labour donations. By November, having received strong signals from labour bodies in southern Ontario that more money would be forthcoming, the NDP decided to retain its existing organizing staff of seven; Doc Ames and Fred Young, of course, were still on the Steelworkers' payroll as staff reps. If the unions came through, the party could then use regular membership revenues to help the weaker areas of the province, through part-time organizers, cash donations, and so on. The party saw financial commitments from the unions, then, as indispensible to its more ambitious, post-founding organization plans.[55]

These commitments acquired an added importance in light of the party's desperate financial straits – once again – in the summer of 1962. The events of the previous three years, particularly the recent electoral contests, had taken their toll financially. In the riding of Greenwood, for example, the NDP spent $4,000 in the 1962 federal election, which was double the highest ever spent by the CCF in a single riding. But what made matters worse was that the NDP's "go for broke" approach resulted in much careless spending at the local level. In November, a concerned Finance Committee reported that "a disturbingly large number of Riding Associations are in debt as a result of the last federal campaign" because "many did not set up proper machinery to authorize expenditures, which, of course, resulted in confusion and lack of economy." Consequently, ridings were not remitting as much to the Provincial Office as they should. This put the latter in the red, as well, and forced the Executive to give notice to four of its full-time organizers, who were not as yet being financed by the Organizing Fund. This decision, though, was strongly opposed by half a dozen party leaders in the Toronto area – including Ken Bryden, Val Scott, Andrew Brewin, and David Lewis – who felt that the party's organizing staff must be expanded, not reduced, even if it meant going further into debt. Under such pressure, and against its better instincts, the Executive withdrew notice for three of the four organizers and added two "special organizers," Marj Pinney and her protegé Lucille Ross, to work in particularly winnable ridings in south-central Ontario. Thus, despite its mounting financial difficulties, the NDP's ambitious organizational strategy for 1963 – with its focus on regional organizers, paid for, in part, by the labour movement and concentrated in promising ridings – remained basically unchanged from 1962.[56]

This strategy did have at least one additional negative repercussion, apart from its financial burden: it made a number of area councils and riding associations more jealous of their presumed autonomy, which in turn put a minor strain on relations between the Provincial Office and the local level. Past disputes between the two levels had usually been slight, revolving around financial issues. The dispute over regional organizers, however, was more serious, insofar as it concerned the distribution of authority within the party. Where the local area council or riding association had raised sufficient funds to entitle it to a regional organizer, it often presumed to have complete authority over this individual as well; such was the case in Hamilton. Morever, the riding's sense of independence was in some cases intensified by its distrust of the Provincial Office, stemming from the belief that the latter was dominated by labour and that its regional organizers, there-fore, were insufficiently impartial to be listened to.[57]

The most serious conflict was between the Provincial Office and the Toronto Area Council. As early as December 1961, the Provincial Executive had been concerned about the independent mentality of the Council, then called the Metro Committee for the New Party. It noted that a portion of the latter's draft constitution submitted to the Executive for approval "ignores the fact that Metro [Council] is part of the Ontario party." The Executive accordingly suggested that the constitution contain a clause stating that "the Council (Metro) shall at all times act in cooperation with the provincial organization and in accordance with its decisions." Trouble with the Council resurfaced in April, shortly before its founding convention. A delegation of Toronto riding representatives who had seen a draft of the constitution complained to the Provincial Office that the ridings had not been consulted by the Council's Secretary, Francis Eady, who was drafting the constitution with the assistance of George Cadbury; they announced that they were "unanimously opposed to the proposed draft on every basic point of principle." Although no precise details were given in the report of the meeting, subsequent comments suggest that the delegates felt (and the NDP Executive agreed) that the constitution assumed too much power *vis-à-vis* the provincial level. The Executive accordingly postponed the founding convention until the fall and instructed the Council to consult with the ridings.[58] That consultation, which took place in September, obviously caused a good deal of disruption on the Council, for both the chair, Bill Sefton, and the secretary, Eady, resigned, and the Executive reported that "the other members are considering resignation." Clearly a sharp division had emerged between the Council – which represented riding associations, affiliated members, and New Party Clubs – and other Toronto representatives, probably over the constitutional amendments proposed by the latter. In a dramatic gesture, the Provincial Executive proceeded to disband the Council and reconstitute it with new representatives, including some from the Provincial Executive.[59]

The founding convention of the Toronto NDP Council occurred in late October, shortly after which the Provincial Office received a letter from Charles Millard, the organization and finance chairperson of the new Council. Intended to reassure the Provincial Office that it need not worry about the loyalty of the new Council, Millard emphasized:

The function of the Council, as stated in the Council constitution, is: "To assist the Provincial Organization ... in carrying out Provincial projects (organization, finance, etc.) within the [provincial] area and at the municipal level." Given adequate leadership and direction [on the part of Council], there should be no tendency or danger of building a 'separate' or 'fourth' level of Party Government ... I will give what help I can in building the Council as I visualize it and [we] will tie in as closely as we can with the Provincial organization. Certainly we don't want to operate on an independent basis.[60]

Shortly after receiving these assurances, the Executive reported that although the Toronto NDP Council was still in the process of reconstruction, "already there is better attitudes [sic] displayed."[61] Millard's letter reveals quite clearly that the entire dispute had indeed centred on the question of which level should have the final authority in directing the organizational and financial resources of the NDP in the Metro area. The root cause, he stated, was primarily the NDP's decentralizing organizational strategy. The regional organizer plan, by encouraging groups of ridings to find and finance their own organizers, had bred a greater sense of autonomy in some areas, particularly Hamilton and Toronto. And although the Provincial Office asserted its authority in the end, a sign that tensions between the constituency associations and the Provincial Office had not completely disappeared by year's end was the latter's quest to "build up a loyalty to the Provincial Office and the movement generally" through better communications between the two levels.[62]

Clearly, the NDP faced more than its fair share of challenges in the twelve or so months following its birth: five by-elections, a federal election, several damaging defections, an anti-socialist propaganda campaign, growing talk about an NDP-Liberal merger, an uneasy and at times turbulent relationship with its labour partner, extreme financial pressures, and dangerous structural tensions. Under the circumstances, the increase in regular and affiliated members in 1962 was quite an achievement. Nevertheless, to those who had worked so diligently to make the new party a success, the number and seriousness of the problems must have seemed part of a deliberate plot to sabotage a magnificent venture – one that, such a short time ago, had held so much promise.

The road ahead was only slightly less challenging, for there were still two major election battles to be fought. The first was the federal election, which everyone expected would be called within a year of the June 1962 election that saw Diefenbaker's government reduced to minority status. Preparations began slowly. Throughout the summer, provincial organizers reported that many ridings were still recovering from the last election, trying to raise money to pay off large debts; otherwise, their members were vacationing for the summer. Indeed, few signs indicated that ridings were holding the two nominating conventions (federal and provincial) suggested by the Provincial Office, signing up new members, or putting together an election team. Not until very late in the year did the ridings show some signs of life, at least in southwestern Ontario. In the east, all was quiet. Ames, reporting from the North, said he was "having a most difficult time ... and not getting much help from the local people"; personality conflicts, second thoughts, and a bitter jurisdictional struggle between Steelworkers and

Mine-Mill workers had spilled over into some riding associations, causing the cancellation of several nominating conventions.[63]

In contrast, preparations in the major metropolitan areas such as Toronto and Hamilton advanced smoothly and efficiently. In part this was because, for once, much of the pre-election work (including the conducting of publicity and fund-raising, the printing of leaflets and arranging of rallies, and the giving of money to needy ridings) was being handled by the area councils. It was also a result of the decision to concentrate most of the provincial organizers in the "promising" ridings – that is, in those areas where the NDP had done well in 1962 and where the state of organization was good (for instance, in Toronto, Peterborough, Hamilton, and a few northern ridings). The remaining ridings, however, were experiencing varying degrees of neglect. For example, many associations had not yet retired their debts; and even where they had, few could turn to members or local unions for more money. The only recourse was to plead with the Provincial Office. Normally, the latter could channel some funds or literature to these less-promising areas, to compensate for the decision to concentrate organizers in major urban areas. But this time, even this option was severely limited by the movement's weak financial position. Except for the donation of the Hamilton Steelworkers Area Council, little money had been contributed to the Organizing Fund. In April, then, the Council was to conclude that "the Regional Organizational Fund never got off the ground except in Hamilton." In addition, efforts to raise money through a Spring Finance Drive were cut short by the calling of the election in March. Nor could the party rely on more money from regular and sustaining memberships, since the number of members actually declined in the months before the election. To cover its election expenses, the party was forced to negotiate a loan.[64]

Once again, however, the efforts of the labour movement eased the NDP's burden. Beginning in the winter of 1962, the OFL turned its attention away from securing affiliations toward electoral activity. As usual, its assistance was both direct and indirect. While OFL affiliates contributed directly by providing candidates and organizers in key ridings, the CLC directed its staff representatives "to devote all the time you can spare from your regular work for the election campaign." In February, the Toronto Labour Council's PEC cooperated with the NDP in recruiting election workers from the unions, using the card registration system devised the year before. With respect to money, the OFL-PEC turned over the remainder of its funds to the NDP, closed its account, and once again allowed the party to appeal directly to labour organizations for funds, rather than through the PEC, as the CCF had done. The money raised was vital in key areas such as Toronto, where 90 percent of all election spending was financed by union contributions.[65]

Indirectly, the OFL-PEC helped the party through its political education and publicity programs. Its medicare campaign, in particular, seems to have been well received by the union membership. In March, the secretary of the Kingston Labour Council, Lloyd Fell, told Lazarus that it was "one of the few political action efforts we have undertaken which has not met with vigourous opposition from supporters of the other parties ... It may very well be an indication that this technique will achieve more by way of introducing people to the NDP than the head-on approach which we have used in past."[66] Information on medicare was supplemented by leaflets on auto insurance, portable pensions, and other prominent aspects of the NDP's program. As well, in January and February, the PEC held its annual series of staff conferences across the province to discuss political issues, including party organization and financing.

As usual, the NDP seemed fairly confident going into the campaign. The electorate, deeply divided over the nuclear weapons issue, did not seem particularly enamoured of the leaders of either major party. In these unsettled circumstances, the NDP hoped that a fair number of the nervous and confused voters, many of whom were obviously disaffected with the Tory government, would settle on the NDP as the alternative. "It's anybody's ball game in Ontario," declared the *New Democrat* in March, predicting "major gains [for the NDP] ... in the industrial heartland of Canada." Certainly the polls did not confirm the paper's talk of "a genuine swing to the new party" or a "phenomenal surge" in NDP support, and, except for the *Toronto Star*, the media paid little attention to NDP pronouncements or to such major events as the huge cavalcade and rally for Tommy Douglas in Toronto in late March.[67]

The polls were right again. On 8 April, the Liberals captured 129 seats and faced a combined majority in opposition of 95 Tories, 24 Social Crediters, and only 17 New Democrats; the 2 percent drop in popular support for the latter since the previous election was matched by a loss of two seats. In Ontario, where it had run slightly fewer candidates than the year before, the NDP was able to retain its six seats and popular vote from the year before, although the disappointing loss of David Lewis in York South was only slightly mitigated by the addition of Hamilton South. Publicly, the party emphasized the silver lining – the fact that it had held its own over the previous election, that it had finished a close second in several northern ridings, and that all three levels of the party structure, as well as the PAC and labour councils, had worked together harmoniously during the campaign. Privately, however, there was deep disappointment. The strategy of convincing the voters that the NDP, and not the Liberals, was the best alternative to the Tories had obviously failed, and again the party found itself a victim of the wasted vote mentality. Party leaders blamed the defeat on several factors, including the Communist smear campaign, the federal NDP's clumsy prediction that it would not form the government, the similarity of the NDP and Liberal platforms, and the last-minute plea by the media for a stable, majority government. To this list could be added the fact that despite the more indirect approach of the PEC, only 21 percent of the labour vote went to the NDP according to party estimates.[68]

Yet the party had little time to sulk over the latest setback. Preparations for the provincial election, expected in the fall, began immediately. In April, the Provincial Office hired seven part-time organizers, mostly university students, to complement its full-time staff of six; they would work throughout the summer in the most winnable ridings. This, of course, meant a further increase in the party's debt, although the chair of the Organization Committee, Stephen Lewis, reassured doubters that "with this sort of potential our movement is big enough and well enough established to take such a calculated risk." The party also decided to hold its first provincial membership drive since the founding convention – and a much-needed drive at that, as almost 7,000 memberships had lapsed by June 1963. Donald MacDonald, looking back, feels that "part of the problem following the founding of the party was that we had so damn many elections that there was no time to build the party." The 1963 membership drive was a case in point. Beginning in May, it was run in almost identical fashion to the former CCF drives, with zone captains, quotas, and prizes; it had to be extended to mid-July, however, because of "post-election lethargy and the difficulty of getting the Drive thoroughly organized." Finally, the party established an Election Committee in June which, as in the past, coordinated all organizing and publicity until election day.[69]

The success of these efforts, however, was limited. The battle weariness of the troops translated into fewer new or renewed members than expected, despite the extended deadline of the drive. At the time of the 1963 federal election, the party had 13,500 members. By the end of July, the total number had dropped to 12,900, and would continue to fall until year's end. Not surprisingly, given the placement of the organizing staff, all of the decrease occurred outside the Toronto ridings. The drive had simply slowed down the organizational contraction which, in any case, meant a smaller pool from which to recruit election workers and raise money. To some extent, this was offset by the OFL's usual contribution of organizers, but because less was forthcoming in the way of financial contributions from this source, funds were in even shorter supply. In his appeal to the UAW for donations, Bury noted that the two recent federal elections had "placed a considerable financial burden on the party," and that the party expected a post-election deficit of at least $21,000.[70]

The official campaign took place during the five or so weeks before the 25 September election; although the NDP's conduct did not differ markedly from previous campaigns, a few interesting changes were evident. The strategy for the party's ninety-seven candidates was to stress the major points in the NDP's 1962 program: medicare, public automobile insurance, portable pensions, and other consumer-oriented issues. Candidates were also told to emphasize the basic conservatism and opportunism of the Tory and Liberal platforms, and by contrast, the "willingness [of the NDP] to act to implement its plans, and to use government action – including public ownership – to get results." The party's campaign slogan was: "New Democrats will do it."[71] The NDP had little choice except to follow this approach, since by 1963 the policy differences among the three major parties were those of degree not kind. Consequently, when it was not emphasizing its willingness to actually come through on its promises, the NDP was busy trying to persuade voters that their policies were "better," that they went further, and so on. This marked one difference from the more programmatically distinct CCF campaigns of the 1950s.

Another, more subtle difference was the performance of the provincial leader. As head of the CCF, MacDonald had clearly played a prominent role in the two previous provincial contests. But in 1963 he really outdid himself. Ably assisted by Federal Secretary Terry Grier, who wrote many of his speeches and planned his itinerary (also a departure of sorts), MacDonald scoured every inch of the province. He drove 10,000 miles, addressed 41 public meetings, issued at least 40 press releases, and spent over 30 hours on the phone with his advisers. And because most of the party's election funds were being put into organizers and expensive radio and television advertising, MacDonald was also forced to raise money along the way to finance his campaign. But as usual, he was the quintessential political warrior, loving almost every minute of his frenetic, dawn-to-dusk schedule. He never seemed to tire, and told reporters on the last day of the campaign that he had never felt more invigorated. "The thing about these elections," he remarked casually, "is that you feel fine up to a day after the election, then you fall apart."[72] Somehow one doubts this was true in MacDonald's case.

Apart from his Herculean efforts, MacDonald's general approach was also perceptibly different. In each of his previous campaigns the theme of government scandal had figured prominently, and had Mac-Donald been given his way this would again have been the focus in 1963. But apparently he was persuaded by the party brass to avoid such a negative approach and to focus, instead, on the highlights of the party's platform, which for the most part he did. Instead, it was Liberal leader John Wintermeyer who harped on the scandal theme, accusing the Tories of profiting from certain public works projects, suggesting that Provincial Secretary John Yaremko was in the back pocket of Ontario gamblers, and questioning the integrity of Mr. Justice Wilfrid Roach, who had headed the recent inquiry into organized crime in the province. Wintermeyer's "scandal-a-day" campaign, however, was simply too enticing for the NDP leader to remain aloof – it was like watching a rival playing with a toy one had been forced to relinquish unwillingly – and so, as the campaign wore on, MacDonald returned frequently to his favourite theme. Lashing out against the Liberal leader's hypocritical and opportunistic conversion to anti-scandal crusader, he reminded the voters that *he* had been the first to charge NONG president, Ralph Farris, with perjury during the NONG affair, a charge that had recently been vindicated by Farris's conviction. Mac-Donald argued that Wintermeyer should have spoken up on the issue four years ago but had not because of his own involvement; that the Roach investigation was incomplete; and that the minister of Municipal Affairs, J.W. Spooner, should resign for allegedly doctoring the report of an investigation into another scandal. Wilfred List of the *Globe* aptly summed up MacDonald's performance: "With one breath he scorned the skeleton rattling of the Liberals, and with the other he renewed and embellished old charges that the Conservatives were scandal-ridden." On the whole, however, the NDP placed only secondary emphasis on government immorality in 1963, another subtle change from previous elections. Commented one journalist, the NDP has adopted a more reasoned, "dignified" approach to electioneering, in contrast to the "colourful campaigns waged under the CCF banner by Donald MacDonald."[73]

One thing that had not changed was the tendency for the NDP and Tories to gang up on the Liberal leader. Wintermeyer, a sometimes staunch conservative who normally exuded the gentlemanly air of a Leslie Frost or a Louis St. Laurent, was completely out of character during the campaign. Party advisers told him to be direct, aggressive, and colourful, not unlike a Mitch Hepburn, and designed his speeches accordingly. So in addition to slinging mud, Wintermeyer called Robarts a "puppet" of the insurance industry, a "liar" for exaggerating his government's achievements, and a "bigot" for not having made French mandatory in the schools. But Wintermeyer was no Mitch Hepburn, and coming from him these sometimes outrageous comments – reminiscent of Walter Thompson in 1951 – seemed incredible. Moreover, his talk of economic planning, creating a more humane society, and reducing the influence of big business on politics, often delivered with a JFK accent, sounded too much like the NDP, and hence smacked of pure opportunism. Surely such histrionics invited retaliation, and, indeed, MacDonald and Robarts had a field day. At one point, MacDonald attacked Wintermeyer as a creation of his speech writer, Globe reporter Harold Greer – all image, and no substance – and compared Wintermeyer to "little orphan Annie on an election tour discussing Einstein's theory." Remember, too, that the Liberal leader's credibility had already been weakened before the campaign by Justice Roach's royal commission report, issued in March, which concluded that Wintermeyer's earlier allegations regarding the attorney-general department's connections to organized crime were unfounded. Neither the NDP nor the Conservatives, in short, had reason to fear the Liberal party on election day.[74]

The NDP did, however, have reason to fear the Conservatives, for although the Tory campaign was not particularly inspiring or exciting, it did succeed in presenting Robarts in an advantageous light. When he was not turning back Wintermeyer's ludicrous statements, defending his government's record, or taking credit for Ontario's growing prosperity, the premier was seen quietly sipping coffee and eating donuts with supporters across the province. He completely ignored the NDP, observed the Globe, preferring not to get "tangled in philosophic or economic in-fighting ... with those ... formidable and earnest debaters, the New Democrats." Above all, he did not let himself get rattled by Wintermeyer's provocations, and was consistently toning down the language of his prepared speeches. As a result, the premier appeared calm, reasonable, mature, strong, and confident. Looking back, MacDonald feels that Wintermeyer "was Robarts's greatest asset: the longer the shrill [scandal] attack went on, the more attractive became the solid, chairman-of-the-board image of Robarts." Robarts' comments on policy reinforced this image of stability. In general, he simply promised expansion in all areas: health care, transportation, law enforcement, social security, education, human rights, and so on.[75]

Equally important was the fact that the Tory machine was able to surround the party's campaign with an aura of "newness," in a deliberate attempt to dispel the lingering suspicion that Robarts was the heir of an old, lethargic Tory dynasty. This was particularly important since both the Liberals and New Democrats were running more youthful candidates than in the past, perhaps hoping to cash in on the Kennedy phenomenon south of the border. Several of the NDP's candidates, for example, were young, enthusiastic left-wingers with university backgrounds, people such as Stephen Lewis in Scarborough West, Vince Kelly in Armourdale, Joe Zbitnew in Cochrane South, and Giles Endicott in St. David's – people who would, in a few years time, take over the reins from the old-time CCFers. It was this new, younger look that the Tories were up against with their rather dull and stodgy leader. Nevertheless, through heavy radio and television advertising, which emphasized the new faces and new initiatives of the Tory cabinet, "the electorate was sold on the proposition that John Robarts was the head of a new government, not simply the leader of a 20-year old regime."[76]

The NDP occasionally criticized the slick Madison Avenue techniques used to such effect by the Tories to make "Mr. Nobody" into a desirable commodity, but the fact is that all three parties were employing similar techniques at this time. The use of television, in particular, to sell party leaders and images (as opposed to party policies) had become very popular, even with the NDP. The overwhelming success of the televised founding conventions, as well as the strains that whirlwind tours placed on Tommy Douglas's health, convinced the federal NDP to devote large chunks of money to radio and television advertising in the 1962 and 1963 federal elections, and to employ the services of a public relations expert in the person of Morden Lazarus.[77] The Ontario NDP soon followed suit. In October 1962, it established a Public Relations Committee, which began consulting with public relations experts to determine the best approach to voters in terms of party image, leadership image, and the "marketing" of its program; in a highly revealing comment on the changing times, the Committee saw itself as "something similar to a brain trust or the old Fabian group"! As a result, the party spent more time analysing public opinion and the basis of its electoral support so that image and policy emphasis could be fashioned accordingly.[78]

For the NDP, the 1963 provincial election was really the first test of these new techniques. In April, the Council concluded that "we should get the candidates known across the Province by [the] use of pictures, etc.," especially television, which the riding associations felt was a more effective tool than door-to-door canvassing. Approximately 40 percent of the Provincial Office's election budget, therefore, was used for television and radio advertising.[79] In addition, the party hired a communications expert, Ken Goldstein, to do public relations work during the campaign, such as designing attractive leaflets and coordinating press releases. The party's new emphasis on properly packaging itself was expressed most clearly in its analysis of the 1963 federal election. "No real progress has been made in breaking down the traditional support of the 'old line parties,'" declared the Council. "Our policy and program won't get us elected; we must look for and devise other tactics to win ... We must start looking at the electorate as [sic] what they are and not what we want them to be ... We must use the element of personality more, (use more of our people, etc.) and put forward the fact that our people would be cabinet material if elected."[80] Certainly the NDP still placed much faith in conveying its policies and in building basic organization, but by 1963 it was clearly more willing to employ modern electioneering techniques that appealed to voters' emotions instead of their minds. For a party that had always placed the intellectual appeal first, this was a noteworthy change. That the Tories went even farther in this respect during the campaign of 1963 was only a reflection of their more extensive resources, and the fact that their leader was more adept at adjusting to the new techniques than were his opponents. As the NDP Election Committee said in its review of the campaign, the major expenditure was on the "utilization of the mass media, press, radio and TV"; it noted, too, that "it goes without saying that this is a recognized need and only lack of finances limited us in this area."[81] In several respects, therefore, the NDP's 1963 provincial campaign marked a shift from the old-style politics to the new.

The success of the Conservative party's campaign became clear on election day. The Tories increased their majority from seventy-one to seventy-seven seats and their popular vote from 46 to 48 percent, thus reversing the gradual decline in support during Frost's last years as premier. The Liberals gained two seats, up to twenty-four, despite a 2 percent drop in popular support, but Wintermeyer lost his own seat in Waterloo North. The NDP once again finished third, but with two additional seats, bringing the total to seven. Its popular vote, however, was 1 percent below what the CCF received in 1959. In the legislature, it lost the veteran Tommy Thomas from the strong union riding of Oshawa, but added three new faces: Stephen Lewis, who had built up an impressive riding organization over the summer, in Scarborough West; Fred Young, the veteran organizer and North York Councillor, in Yorkview; and Ted Freeman, a small businessperson, in Fort William.[82]

As for a post-mortem analysis by the party, there was an almost eerie silence. Even the NDP's official report on the election simply alluded to general problems that had plagued the NDP since its founding and that would have to be corrected before real progress was made – things such as inadequate finances, lapsed memberships, too little support from union members, a poor party image, insufficient media coverage, policies too similar to those of other parties – without getting down to specifics. Perhaps this was because the NDP had not expected to do better, and so was not driven to explain its defeat in specific terms. As MacDonald states in his memoirs, "The party approached the election with moderately higher hopes ... There had not been time to consolidate the wider public support which the new party had evoked, [but] it was hoped that the popular vote would increase, and produce a few more seats."[83] So while the NDP was disappointed, and certainly frustrated, it was not shocked. The loss in 1963 was, indeed, a consequence of the general problems cited above. But to this list one could add the Election Committee's delay in getting literature out to the ridings; MacDonald's occasional scandal mongering; the persistence of the Communist smear campaign in some ridings; low voter turnout in several industrial wards; public complacency based on both economic revival and the heat of a summer campaign; and the war of words between Robarts and Wintermeyer, which focused voter attention away from the NDP.[84]

The two years from the founding convention of the Ontario NDP in October 1961 to the 1963 provincial election are very exciting ones for those concerned with describing and understanding the evolution of the "new" party. They were filled with high drama and collective fortitude every step of the way. But it was the sort of excitement that the much heralded new party could easily have done without as it tried to get its bearings in those first few months of life. The string of debilitating elections; the Argue defection; the internal strife, especially between labour and non-labour elements; and the attacks on the party from without – all were major challenges. And each accounts in some part for the failure of the NDP to become the alternative party in Ontario.

In addition to this adversity, the period was striking for its mixture of continuity and change within the party. Much remained the same in the transition from the CCF to the NDP. The broadly based image of the New Party had failed to attract, as full members, significant numbers of farmers, unionists, or "liberal-minded" persons; relations with labour remained cool, at best; the party continued to concentrate its resources in key ridings; and the basic ideology of the party persisted. On the other hand, there was change. The NDP adopted a bold, deficit-financing policy toward basic organization, combined with a more positive, sophisticated approach to the voters; the affiliated wing of the party grew quickly, thereby strengthening the financial base of the party; the party program underwent subtle changes that de-emphasized economic policy and public ownership, thus making it less distinct from the Liberal party; the Provincial Office gave more organizing responsibility to area councils and riding associations; and finally, the period witnessed the emergence of a new breed of young, aggressive party members who infused the movement with a greater sense of realism, especially about what it took to win.[85] But despite these differences, there was one inescapable constant: in terms of its proportion of popular support and legislative representation, the NDP was as deep into Ontario's political wilderness in late 1963 as it had been exactly twelve years before.

10 Conclusion

This study has focused on the history of the Ontario CCF/NDP during what was, if one excludes the inevitable growing pains of the 1930s, the party's worst period. Between 1951 and 1963, the CCF/NDP experienced few highs and many lows. Despite the rapid growth in the province's population after the war, party membership levels fell sharply and did not reach their pre-1951 level until late in the period; party morale, especially at the grass roots, experienced a similar downward trend; money was hard to come by; and election after election yielded little in the way of popular support or legislative representation. These were indeed, as Marjorie Pinney recalls, "desperate" years.[1]

The rapid decline of the Ontario CCF/NDP and the long period of stagnation that followed undermines several myths about postwar Ontario politics. Scholars of the subject are fond of asserting two things in particular: first, that the postwar period, at least until the mid-1980s, was one of remarkable political stability; and second, that the province's three-party system was born at the start of this period.[2] But the dismal experience of the Ontario CCF/NDP after World War Two (not to mention its quick return to respectability in the late 1960s) clearly weakens both of these characterizations. Without putting too fine a point on it, it is worth keeping in mind that in 1948 when the CCF/NDP again formed the Official Opposition, it captured 27 percent of the popular vote and twenty-one seats; by 1963, however, it had dropped to 16 percent and only seven seats, and this in an enlarged legislature – hardly a portrait of stability. By the same token, it is hard to discern the existence of a veritable three-party system in Ontario during this period. For such a system to exist, the least competitive of the three parties would have had to be at least a "minor" party. McCormick defines minor parties as those receiving between 15 and 30 percent of the popular vote, while Gagnon and Tanguay define them as "those political formations that present candidates in federal or provincial elections but fail to obtain one of the two largest blocs of seats in the legislature."[3] By both definitions – each being fairly generous in scope – the CCF can, indeed, be considered a minor party, but just barely so. A less generous definition, one that requires a minor party to be truly competitive, would yield a different conclusion. In a recent article, for example, MacDonald defines a "mature" three-party system as one in which *any of the three parties* might win."[4] This is a more reasonable definition, and yet Macdonald repeats the conventional wisdom that such a system was born in 1943. It seems more plausible to argue that the CCF was a fringe party in the period 1951 to 1963 and, therefore, that the competitive three-party system that marks Ontario as unique among provincial party systems in Canada did not appear in earnest until 1967, when the NDP tripled its seats and attracted the support of one in four Ontario voters; thereafter, and until it formed Ontario's first NDP government in 1990, it held an average of 25 seats and 26 percent of the popular vote.[5]

If its uncompetitiveness in postwar Ontario politics makes the label of even a minor party hard to apply to the CCF/NDP, the organization's internal weakness makes its characterization as a genuine "mass" party just as difficult, even though such a characterization has been consistently applied. Duverger and others use several criteria to distinguish a mass party from a "cadre" party, such as a high and stable membership, a high level of organizational activity between elections, a preoccupation with political education, a broad financial base, substantial links with mass organizations such as labour unions, and a tendency over time toward bureaucratization and oligarchy.[6] During the years 1951 to 1963, however, the CCF/NDP falls short on all counts. Its membership levels were anything but high and stable (see Appendix); little in the way of grass-roots activity could be seen between elections; political education was important but not paramount; the party's financial base narrowed, relying more heavily on ad hoc contributions from large labour bodies; links with mass organizations, including unions, were weak; and no noticeable shift occurred toward a more bureaucratic, oligarchical party structure. Of course the CCF/NDP cannot be labelled a cadre party either, given its essentially democratic and highly articulated structure. Nevertheless, the circumstances of the postwar years did cause the party to diverge quite noticeably from the mass party model.

Beyond these iconoclasms stands the decrepit state of the Ontario CCF/NDP in these years – a central theme of this study and one that requires little additional comment. What *is* worthy of synthesis and further analysis, however, are the reasons why this was so. Certainly the Cold War atmosphere of the period was one reason. The widespread fear of communism tended to mute notions of class conflict, government intervention, or the socio-economic equality upon which much of the CCF/NDP's philosophy and program was based. In fact, most Ontarians called for an "end to ideology" and for a united front in the face of the so-called international communist threat. Dissent was viewed as dangerous, even subversive, especially if it took the form of left-wing agitation. Without question, the CCF/NDP suffered greatly as a result of this widespread phobia – as did left-wing parties throughout the Western world – and even more so when enemies of the party openly linked it with the communists at home, as they did before and during the 1955 election and at various times in 1962 and 1963. During the pre-Cold War period, when the ideological battle lines in Western society were drawn largely between capitalism and socialism – with the former discredited and the latter emerging as more appealing – the CCF made gains. When the ideological struggle was redefined in the postwar years, as being one between freedom and totalitarianism, the CCF suffered losses.

Another key factor in the decline of the CCF was the tremendous economic prosperity Ontarians enjoyed between 1945 and 1975, a period in which unemployment averaged below 4 percent, real incomes tripled, and the amount of available leisure time in which to enjoy these gains increased substantially.[7] But the relationship between economic growth and the popularity of left-wing parties is not that straightforward. The traditional model of this relationship posits that economic growth is inversely related to the success of parties that promise to take the economy in new directions.[8] Even intuitively this makes sense, for there would seem to be little reason for voters to support a socialist party in times of significant economic growth. Recent studies, however, have questioned this theory as far as Canada is concerned. Monroe and Erikson, for example, found that although economic developments had a significant impact on the support given to third parties in Canadian federal elections between 1954 and 1974, the relationship between economic growth and CCF/NDP support was the *opposite* of that predicted by the traditional model.[9] Numerous others, as well, have made the point that the CCF/NDP has done better in *goods times* than in bad, such as during the mid-forties, early seventies, and late eighties. In the end, one is left with the conclusion that economic conditions are a rather poor predictor of CCF/NDP support.

This study, while it does not purport to provide a detailed analysis of the relationship between the business cycle and CCF/NDP support, nevertheless tends to confirm the conventional model, namely that prosperity hurt the CCF/NDP electorally. After having endured six long years of sacrifice, self-restraint, and government regulation in the name of noble principles during World War Two, Ontarians were in no mood come peacetime to create a socialist heaven on earth, especially one directed by bureaucrats. Most wanted only to drive their new cars down one of Ontario's many new expressways, mow their suburban lawns, or watch their new television sets. And many more could afford to do these "frivolous" things because jobs were plentiful, wages were rising, and inflation was low. "We seemed to wither on the vine [in the 1950s]," recalls MacDonald, "partly by reason of the whole atmosphere of the time and the apathy of the Eisenhower period ... Everybody just wanted to relax. The normal apathy of the electorate *vis-à-vis* politics became even more pronounced with relatively good times."[10]

But clearly economic growth *by itself* is an insufficient explanation for the party's decline, as the more recent studies prove. To account for the apparent contradictoriness of the studies surrounding this question, we need to look more closely at how the CCF/NDP was perceived by the voters at different times in its history. It could be argued, for example, that as long as the party's image was largely that of an *economic reform-oriented* party, economic growth tended to *hurt* the party's support. This stands to reason, for voters during good times are unlikely to elect a party whose main goal is to restructure the economy. Such was the case in the period 1951 to 1963, when the CCF/NDP in Ontario and across much of Canada still emphasized comprehensive economic planning as the answer to society's ills. Since becoming the NDP, however, the party's emphasis has shifted. Realizing the unpopularity of its economic agenda, particularly the concept of state-owned industries, the NDP devoted greater attention to social security issues, such as medicare and pensions, and expanded social services.[11] In any case, the NDP was perceived by voters as being very good on social policy concerns, although less competent with respect to economic questions.[12] This, in turn, would account for the success the party enjoyed across Canada during the still prosperous years of the early 1970s and the renewed prosperity of the late 1980s. Studies show that, in good times, voters seem to be quite comfortable with supporting a democratic socialist party that emphasizes social programs; they know these programs can be afforded. As Monroe and

Erikson note, "Support for the NDP increases as personal income and employment rise, suggesting the NDP's social welfare programs may be viewed as luxury goods reserved for times of economic prosperity."[13] Depending on how a democratic socialist party's agenda is perceived by the electorate, therefore, economic growth can either benefit or harm the party.

But if this theory is valid, how do we explain the massive support for the CCF during the rapidly rising prosperity of World War Two, when the CCF was clearly an economic reform-oriented party, its ideology still firmly rooted in the Regina Manifesto's call to replace capitalism with a more state-managed system? This can be explained by the unique circumstances of the war, when recent memories of the Depression and widespread fear of postwar recession made voters favour comprehensive economic planning such as the CCF proposed. This feeling of uncertainty about the future simply delayed the negative impact of renewed prosperity on the CCF's popularity. As the fear of recession was slowly dissipated by the tremendous growth of the postwar years, so was support for the CCF. By the early fifties, the CCF's talk of imminent recession and comprehensive planning seemed very much out of place. The only province in which the party was able to retain its popularity was Saskatchewan, and this was due to the Douglas administration's de-emphasis on traditional socialist economic policies. As McLeod and McLeod note in their recent biography of the CCF/NDP leader, "Douglas came to symbolize a government that was activist rather than overtly socialist" in its approach to the economy.[14] In short, barring the presence of unusual historical circumstances, it is possible that economic growth tends to harm support for socialist parties advocating fundamental economic reforms – the Ontario CCF/NDP situation after the war – while benefiting those favouring government-run, redistributive, social security programs.[15]

It is impossible, in any event, to explain the CCF/NDP's weakened state in the period 1951 to 1963 without reference to international and domestic currents. And yet, so little mention is made of these influences in the existing literature on the party. Instead, these studies tend to focus on internal party dynamics to explain the party's decline, whether they be poor organization, "secularization," low morale, or the tensions between movement and party adherents. Although some of these internal factors may explain why the CCF/NDP never became more popular at any one point in time, they do not explain the abyss into which the party fell after 1950 – not just in Ontario but across Canada. The CCF lost seats, members, and popular support in all provinces after the war; even the indomitable Saskatchewan CCF suffered: as its membership fell to less than one-third its 1944 level, it lost fourteen seats in the 1948 election.[16] Federally, the CCF went from an all-time high of 29 percent of popular support in a September 1943 Gallup Poll to only 9 percent by 1958.[17] In view of this widespread and rapid descent, Walter Young's powerfully alluring statement that "the failure of the party was largely through the crippling effects of the movement" is far too reductionist. Furthermore, and this is key, many of the internal factors contributing to the party's decline were themselves simply products of external conditions, such as the Cold War and postwar prosperity. Looking at the party's weak organization, for example, it is clear that the growing east-west tension was very demoralizing for grass-roots CCFers, especially insofar as it reduced popular support. This, in turn, bred apathy and indifference among the activists. The result was a weakening of efforts to sign up or renew memberships, raise money, hold meetings, and find candidates, and in many ridings the party organization fell into serious disrepair. The postwar economic boom can be said to have had the same harmful effect.[18]

Once set in motion, the process of organizational collapse was hard to reverse. Fewer members and financial contributions meant a smaller pool of constituency workers, funds, and capable candidates from which the party could draw during elections. This meant a poorer showing, notwithstanding the unfavourable "climate" of the period; repeated defeats bred further disillusionment and apathy. While strong organization is no guarantee of political success, a weak organization will, in many instances, spell political failure, as it did in this case. "Between elections," notes Carty, "the life of the party is in the hands of its local membership. If they are keen and busy, it generally prospers; if they are apathetic and inactive, it is more likely to atrophy."[19] Even signs of renewed spirit and vitality *between* elections, however, rarely translated into overall organizational expansion or electoral success, as growth in some areas was inevitably matched by decline in areas that provincial organizers had been forced to neglect. Hopes would be revived somewhat as an election approached, resulting in a flurry of last-minute preparations and an improvement in membership levels and finances. Expectations would be further inflated by promises of PAC assistance or a juicy election theme, such as a government scandal. But this eleventh-hour activity was never enough to stave off defeat, after which the cycle would resume.

The fact that the CCF/NDP declined and stagnated in this period, and that this uniform decline was, at root, the result of macro variables such as the economy and foreign affairs has implications for the study of Canadian voting behaviour. What the postwar experience of the CCF/NDP suggests is that students of politics should not exaggerate the influence of relatively static micro variables such as class, ethnicity, region, and political culture when seeking to explain Canadian voting behaviour; clearly, the decline and stagnation of the party in this case cut across such sociological, territorial, and cultural cleavages. Some attention must be given to macro forces, particularly when, as many social scientists readily concede, micro variables seem to have had (and continue to have) only a marginal influence on the political ideas and behaviour of Canadian voters, and party loyalties in Canada were becoming increasingly fluid.[20] Traditional analyses of voting behaviour have been criticized, as well, for failing to explain the rapid shifts in voting patterns from one election to the next.[21] While micro variables undoubtedly *mediated* macro ones – a good example being the particular harshness with which Canada's first-past-the-post electoral system distorted the Ontario CCF's legislative representation in the 1950s, thus exaggerating its decline – they were of minor import when weighed against the high levels of prosperity and international tension that prevailed in this period, or against other phenomena specific to the era.[22]

The overriding influence of postwar national and international influences on the fate of Canadian socialism may also provide the basis for questioning a popular theory concerning the evolution of Ontario's party system and political culture in the modern era. The theory, first presented by political scientist John Wilson some twenty years ago, holds that urbanization and industrialization, and in particular the growth and concentration of the working class, will tend to benefit social democratic parties because of their more secular, progressive, class-oriented appeal.[23] In view of the province's rapidly expanding urban-industrial base after the war, one might therefore have expected the Ontario CCF's popularity to *increase* in the urban centres.[24] Yet this was not the case. The CCF's popular vote in those ridings that grew quickest economically and demographically after the war fell at least as much, and probably more, than its vote in the rest of the province.[25] Why this was so requires a far more sophisticated analysis than can be presented here. It may be, as some have suggested, that proletarian support for the CCF in the growing urban areas was offset by the even more rapid growth of the new middle class, a class more predisposed to liberalism than democratic socialism.[26] Just as likely, though, is the uniformly negative effect that unprecedented prosperity and Cold War paranoia had on the party's potential supporters.

This is not to discount the impact of key structural change on CCF support. It *is* possible, for example, that socio-economic changes affected CCF support in *rural* Ontario as they did in rural areas elsewhere. Studies of the CCF out West have concluded that the loss of the party's rural base of support after the war was due largely to the decline of the small family farm and the rise of larger, more mechanized farms, where farmers came to see themselves more as entrepreneurs and "less as victims of capitalism," particularly with the return of prosperity.[27] Ontario farmers underwent a similar transformation, and electoral returns for the ridings closest to the Hamilton-Toronto nexus in the period 1951 to 1963 indicate that this transformation may have exacerbated the CCF's declining support in rural Ontario.[28] It should be remembered, though, that outside of the isolated mining towns of the north, the party's rural base was not very significant to begin with.

Another influential factor in the CCF/NDP's fall to fringe party status was, without question, the flexibility – some would say opportunism – of the Ontario Conservative party. If, as some have argued, it is true that third parties flourish when traditional parties fail to represent, or are unresponsive to, the interests of large segments of the electorate,[29] then it is equally true that traditional parties flourish – and protest parties suffer – when they *are* responsive to new public concerns. And Ontario Tories were nothing if not responsive during these years. During the war and for a short while after, Ontarians joined many others in the Western world in embracing the concept of "economic planning," part of a relatively new economic doctrine called Keynesianism, that emphasized the role of government in maintaining near-full employment through regulation and manipulation of the economy; alongside this emerged the belief that governments also had an obligation to buffer the individual from the vissicitudes of life by providing a social safety net for those in need.[30] The meteoric rise of the CCF across Canada in the early forties owed almost everything to this new way of thinking.

Unfortunately for the CCF, the traditional parties proved quite adept at accommodating themselves to the new intellectual climate. One month after the Ontario CCF's stunning second-place finish in the 1943 election, the new premier, George Drew, issued his now-famous "Twenty-two Point Program," promising cradle-to-grave social security and a greater role for government in the economy. It included universal health care insurance, income supplements to mothers and the elderly, a substantial increase in funding for schools and hospitals, increased encouragement and regulation of the province's farming and natural resource sectors, extensive public works projects, and even greater protection to organized labour. It was a far-reaching program for its time, strikingly similar to what the CCF had been preaching for years; and the rapid implementation of a good part of it helped the Tories win re-election in 1945 and again in 1948.[31]

When Frost took over from Drew in 1949 he continued where his predecessor had left off, pouring millions of dollars into the province's infrastructure and social services. Provincial spending on goods, services, and capital formation as a percentage of the Gross Provincial Product increased from 7.4 percent in 1951 to 13.5 percent in 1963, with the bulk of this going into education, health care, and transfers to individuals.[32] Admittedly such measures were far from the sort of comprehensive economic planning or social security that had been foreseen during the latter part of the war – "economic planning in this broad sense did not survive the immediate post-war years," notes Rea.[33] But, then, by the 1950s, the public mood had changed. A buoyant economy and growing suspicion of centralized economic planning, the latter abetted by the Cold War atmosphere of the day, had made the CCF's program largely passé.[34] A more moderate, pragmatic form of state intervention was in vogue. Focusing increasingly on creating the conditions favourable to private investment and on piecemeal improvements to the social security net, this approach also fit more neatly into the province's long-standing "progressive conservative" political culture.[35] The successive Frost administrations accommodated the new mood well, or at least well enough to get re-elected time and again. The CCF/NDP, meanwhile, came dangerously close to confirming American historian Richard Hofstadter's well-known maxim that "third parties, like bees, having stung, must die."[36]

In addition to the Tory party's skill in stealing the CCF/NDP's thunder, there was the immense personal popularity and cunning of Leslie Frost, another key factor specific to the period in question. By carefully cultivating the down-to-earth, folksy public image that was his trademark and diffusing his opponents' assaults with his fulsome stock of charm and anodynes, he carried the Conservative party to massive victories in these years. Donald MacDonald explains:

There were many Leslie Frosts. One, the most familiar to the public, was the grandfather figure, usually viewed from afar, but seen in closer proximity only at meetings or on television, rarely attacking his political opponents, but rather chatting about local history and the merits of the province of Ontario in general ... Another was the charmer, who subjected visiting delegations ... to a process of political seduction that became legendary ... They were greeted with warm hand-shakes, softened with the friendly arm-around-the-shoulder confidentiality, and out-talked from start to finish ... I dubbed him the Great Tranquilizer.[37]

Frost's successor, John Robarts, was also a very capable and appealing figure. Although less the politician than Frost, Robarts' low-key, pragmatic management style was appropriate to the even bigger role government was being asked to play by the early sixties. Both Tory leaders were well served, as well, by capable provincial organizers: Alex McKenzie and Eddie Goodman under Frost, and Ernie Jackson under Robarts.[38]

To some extent, therefore, the decline and stagnation of the CCF/NDP was due to the exceptional political and organizational leadership with which it had to contend in those years.

In view of these powerful exogenous factors – the Cold War, economic prosperity, and co-optation of the Left's agenda – factors clearly beyond the party's control, it is difficult to see how the CCF/NDP could have done anything differently to improve its position in this bleak period. "Looking back," David Lewis states in his memoirs, "I am confirmed in the feeling I had at the time that the CCF decline could not be reversed. With MacDonald as the leading CCF organizer and Weisbach as head of political action in the CCL, our talent simply could not be improved upon."[39] What is more, the CCF tried almost everything to revitalize itself. Yet the impact on its popular support was minimal. Perhaps if it had harped less on government immorality, and thus appeared less negative and self-righteous, it could have helped its own cause. But it is hard to believe that this was an important factor in curbing the CCF/NDP support. It is difficult to prove the effect either way, of course, but it was more likely a positive force. First, in most cases the party was quickly vindicated. Second, it brought the CCF/NDP much-needed publicity. And finally, the series of scandals tarnished the government's image and helped diminish its popularity in the late 1950s.

Another noteworthy theme in this period was internal dissent. To some extent, however, this is to be expected, for left-wing parties have traditionally suffered from divisions over methods and ideology and other CCF/NDP provincial parties experienced their share after the war.[40] Moreover, dissent only became prominent in the Ontario CCF/NDP for brief moments – in 1952, 1956, 1958–59, and 1962–63. Generally speaking, the party was very united in these years, a quite remarkable feat given the number of its electoral setbacks. Nevertheless, there was always a portion of the membership that was dissatisfied with the direction it thought the party was taking and, at times, this dissatisfaction would flare up. In 1952, the born-again Ginger Group opposed what it felt was the bureaucratization and centralization of the movement. Partially rooted in actual developments, these nostalgic longings for the "movement" were largely shaped by Cold War paranoia. In 1956, a small coterie of CCFers criticized the Winnipeg Declaration as a dilution of democratic socialist principles; they also questioned the high-handed methods used to expedite its passage by the national convention of that year. In 1958–59, a much larger number of party members, especially in northern Ontario and among old-time CCFers, opposed the decision to join with organized labour to form a "new" party. Like their predecessors in the Ginger Group, they feared that power within the party was shifting from the grass roots to higher levels, particularly to union leaders, and that, in general, the essential character of the movement was being transformed. These fears were temporarily swept away in the euphoria of the NDP's birth, but they resurfaced in 1962–63, when it became apparent that the promise of the new party had not materialized but the earlier predictions of labour domination had.

If one is looking for common elements in these instances of dissent, it can be said, first of all, that CCF/NDP dissenters tended to share a fear of change, especially when that change appeared to undermine the key "movement" aspects of the party: the role of political education, the democratic socialist ideology, and party democracy. These were the true conservatives of the party – the "tories" as Ken Bryden calls them.[41] Furthermore, their fears were often the result of misperceptions shaped by historical circumstances, be it the Cold War of the early fifties or the growing anti-labour sentiment later on. Finally, the evidence strongly suggests that, in all cases, these fears were either groundless or quite exaggerated.

The third theme to note is the CCF/NDP's attempt to broaden its organizational base among farmers, organized labour, and the middle class. Actually, the efforts to attract the middle class, or the "liberal-minded" as they were called, were half-hearted at best. Although most of the party's top leaders came from middle-class families of ministers, social workers, teachers, and lawyers, as did a substantial percentage of the rank and file, the CCF/NDP did not target the middle class, either in its election propaganda or its organizational efforts. There was, for example, no middle-class equivalent of the CCF Trade Union Committee or Farm Committee within the party's organizational apparatus. There was, it is true, the Woodsworth Foundation, which had at first hoped to attract middle-class members to the CCF; but this body was not formally part of the CCF and, after 1952, it shifted its educational emphasis toward the working class. Indeed, it was not until the new party movement of the late fifties that the liberal-minded people officially become a target group, and, even then, as this study has demonstrates, the effort to mobilize their almost meteoric rise in support of a "new party" was mostly symbolic. Any possibility that large numbers of liberal-minded people would join the NDP after its birth, moreover, was likely dashed by the continuing organizational neglect and widespread rumours of labour domination.

Instead, the CCF/NDP reached out in earnest to other occupational groups, such as farmers and blue-collar workers, groups with mass organizations in place that could more easily be tapped for support and that were more likely to sympathize with the party's philosophy and program. The attempt to attract farmers, however, was largely unsuccessful. The suspicion among farmers that the CCF had a hidden, communist agenda; their long-standing antagonism toward organized labour; the non-partisanship of the leading farm organizations in the province; and the CCF/NDP's shortage of rural organizers – all contributed to the party's perpetually low membership and weak performance in rural ridings.

The party enjoyed much more success among organized labour, but even here its record was unenviable. The CCF's relationship with labour, always rather tenuous, began to deteriorate in the early 1950s. Fears in some quarters of the party that labour was trying to gain an unduly large voice in party affairs – one that many felt would render the CCF less democratic and less socialist – without first committing itself more formally and permanently to the party, were met with resentment from the many non-affiliated unions who felt that the CCF, although quite willing to take their money and assistance during elections, was unwilling to give them a say in matters of policy, candidate selection, and party affairs generally. There was truth in each perspective. As the decade progressed this mutual antagonism became less overt, but did not disappear altogether. It resurfaced briefly in northern Ontario during the New Party development, at a time when unions were increasingly viewed as corrupt and violent, and grew to fever pitch in the twenty-four months following the NDP's founding convention, as old fears of "labour domination" took hold once again.

This mutual antagonism naturally soured relations at all levels between the two organizations. Even during the New Party development, the essence of which was to finally make labour an integral part of a "new" left-wing realignment, the two sides had a hard time cooperating and pooling resources. The serious conflict within the OCNP over part-time organizers was ample testimony to the mutual suspicion and organizational rivalry between labour and the party, as each side scrambled to ensure itself sufficient representation at the founding conventions. In the months following the birth of the NDP, relations worsened. Unfounded charges that labour was controlling the new party, combined with the reluctance of labour to get involved with the party, led many party members to question the wisdom of the NDP-labour connection. In the end, people like Doug Fisher, Arnold Peters, and Hazen Argue, who predicted that the New Party would not mean a more organic CCF-labour relationship and that the New Party would only gain the bad image that a closer association with labour entailed, were correct.

In the final analysis, the strained relations between labour and the CCF/NDP meant that for the period 1951 to 1963 joint political action was restricted to election campaigns. Although some informal consultation *between* elections did occur at the highest level, and even some formal cooperation through the TUC for a short while, it rarely extended to the local level. Where unionists did get involved with CCF at the riding level, they more often than not formed a majority in the riding association; in fact, then, there was little mixing of unionists and non-unionists. After 1952, moreover, the PAC seemed more attuned to municipal politics than to either provincial or federal politics. Thus Zakuta's assertion that "the dominant trend throughout the whole period was the growing role of the trade unions in party affairs and the steady meshing of the two organizations in conducting the operations of the CCF" is not very persuasive.[42]

What is sadly ironic about the poor state of affairs between the party and labour in this period is that it probably represented the high point in CCF/NDP-labour relations. Since 1963, when the rate of union affiliation to the party peaked, union support for the NDP has apparently been falling.[43] The recent actions of the Ontario NDP government with respect to the "social contract" and the dismal showing of the federal NDP in the 1993 election have only aggravated the problem, alienating segments of the province's labour movement to the point where parts of it have officially withdrawn their support.[44] The relatively poor record of the CCF/NDP in its efforts to integrate organized labour with the party is all the more unfortunate in view of a recent study suggesting that closer integration, particularly union affiliation to the party, would translate into more votes from union members.[45]

Several additional points are worth noting to round out the picture of the party's relationship with labour. First, although mutual suspicion and resentment were key reasons for the sporadic cooperation between both sides, they were not the only reasons. Union leaders, particularly in the immediate postwar years, were very busy with their own union affairs – establishing new unions, winning the right to check off union dues, negotiating contracts with employers – and this usually left little time for political action. As a result, the party was regularly deprived of capable local leaders, candidates, and organizational assistance. Furthermore, union leaders sympathetic to the CCF were often reluctant to disrupt newly established (and sometimes well-established) unions by introducing the always divisive issue of political action. And where political action *was* encouraged, by local PACs for example, rank-and-file unionists frequently complained of having the CCF shoved down their throats. All of these factors militated against sustained and substantial political action by the labour movement and, in turn, gave rise to the sometimes bitter feeling among CCFers that when it came to helping the party, labour was all talk and no action.

The second point is that despite its arm's-length relationship with the CCF/NDP, labour's contribution to the party must not be understated. Many of the party's members and local leaders, for example, were unionists, and they often used what influence they had in their own organization to win adherents to the party. As well, in election after election, the OFL-PAC raised large sums of money for the CCF/NDP (most of which paid for its advertising), distributed leaflets, provided candidates and organizers, and brought out the union vote on election day. Bryden points to the generosity of the Steelworkers, in particular; if they had not agreed in 1952 to pay the salaries of the party's only full-time organizers, Ames and Young, he doubts the CCF would have survived.[46] Finally, the labour movement played a leading role in the formation of the NDP, as seen in the large number of union delegates at the founding convention and the sudden rise in affiliations that followed.

Third, the argument that feelings of tension were a significant feature of the labour-CCF/NDP relationship between 1951 and 1963 does not appear in the existing studies of either the Ontario party or the national party. Neither Morley nor Zakuta, for example, deals with the issue directly, although they strongly imply that compatibility and cooperation were touchstones of the relationship. Horowitz, while conceding that relations between labour and the party were poor in the *early* fifties, suggests that – at the highest levels, at least – the two sides enjoyed an increasingly warm and close relationship thereafter, culminating in the joining of hands under the NDP banner in 1961. What this study has shown, however, is that the tensions which emerged forcefully in the early 1950s persisted and were manifested just as forcefully during the New Party development and the honeymoon that followed.

Having said this, some qualification is necessary, for it is clear that party leaders at the provincial level did not harbour strong feelings against labour and, in fact, saw the alliance as a prerequisite to the CCF/NDP becoming a major force in provincial politics. Instead, much of the anti-labour sentiment seems to have been concentrated at the local level, particularly among the sizeable minority of old-time CCFers who felt they had a vested interest in preserving, unchanged, the party they had done so much to build. As for the majority of (non-union) party members, labour was likely viewed with indifference or, at worst, grudging acceptance. This would account for the New Party's proposal being accepted almost unanimously by the membership, but without much enthusiasm and, as the later debate over voting rights for affiliated members demonstrated, with a good deal of anxiety. In short, the tension between labour and the CCF/NDP in this period should not be overstated. But neither should it be understated.

Finally, it should be noted that the factors cited above to explain the arm's-length relationship between labour and the party do not necessarily explain why most members of Ontario's working class did not vote CCF/NDP. They only explain why union leaders and their followers who sympathized with the CCF/NDP – that is, who voted in favour of resolutions endorsing the party at each OFL convention, or who voted for the party on election day – did not cooperate more closely and regularly with the party in the period 1951 to 1963. The more general issue of working class political loyalties has been dealt with elsewhere.[47]

The most important theme in the evolution of the CCF/NDP in this period, contrary to the conventional wisdom, is *not* that the party became less of a "movement" and more of a "party" over time, but that its evolution was marked above all by *centrally directed efforts to rebuild and expand the party's basic organization by whatever means necessary*, whether these were "movement"-type methods or "party"-type methods. The standard interpretation, as revealed in the words of its leading proponent, Walter Young, affirms that "the increasing attention that was paid to electoral activity, the increasing emphasis on organization, and the lessened emphasis on education marked the decline of the movement aspect of the CCF and the pre-dominance of the party aspect."[48] This explanation does not seem to apply, however, to the Ontario CCF/NDP in the period 1951 to 1963. First, the attention paid to organization (and, by extension, elections), defined by Young and others to exclude political education, did not increase in these years. In fact, depending on the circumstances, edu-cation was sometimes emphasized over other activities. The rank and file spent a good deal of time, for example, discussing drafts of the party's 1955, 1959, and 1962 programs, as well as the Winnipeg Declaration and drafts of the New Party constitution and program. This enthusiastic, widespread participation at the grass-roots level served the party's organizational purposes well, insofar as it stimulated interest in the party, increased understanding of democratic socialism, and, in general, motivated members to do more. At other times, mem-bership recruitment and fund-raising – that is, basic organization – were emphasized over education. This was especially the case in 1952–53, when the party was trying to recover from the significant loss of members and money preceding the 1951 election, and during the development of the New Party, when it was struggling to ensure that it would enter the New Party with a strong membership base.

Another criterion employed by proponents of the movement/party thesis to support the view that the CCF/NDP paid more attention to organization than to education is the number of paid employees working out of the Provincial Office. And, related to this, is the distribution of organizing responsibility within the party. Zakuta, for instance, argues forcefully that the party was becoming more bureaucratic in this period. But in fact, the number of organizers tended to fluctuate depending on the party's financial resources. In 1952, there were two full-time provincial organizers. For a while in 1954, there were four. For the remainder of the decade, however, the staff was again reduced to two. And it stayed at that level until 1962, when the number of organizers was expanded to six, thanks in small part to the influx of funds for the regional organizer plan – a plan not unlike the one attempted in the mid-fifties, without success. In short, the impetus to hire more organizers was not something that grew stronger in this period. The will was present from the start, the money was not. Even the 1953 decision to pay a salary to the provincial leader was purely pragmatic and did not reflect a fundamentally new orientation in the party. Because there was no guarantee that the provincial leader would be elected and thus receive a legislative stipend, as was the case with Ted Jolliffe between 1945 and 1948, and again between 1951 and 1953, the party decided that it would only be fair (and democratic), particularly in cases where the leader lacked independent financial means, to ensure his or her livelihood.

As well, it cannot be said, because greater responsibility for organizing the party was assumed by the Provincial Office in the 1950s, that the CCF/NDP was becoming a typical cadre-like party, organized, financed, and run by a small coterie of prominent individuals. There were very good reasons why this centralization occurred; there was nothing inevitable or machiavellian about it, notwithstanding the views of Michels and others who see the drive for personal power as endemic to mass parties. The Provincial Office was simply forced to assume more of the burden of fund-raising, recruiting members, promoting membership education, and so on, because fewer people at the grass-roots level were willing to do it. Rank-and-file apathy, and not the inexorable laws of party evolution, led to the centralization of responsibility in the 1950s. Moreover, rather than covet power, CCF/NDP leaders were forever trying to return the burdens of organizing the party to the local level. They finally succeeded, to some extent, with the regional organizer plan of the early 1960s, as well as the accretion of campaigning responsibilities at the constituency association and area council level.

With the exception of Morley, the movement/party theorists point, as well, to the so-called rightward shift in the party's ideology and program to support their case. But even here the standard interpretation is not helpful. It is clear from the analysis presented in the preceding chapters that the party's democratic socialist philosophy of placing human need before profit and cooperation before competition, and of redistributing wealth more equitably, remained unchanged through three programmatic revisions between 1951 and 1962. Nor did the program for achieving these ultimate goals change very much. Only in 1962 was there a de-emphasis on public ownership as a means of achieving a socialist society, combined with a less economic and less class-oriented analysis; the emphasis on government as a key instrument in achieving reform, however, was no less salient in 1962 than in 1948.

In fact the only indication that the CCF/NDP had become more opportunistic in its quest to win elections (opportunistic in the sense of subverting something essential about itself for the sake of votes), and therefore more like a typical "party," as Young defines it, was its adoption of modern electioneering techniques in 1963. These included the use of polls and slick advertising, and the increased use of radio and television; the goal here was not to "sell" the party's program or philosophy, as it had generally been in the past, but to sell a particular policy or leader according to what the polls said would win votes. The Council expressed this new direction in no uncertain terms when it stated before the 1963 provincial election that "our policy and pro- gram won't get us elected; we must look for and devise other tactics to win."[49] In other words, the CCF/NDP's intellectually based appeal was subordinated to the emotional-visual appeal of manipulative advertising.

For the most part, however, the much-heralded movement/party thesis does not explain the CCF/NDP's evolution between 1951 and 1963. Perhaps a broader time frame would yield the movement-to- party shift, although adherents would likely be hard-pressed to find examples of how, over time, the CCF subverted its basic beliefs for the sake of gaining power – this being perhaps the essential difference between a movement and a party, the rest being simply a question of tactics. Even if the concept of "movement" is defined narrowly to mean a preoccupation with preaching and discussing socialist theory over more pragmatic matters such as fund-raising and membership-recruitment, a strong case could be made that early CCF leaders, in addition to their devotion to socialist education, were also incredibly skilled grass-roots organizers and fund-raisers.[50] In the end we may well conclude, as does David Lewis, that "the CCF was never a movement which degenerated into a party; it was always both at the same time."[51] For the period 1951 to 1963 in Ontario, at least, the transformation is not very discernible.

Rather, the dominant theme, as stated, was the party's sustained effort to rebuild and expand its basic organization. The organization impulse was the engine of the CCF/NDP's evolution in this period. Virtually every action or initiative the party took – the membership drives, the fund-raising campaigns, the political education conferences, the revised programs, and even the publicity (especially the focus on government scandals) – related to the necessity of rebuilding membership and finances. In almost every case, the goal was to wrest members from their apathetic state so that they would take responsibility for organization at the constituency level; that meant holding regular meetings, electing delegates to Council and conventions, discussing party policies, finding new members and renewing old ones, raising money, establishing zone and poll committees, nominating candidates, and assembling campaign teams. Even the formation of the NDP, a federal initiative, was manipulated to serve the party's basic organizational needs of expanding the membership and financial base, even if this involved a degree of deception.

That the emphasis on basic organization was so strong in this period should come as no surprise. After all, the CCF lost almost half of its members between 1948 and 1951, and after the 1951 election lost all but two of its M.P.P.s. The implications of this for a left-wing, mass party, which depended heavily on its regular members for money, recruitment, publicity, and electioneering, were readily apparent. If the party was to avoid extinction, the only option was for it to intensify its basic organizational efforts. Consequently, the twelve years that followed mark a distinct phase in the party's history. Unlike the 1940s, when policy research and legislative performance were important elements of the party's organizational strategy, and unlike the late 1960s and beyond, when modern campaigning methods were combined with the maturation of the zone and poll structure and greater attention was given to producing party literature, the 1950s and early 1960s were heavily coloured by techniques, gimmicks, and plans aimed at reinforcing the very foundations of the party. Sometimes the methods were desperate and crude, like the CCF Brigade; sometimes rational and sophisticated, like the zone and poll structure; and sometimes grand and deceptive, like the formation of the NDP. But they were always essential.

Closely related to the "organization" theme is the dominant role played by party leaders in attempting to restore the CCF/NDP's organizational vitality. This has been alluded to above, but is worth reiterating, for there can be no question that the party owes its very survival to those individuals who were willing to take hold of the party at a most difficult time in its history. The circumstances need not be repeated, except to say that few rank-and-file members were willing to assume the burden of rebuilding the party after the collapse of the late forties, early fifties.[52] This was understandable. Even the provincial leaders could have been forgiven for joining the grass roots in their apathy and demoralization, or for abandoning the party altogether. After all, many leaders had young families and first mortgages, and with their drive and intelligence could easily have found more lucrative and secure employment in the private sector. Moreover, at a time when to be a democratic socialist was more difficult, socially, than it had ever been before, it would have been much easier to opt for political inactivity. But many did not. Instead, driven by a burning belief in the righteousness of what the movement stood for and by the loyalty and love they felt for one another, they redoubled their efforts and continued to make the sacrifices required to save the CCF/NDP from extinction. Fred Young recalls, without regret, the endless hours he spent criss-crossing the province as a CCF organizer: "You were always travelling, living in hotels, or sleeping in cots in spare rooms, and on the floor sometimes and in the back seat of the car ... trying to keep your expenses as low as you could ... It was just a case of digging in your heals, all the time. You were just struggling to keep the membership, struggling to keep leadership, and I just had the feeling all those years, up until the early '60s, of just standing there, pushing ... It was a desperate holding action."[53] On top of all this, Young had to endure the loneliness of constant travelling, the disappointment of successive electoral defeats, and a wife who, while supportive, was not altogether pleased that he had left the ministry to do CCF work. Marjorie Pinney also recalls the tribulations of the period: "The fifties, especially, were tough years. Nobody knows how close the party came to going under in Ontario in the fifties it was so bad. But it was mainly because most of us were there working our heads off ... so you admire all the people you remember from then ... I have thought that this party, if it means anything today, is here because of that group of people in that period, because we could easily have packed it in."[54] And then, of course, there was the party's chieftain, Donald MacDonald, whose Herculean feats and tireless dedication have been well documented in the foregoing pages. Morley's observation that MacDonald "almost single-handedly ... kept the party alive in the darkest days" is only a slight exaggeration.[55]

Some of the leading political theorists of this century would have us believe that what drove these individuals to make such sacrifices was a ruthless desire for power and self-aggrandizement.[56] In fact, what kept Young, Pinney, MacDonald and many others, including the small core of dedicated, grass-roots CCFers going through these tough times was, first and foremost, their unshaken belief in democratic socialism. "The Kingdom of God ... was still a beacon there that you were working towards," remembers Young.[57] Dudley Bristow, a two-time CCF candidate in Toronto and chair of the Organization Committee in the early fifties, echoes the sentiment: "The question of whether we would win wasn't important. I was elated when we did well and disappointed when we did poorly, but it didn't affect my level of activity because I believed strongly in what we were doing."[58] No doubt it was people such as Young, Pinney, Ames, MacDonald, and Bristow whom the party's prescient national secretary had in mind when he wrote, shortly after the 1951 election disaster, that CCF activists "have a conviction in the justice of their cause and the leadership and spirit necessary to tackle anew the task of building the organizational foundation which can one day win power in Ontario."[59]

Some theorists also argue that feelings of solidarity and devotion are not enough to keep a left-wing party organization alive – that there must be material incentives.[60] In fact, the other main motive of CCF/ NDP activists was *precisely* the feeling of comradery and devotion, of not wanting to let one's colleagues down by doing any less than they were for the cause. Young recalls with warm affection the "people who were willing to spend time, energy, and money to hold on to what we had," and that this inspired him to make similar sacrifices. Doc Ames was one such individual. "Everybody loved Doc," recalls Pinney. "He was always up. I never knew him to be down. He was marvellous. It was a joy to go up there [to northern Ontario] ... because you could just feel all the love and warmth. It was the kind of feeling you felt that this party was about and which was very much there all through the forties and fifties ... He exemplified the fellowship, the human love between people working for a cause. And that's what you felt with people like Doc, and Fred, and Donald, and Ken [Bryden]. That's what nurtured us."[61] It is out of this same sense of fellowship that Donald MacDonald dedicates his memoirs, in part, to "the thousands of working people who shared the vision of the Co-operative Commonwealth Federation and the New Democratic Party," adding that "their labours and sacrifice were an inspiration for those to whom they entrusted the responsibilities of leadership" and that "I shall always treasure the memories of their comradeship." Surely Tommy Douglas's biographer is way off the mark, then, when she states flatly that while "the old concepts of political brotherhood were alive" in Saskatchewan in the 1950s, "in Ontario they were sour, irrelevant, and empty, a poor joke."[62]

The qualities of self-sacrifice and perseverance in the name of high principles and fellowship, which many leaders and certain followers in the party displayed in these difficult times, clearly distinguished the CCF as something more than just another political party driven by the potential spoils of office. "Movements have a vitality and a tenacity which parties lack," writes Walter Young, "because they are organizations of like-minded people dedicated to a cause that is predicated on what are seen as high moral values."[63] By his own criteria, then, Young would be forced to admit that in at least one important respect – ideologically based vitality and tenacity – the "movement" aspect of the CCF was stronger in the 1950s and early 1960s than before.

Those who see *only* the decline and stagnation of the CCF/NDP in this period, therefore, are missing an important element; namely, the commitment and tenacity of those who remained to fight on, who struggled to keep the dream of the cooperative commonwealth alive against overwhelming odds. More than just dedicated dreamers, however, CCF/NDP activists possessed an ingenuity and hard-headed pragmatism, expressed time and time again through the wide variety of strategies they devised to maintain and expand the party's organizational foundation. As a result, the party lived to fight – and eventually win – another day. But the significance of these central characteristics of the Ontario CCF/NDP's history lies beyond the party and the period, for in the final analysis they entailed the survival of an organization that, many have argued, has made a significant contribution to Canadian life. Viewed in this light, both partisans and non-partisans are to some extent indebted to this tiny lot of dedicated dreamers.

Appendix:
Ontario CCF/NDP Membership Levels and Election Returns, 1945–1963

ONTARIO CCF/NDP REGULAR
MEMBERSHIP LEVELS 1948–1963

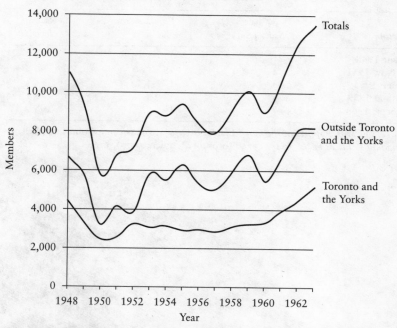

Source: Membership Reports, appended to Minutes of Provincial Council/Executive, CCF/NDP, 1948–1963, CCF/NDP Papers.

ONTARIO CCF/NDP AFFILIATED MEMBERSHIP LEVELS 1945–1962

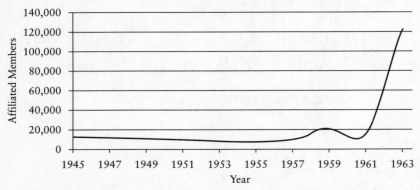

Source: Membership Reports, appended to Minutes of Provincial Council/Executive, CCF/NDP Papers, 1949–1962: Young, *Anatomy,* page 86.

CCF/NDP PROVINCIAL GENERAL ELECTION RETURNS, 1948–1963

Election	Seats won	Popular vote (%)	Size of legislature
7 June 1948	21	27	90
22 Nov. 1951	2	19	90
9 June 1955	3	17	98
11 June 1959	5	17	98
25 Sept. 1963	7	16	108

Source: Ontario, *Reports of the Chief Electoral Officer, 1948–1963;* Colin Campbell, *Canadian Political Facts, 1945–1976* (Toronto: Methuen, 1977), 116.

Notes

INTRODUCTION

1 Caplan, *The Dilemma of Canadian Socialism*; Horowitz, *Canadian Labour in Politics*; Zakuta, *A Protest Movement Becalmed*; Morley, *Secular Socialists*.

2 Zakuta bases his study in large part on his experience as "a deeply involved 'CCFer'" and member of a Toronto riding association executive who, it is clear, was subject to much criticism from the provincial leadership in the 1950s for being what the latter called "deadwood." Clearing his name, therefore, seems to be an important rationale for his study. Zakuta, *A Protest Movement Becalmed*, 5–6.

3 Ibid., 25–30.

4 James Bryce, "Introduction," in Ostrogorski, *Democracy and the Organization of Political Parties*, lxvii.

5 See, for example, Sangster, "'Women and the New Era'"; MacPherson, "The 1945 Collapse of the CCF in Windsor"; and Young, "The Peterborough By-Election." Two useful dissertations on the CCF in Ontario at the local level are Campbell, "'Truly Grass Roots People'" and Szmigielski, "Constituency Level Politics."

6 Lipset, *Agrarian Socialism*; Lewis, *The Good Fight*; MacDonald, *The Happy Warrior*.

7 In his classic study of political parties, Robert Michels contends that all organizations are subject to centralizing tendencies that result sooner or later in the establishment of an oligarchy. "Organization implies the tendency to oligarchy," he writes. "In every organization,

whether it be a political party, a professional union, or any other association of the kind, the aristocratic tendency manifests itself very clearly. The mechanism of the organization, while conferring a solidity of structure, induces serious changes in the organized mass, completely inverting the respective position of the leaders and the led." Michels calls this a "sociological law" and those who deny it, dangerous liars. Michels, *Political Parties*, 32–5.

8 See Whitaker, *The Government Party*, perhaps the best account of Canadian party organization written to date, in which he argues that the Liberal party and the state became one and the same over time as the latter was mobilized to serve the partisan purposes of the party.

9 Young, *The Anatomy of a Party*, 60.

10 See, for instance, Zakuta, *A Protest Movement Becalmed*; Cross, *The Decline and Fall of a Good Idea*; McNaught, *A Prophet in Politics*, chap. 19; and Sinclair, "The Saskatchewan CCF"; Stinson, *Political Warriors*, 7; and Penner, *From Protest to Power*, 87–90.

11 For a more general critique of the movement-to-party thesis, see Whitehorn, *Canadian Socialism*, chap. 2; and Azoulay, "'A Desperate Holding Action.'"

CHAPTER ONE

1 "Frost Victory Sets Record; Salsberg Lone Red Returned," *Globe and Mail (GM)*, 23 November 1951.

2 Alex Barris, "Jolliffe Beaten; Rallies Backers With Pep Talk," GM, 23 November 1951.

3 *CCF News* (Ontario), December 1951, Woodsworth Memorial Collection (WMC), Thomas Fisher Rare Book Library (TFRB), University of Toronto, Toronto, (hereafter cited as simply *CCF News*); Ontario, Chief Electoral Officer, *Returns from the 1951 General Election*.

4 "PC's Blanket Hamilton, Rout CCF Members," GM, 23 November 1951"; Frost Victory," GM, 23 November 1951.

5 CCF, Ontario, Minutes of Joint OFL-CCF Committee on Political Action, 15 May [1951], CCF/NDP Papers, National Archives of Canada (NA), Ottawa; *CCF News*, July 1951; "Predictions Foolishness, Jolliffe Not Having Any," GM, 9 Nov 1951. See editorial in *CCF News*, April 1951, on party's 1951 legislative performance, and Bert Leavens' (CCF M.P.P., Woodbine) comments in the May issue.

6 GM, 5, 7, 10, 12, 20, 21 November 1951.

7 GM, 8, 9, 10, 12, 16, 17 November 1951; McDougall, *John P. Robarts*, 28.

8 See Caplan, *The Dilemma of Canadian Socialism*, chaps. 8–10.

9 GM, 20 November 1951. The standings as of 10 November were: Conservatives 44 percent, Liberals 32 percent, and CCF 23 percent; Donald MacDonald [CCF National Treasurer] to Mrs Howard MacCordick, 16 January 1952, CCF/NDP Papers.

10 CCF, Ontario, Minutes of Provincial Council, 10, 11 February, and of Provincial Executive, 5 May 1951, CCF/NDP Papers; CCF, Ontario, "Report of the Eighteenth Annual Convention," 10–12 April 1952, Woodsworth Memorial Collection, TFRB.

11 CCF, Ontario, Report of the Organization Committee to Provincial Council, 29, 30 September 1951, CCF/NDP Papers (quote); CCF News, July 1951; CCF, Ontario, Minutes of Provincial Council, 29, 30 September 1951, 12 January 1952, Ontario CCF/NDP Papers, Queen's University Archives (QUA); Kingston, Ontario; MacDonald to Lazarus, 14 May 1951, CCF/NDP Papers; CCF, Ontario, Minutes of Provincial Council, 29, 30 September 1951, CCF/NDP Papers.

12 Ontario Federation of Labour (OFL) Papers, NA, Report to OFL Executive, December 1951, OFL Papers, NA.

13 OFL, Report to OFL Executive, 27 July and December 1951, OFL Papers; Morden Lazarus to Lorne Ingle, 22 May 1951, CCF/NDP Papers.

14 The total number of CCF candidates who were union members was actually forty-five, as several TLC unionists ran for the party. GM, 21 November 1951 (quote); CCF News, September 1951, January 1952; CCF, Ontario, Minutes of Provincial Council, 29, 30 September 1951, CCF/NDP Papers; Minutes of Provincial Council, 12 January 1952, Ontario CCF/NDP Papers; GM, 21 November 1951; CCF News, November 1951, Election Issue; OFL, "Report of the OFL-PAC Director," December 1951, Canadian Labour Congress (CLC) Papers, NA.

15 CCF News, November 1951; CCF, Ontario, Minutes of Provincial Council, 29, 30 September 1951, CCF/NDP Papers; GM, 21 November 1951.

16 CCF, Ontario, "Report of the Eighteenth Annual Convention," 10–12 April 1952, WMC; Fred Young, interview by author, 29 April 1990, Toronto, tape recording; Donald MacDonald, interview by author, 16 May 1990, Toronto, tape recording; MacDonald, The Happy Warrior, 43–4.

17 CCF, Ontario, Minutes of Provincial Executive, 31 July 1951, and Donald MacDonald, Organization Report to National Council, 1, 2 March 1952, CCF/NDP Papers.

18 CCF, Ontario, Riding Report to Provincial Council, 14 April 1951, Ontario CCF/NDP Papers; Report of Organizing Committee to Provincial Council, 29, 30 September 1951, CCF/NDP Papers.

19 Ron Cheffins, "Report from Ron Cheffins-Cornwall," to Lazarus, 6 June 1951, and Matt Quinn, Eganville, Ontario, to MacDonald, 4 April 1951, CCF/NDP Papers.

20 CCF, Ontario, Riding Report to Provincial Council, 14 April 1951, Ontario CCF/NDP Papers; MacDonald, interview by author.

21 CCF, Ontario, Minutes of Provincial Council, 10, 11 February, and 29 September 1951; Loretta LePalm, Smiths Falls, Ontario, to Mac-Donald, 19 April 1951, CCF/NDP Papers.

22 CCF, Ontario, Membership Report to Provincial Convention, [1952], Ontario CCF/NDP Papers.

23 CCF, Ontario, Report of Organizing Committee to Provincial Council, and Minutes of Provincial Council, 29, 30 September 1951, CCF/NDP Papers.

24 CCF, Ontario, Report of Electoral Committee to Provincial Council, 29, 30 September 1951, Ontario CCF/NDP Papers; Lazarus to Ingle, 17 September, 13, 23 October, 1951; Ingle to Lazarus, 25 October, 6 November; CCF, Ontario, Minutes of Provincial Council, 29, 30 September 1951, CCF/NDP Papers.

25 MacDonald to Lazarus, 9 March 1951, CCF/NDP Papers.

26 Lazarus to MacDonald, 2, 26 January 1951; MacDonald to Lazarus, 30 July 1951; CCF, Ontario, Minutes of Provincial Executive, 8 March 1952, CCF/NDP Papers; CCF, Ontario, Report of NED Planning Conference, 4 February 1951, Ontario CCF/NDP Papers.

27 CCF, Ontario, Minutes of Provincial Executive, 28 August 1951, and Provincial Council, 12, 13 January 1952, CCF/NDP Papers; CCF, Ontario, "Election Memo #1," 5 October 1951; Report of Electoral Committee to Provincial Council, 29, 30 September 1951, Ontario CCF/NDP Papers.

28 MacDonald to Leo Lalonde, Timmins, Ontario, 8 May 1951; Mac-Donald to Arnold Peters, Timmins, Ontario, 10 May 1951, and MacDonald to Lazarus, 12 September 1952; Quinn to MacDonald, 3 November 1951, CCF/NDP Papers; CCF, Ontario, "Report of the Eighteenth Annual Convention, 10–12 April 1952," WMC. Emphasis added.

29 CCF, Ontario, Report of NED Planning Conference, 4 February 1951, Ontario CCF/NDP Papers (quotes); OFL, Report of PAC Director to OFL Executive, December 1951, Ontario Federation of Labour (OFL) Papers, National Archives of Canada; Horowitz, *Canadian Labour in Politics*, 132; Graham, *Old Man Ontario*, 133–4; Ken Bryden, interview by author, 9 July 1990, Toronto, tape recording.

30 Graham, *Old Man Ontario*, 184–7; George Bain, "Frost Speeches Draw Large Enough Crowds, But Calmness Keynote," GM, 14 November 1951.

31 Ontario, Chief Electoral Officer, *Returns from the General Election, 1945, 1948.*

32 Ontario, Chief Electoral Officer, *Returns from the General Election, 1943, 1945, 1955.*

33 CCF, Ontario, Minutes of Provincial Executive, 1 December 1951, and Provincial Council, 12, 13 January 1952, CCF/NDP Papers; *CCF News*, December 1951 and February 1952; CCL-PAC, *Newsletter*, December 1951, Canadian Labour Congress (CLC) Papers, National Archives of Canada.

34 OFL, Report of PAC Director to OFL Executive, December 1951, OFL Papers.

35 See Young, *Anatomy of a Party*, chap. 7, and Leo Zakuta, *A Protest Movement Becalmed*, 112–37.

36 *CCF News*, December 1951.

37 For more on Ontario's tremendous economic growth after 1945, see K.J. Rea, *The Prosperous Years*.

38 CCF, Ontario, Minutes of Provincial Council, 12, 13 January 1952, and "Report of the Eighteenth Annual Convention," CCF/NDP Papers; MacDonald, interview by author.

39 *CCF News*, December 1951; CCF, Ontario, "Report of the Eighteenth Annual Convention."

CHAPTER TWO

1 CCF, Ontario, "Report of the Eighteenth Annual Convention"; Lazarus to MacDonald, 17, 21 December 1951; CCF, Ontario, Minutes of Provincial Executive, 5 January 1952, CCF/NDP Papers.

2 Sustaining members were those who made a lump sum contribution of at least five dollars to the party once each year over and above regular membership fees. Lazarus to MacDonald, 17 and 21 December 1951, CCF/NDP Papers; *CCF News*, April 1952. Bryden was still officially the caucus research director, but was a *de facto* provincial organizer. He recalls approaching Lazarus, shortly after the 1951 election, and saying, "Look, we can't afford the luxury of research. We have to try and hold this damn thing together and try and build it and keep the membership at least functioning so we can pay the rent and pay the staff." Ken Bryden, interview by author, Toronto, Ontario, 9 July 1990, tape recording.

3 CCF, Ontario, Minutes of Provincial Executive, 12 January 1952, Ontario CCF/NDP Papers.

4 It should be noted that riding "clubs" were distinct from riding "associations." The CCF constitution stated that "CCF members in any locality with the approval of the constituency association or the provincial council may form themselves into a CCF club for social, educational and political purposes, hold meetings, elect officers and raise from among themselves the necessary monies to carry on local activities, provided that, for the purposes of electing candidates and fighting election campaigns, members of all clubs in the constituency shall act through the

constituency association." CCF, Ontario, "Constitution of the CCF (Ontario Section), April 1955," in Zakuta, Appendix B.

5 MacDonald, Memorandum on Proposals for Ontario Organization, January 1952, CCF/NDP Papers.

6 Ibid.; CCF *News*, April 1952.

7 CCF, Ontario, Minutes of Provincial Council, 12 January 1952, Ontario CCF/NDP Papers; MacDonald to Lazarus, 10 March 1952, CCF/NDP Papers.

8 The exact composition of the Ginger Group is uncertain, since only four official meetings of the Group were held in 1952 and attendance varied. Nineteen different persons attended at least half of the meetings, while twenty-seven attended at least one meeting. Only six were present for all four. Ontario CCF Ginger Group, Minutes of Special Meetings, 16 March to 6 April, 1952, Ontario CCF/NDP Collection, McMaster University Archives (MUA), Hamilton, Ontario.

9 Ontario CCF Ginger Group, "Proposed [policy] Suggestions," "Where Are We CCF Socialists Going?" (an open letter), and "The Ginger Group of the Ontario CCF," (first newsletter), 1950, Ontario CCF/NDP Collection; CCF, Ontario, Minutes of Provincial Council, 21, 22 October 1950, CCF/NDP Papers.

10 Ontario CCF Ginger Group, "Where are We Socialists Going?", Ontario CCF/NDP Collection.

11 Ontario CCF Ginger Group, Resolutions adopted at meeting, 14 January 1951, Ontario CCF/NDP Collection; Cotterill to Pat Conroy (CCL secretary-treasurer), 28 March 1951, CLC Papers.

12 Ontario CCF Ginger Group, Minutes, 16 March 1952, Ontario CCF/NDP Collection.

13 The original Ginger Group was also concerned with the bureaucratization of the CCF. In 1950, for example, it passed a resolution calling for the exclusion of paid officials from the national CCF's Resolutions Committee since volunteer officials, they reasoned, would be less likely to toe the party line. Ontario CCF Ginger Group, "The Ginger Group of the Ontario CCF."

14 CCF, Ontario, Minutes of Provincial Executive, 5 January 1952, CCF/NDP Papers (quotes); Ontario CCF Ginger Group, Minutes, 30 March 1952, Ontario CCF/NDP Collection.

15 Ontario CCF Ginger Group, Minutes, 16 March 1952, Ontario CCF/NDP Collection.

16 Ontario CCF Ginger Group, Minutes, 16, 23, 30 March 1952, Ontario CCF/NDP Collection.

17 Ontario CCF Ginger Group, Minutes, 16 March 1952, Ontario CCF/NDP Collection.

18 CCF, Ontario, Minutes of Provincial Executive, 4 March, 3 October 1950 (quotes); Donald MacDonald to William Powell, Smiths Falls, Ontario, 17 February 1950, CCF/NDP Papers.

19 CCF, Ontario, Minutes of Provincial Council, 29, 30 September 1951, and Report of Literature Committee to Provincial Convention, 10–12 April 1952, Ontario CCF/NDP Papers.

20 Avakumovic, *Socialism in Canada*, 141–3; Bryden, interview by author. For more on the League for Social Reconstruction, see Horn, *The League for Social Reconstruction*.

21 Ontario CCF Ginger Group, Minutes, 16, 23, 30 March 1952, Ontario CCF/NDP Collection (quotes); CCF, Ontario, Minutes of Provincial Executive, 1, 18 December 1951, 5 January 1952, CCF/NDP Papers.

22 CCF, Ontario, "Constitution of the CCF, Ontario Section, 1955," in Zakuta, Appendix B; CCF, Ontario, Minutes of Provincial Council, 12 April 1952, CCF/NDP Papers. See also Engelmann, "Membership Participation in Policy-making in the CCF", and n. 67 below.

23 Ontario CCF Ginger Group, Minutes, 23 March, 6 April 1952, Ontario CCF/NDP Collection.

24 *CCF News*, May 1952.

25 *CCF News*, May 1952; "Ontario CCF Split Buried as Temple Loses in Vote," *Toronto Star (TS)*, 12 April 1952.

26 Moore was one of the many Ginger Group members who eventually resigned from the CCF rather than accept the new thrust of CCF organizational policy. "Ontario CCF Split," *TS*; CCF, Ontario, Minutes of Provincial Executive, 20 June 1952, CCF/NDP Papers; "Jolliffe Stays CCF Leader; Revolt Fails," *Toronto Telegram (TT)*, 12 April 1952.

27 "Ontario CCF Split," *TS*; CCF, Ontario, "Report of the Eighteenth Annual Convention."

28 "Ontario CCF 'Bevanites' seek to Oust Leaders 'Not Socialist Enough,'" *TS*, 10 April 1952; "Ontario CCF Split," *TS*.

29 Doc Ames, a party vice-president and soon-to-be provincial organizer, believed strongly in educating CCF members in socialist principles so that they might be more effective in reaching out for new members. CCF, Ontario, Minutes of Provincial Council, 12 April 1952; Ames to MacDonald, 4 May 1952, CCF/NDP Papers.

30 CCF, Ontario, Minutes of Provincial Executive, 8 September 1952, CCF/NDP Papers.

31 CCF, Ontario, Minutes of Provincial Executive, 1 December 1951, 26 April 1952; Lazarus to Ingle, 3 December 1951, CCF/NDP Papers; Minutes, Provincial Council, 3, 4 May 1952, Ontario CCF/NDP Papers.

32 Actually, the York East CCF had tabled a motion of non-confidence, but did not actually decide anything. That same month, however, the

West York CCF informed the Executive that it had passed a motion asking that the provincial leader be withdrawn before the next election. CCF, Ontario, Minutes of Provincial Executive, 20 June 1952, CCF/NDP Papers.

33 There is a sad epilogue to this whole affair. Although three large unions had initially expressed interest in contributing to the fund, by September of 1952 the CCF had been unable to raise enough money to sustain the leader for one year. Therefore, with Jolliffe's concurrence, the Executive agreed to pay only his CCF-related expenses with whatever was currently in the Fund. CCF, Ontario, Minutes of Provincial Executive, 8 September 1952, CCF/NDP Papers.

34 Bernard Loeb, untitled document constituting "a short history of the development of the … Foundation," [1950], Ontario CCF/NDP Collection; Ontario Woodsworth Memorial Foundation (OWMF), "The Ontario Woodsworth Memorial Foundation," n.d.; Dr. H.N. Wilkinson, Resignation Letter, March 1953; Loeb, "A Short History," OWMF Papers, McMaster University Archives (MUA), Hamilton, Ontario.

35 Dr. H.N. Wilkinson, Resignation letter, March 1953; Loeb "A Short History," OWMF Papers (quote).

36 Francis, "The Ontario Woodsworth House Controversy", 28–9.

37 Loeb, "A Short History"; OWMF, Report of the Annual Meeting, 17 April 1950, and Minutes of Special Board Meeting, 2 November 1951; Grube to Wilkinson, 7 November 1950, OWMF Papers.

38 Lewis, *The Good Fight*, 420; Francis, "The Ontario Woodsworth House Controversy", 28–31; OWMF, "Basis for Discussion of Foundation Activities," undated document, and Minutes of Special Board Meeting, 2 November 1951, OWMF Papers.

39 OWMF, "Comments on the First News Letter," [October] 1951, OWMF Papers.

40 Underhill, "What's Left," 243–4.

41 It should be emphasized that the *coup* was organized primarily by a group of well-known party leaders, but did not have the CCF's official sanction. As Bryden states, "It wasn't a party initiative, but it was an initiative of people in the party." OWMF, Minutes of Special Board Meeting of Woodsworth Foundation, 25 February 1952, OWMF Papers; OWMF, Minutes of Annual Meeting, 27 February 1952, Ontario CCF/NDP Papers; Bryden, interview by author.

42 OWMF, Minutes of Special Board Meeting of Woodsworth Foundation, 25 February 1952, OWMF Papers.

43 OWMF, Minutes of Annual Meeting, OWMF Papers.

44 Ibid.; Ken Bryden recalls that Lewis did not play a leading role in organizing the coup, but was simply a "front man" for the unofficial group of CCFers intent on removing the old guard from the Board. Lewis

confirms this in his memoirs. Bryden, interview by author; Lewis, *The Good Fight*, 422.

45 It is difficult to identify with certainty the loyalties of several of the new directors. But according to CCF Secretary Morden Lazarus, CCF partisans were still in a minority since only six of the twelve director positions were open for election that year. Lazarus to Ingle, 6 March 1952, CCF/NDP Papers; OWMF, Minutes of Board of Directors Meeting, 12 March 1952, OWMF Papers.

46 See undated newspaper clipping from *Toronto Telegram* in OWMF Papers entitled "Reveal 2 Groups Split on Running of CCF Centre"; Ingle to Lazarus, 5 March 1952; Lazarus to Ingle, 6 March 1952, CCF/ NDP Papers; see also Andrew Brewin, "Woodsworth Foundation," *Canadian Forum* 32 (May 1952): 34–7, the party's official response to the whole affair.

47 OWMF, Minutes of Annual Meeting; Memorandum found in file entitled "The Internal Struggle, 1952–53," OWMF Papers"; Reveal Two Groups Split" (quote); see also reports by Wilkinson and Fowke to Foundation's 1952 Annual Meeting.

48 CCF, Ontario, Minutes of Provincial Executive, 18 March 1952, CCF/ NDP Papers; Brewin, "Woodsworth Foundation."

49 Brewin, "Woodsworth Foundation."

50 Underhill, "Power Politics in the Ontario C.C.F.," 7–8.

51 For a similar critique of the party, see Harrington, "What's Left," 269– 70, and Mark Cohen's memo, "The Internal Struggle," OWMF Papers.

52 Brewin, "Woodsworth Foundation." In 1952, the CCF had only three full-time employees: Bryden, Young, and Lazarus. Brewin was also correct in noting that "very few members ... of the present provincial executive have served for more than four or five years. Quite a few new members are elected to the executive every year." Between 1943 and 1951, at least sixty different individuals served on the Executive, which in the same period grew in size from sixteen to nineteen persons. In those eight or so years, only two people sat on the Executive each year: Ted Jolliffe, the provincial leader, and Morden Lazarus, the provincial secretary. As for the rest, forty people served for two years or less, eighteen for more than three, and only seven people (including Jolliffe and Lazarus) served for more than five years. This indicates a substantial turnover in the composition of the CCF's highest body of between six and eight completely new members *each* year. Figures derived from *The New Commonwealth* (later CCF *News*), 1943–51.

53 Ibid.

54 OWMF, document relating to meeting prior to 1953 Annual Meeting; Minutes of Board of Directors, 12 March 1952; Wilkinson, resignation letter; Minutes of Annual Meeting, 12 March 1953, OWMF Papers.

55 OWMF, Minutes of Annual Meeting, 12 March 1953; document relating to meeting just prior to 1953 Annual Meeting, OWMF Papers; "Foundation Officials Issue Statement," GM, 19 March 1953.

56 See Young, *Anatomy of a Party*, 281–4; Horowitz, *Canadian Labour in Politics*, 148–9; and Morley, *Secular Socialists*, 84–6.

57 Zakuta, *A Protest Movement Becalmed*, 11–22.

58 See TT, 22 March to 1 April, 1952.

59 Several interpretations have been advanced for Underhill's virulent attacks on the party he helped to found in the early 1930s. Ken Bryden, for example, argues that Underhill began attacking the CCF in such harsh terms because he was no longer being consulted by party leaders and his ego was bruised. A more plausible explanation is offered by Underhill's biographer. "Underlying Underhill's attacks on the CCF," writes Douglas Francis, "lay an uneasiness, almost a paranoia, about communism ... His search for 'communistic' tendencies within the CCF could be viewed as a moderate Canadian version of the 'Red Scare' in the United States." Francis, *Frank Underhill*, 153–4. The evolution in Underhill's thinking is spelled out more thoroughly in his book, *In Search of Canadian Liberalism*.

60 Underhill, "Power Politics"; "Foundation Officials Issue Statement"; Cohen memorandum, 1952; OWMF, Report of Annual Meeting, 27 February 1952; untitled document found in "1953 Annual Meeting" file, which seems to be notes on the Board of Director's meeting just prior to the Annual Meeting, OWMF Papers.

61 From undated newspaper clipping in OWMF Papers entitled "CCF-ers Say 'Red' Charge 'Tempest in Pink Teacup.'"

CHAPTER THREE

1 CCF, Ontario, "Report of the Eighteenth Annual Convention."

2 CCF, Ontario, Minutes of Provincial Executive, 2 June 1952, CCF/NDP Papers; Minutes of Combined Finance and Organization Committee, 3 May, and Provincial Council, 3, 4 May 1952, Ontario CCF/NDP Papers.

3 Ibid.

4 Lazarus to MacDonald, 11 September 1952, CCF/NDP Papers.

5 *The Canadian Parliamentary Guide, 1938–1952* (Ottawa: n.p.); Lazarus to MacDonald, 16 April 1952; CCF, Ontario, "Minutes of Executive Committee Meeting," 26 April 1952; MacDonald to Lazarus, 18 April 1952, CCF/NDP Papers; *CCF News*, June 1952.

6 CCF, Ontario, Report of Organization Committee to Provincial Council, 4, 5 October 1952, Ontario CCF/NDP Collection; MacDonald, *The Happy Warrior*, 43–4.

7 CCF, Ontario, Report of Organization Committee to Provincial Council, 4, 5 October 1952, Ontario CCF/NDP Collection, and 17, 18 January 1953, Ontario CCF/NDP Papers; "Membership Report," 25 June 1952, CCF/NDP Papers; *CCF News*, June, October, and November, 1952; MacDonald to Lazarus, 9 September 1952; Minutes of Provincial Executive, 6 December 1952, CCF/NDP Papers; Membership Report, 25 June 1952, appended to Minutes of Provincial Executive, 8 July 1952, CCF/NDP Papers.

8 *CCF News*, June 1952; Lazarus to Ralph Carlin, 10 September 1952; CCF, federal, "Organizer's Report – Fred Young," 20 October 1952, CCF/NDP Papers.

9 *CCF News*, November 1952.

10 CCF, Ontario, Report of Organization Committee to Provincial Council, 17, 18 January 1953, and Minutes of Provincial Executive, 6 December 1952, CCF/NDP Papers; Report of Organization Committee to Provincial Council, 4, 5 October 1952, Ontario CCF/NDP Collection; *CCF News*, July and October 1952.

11 CCF, Ontario, Report of Organization Committee to Provincial Council, 4, 5 October 1952, Ontario CCF/NDP Collection; Minutes of Provincial Executive, 10 January 1953, and Provincial Council, 9 May 1953, 16, 17 January 1954, CCF/NDP Papers; *CCF News*, 1953.

12 CCF, Ontario, Minutes of Provincial Council, 12, 13 January 1952, and Provincial Executive, 8 March 1952, CCF/NDP Papers.

13 OFL, PAC, Report to OFL Executive, December 1951; OFL, Minutes of Executive Committee, 9 January 1952; Report of Annual Convention, 1, 2 February 1952, OFL Papers.

14 *CCF News*, February 1952; CCF, Ontario, Minutes of Provincial Executive, 19 February, 1 April 1952, CCF/NDP Papers.

15 CCF, Ontario, Minutes of TUC, 7 June 1952, CCF/NDP Papers; *CCF News*, May 1952.

16 CCF, Ontario, Report of TUC to Provincial Council, 4, 5 October 1952, Ontario CCF/NDP Collection; CCF, Ontario, Minutes of Provincial Executive, 1 November 1952, CCF/NDP Papers; Young interview by author; Murray Cotterill, interview by author, Toronto, Ontario, 4 June 1990, tape recording: Bryden, interviews by author.

17 CCF, Ontario, Minutes of Provincial Council, 4, 5 October 1952; Minutes of First Meeting of Toronto Area CCF-Labour Organizing Committee, 25 June 1952, CCF/NDP Papers; *CCF News*, August 1952.

18 MacDonald to Lazarus, 24 January 1952, CCF/NDP Papers; CCF, Ontario, Minutes of TUC, 15 December 1953, Ontario CCF/NDP Papers.

19 Weisbach to Donald MacDonald (of CCL), 1 May 1952; MacDonald to Ralph [Carlin], 13 September 1952; Matt Quinn to MacDonald,

3 November 1951; MacDonald to Fred [Young], 6 February 1952, CLC Papers; Donald C. MacDonald to Lazarus, 12 September 1952, CCF/ NDP Papers.

20 See, for instance, the letter from Norm Chalmers, a provincial councillor, in the CCF News, April 1953.

21 OFL, Report of Annual Convention, 6, 7 February 1953, OFL Papers; CCF News, December 1952 and July 1953.

22 CCF, Ontario, Minutes of Election Committee, 23 May 1953, Ontario CCF/NDP Papers; "Minutes of Executive Committee Meeting," 18 July and 15 August, 1953, CCF/NDP Papers; OFL, PAC, Report to Executive Committee, 10 July 1953, OFL Papers; "PC's Appealing to Selfish Side of Human Nature," and "PC Lauds CCF Methods, Calls Liberals Fiendish," GM, 5 August 1953; CCF News, July 1953.

23 CCF News, July 1953; OFL, PAC, Report to the Executive, 10 July 1953, OFL Papers.

24 CCF News, July 1953; GM, 15 July-6 August, 1953.

25 Ralph Hyman, "PC's Gain Six Seats in Ontario," GM, 11 August 1953; Young, Anatomy of a Party, Appendix B; CCF, Ontario, Minutes of Provincial Council, 5 September 1953, CCF/NDP Papers.

26 CCF, Ontario, Minutes of Organization Committee, 4 September 1953; "Program of Action," [1953], Ontario CCF/NDP Papers.

27 CCF, Ontario, Minutes of Organization Committee, 4 September 1953, Ontario CCF/NDP Papers; Minutes of Provincial Executive, 17 October 1953, and Provincial Council, 4, 5 October 1952, and Financial Statement, appended to Council Minutes, 16, 17 January 1954, CCF/NDP Papers; CCF, Ontario, Minutes of Finance Committee, 13 August 1953, Ontario CCF/NDP Papers; CCF, federal, Provincial Reports to National Council, 1953, CCF/NDP Papers.

28 CCF, Ontario, Minutes of Provincial Executive, 23 September 1952, Provincial Council, 17 January 1953, 16, 17 January 1954; Mary Ramsay (Literature Committee Chairperson), to Lorne Ingle, 5 April 1952, CCF/NDP Papers; CCF, Ontario, Minutes of Membership Education Committee, 4 October 1952, and Report of same to Provincial Council, 4, 5 October 1952, Ontario CCF/NDP Collection; CCF, Ontario, Minutes of Membership Education Committee, 17 October, 3 November 1953, and Report of Literature Committee to 1952 convention, Ontario CCF/NDP Papers.

29 CCF News, September 1953; Jolliffe to Bryden, "Letter of Resignation of E.B. Jolliffe," 15 August 1953, CCF/NDP Papers.

30 CCF, Ontario, Minutes of Provincial Council, 5 September 1953, CCF/ NDP Papers.

31 "Ontario Tour Planned by New Leader of CCF, Donald C. Mac-Donald," GM, 23 November 1953; "Donald MacDonald Elected CCF Leader," TS, 23 November 1953; Young interview by author, Marjorie

Pinney, interview by author, Toronto, Ontario, 1 June 1990, tape recording; and Bryden, interview by author.

32 *CCF News*, December 1953; MacDonald, *Happy Warrior*, 29–38.

33 "Donald MacDonald," TS.

CHAPTER FOUR

1 CCF, Ontario, Minutes of Provincial Council, 27, 28 March 1954, CCF/NDP Papers; *CCF News*, February 1954.

2 CCF, Ontario, Program of Action; Report of Annual Convention, 22–24 May 1954; Minutes of Provincial Council, 27, 28 March 1954, CCF/NDP Papers; *CCF News*, December 1953, June 1954; MacDonald, interview by author.

3 CCF, Ontario, "Looking to the Future: The CCF Program for Ontario, (1955)," CCF/NDP Papers.

4 See chap. 2, 88–95.

5 *CCF News*, January, February, September 1954.

6 CCF, Ontario, Minutes of Organization Committee, 9 January 1954, Ontario CCF/NDP Papers; Minutes of Executive Committee, 16 March, 15 May 1954, and Membership Report, June 1954, appended to Minutes of Provincial Council, 26, 27 June 1954, CCF/NDP Papers.

7 CCF, Ontario, Minutes of Provincial Council, 26, 27 June 1954, CCF/NDP Papers; *CCF News*, August 1954.

8 Marjorie Pinney, interview by author; CCF, Ontario, Minutes of Organization Committee, 31 August 1954, George Grube Papers, Queen's University Archives (QUA), Kingston, Ontario.

9 *CCF News*, July 1954.

10 *CCF News*, November 1954, January 1955; CCF, Ontario, Minutes of Executive Committee, 13 November 1954; Membership Report, October 1954, appended to Minutes of Executive Committee, 13 November 1954, CCF/NDP Papers.

11 Bryden to riding presidents and secretaries, 15 June 1954; "Canvass Plan for Toronto Area, January 7 to February 15, 1955," Ontario CCF/NDP Papers; CCF, Ontario, Organization Report to Ken Bryden et. al. from Doc Ames, 28 January 1955, Donald C. MacDonald Papers, Queen's University Archives (QUA), Kingston, Ontario; *CCF News*, January, February 1955.

12 For more on Communist tactics, see Oliver, *Unlikely Tory*, 65–9, and Lewis, *The Good Fight*, 231–2.

13 See Young, *Anatomy of a Party*, 255–84; Sefton, "Some Thoughts following the Ontario Election of June 11, 1959," United Steelworkers of America (USA) (District 6) Papers, McMaster University Archives (MUA), Hamilton, Ontario; Young, interview by author.

14 Wilfred List, "Canadian Trotskyites Now Out of Business, Workers Turn to CCF," *GM*, 19 April 1952; CCF, Ontario, "Report of Provincial Council on Certain Charges Dealt with at Meeting of October 30 & 31, 1954," Ontario CCF/NDP Papers; Minutes of Executive Committee, 26 April, 23 September 1952, CCF/NDP Papers.

15 CCF, Ontario, "Summary of Report of Committee of Provincial Executive," Ontario CCF/NDP Papers; "Oust 15 Reds as CCF Breaks Trotskyites," *TS*, 9 April 1955; "Statement of Leslie G. Dawson," 8 September 1954, Grube Papers.

16 CCF, Ontario, Minutes of Special Meeting of Executive Committee, 17 October 1954, CCF/NDP Papers; CCF, Ontario, *Constitution*.

17 CCF, Ontario, Report of Provincial Council on Certain Charges, CCF/NDP Papers.

18 CCF, Ontario, Report of Committee appointed by Provincial Executive to hear and report on charges, Ontario CCF/NDP Papers; Ingle to Bryden, 7 October 1954; Minutes of Provincial Council, 11 December 1954, CCF/NDP Papers.

19 "Revolutionary Workers: 14 Expelled by Ontario CCF as Members of Alien Party," *GM*, 9 April 1955; *CCF News*, May 1955; LABEL, "Onward and Upward with the Revolution," 58–9; CCF, Ontario, "Report of the Twenty-First Annual Convention," 7–9 April 1955, CCF/NDP Papers.

20 Bryden to Leslie Lawlor (secretary, St. Paul's CCF Association), 10 November 1954; "Oust 15 Reds As CCF Breaks Trotskyites," *TT*, 9 April 1955; "Revolutionary Workers: 14 Expelled by Ontario CCF As Members of Alien Party," *GM* 9 April 1955; "Take Over CCF, Then Revolution, said Aim of Trotskyite Group," *TS*, 9 April 1955; "The CCF Purge," *TS*, 11 April 1955.

21 "The CCF Purge," 11 April 1955; "A Statement from Colin Cameron ... to the delegates at the 1955 Convention of the Ontario Section of the CCF," 4 April 1955, Grube Papers.

22 Lewis, *The Good Fight*, 429; "Oust 15 Reds"; LABEL, "Onward and Upward with the Revolution"; "Revolutionary Workers"; *CCF News*, July 1955.

23 Statistics found in letter from Bryden to CCF riding associations, 25 April 1955, Ontario CCF/NDP Papers.

24 Ontario, Chief Electoral Officer, *Returns of By-Elections, 1947–1955*; Canada, Chief Electoral Officer, *By-Election Report, 1954*.

25 *CCF News*, September 1954.

26 CCF, Ontario, "Report of the Twenty-first Annual Convention," 7–9 April 1955; *CCF News*, June, December 1954; OFL, "Report of the Annual Convention," 3–5 February 1955; "Election Guide for Labour

Council and Local Union PACS," 1955; and "Report of the Annual Convention," OFL Papers; CCF, Ontario, Minutes of Provincial Council, 22, 23 January, 25 June 1955, and Executive Committee, 31 March, 16 June 1955, CCF/NDP Papers; Francis Eady (organizer, Toronto CCF) to CCF Riding Associations in Toronto and District, 13 May 1955, Ontario CCF/NDP Papers; "Blame Worker Apathy For Showing of CCF," GM, 10 June 1955; "Union Leader Criticizes Quest To Pick Winner," GM, 8 June 1955.

27 Graham, *Old Man Ontario*, 289–97;"No Closing Off of Witnesses in Roads Probe," GM, 7 June 1955; MacDonald, *The Happy Warrior*, 55–6"; CCF Raps Punishment in Highways Scandal," GM, 11 April 1955; *CCF News*, June 1954.

28 CCF, Ontario, Minutes of Provincial Council, 27, 28 March 1954, CCF/NDP Papers; OFL, "Speech by Donald C. MacDonald, Provincial C.C.F. Leader, Ontario Federation of Labour Convention, February, 1954," OFL Papers.

29 *CCF News*, June 1954, March, April, May 1955; CCF, Ontario, "Press Release," [February] 1955, CCF/NDP Papers; Ontario, Legislative Assembly, *Debates of the 24th Legislature, Session 4, 1954, and Session 5, 1955*, quote on 430; see also Graham, *Old Man Ontario*, 289–300.

30 GM, 9, 12, 16, 19, 21 May, 3 June 1955.

31 MacDonald, "The Happy Warrior," rough draft of memoirs, in author's possession, 146–7; GM, 11, 21, 27 May 1955.

32 "PC's Play the Game in Presenting Facts," GM, 10 May 1955.

33 "Frost Ends Speaking Tour, Puts Future Up to Voters," GM, 8 June 1955; Ontario, Chief Electoral Officer, *Returns From 1955 General Election*; see also GM, 9, 11 June 1955.

34 Graham, *Old Man Ontario*, 288; Oliver, *Unlikely Tory*, 81; "Blame Worker Apathy For Showing of CCF," GM, 10 June 1955.

35 "Frost Betrayed North on Pipeline," GM, 2 June 1955; "Leader of CCF Bids For Liberal Support," GM, 3 June 1955; CCF, Ontario, Minutes of Provincial Executive, 16 June, 17 August 1955, CCF/NDP Papers.

36 *Returns*. Across the province the voter turnout was 61 percent. In Toronto and the Yorks, it was 54.9 percent; in the eighteen ridings containing 5,000 union members or more, the figure was 58.4 percent. Canada, Department of Labour, Economics and Research Branch, *Forty-Second Annual Report on Labour Organizations in Canada, 1953–55* (Ottawa, 1954), 15.

37 "Blame Worker Apathy"; *CCF News*, July 1955.

38 *CCF News*, December 1956; Graham, *Old Man*, 288.

39 CCF, Ontario, Minutes of Provincial Executive, 16 June 1955, CCF/NDP Papers.

CHAPTER FIVE

1 CCF, Ontario, Minutes of Provincial Executive, 16 June 1955, CCF/NDP Papers.
2 Ibid.
3 CCF News, July, August 1955.
4 CCF, Ontario, Minutes of Provincial Executive, 16 June 1955, CCF/NDP Papers.
5 CCF, Ontario, Minutes of Organization Committee, 4 October 1952, Provincial Council, 25 June 1955, Provincial Executive, 16 June 1955, CCF/NDP Papers.
6 Wrong, "Preliminary Survey," 400.
7 CCF, Ontario, Minutes of Provincial Council, 25 June, 5 November 1955, Provincial Executive, 21 September 1955, CCF/NDP Papers.
8 CCF News, December 1955 (quote), January 1956; CCF, Ontario, Minutes of Organization Committee, 30 August 1955, CCF/NDP Papers. The figures on poll organization, coming as they do from the habitually optimistic News, should be taken cautiously, since they sometimes contradicted simultaneous reports from provincial organizers. See, for instance, Doc Ames, Organizational Report, 29 January 1956, MacDonald Papers.
9 CCF, Ontario, Minutes of Provincial Council, 5 November, 25 June 1955, CCF/NDP Papers; CCF News, August 1955.
10 CCF News, January 1956; CCF, Ontario, "Membership Report, August 1956," appended to Minutes of Provincial Council, 8 September 1956, Ontario CCF/NDP Papers; see also Appendix.
11 CCF, Ontario, Minutes of Provincial Council, 8 September, 8 December 1956, Ontario CCF/NDP Papers; Minutes of Provincial Executive, 21 November 1956, CCF/NDP Papers. As of September 1956, the party knew of over 3,000 lapsed memberships, dating back eighteen months, which had not been renewed.
12 CCF News, November 1955, November 1956. See also Bryden to Ingle, 30 December 1955, CCF/NDP Papers. In addition to singling out the "Ginger Group" mentality and apathy of CCFers as the root cause of the party's organizational decline, Pinney, for one, was convinced that the problem lay partly in the upper echelons of the party structure. In November 1955, she informed the National Secretary Lorne Ingle that she was "appalled at the number of 'top' people who will put so much ahead of the CCF ... [and] who do little or no work in the riding they live in ... We cannot inspire our average CCFer to do more without examples of sacrifice of time and money such as were given by people like Woodsworth." While not as quick to generalize, Ingle agreed that too many CCF leaders were complacent and lazy. Pinney to Ingle,

18 November 1955, and Ingle to Pinney, 28 December 1955, CCF/NDP Papers.

13 CCF, Ontario, "Membership Report, August 1956"; "Membership Report, July 31, 1957," appended to Minutes of Provincial Executive, 8 August 1957, CCF/NDP Papers.

14 Between May 1954 and June 1955, the Brigade brought in 1,600 members. The figure for the period June 1955 to January 1956 was 400. CCF, Ontario, Minutes of Provincial Council, 25 June 1955, CCF/NDP Papers; CCF News, January 1956.

15 In an organizational report to the Provincial Office in January 1956, Doc Ames wrote: "Enclosed are the following memberships picked up [i.e. renewed] in our travels. I may point out that they may seem disappointing but I have been concentrating on selling the [poll] organizational plan as our first objective and working with the local [CCF] groups to show them that it can be done." Doc Ames, Organizational Report, January 29, 1956, MacDonald Papers.

16 Ames, Organizational Report, February 8, 1956, MacDonald Papers; Young, interview by author.

17 CCF, Ontario, "Membership Report, June 1955," appended to Minutes of Provincial Council, 25 June 1955, CCF/NDP Papers; "Membership Report, August 1956," appended to Minutes of Provincial Council, 8 September 1956, Ontario CCF/NDP Papers.

18 CCF, Ontario, Minutes of Provincial Council, 22, 23 January, 5 November 1955; Minutes of Provincial Executive, 14 February 1956, 9 January 1958, CCF/NDP Papers.

19 CCF, Ontario, "Report of the Twentieth Annual Convention, May 22–24, 1954"; "Report of the Twenty-First Annual Convention, April 7–9, 1955"; "Report of the Twenty-Second Annual Convention, 19–21 May 1956"; Minutes of Provincial Executive, 12 June, 16 September, 1954, 14 February 1956, 21 November 1956, and Provincial Council, 25 June 1955, CCF/NDP Papers; Minutes of Provincial Council, 30, 31 October 1954, 8 September 1956, Ontario CCF/NDP Papers.

20 CCF, Ontario, Minutes of Provincial Council, 25 June 1955, CCF/NDP Papers.

21 CCF, Ontario, "Report on the Business Adminstration of CCF News," appended to Minutes of Provincial Executive, 20 July 1955, 18 July 1956; Minutes of Provincial Executive, 9 January 1958, CCF/NDP Papers.

22 CCF, Ontario, Minutes of Provincial Council, 14, 15 December 1957, Ontario CCF/NDP Papers.

23 The CCF placed fourth in the October 24, 1955, federal by-election in Spadina riding, with a lower popular vote than in 1953, and this despite the support of the needle trades unions in the riding and the

assignment of the capable Fred Young as campaign manager. CCF, Ontario, Minutes of Provincial Executive, 21 September 1955, CCF/ NDP Papers; "Conservative Wins Spadina," GM, 25 October 1955. Gallup poll results cited in Young, *Anatomy of a Party*, Appendix B.

24 CCF, Ontario, Minutes of Provincial Executive, 20 December 1955, CCF/ NDP Papers.

25 Ibid.; CCF, Ontario, Minutes of Provincial Executive, 10 January 1956, CCF/NDP Papers.

26 Remarks of National Council cited in CCF, Ontario, Minutes of Provincial Council, 17, 18 March 1956, CCF/NDP Papers.

27 J.B. McGeachy, "Whither, if Anywhere, the CCF?," *Financial Post*, 11 August 1956, 7.

28 "Try to Resurrect CCF in Ontario After Right Turn," TS, 3 August 1956; McGeachy, "Whither"; "CCF Meeting Cuts Off Nationalization Debate," GM, 4 August 1956. On dissent see CCF *News*, September, December 1956, January, February 1957, and for more on the content and formation of the Winnipeg Declaration, see Azoulay, "The CCF's Winnipeg Declaration."

29 "Try to Resurrect CCF in Ontario after Right Turn," TS, 3 August 1956; CCF, Ontario, Minutes of Provincial Council 8 September 1956; OWMF, Annual Meeting Report, 20 March 1957, Ontario CCF/NDP Papers; CCF, Ontario, "Membership Education and Organization, Plans for Conferences, 1956–57," n.d., MacDonald Papers; CCF *News*, December 1956.

30 CCF, Ontario, Minutes of Provincial Executive, 20 July, 20 December 1955, CCF/NDP Papers; CCF, Ontario, "Report of the Twenty-second Annual Convention, 19–21 May 1956," Ontario CCF/NDP Papers; CCF, Ontario, Minutes of Provincial Council, 24, 25 August, 8 September, 8 December 1956; Minutes of Provincial Executive, 21 November 1956, CCF/NDP Papers.

31 CCF, Ontario, Minutes of Provincial Executive, 8 August 1957, CCF/ NDP Papers. Nor did it result in any immediate increase in popularity. In the provincial by-election in York West on 18 October 1956, the CCF finished a distant second behind an unknown Conservative candidate with limited funds, and this despite substantial assistance from the labour movement and the fact that the CCF had won the riding twice in the past. Even in 1955, it had finished a strong second. Ontario, Chief Electoral Officer, *Returns of By-elections, 1956–62*; CCF *News*, October 1956.

32 Ames, Organization Report, 18 January, 7 February, 9 July 1956, MacDonald Papers; CCF *News*, July 1956; CCF, Ontario, Minutes of Provincial Council, 8 September 1956, Ontario CCF/NDP Papers; Minutes of Provincial Executive, 8 August 1956, CCF/NDP Papers; Ames,

Organization Reports, 18 January, 8 December 1956, [September], 9 November 1957, MacDonald Papers.

33 CCF, Ontario, Minutes of Provincial Executive, 21 November 1956, Minutes of Provincial Council, 8 December 1956, CCF/NDP Papers; Ames, Organization Report, 9 July 1956, MacDonald Papers.

34 CCF, Ontario, Minutes of Provincial Executive, 8 August 1957, CCF/NDP Papers; Meisel, *The Canadian General Election of 1957*, 217. The OFL spent an additional $7,000 on CCF advertising in its own literature. CCF, Ontario, Minutes of Provincial Executive, 29 April 1957, CCF/NDP Papers.

35 CCF, Ontario, "Report on Conduct of 1957 Federal Election [in Ontario]," 6 August 1957, Grube Papers; "Liberals Hit by Landslide in Ontario," GM, 11 June 1957; Fisher, "An Interesting Campaign," 121, 143–4; CCF *News*, July 1957. For a detailed analysis of the 1957 election, see Meisel, *The Canadian General Election of 1957*.

36 CCF *News*, July 1957; CCF, Ontario, Minutes of Provincial Council, 24, 25 August 1957, CCF/NDP Papers.

37 CCF, Ontario, "Report of the Twentieth Annual Convention"; CCF *News*, December 1955.

38 The three-man CCF caucus had twenty-two departments to cover. Gisborn and Thomas took two apiece, while MacDonald took the remaining eighteen. MacDonald, *The Happy Warrior*, 70–1.

39 CCF, Ontario, "Report of the Twenty-second Annual Convention"; "Report of the Nineteenth Annual Convention, 2–4 April 1953," Woodsworth Memorial Collection; Minutes of Provincial Council, 8 September 1956, Ontario CCF/NDP Papers; Oliver, *Unlikely Tory*, 81; MacDonald, "Happy Warrior," chap. 6, 14–15.

40 CCF *News*, March 1956.

41 MacDonald, "Happy Warrior," 14–16 (quote); CCF, Ontario, Minutes of Provincial Council, 17, 18 March 1956, CCF/NDP Papers.

42 See Goodman, *Life of the Party*, 63.

43 Ames, Organization Report, 29 February 1956, MacDonald Papers; CCF *News*, April, June 1956.

44 CCF, Ontario, Minutes of Provincial Executive, 14 November 1957; Minutes of Provincial Council, 25 June 1955, CCF/NDP Papers.

CHAPTER SIX

1 CCF *News*, July 1957.

2 Minutes of Provincial Council, 24, 25 August 1957, CCF/NDP Papers. All of the top CCF leaders in Ontario seem to have been infected with this optimism, based on a perceived Liberal decline. As Donald MacDonald told the CCF Co-ordinating Council after the 1957 federal

election, "The CCF is now faced with what may prove to be the most critical period in its history. With the remarkable eclipse of the Liberal party, there are hundreds of thousands of voters seeking a new political home. If we do our job effectively in the months ... ahead we may well have the best opportunity in our history to establish the CCF on a genuine national basis as the only alternative to the old parties holding power." MacDonald to CCF Co-ordinating Council, June 1957, Ontario CCF/NDP Papers.

3 Subsequent scholarly research on voting behaviour in Ontario suggests that this is indeed an element of the province's political culture – that is, that party loyalties are weak and that voters have a tendency to vote *against* governments and *for* the party with the best chance of replacing them. See Drummond, "Voting Behaviour: The Blueing of Ontario."

4 CCF, Ontario, Minutes of Provincial Council, 24, 25 August 1957, CCF/NDP Papers.

5 CCF, Ontario, Minutes of Provincial Executive, 13 June, 8 August, 14 November 1957, CCF/NDP Papers; *CCF News*, September 1957. The younger Lewis was an outstanding organizer. He began organizing at a young age, and by the mid-fifties was running constituency campaigns for CCF candidates in Toronto and the western provinces. According to his biographer, Lewis's success lay primarily in his ability to articulate and impose his will on party workers. Smith, *Unfinished Journey*, 350–3.

6 CCF, Ontario, Minutes of Provincial Council, 24, 25 August 1957; Minutes of Provincial Executive, 8 August 1957, CCF/NDP Papers.

7 CCF, Ontario, "Report of Meeting of Certain Committee Chairmen," 19 June 1957, and Minutes of Provincial Executive, 14 November 1957, CCF/NDP Papers.

8 CCF, Ontario, Minutes of Provincial Executive, 9, 27 January, 27 February, 27 March 1958; Minutes of Provincial Council, 1, 2 February 1958; "Membership Report," July 1958; Pinney to riding presidents et al., 16 January 1958, CCF/NDP Papers.

9 Camnitzer to Hamilton, 12 February 1958, MacDonald Papers.

10 See, for instance, "Road to Oblivion," GM, 8 February 1958.

11 CCF, Ontario, Minutes of Provincial Executive, 9 January, 27 March 1958; Minutes of Provincial Council, 24, 25 August 1957, 1, 2 February 1958, CCF/NDP Papers; *CCF News*, January, February 1957, February 1958.

12 OFL, "Report on PAC Election Campaign – March 31, 1958"; Minutes of OFL-PAC Advisory Executive, 28 February 1958, OFL Papers; "2-Party System in Politics is Aim of Current Drive," GM, 10 March 1958.

13 "Knowles Predicts Election will give CCF Major Role," GM, 6 March 1958; "Road to Oblivion." For additional indications of the party's

optimism, see Trofimenkoff, *Stanley Knowles: The Man From Winnipeg North Centre*, 143–6.

14 "Liberal Ship is Sinking: Coldwell," GM, 4 March 1958.

15 Young, *Anatomy of a Party*, Appendix B; "Members Doubled, Claims CCF," GM, 25 March 1958.

16 The final standings were: Conservatives 208, Liberals 48, CCF 8, Liberal Labour 1. The Social Credit party lost all 19 of the seats it had held in the previous Parliament. In Ontario the standings were: Conservatives 67, Liberals 14, CCF 3, Liberal Labour 1. Leacy, ed., *Historical Statistics of Canada*.

17 Young, *Anatomy of a Party*, Appendix B; "Last Liberal Foothold Lost in City," GM, 1 April 1958.

18 When the Ontario CCF was founded in 1933, it was originally constituted as a federation of three quite autonomous organizations: the United Farmers of Ontario (UFO), the Labour Conference, and a group of CCF Clubs dominated by white collar intellectuals and professionals. However, strong philosophical differences and suspicions within and among the three sections, exacerbated by the almost complete autonomy of each section, led to the departure of the UFO in 1934 and to the decision by the National Leader, J.S. Woodsworth, to centralize the party structure. Under the new constitution, the majority of CCF members no longer belonged to the CCF *indirectly*, through a largely autonomous section acting in concert with other members of the federation, but participated *directly*, as individual members of the party, through their local riding association. See Caplan, *The Dilemma of Canadian Socialism*, 1–77, passim.

19 Young, *The Anatomy of a Party*, 76–82.

20 Abella, *Nationalism, Communism, and Canadian Labour*, 73; Lewis, *The Good Fight*, 299. For more on the internal divisions created by the issue of labour and political action, in both the craft and industrial unions in Ontario, see Robin, "The Trades and Labour Congress of Canada and Political Action"; Piva, "The Toronto and District Labour Council and Independent Political Action: Factionalism and Frustration, 1900–1901"; Roberts, "Artisans, Aristocrats and Handymen"; MacPherson, "The 1945 Collapse of the CCF in Windsor," 205; and Horowitz, *Canadian Labour in Politics*, chaps. 2, 3.

21 Mosher cited in Young, *The Anatomy of a Party*, 83; Larry Sefton, "Memo on Political Action by CC of L Unions and proposals for organization, 1947," Oliver Hodges Papers, York University Archives (YUA), York University, North York, Ontario; Horowitz, *Canadian Labour in Politics*, 138–50, 156.

22 CCF, Ontario, "Report of the TUC to the Annual Convention," 23 November 1945, Grube Papers; Oliver Hodges [Ontario Trade Union

Committee (TUC) organizer] to Larry Sefton, 16 June 1948, Hodges Papers; Young, *The Anatomy of a Party*, 85–6.

23 Horowitz, *Canadian Labour in Politics*, 132–3.

24 Young, *The Anatomy of a Party*, 85–6, 121–2; Horowitz, *Canadian Labour in Politics*, 133–4.

25 CCF, federal, Minutes of Provincial Executive, 10 May 1952, CCF/NDP Papers; Ingle to Weisbach, 2 May 1952; CLC, "Memorandum Re CLC Convention Resolution on New Political Party," [1958], CLC Papers. This antipathy toward a more organic relationship with the CCF, along the lines of European socialist parties, for example, was exemplified by the PAC's director, Murray Cotterill. Cotterill's idea of political action was to build the PAC into a strong organization that could be used to influence, or hopefully dominate, *any* political party. This flexibility was preferable to, and in his view more realistic than, committing labour to one particular party and its ideology. Thus the CCL-PAC's attitude toward affiliation was lukewarm, at best. Murray Cotterill, interview by author, 4 June 1990; MacDonald, *The Happy Warrior*, 383; Lewis, *The Good Fight*, 415; Horowitz, *Canadian Labour in Politics*, 139.

26 Cotterill, interview by author.

27 David Lewis, *The Good Fight*, 301. For a detailed account of these internal struggles, see Abella, *Nationalism, Communism and Canadian Labour*, especially chaps. 6, 8, and Campbell, "'Truly Grass Roots People,'" 120–47. It is also likely that much of the anti-labour sentiment among old-time CCFers in the 1950s stemmed from the authoritarian tactics used by the CCL leadership in its struggles against the Communists in the late 1940s. See E. Fowke to J.E. McGuire [March 1952], OWMF Papers.

28 Bill Sefton neatly summarized this problem in a letter to his brother in 1959: "The CCF was imposed on the Labour movement – and for very good reason, i.e. our need for political action. All kinds of subterfuges were then resorted to ['in lieu of direct political action'] in order to rally support for the C.C.F., such as P.A.C., P.E.C., a buck for the P.A.C., 10 cents per capita in the Steelworkers, some of which was siphoned off into the C.C.F., the direct affiliation etc. ... The total effect was to leave the impression with the Unions that their support was wanted and welcome but no impression was created that this was Labour's party." Bill Sefton to Larry Sefton, 18 June 1959, USA Papers.

29 Young and Cotterill, interviews by author; Caplan, *The Dilemma of Canadian Socialism*, chap. 2; MacPherson, "The 1945 Collapse of the CCF in Windsor," 203–5.

30 Young, *The Anatomy of a Party*, 86; CCF, Ontario, "Unions Affiliated with the CCF – 1956," CCF/NDP Papers.

31 Weisbach, "Memorandum to Cleve Kidd for the OFL Executive," 27 October 1952, CLC Papers. Weisbach told Kidd that since February, "we have not done a great deal to implement and advance PAC work in Ontario ... mainly [because] the PAC Director, due to his appointment as Executive Secretary [of CCL-PAC] had been heavily engaged in election work in the western provinces."

32 Young, interview by author; CCL, "Report of the Political Action Department," 15 June 1954; "Report of the PAC to the Executive Council of the CCL," [1955], CLC Papers.

33 Such comments drew a barrage of criticism from other CCFers. "If members of the CCF working in trade unions are not prepared to supply the inspiration and push," snapped one member, "it's hard to expect it to come from any other source." A CCF unionist who spoke in favour of the resolution at the convention asked "When, pray, will the time ever be more suitable than right now?" CCF News, February, March 1954.

34 CCF News, January 1956.

35 CCF News, February, June 1954; Horowitz, Canadian Labour in Politics, 162–9; See also "Political Activity Seen Rising Force for Labour Unity," GM, 8 March 1958.

36 Smith, Unfinished Journey, chap. 20; Lewis, The Good Fight, 437. Informally, the idea of a new political alignment was probably bandied about earlier than this. David Lewis, for example, claimed to have struck an informal agreement with Jodoin in July 1955 whereby pro-CCF political action would be taken by the CLC "through the CCF or through some broader political alignment" within three years. Cited in Horowitz, Canadian Labour in Politics, 168–9, 172, 175–8.

37 Horowitz, Canadian Labour in Politics, 170–1, 175–9; "First Constitutional Convention of the Canadian Labour Congress," Labour Gazette, 56 (June 1956): 643–7; "2-Party System in Politics is Aim of Current Drive," GM, 10 March 1958.

38 Horowitz, Canadian Labour in Politics, 185–92.

39 Cited in Horowitz, Canadian Labour in Politics, 192 n.

40 Ibid., 193–4. A further indication of the close CCF-CLC relationship formalized at the convention was the election of two veteran CCFers, Stanley Knowles and William Dodge, as general vice-presidents of the Congress.

41 Knowles, The New Party, 19–20; Ken Bryden, interview by author, 18 July 1984, Toronto, Ontario, tape recording; Horowitz, Canadian Labour in Politics, 194.

42 CLC-CCF JNC, A New Political Party for Canada, 21–2.

43 David Lewis claims that the Ontario CCF's Donald MacDonald was involved in the informal discussions beginning in 1957, but MacDonald

has no recollection of this. Lewis, *The Good Fight*, 493; MacDonald, interview by author.

44 CCF, Ontario, "Unions Affiliated with the CCF – 1956"; Minutes of Provincial Council, 1, 2 February 1958, CCF/NDP Papers.

45 CCF *News*, October 1956.

46 CCF, Ontario, Minutes of Executive Committee of the Toronto and District CCF Council, 11 December 1957; Minutes of Provincial Council, 5 November 1955; "Report of the Twenty-fourth Annual Convention, 11–13 October 1958," CCF/NDP Papers; Minutes of Provincial Council, 8 September 1956; "Report of the Twenty-Third Annual Convention, 18–20 April 1957," Ontario CCF/NDP Papers; CCF, Minutes of TUC, 22 October 1956, MacDonald Papers; Weisbach, OFL-PAC Director, "Report to OFL Executive," 10 May 1956, OFL Papers; CCF, Ontario, Minutes of TUC, 6 September 1956, Grube Papers; letter from Bill Sefton to his brother Larry entitled "Some Thoughts on the Ontario Election of June 11, 1959," 18 June 1959, USA Papers.

47 Graham, *Old Man Ontario*, 275–83; Epstein, *Political Parties in Western Democracies*, 160–1.

48 MacDonald to Ames, 14 November 1957; Doc Ames, Organization Report, 5 November 1957, MacDonald Papers. See also Ames's report of 11 November, in which a union organizer in the bush camps around Geraldton agrees with Ames that a less partisan approach to labour was required.

49 OFL, "Report of the Annual Convention, 6–8 February, 1956," OFL Papers; Weisbach to MacDonald, 27 August 1958, CLC Papers.

50 "Political Activity Seen Rising Force for Labour Unity," GM, 8 March 1958. Another factor was the influx of British working-class immigrants in the 1950s who, according to the PAC, "have been seeking in Canada a counterpart of the British Labour Party." OFL, "Confidential Memo for OFL-PAC Special Meeting, 26 May 1958," OFL Papers.

51 Most TLC union locals were forbidden by their constitutions to take partisan political action. "Politics Said Drawing Unions Closer Together," GM, 13 March 1958. See also "Political Activity Seen Rising Force for Labour Unity," and "2-Party System in Politics".

52 OFL, "Report of the First OFL-CLC Convention, 27–29 March 1957," OFL Papers; Canada, Department of Labour, "New Ontario Labour Federation Formed at Merger Convention," *Labour Gazette* 57 (May 1957): 48–52.

53 "New Ontario Labour Federation," 50.

54 OFL, "Report of the First OFL-CLC Convention" (emphasis added). See also Smith, *Unfinished Journey*, 234, for an unequivocal indication of Cotterill's desire to control a political party with union money.

55 "New Ontario Labour Federation," 48; Horowitz, *Canadian Labour in Politics*, 189. For the clearest statement of the CLC's views on the role of labour in the New Party, see CLC, "Memorandum Re CLC Convention Resolution on New Political Party, [1958], CLC Papers.

56 OFL, Minutes of Advisory Council, 12 April 1957, OFL Papers; OFL, *Ontario Labour Review* 1 (October-November 1957): passim; CCF, Ontario, Minutes of Provincial Executive, 12 September 1957, CCF/NDP Papers; Cotterill, interview by author.

57 OFL, "Confidential Memo for OFL-PAC Special Meeting, 26 May 1958," OFL Papers; Ontario, Department of Labour, "Second Annual Convention of OFL," *Labour Gazette* 58 (December 1958): 1370–72.

58 OFL, "Confidential Memo"; CCF, Ontario, "Report of the 24th Annual Convention, 11–13 October 1958," CCF/NDP Papers.

59 Ibid.

60 Ibid; Horowitz, *Canadian Labour in Politics*, 193–4.

CHAPTER SEVEN

1 CCF, Ontario, "Report of the Twenty-Fourth Annual Convention, 11–13 October 1958"; Minutes of Provincial Executive, 26 June 1958, CCF/NDP Papers; OFL, Confidential memo for OFL-PAC special meeting, 26 May 1958, OFL Papers; CLC-Political Education Department, "Political Education Information: National Seminar, August 28–30, 1959," CCF/NDP Papers, 47–8.

2 *CCF News*, February, March 1959; Weisbach, "The First CLC Ontario Provincial Education Conference," 73–4.

3 CLC-CCF JNC, *A New Political Party for Canada*, 1–16.

4 OFL-PAC, Report to Executive Council, 20 March 1959, OFL Papers; *CCF News*, February, April, 1959; CLC-PEC, "Political Education Information," 52; Bryden, interview by author, 18 July, 1984.

5 OFL-PAC, "PAC Report, 10 July 1959," OFL Papers; CCF, Ontario, Minutes of Joint OFL-CCF Election Committee, 18 February 1959, Ontario CCF/NDP Papers.

6 Sefton to Dodge, 19 December 1958; "Confidential Memo," OFL Papers; Dodge to Sefton, 8 January 1959, CCF/NDP Papers.

7 See GM, May, June 1959; MacDonald, *The Happy Warrior*, 75–96; Graham, *Old Man Ontario*, 339–50.

8 "MacDonald Called Reckless, Absurd In Attack by Frost," GM, 28 May 1959.

9 Ontario, Chief Electoral Officer, *Returns of the 1959 Ontario Election*; OFL-PAC, "PAC Report, 10 July 1959," OFL Papers. The CCF finished second in six ridings and third in sixty-nine ridings, compared with

nineteen and fifty-seven, respectively, in 1955. This, too, suggests that Ontario voters were becoming even less inclined to view the CCF as an alternative to the ruling party.

10 Sefton to Dodge, 19 December 1958, OFL Papers.

11 Sefton's elaborate plans for organization in Toronto using "regional" organizers, paid for by local labour councils and unions to work in urban industrial areas, would eventually be realized under the NDP. Bill Sefton to Larry Sefton, 25 June 1959, USA Papers.

12 CCF News, July 1959.

13 On subsequent convictions, see MacDonald, *The Happy Warrior*, 135–7; for examples of MacDonald's questionable methods, see Graham, *Old Man Ontario*, 347–50.

14 "A Noisy Nuisance," GM, 28 May 1959.

15 Ames to MacDonald, 20 August 1958, MacDonald Papers. In a 1972 interview, MacDonald admitted that his emphasis on government scandals during the 1950s probably backfired. First, it made people vote for Frost, who was considered the only person capable of cleaning up the Tory party. Second, it allowed Frost to respond with vehement indignation to the various accusations, which fostered the notion that the CCF was wrong and was simply being opportunistic. MacDonald Interview, for the Ontario Historical Studies Series, 6 June 1972, transcript, OHSS, Public Archives of Ontario (PAO), Toronto.

16 CCF, Ontario, Minutes of Provincial Council, 28 May 1960, Ontario CCF/NDP Papers; OFL-PAC, Report of preconvention meeting, 1 November 1959, CCF/NDP Papers.

17 CCF, Ontario, Minutes of Organization Committee, 25 October 1959; Minutes of Provincial Executive, 17 November 1959; "Report of the 25th Annual Convention, 10–12 October 1959"; National Committee for the New Party (NCNP), *New Party Newsletter*, March 1960, Ontario CCF/NDP Papers.

18 OFL, "Report of the Annual Convention, 2–4 November 1959"; OFL-PAC, Report to Executive Council, 15 January 1960, and to Executive Board, 11 December 1959, OFL Papers; Ontario, Department of Labour, "Third Annual Convention of the Ontario Federation of Labour(CLC)," *Labour Gazette* 59 (December 1959): 1279.

19 CCF News, August, September, November 1959. The name of the Joint National Committee (JNC) was changed to reflect the possibility of broader representation on the Committee.

20 Peg Stewart to Bill Sefton, 15 September 1960; Sparham, Report of New Party Clubs, 14 March 1960, Ontario CCF/NDP Papers; NCNP, *Study Paper on Constitution of the Proposed New Political Party for Canada*, and *Study Paper on Programme of the Proposed New Political Party for Canada*.

21 CCF, Ontario, Minutes of Organization Committee, 25 October 1959, Ontario CCF/NDP Papers.

22 Ibid.

23 MacDonald, "Memorandum: Basic CCF Organization and New Party Clubs," 4 November 1959, MacDonald Papers.

24 Peg Stewart to Carrol Coburn, Confidential notes on discussion at Provincial Committee for New Party meeting, 7 December 1959; Donald MacDonald, "Basic CCF Organization and New Party Clubs"; Kari to Ames, 29 January 1960, Ontario CCF/NDP Papers.

25 CCF, federal, "Single Constituency Areas," [1961], analysis of CCF and New Party Club organization in all Ontario ridings, CCF/NDP Papers.

26 CCF News, November 1957; CCF, Ontario, Minutes of Provincial Council, 22 November 1953, Ontario CCF/NDP Papers. For an analysis of the relations between farmers and the CCF in the early years of the party, see Caplan, *The Dilemma of Canadian Socialism*, 50–63.

27 CCF News, November 1957. For a lengthy analysis of the political activities of Ontario farmers before 1950, see Bristow, "Agrarian interest in the politics of Ontario."

28 CCF, Ontario, Minutes of Farm Committee, 20 May 1950; Minutes of Provincial Council, 22 October 1950, 14 April 1951, 12, 13 January 1952, 5 November 1955, CCF/NDP Papers.

29 MacDonald, *The Happy Warrior*, 265–88.

30 Apart from the handful of farm "representatives" on the CCF Farm Committee and the executive officers of the small UFO, all of whom were dues-paying members of the CCF by 1954, support in rural areas by the early 1950s was minimal. CCF, Ontario, Minutes of Provincial Council, 11 December 1954, CCF/NDP Papers; "Report of the Eighteenth Annual Convention, 10–12 April 1952," WMC; Farm Committee Report to Provincial Council, 4, 5 October 1952, Ontario CCF/NDP Collection.

31 CCF, Ontario, Farm Committee Report; Minutes of Provincial Council, 4, 5 May 1952, Ontario CCF/NDP Papers; Minutes of Provincial Council, 16, 17 January 1954, 4, 5 October 1952; "Report of the 23rd Annual Convention," CCF/NDP Papers. See also CLC, *Can Farmer and Labour Co-operate?*; OFL, *Ontario Labour Review* 1 (October–November 1957); "Report of the Annual Convention, 6–8 February 1956"; "PAC Report, 10 July 1959," OFL Papers; CCF News, July 1954.

32 CCF, Ontario, Minutes of Provincial Council, 4, 5 October 1952, 16, 17 January 1954, CCF/NDP Papers; Farm Committee Report to Provincial Council, 4, 5 October 1952, Ontario CCF/NDP Collection; David Lewis, interview by Paul Fox, 1961, transcript, Paul Fox Collection, York University Archives (YUA), North York, Ontario; Von Pilis to Bell, 8 May 1954, and Bell to Von Pilis, 10 May 1954, CCF/NDP Papers.

33 CCF, Ontario, Minutes of Farm Committee, 20 May 1950; Minutes of Provincial Council, 11 December 1954, CCF/NDP Papers; MacDonald, "Happy Warrior," chap. 17; *CCF News*, June 1953.

34 CCF, Ontario, Minutes of Provincial Council, 22 November 1953, 8 September, 8 December 1956; "Report of the Twenty-Third Annual Convention, 18–20 April 1957," Ontario CCF/NDP Papers; Minutes of Provincial Council, 16, 17 January 1954, CCF/NDP Papers.

35 See MacDonald, *The Happy Warrior*, 268–75.

36 NCNP, Minutes, 30 January 1960, CCF/NDP Papers; Ontario Committee for the New Party (OCNP), Minutes, 16 June 1960, Ontario CCF/NDP Papers. Des Sparham, "Final Report upon the development of the third section of the movement to found a new Canadian political party," [July 1961], Ontario CCF/NDP Papers.

37 Stewart to CCF Farm Committee Executive, 19 February 1960; Stewart to Tait, 25 March 1960; letter from Stewart to CCF Farm Committee Executive, 29 February 1960, Ontario CCF/NDP Papers; CLC, *Can Farmer and Labour Co-operate?* 24.

38 CCF, Ontario, Minutes of Provincial Council, 14, 15 December 1957; OCNP, Minutes, 16 November 1960; "Report: Farm Forum," 9 April 1960; Bowman to Stewart, 10 May 1960, Ontario CCF/NDP Papers; Stewart to Terence Grier, 20 June 1960; Stewart to Carl Hamilton, 26 October 1960, CCF/NDP Papers; Eldon Stonehouse, "Delegates Ask Questions, Put off Debate," GM, 25 October 1960.

39 Don Ellis (Hamilton East CCF President) to Ingle, April 1951; Eve Silver to G. [Rombeck-Masten], 12 March 1952; Ingle to Bryden, 2 September 1954; Minutes of Provincial Executive, 18 July 1953; MacDonald to Peters, 10 May 1951; Lazarus to Massey, 31 March 1952; Parkdale CCF, "Parkdalian," newsletter, January 1958, CCF/NDP Papers; Avakumovik, *The Communist Party in Canada*, 22–53 passim; CCF, Ontario, "Report of Annual Convention, 22–24 March 1951," WMC.

40 During the 1958 federal election campaign, for example, the CCF had evidence that Liberal candidates were using "Information Centres for New Canadians" to warn newcomers that CCF candidates were communists. The Liberals denied that the centres were being used for this purpose. "Information Frauds Charged to Liberals," GM, 11 March 1958.

41 Bryden to Ingle, 1 March 1957, CCF/NDP Papers; CCF, Ontario, Minutes of Provincial Council, 8 December 1956, 14, 15 December 1957, Ontario CCF/NDP Papers; Whitaker, *Double Standard*, 1–24.

42 The Conservatives were much more successful in attracting urban ethnic support, especially among anti-communist Ukrainians and those looking to the provincial government for jobs, contracts, and other favours. CCF, Ontario, Minutes of Ethnic Council, 17 June, 8 December 1956, MacDonald Papers; Minutes of Provincial Council, 24,

25 August 1957, CCF/NDP Papers; see also Oliver, *Unlikely Tory*, 144–73, for an excellent account of Allan Grossman's activities among New Canadians.

43 *CCF News*, August 1956; CCF, Ontario, "Report of Meeting of Representatives of Ethnic Groups," 19 January 1955, and Minutes of Ethnic Council, 17 June 1956, MacDonald Papers; Minutes of Provincial Council, 8 December 1956, Ontario CCF/NDP Papers; Minutes of Provincial Council, 9 February 1957, and of Provincial Executive, 29 April 1957, CCF/NDP Papers.

44 Sefton to Stewart, 19 September 1960; ONCP, Minutes, 10 May, 6 June 1961, 24 May 1960; OFL, "Report of Annual Convention, 7–9 November 1960," OFL Papers.

45 Des Sparham, "Final Report upon the Development of the Third Section of the Movement to Found a New Canadian Political Party," [1961]; CCF, Ontario, summary of meeting regarding role of Ethnic Council in New Party movement, 18 September 1959, Ontario CCF/NDP Papers.

46 NCNP, *New Party Newsletter*, March 1960; Sparham, "Brief Report on New Party Clubs," 14 March 1960; OCNP, Minutes, 24 May 1960, Ontario CCF/NDP Papers; *CCF News*, July 1960.

47 Stewart to Hamilton, 19 February 1960, Ontario CCF/NDP Papers.

48 This was, indeed, a very real fear. In September 1960, for example, the Ontario Hydro Commission sent a threatening letter to its employees discouraging virtually all forms of political activity. See *CCF News*, September 1960, for copy of letter; Sparham, "A Case for New Party Clubs"; CCF, Ontario, Minutes of Provincial Executive, 18 October 1960, Ontario CCF/NDP Papers; Kari to Stewart, 13 January 1961, CCF/NDP Papers.

49 OCNP, Notes regarding meeting of representatives of New Party Clubs, 7 June 1960; Minutes, 28 June 1960; Sparham, "Report on Metro Toronto New Party Clubs Co-ordinating Committee," 13 July 1960, Ontario CCF/NDP Papers.

50 NCNP, "Progress Report on Regional Conferences," [1960], CCF/NDP Papers; CCF, Ontario, Minutes of Provincial Executive, 18 October 1960; Minutes of Provincial Council, 24, 25 September 1960, Ontario CCF/NDP Papers.

51 Stewart to Bill Sefton (chair of Toronto and District Labour Council-Political Education Committee [TDLC-PEC] and Metro Toronto Committee for the New Party), 27 September 1960, Ontario CCF/NDP Papers.

52 Stewart to Reg Gisborn, 7 July 1960, Ontario CCF/NDP Papers.

53 Incidentally, the NCNP agreed with this policy wholeheartedly. The chairman of its Subcommittee on the Liberal-minded, Donald MacDonald, informed his colleagues that "to create an acceptable public 'image' for

the new party we must have attached to the movement a body of people who are not CCFers and not Trade Unionists." NCNP, "Memorandum to Members of Sub-Committee on Participation of Other Liberal-minded People," 23 August 1960, CCF/NDP Papers; Doc Ames, Organization report, 29 February 1960; CCF, Ontario, Minutes of Provincial Executive, 13 September 1960; OCNP, Minutes, 20 September 1960; Stewart to Carrol Coburn, Ontario CCF President, "Confidential notes on discussion at Provincial Committee for the New Party Meeting," 7 December 1960, Ontario CCF/NDP Papers (emphasis added).

54 Sparham, "Final Report"; OCNP, Minutes, 13, 20 March 1961; OCNP and Metro Toronto Committee for the New Party, Minutes of Meeting between Executives, 27 March 1961, Ontario CCF/NDP Papers.

55 Stewart to Hamilton, 19 February 1960; OCNP, Minutes, 12 February 1960, Ontario CCF/NDP Papers.

56 Stewart to Bowman, 21 April 1960, Ontario CCF/NDP Papers.

57 OCNP, Minutes, 24 May 1960, Ontario CCF/NDP Papers.

58 OCNP, Minutes of Table Officers, 24 May [1960]; Stewart to Robinson, 10 June 1960; Stewart to Coburn, 13 June 1960, Ontario CCF/NDP Papers.

59 NCNP, "Report of the NCNP," n.d.; Stewart to Hamilton, 13 January 1961; OCNP, Minutes, 20 March, 14 June 1961; CCF, Ontario, Minutes of Provincial Executive, 18 July 1961; "Press Release," 26 July 1961, Ontario CCF/NDP Papers.

60 OCNP, Minutes, 5 January 1961, 28 June 1960, Ontario CCF/NDP Papers; MacDonald, interview by author, Toronto, 4 July 1984, tape recording.

61 OFL, "Report of the Annual Convention, 2–4 November 1959"; "PAC Report, 10 July 1959"; OFL-PAC, *Memo*, October 1959, OFL Papers; *CCF News*, December 1960.

62 OCNP, Minutes, 12 February 1960; *New Party Newsletter*, Summer 1960, Ontario CCF/NDP Papers; *CCF News*, August 1960; CCF, Ontario, Minutes of Provincial Council, 23, 24 January 1960, 14, 15 January 1961, Ontario CCF/NDP Papers; see also Appendix.

63 OFL-PAC, Report to Executive Council, 20 March 1959, OFL Papers.

64 OFL-PAC, Report to Executive Council, 17 June 1960; OFL, Report of the Annual Convention, 1959, 1960, OFL Papers.

65 *CCF News*, December 1960.

66 Ames to Lazarus, 21 July 1960, Ontario CCF/NDP Papers.

67 OCNP, Minutes, 12 September 1960; Sefton to Dodge, 19 December 1958; OFL, Minutes of Executive Council, 17 June 1960, OFL Papers.

68 *CCF News*, April 1960; Stewart to Chapman, 7 March 1960; CCF, Ontario, Minutes of Provincial Executive, 18 October 1960, Ontario CCF/NDP Papers.

69 OCNP, Minutes, 24 May 1960; CCF, Ontario, Minutes of Provincial Council, 24, 25, September 1960; Stewart to Bowman, 21 April 1960, Ontario CCF/NDP Papers.

70 CCF, Ontario, Minutes of Provincial Executive, 21 June 1960, Ontario CCF/NDP Papers; Minutes of Provincial Executive, 26 June 1958; Minutes of Organization Committee, 24 June 1960, CCF/NDP Papers; Minutes of Organization Committee, 20 July 1960; "Membership Report," [1960], CCF/NDP Papers.

71 Stewart to Gisborn, 7 July 1960; CCF, Ontario, Minutes of Provincial Executive, 21 June 1960, Ontario CCF/NDP Papers; OFL-PAC, Report to Executive Council, 17 June 1960, OFL Papers.

72 Stewart to Ames, 21 July 1960, Ontario CCF/NDP Papers.

73 Stewart to Ames, 29 July 1960, Ontario CCF/NDP Papers.

74 OFL-PAC, "Summary of Organizers Reports, October to December inclusive, 1960," 24 January 1961, Ontario CCF/NDP Papers; CCF, Ontario, Minutes of Provincial Council, 14, 15 January 1961; Ames, Organizational report, January-February, 1961, Ontario CCF/NDP Papers.

75 OCNP, "Rough Draft for OCNP," [1960], Ontario CCF/NDP Papers (emphasis added).

76 OCNP, Minutes, 12 April 1961; OCNP, "How to Co-ordinate New Party Activities," sent to Councils and Clubs in multi-constituency areas, n.d., Ontario CCF/NDP Papers.

77 Le Devoir cited in CCF News, December 1960; NCNP, New Party Newsletter, October-November 1960, April 1961. For more on the Peterborough by-election, see MacDonald, The Happy Warrior, 117–19; Walter Pitman, interview by OHSS, 26 November 1973, transcript; and Young, "The Peterborough By-Election," 505–19.

78 Sparham to Pitman, 4 November 1960, CCF/NDP Papers; MacDonald to Stewart, 22 July 1960, Ontario CCF/NDP Papers.

CHAPTER EIGHT

1 OCNP, Report of Sub-Committee on Organization, 3 March 1961; Minutes, 10 May 1961; Stewart to Francis Eady, secretary-treasurer of Metropolitan Toronto Committee for the New Party, 22 February 1961, Ontario CCF/NDP Papers.

2 OFL-PAC, Report to Executive Council, 16 June 1961; Report to Executive Board, 17 March, 15 September 1961, OFL Papers; "New Party Fund now $160,000," GM, 20 April 1961; OFL-PAC, Memo, September-October 1961; CCF, Ontario, Minutes of Provincial Council, 14, 15, January 1961; OCNP, Minutes of Organization Committee, 2 May 1961, Ontario CCF/NDP Papers.

3 *CCF News*, June 1961; NDP, Ontario, Membership List, 21 June 1962, Ontario CCF/NDP Papers.

4 CCF, Ontario, Minutes of Provincial Executive, 21 February 1961; Minutes of Provincial Council, 26, 27 August 1961; "Report of New Party Clubs in Ontario, May-September 1961; Ames, Organization Reports, January, 10, 28 February, 16 March, 12 June 1961, Ontario CCF/NDP Papers; *CCF News*, June 1961; NCNP, *New Party Newsletter*, May 1961.

5 Kari to Stewart, 21 February 1961; Guilford to "Gentlemen," [January 1961]; Levert to Sparham, 25 March 1961; Kari to Fred Schindeler, 20 September 1961, CCF/NDP Papers; OCNP, Minutes, 12 April 1961; Stewart to Eady, 22 February 1961, Ontario CCF/NDP Papers.

6 Stewart to Sparham, 8 June 1961, Ontario CCF/NDP Papers. For a clear indication of the intentions of the Communists, see document entitled, "The Role of the L.P.P. and its sympathizers in relation to the formation of the New Political Party," n.d., CLC Papers.

7 Stewart to Kari, 13 June 1960; Sparham to Stewart, 21 June 1960; Kari to Stewart, 23 November 1960, CCF/NDP Papers; Stewart to Sparham, 29 June 1960, Ontario CCF/NDP Papers.

8 MacDonald to Armstrong, 24 January 1961, MacDonald Papers.

9 OCNP, Minutes of Provincial Executive, 15 August 1961; CCF, Ontario, Minutes of Provincial Council, 14, 15 January 1961, Ontario CCF/NDP Papers.

10 OFL-PAC, Report to Executive Board, 17 March 1961, OFL Papers; OCNP, Minutes, 13 March 1961, Ontario CCF/NDP Papers.

11 Sparham to Stewart, "Report on New Party Clubs in Northern Ontario," 24 April 1961. There were also several Clubs comprised entirely of CCF members, of which the OCNP was undoubtedly aware.

12 Sparham, "Final Report," [July 1961]; OCNP, Minutes, 16 August 1961, Ontario CCF/NDP Papers.

13 OCNP, Minutes, 12 April 1961, and Appendix to Minutes of Meeting, 10 May 1961, Ontario CCF/NDP Papers; *CCF News*, June 1961.

14 OCNP, Minutes, 5 January 1961; MacDonald to Stewart, 19 July 1961, Ontario CCF/NDP Papers; MacDonald, interview by author, 1984.

15 MacDonald, interview by author, 1984; *CCF News*, November 1961; OCNDP, Minutes, 13 September 1961, Ontario CCF/NDP Papers. Not only did the OCNDP grant Committee members "delegate" status, it also paid for their convention registration fee, subsidized their travel costs, and provided them with spending money – all clear indications of how eager the OCNDP was to ensure that the farm "delegation" be present at the founding convention, and in significant numbers.

16 Robert Rice, "Internal Party Strife Dangerous – Douglas," *Ottawa Citizen*, 29 July 1961; "Knowles Assails New Party Rift," *Ottawa Citizen*, 27 July 1961; "Bitter Split over New Party Leader," *TS*, 27 July 1961; "The New Party puts big Freeze on Argue," *TT*, 11 July 1961; Peter

Dempson, "Well-Healed Labour splurges at 'Wedding,'" *TT*, 31 July 1961; "$161,000 from Labour to New Party," *TT*, 20 July 1961; "Raising Money for Socialism," *Kitchener-Waterloo Record*, 7 March 1961; "New Party Fund now $160,000," *GM*, 20 April 1961; David Lewis to Claude Jodoin, 4 September 1959, CLC Papers.

17 "Tory, Liberal Financing Hit," *Niagara Falls Review*, 13 June 1961; "Party Check-off," *St. Catherines Standard*, 7 June 1961; Lucas, "Will New Party financing threaten secret ballot rights?"; "The CLC had much to lose and little to gain by declaring itself politically," *Port Arthur News Chronicle*, 14 October 1960; "CLC Role Questioned," *Windsor Star*, 27 March 1961; "Convention Follies," *Financial Post*, 19 August 1961; J.B. McGeachy, "Canada's New Party is still living in 1890," *Financial Post*, 22 April 1961; "In other words – still CCFers," *Sudbury Star*, 24 March 1961; "One thing in common," *Kirkland Lake Northerly News*, 27 June 1961.

18 This feeling was no doubt shared by a good many CCFers. At the party's annual summer school in Port Elgin in 1959, one of every six CCFers in attendance felt that the trade unions were politically immature. Reg Gisborn to Carl Hamilton, 3 August 1959, CCF/NDP Papers; *CCF News*, November 1959.

19 "CCFer sees New Party's Doom," *TS*, 4 January 1961; "Discord in the Overture," *Stratford Evening Herald*, 7 January 1961.

20 Douglas Fisher, "Energetic Builder of New Party," *TT*, 31 July 1961; Fisher, "The Last CCF Roundup," 122.

21 Fisher, 122.

22 Young, *The Anatomy of a Party*, 234–6; Cross, *The Decline and Fall of a Good Idea*, 14; Walter Pitman, interview by OHSS, 26 November 1973, transcript, OHSS.

23 Morley, "Socialist Secularization," 444; MacDonald to Irene Ames (wife of Doc), 10 September 1958, MacDonald Papers; CCF, Ontario, "Confidential By-Election Analysis," 3 October 1960, Ontario CCF/NDP Papers; MacDonald to Hamilton, 1 December 1959; Murdo Martin, "Report to CCF National Executive," 20 June 1959, CCF/NDP Papers; see also Campbell, "'Truly Grass Roots People,'" 114–18, for a discussion of northern Ontario's fear that an increasingly powerful labour movement would dominate the New Party.

24 Bryden, interview by author, 1984.

25 Stewart to Ames, 25 May 1960, Ontario CCF/NDP Papers.

26 Ames to Stewart, 14 March 1960, CCF/NDP Papers.

27 OCNP, Minutes, 12 February, 24 May 1960; OCNP, Minutes of Organization Committee, 2 May 1961, Ontario CCF/NDP Papers; Ames to Kari, 25 March 1961, CCF/NDP Papers; "CCF Policies retained in New Party formation," *Sudbury Star*, 3 July 1961.

28 Ames to Hamilton, 25 January 1960, CCF/NDP Papers.

29 CCF, Ontario, "Confidential By-Election Analysis," 3 October 1960, Ontario CCF/NDP Papers.

30 Ames to Stewart, 24 July 1960, Ontario CCF/NDP Papers.

31 NCNP, *New Party Newsletter*, May 1960 (emphasis added).

32 Peg Stewart, Confidential memo to CCF members of OCNP, [July 1961], Ontario CCF/NDP Papers.

33 "Constitution of the Proposed new political party for Ontario," appended to letter from Archer to Stewart, 7 June 1960; MacDonald to Archer, 16 July 1961, Ontario CCF/NDP Papers.

34 Stewart to Archer, 25 July, and Archer to Stewart, 26 July 1961, Ontario CCF/NDP Papers.

35 OCNDP, Minutes, 16 August 1961, Ontario CCF/NDP Papers.

36 OCNDP, Minutes, 13 September, 6 October 1961; Stewart, Confidential memo, Ontario CCF/NDP Papers.

37 Bryden, interview by author, 9 July 1990.

38 *New Democrat*, (formerly *CCF News*), September 1961; "Canada's Best Road to Reform," *TS*, 1 August 1961; Shackleton, *Tommy Douglas*, 257; Morton, *The New Democrats 1961–1986*, 22–7.

39 *New Democrat*, November 1961.

40 TDLC, "Report of NDP-Ontario Founding Convention," appended to Minutes of Council, 19 October 1961, TDLC Minutes, Labour council of Metro Toronto and York Region (LCTY), Don Mills, Ontario; Pat McNenly, "MacDonald Heads on New Party," *TS*, 10 October 1961.

41 Debate on program-related matters was limited, however, by the fact that a new general program was not submitted to the delegates. The OCNDP had decided beforehand that the formulation of a new constitution was more important. A draft program would be prepared for the 1962 convention.

42 NDP, Ontario, "Capsule Report on Founding Convention, October 7–9, 1961," WMC.

43 The convention also decided, thanks to the strong backing of labour delegates, that the secretary-treasurer, plus fifteen Executive Committee members, would from then on be elected by the convention rather than by the Provincial Council.

44 OCNDP, Minutes, 16, 29 August 1961, Ontario CCF/NDP Papers; CCF, Ontario, Minutes of Provincial Council, 26, 27 August 1961, Ontario CCF/NDP Papers.

45 OCNDP, "Convention Call," n.d.; Minutes, 29 August 1961, Ontario CCF/NDP Papers; NDP, Ontario, "Capsule Report."

46 *New Democrat*, November 1961; Pat McNenly, "New Party Spurns CCF 'Tory' Set-up," *TS*, 7 October 1961; Frank Drea, "Destiny Lies in Farm Vote," *TT*, 10 October 1961. The *Globe* reported that MacDonald's organizing efforts among the farmers during the summer had

produced "at least the *semblance* of farm support for the NDP." In fact, there were only 35 registered farm delegates, of more than 1,000 delegates total, registered at the convention. "The New Party and the Farmers," *GM*, 11 October 1961; "New Party Farmers," 10 October 1961 (emphasis added).

47 MacDonald, interview by author, 1984.

48 *CCF News*, August 1961.

CHAPTER NINE

1 NDP, federal, "That Brand New Democratic Party Train," in NDP *Songbook*, issued for the federal founding convention, Grube Papers.

2 *New Democrat*, December 1961, January 1962; NDP, Ontario, Minutes of Provincial Executive, 29 October 1961, Ontario CCF/NDP Papers.

3 NDP, Ontario, Minutes of Provincial Council, 20, 21 January 1962, Ontario CCF/NDP Papers; *New Democrat*, January, February 1962; Pinney, interview by author; "NDP Beaches Candidate Knocks on 6,000 Doors," *TS*, 5 January 1962.

4 Ames to Stewart and Young, 30 January 1962; NDP, Ontario, Minutes of Provincial Council, 8, 9 December, 20, 21 January 1962, Ontario CCF/NDP Papers; MacDonald, *The Happy Warrior*, 130–2; McDougall, *John P. Robarts*, 79–81.

5 NDP, Ontario, Minutes of Provincial Council, 20, 21 January 1962, Ontario CCF/NDP Papers. Murdo Martin, the NDP M.P. from Timmins, did a quick analysis of the effect of the Communist smear campaign on the by-election results. He found that in the ridings where it had not occurred, the NDP increased its popular vote 8.7 percent, but where it had occurred, the NDP gained only 1 percent. Martin to Stewart, 24 January 1962, Ontario CCF/NDP Papers; Pinney, interview by author.

6 Oliver to Larry Sefton, 1 December 1961, USA Papers.

7 Pinney, interview by author.

8 Bryden, interview by author, 1990.

9 Stewart to "Friends," 9 January 1962; NDP, Ontario, Minutes of Provincial Executive, 1 April 1962, 10 December 1961, Ontario CCF/NDP Papers; Morton, *The New Democrats 1961–1986*, 29.

10 Stewart to MacMillan, and to Douglas, 16 April 1962; Ontario, CCF, Minutes of Provincial Council, 23, 24 June 1962, Ontario CCF/NDP Papers.

11 NDP, Ontario, Minutes of Provincial Council, 20, 21 January 1962; Ames to Stewart and Young, 30 January 1962, Ontario CCF/NDP Papers.

12 It should be noted that the NDP began deficit financing in a big way after the founding convention. It adopted a "go for broke" attitude

toward spending money in the hope that success at the polls would bring its own financial rewards in the form of more members and donations, which could then be used to repay loans. Unfortunately, this strategy did not work and the string of elections the NDP was forced to contest gave the party too little time to recover financially. NDP, Ontario, Minutes of Provincial Council, 20, 21 January 1962; Minutes of Provincial Executive, 6 January, 1 April 1962; Young to Ames, 13 March 1962, Ontario CCF/NDP Papers.

13 After the founding of the NDP, the OFL created two bodies in place of the former OFL-PAC: the Political Education Department and the Political Education Committee. Presumably this was done to de-emphasize the PAC as the focal point or clearing house for labour's political activities and to highlight its purely educational role.

14 NDP, Ontario, Report of election committee, n.d., CCF/NDP Papers; "Report of the Annual Convention, 6–8 October 1962," WMC; OFL-PED, Report to Executive Council, 15 June 1962, OFL Papers.

15 Morton, *New Democrats*, 37. For more on the 1962 federal election, see Meisel, eds., *1962 Election*.

16 Across Canada, 83 percent of organized labour voted for other parties: 38 percent for the Liberals, 31 percent for the Conservatives, 14 percent for Social Credit. Meanwhile, between January and October 1962, the number of union members affiliated to the NDP increased from 58,000 to 133,000. Stewart to Terry Grier (federal secretary), 13 August 1962, Ontario CCF/NDP Papers; Bill Reader (District Representative of American Federation of Grain Millers) to Lazarus, 25 June 1962; OFL, "Record of Union Affiliations to NDP-Ontario-October 18, 1962," OFL Papers; *New Democrat*, September 1962.

17 "Communists Pledge Support for NDP," GM, 27 April 1962; NDP, Ontario, Minutes of Election Committee, 24 May 1962; Minutes of Provincial Executive, 3 March, 2 June 1962; Minutes of Provincial Council, 23, 24 June 1962; MacDonald to "All Publishers," 1 June 1962; J.S. Midanik, Solicitor, to Nelson Castonguay, Chief Electoral Officer, 5 June 1962; Stewart to Midanik, 25 May 1962, Ontario CCF/NDP Papers; *New Democrat*, April 1962.

18 A detailed account of this campaign may be found in the author's unpublished research paper, "'Operation Freedom': The Canadian Chamber of Commerce and the Cold War, 1961–1962," York University, 1985. Most of the information in this section is from this source.

19 According to a former member of the Chamber's Secretariat, William G. Browne, "Operation Freedom" was launched after C.T. Hazen, a Saskatchewan member of the Chamber's Board of Directors, urged the Chamber to initiate a campaign against the newly-formed NDP. Ibid., 23 n.

20 Cited in Azoulay, "'Operation Freedom,'" 21.

21 Ibid., 22 n.

22 Ibid., 55.

23 The NDP's intense determination to avoid any association with the Communists also manifested itself in the expulsion of over a dozen members of the NDP and its youth section accused of being members of "other [i.e. Communist] political parties": the League for Socialist Action and the Young Socialist Alliance. NDP, Ontario, Minutes of Provincial Executive, 19 April 1963; Stewart to "Presidents", 9 April 1962, Ontario CCF/NDP Papers.

24 Cited in Horowitz, *Canadian Labour in Politics*, 260; for a more complete statement, see "Argue Leaves NDP, Says Labour Clique Rules," GM, 19 February 1962.

25 "Departure of Mr. Argue," GM, 20 February 1962.

26 Arnold Peters to Peg Stewart, 26 February 1962; Stewart to "NDP Federal Candidates," 22 February 1962; NDP, Ontario, "Press Release," Ontario CCF/NDP Papers; *New Democrat*, March 1962.

27 *New Democrat*, March 1962; Carberry to "Ontario Presidents and Secretaries," 16 March 1962, Ontario CCF/NDP Papers. See also open letter from Tommy Douglas to Ontario membership in the *New Democrat*, April 1962.

28 TS, 9 May 1962.

29 "Millard Out to Topple Tory M.P.," TS, 7 April 1962; "Claims Unions Pay Donald MacDonald," TS, 23 January 1962; NDP, Ontario, "Press Release," 20 February 1962, MacDonald Papers.

30 NDP, Ontario, Minutes of Provincial Executive, 3 March, 1 April 1962; "Membership report," appended to Minutes of Provincial Council, 23, 24 June 1962; Clarke to Young, 21 February 1962; Stewart to Clarke, 27 February 1962, Ontario CCF/NDP Papers.

31 Clarke to Young, 21 February 1962; Stewart to Clarke, 27 February 1962, Ontario CCF/NDP Papers; newspaper clipping entitled "Ex-MLA Blasts 'Brazen Hazen' for Defection," [February] 1962, found in G.M.A. Grube Papers, Trinity College Archives (TCA), University of Toronto; *New Democrat*, April 1962; "Martin Quits NDP, Charges Officials Were Rude to Gauthier," GM, 3 January 1963; Smith, "The Campaign in Eglinton," in *Papers on the 1962 Election*, ed. J. Meisel, 68–90.

32 Cited in Horowitz, *Canadian Labour in Politics*, 260.

33 Archer to Stewart, 21 March 1962, Ontario CCF/NDP Papers; OFL, Minutes of Executive Council, 14 September 1962, OFL Papers.

34 Speech by Morden Lazarus to Brantford and District Labour Council, Labour Day 1962, OFL Papers.

35 NDP, Ontario, Minutes of Provincial Executive, 10 December 1961, 6 January 1962; Minutes of Provincial Council, 20, 21 January 1962,

Ontario CCF/NDP Papers; OFL, "Report of Annual Convention, 6–8 November 1961"; "Record of Union Affiliations to NDP – Ontario," 2 July, 18 October 1962, OFL Papers.

36 Jodoin, interview by Paul Fox, 1 June 1961, Fox Collection; see also speech by David Archer to OFL Convention, 6 November 1961, OFL Papers.

37 In 1959, the CCF received approximately $6,400 in the form of affiliation dues from unions, which represented 17 percent of its total revenues. In 1963, the amounts were $34,300 and 44 percent respectively. CCF/NDP, Ontario, Statement of revenue and expenditure, 1959, 1963, Ontario CCF/NDP Papers.

38 *New Democrat*, December 1961, March 1962; OFL-PED, Report to Executive Board, 16 March 1962; OFL, "Report of the Annual Convention, 5–7 November 1962"; "Reports on Participation in 1962 Federal Election by Labour Council and Local Union PECs," n.d., OFL Papers; Ames to MacDonald, 1 October 1962; Ames to Bury, 13 November, 14 December 1962; Olive Smith to Bury, 6 December 1962, Ontario CCF/NDP Papers.

39 Pinney, interview by author.

40 NDP, Ontario, Minutes of Provincial Executive, 3 February, 7 July 1962; Minutes of Provincial Council, 20, 21 January 1962; "Report of the Annual Convention, 6–8 October 1962," Ontario CCF/NDP Papers.

41 Grube to Stewart, 4 November 1961; Stewart to Grube, 14 November 1961, Grube Papers; NDP, Ontario, Minutes of Table Officers, 10 November 1961; Minutes of Provincial Executive, 10 December 1961, Ontario CCF/NDP Papers.

42 "NDP Nominates Man President Never Met," TS, 27 March 1962; NDP, Ontario, Minutes of Staff Meeting, 27, 28 December 1962, Ontario CCF/NDP Papers.

43 Lazarus to Bury, 14 November 1962; Bury to Lazarus, 3 December 1962, Ontario CCF/NDP Papers.

44 *New Democrat*, August 1962. Scott would pursue this theme with more vigour in the near future. See "Revamp party or be wiped out, NDP official Warns," TS, 13 November 1963.

45 *New Democrat*, September 1962.

46 NDP, Ontario, Minutes of Provincial Council, 18, 19 August 1962, Ontario CCF/NDP Papers.

47 Sheffe to MacDonald, 16 October 1962, Ontario CCF/NDP Papers.

48 *New Democrat*, November 1962.

49 NDP, Ontario, Minutes of Provincial Council, 8, 9 December 1962, Ontario CCF/NDP Papers.

50 NDP, Ontario, *A New and Democratic Program for Ontario* (1962), CCF/NDP Papers.

51 CCF, Ontario, *Challenge for Ontario* (1958), CCF/NDP Papers. The sections dealing with labour and farmers were left to the last three pages of the 1962 program, but figured prominently in the first two sections of the 1958 program. Perhaps the change was due to the NDP's wish to rid itself of the "class" party image, particularly in relation to organized labour.

52 "Provincial NDP Pledges Aid to Consumers," GM, 8 October 1962; "Unionists in NDP Kill Bill to Replace Strike," GM, 9 October 1962.

53 NDP, Ontario, Minutes of Provincial Executive, 17, 18 November 1962, Ontario CCF/NDP Papers; Archer to Jodoin, 3 August 1962; Ames to Lazarus, 13 October 1962, OFL Papers.

54 NDP, Ontario, Minutes of Table Officers, 23 July 1962; Minutes of Provincial Executive, 2 August 1962, Ontario CCF/NDP Papers.

55 NDP, Ontario, Finance Committee report to Provincial Executive, 17 November 1962, CCF/NDP Papers; Young to Grier, 8 August 1962; NDP, Ontario, "Notes on Meeting of Members of the Organizing Committee," 5 September 1962, Ontario CCF/NDP Papers.

56 "NDP Budgets $4,000 for Greenwood Riding," GM, 27 April 1962; NDP, Ontario, Minutes of Provincial Executive, 20 October 1962; "Submission to Provincial Executive," 2 August 1962; Cadbury to Brigden, 9 July 1962, Ontario CCF/NDP Papers.

57 Some ridings even refused to participate in the federal finance drive in February, and instead held their own drives. NDP, Ontario, "Finance Drive," [1962]; Theobald to Young, 16 February 1962, Ontario CCF/NDP Papers.

58 NDP, Ontario, Minutes of Provincial Executive, 10 December 1961, 1 April 1962; Ted Theobald to "All Metro Toronto NDP Riding Presidents and Secretaries," 29 March 1962; Cadbury to Bill Sefton, 29 January, 25 July 1962, Ontario CCF/NDP Papers.

59 NDP, Ontario, Minutes of Provincial Executive, 8, 9 September 1962, Ontario CCF/NDP Papers. Ken Bryden lays most of the blame for this incident on Bill Sefton who, he alleges, was forever trying to expand his power base in Toronto, this time through the Metropolitain Toronto Committee for the New Party (MTCNP). Bryden, interview by author, 1990.

60 Millard to Cadbury, 15 November 1962, Ontario CCF/NDP Papers.

61 NDP, Ontario, Minutes of Organization Committee, 7 December 1962, Ontario CCF/NDP Papers. Another manifestation of the more independent mentality at the local level was the request of several ridings, in July 1962, that they be given more power over the collection and distribution of funds, as was the practice in the British Labour Party. Evidently they were fed up with having to consistently finance the weaker ridings through their rebates to the Provincial Office. The request was

rejected by the Finance Committee. NDP, Ontario, Minutes of Provincial Executive, 7 July 1962, Ontario CCF/NDP Papers.

62 NDP, Ontario, Minutes of Staff Meeting, 27, 28 December 1962, Ontario CCF/NDP Papers.

63 George Richer, Report on organization, 25 August 1962; NDP, Ontario, Minutes of Organization Committee, 7 December 1962, Ontario CCF/NDP Papers.

64 NDP, Ontario, "Membership Report," 31 March 1963; Minutes of Table Officers, 24 January 1963; Minutes of Provincial Council, 20, 21 April 1963; Erna Fox (Secretary of Cochrane NDP) to Bury, 14 February 1963; Ontario CCF/NDP Papers; Michael Oliver to Cadbury, 4 February 1963, CCF/NDP Papers.

65 Harry Simon (CLC Regional Director of Organization) to Staff representatives, 12 February 1963; NDP, Ontario, "Report of the Election Campaign Committee," 1962, CCF/NDP Papers; Minutes of Toronto Area Council, 27 April 1963, Ontario CCF/NDP Papers; New Democrat, September 1963.

66 OFL-PEC, Minutes, 18 March 1963, OFL Papers.

67 New Democrat, March, April 1963.

68 NDP, Ontario, Report on results of 1962 and 1963 federal elections; Minutes of Provincial Council, 20, 21 April 1963; Toronto Area Council Election Committee to George Cadbury, 13 April 1963, Ontario CCF/NDP Papers; OFL-PEC, Report to Executive Council, 21 June 1963, OFL Papers; TDLC, Minutes, 21 March 1963, TDLC Minutes.

69 New Democrat, June 1963; MacDonald, interview by author, 1990; Young to Riding Presidents etc., 25 June 1963, Ontario CCF/NDP Papers.

70 NDP, Ontario, "Membership report," 29 May 1964, Ontario CCF/NDP Papers; Minutes of Campaign Committee, 13 August 1963; "Suggested Procedure for Raising and Controlling Election Funds," n.d.; Bury to George Burt (Canadian United Automobile Workers [UAW] director), 28 June 1963, Ontario CCF/NDP Papers.

71 NDP, Ontario, Memorandum from George Cadbury entitled "The Real Alternative: Vote New Democrat," 16 July 1963; Minutes of Election Campaign Committee, 11 June, 13 August 1963, Ontario CCF/NDP Papers.

72 "MacDonald's Day Spent on Foot Greeting Electors in York South," GM, 25 September 1963.

73 GM, 6, 10, 11, 12, 16, 17, 19, 25 September 1963.

74 GM, 6, 11, 12, 18, 19 September 1963; McDougall, Robarts, 97, 108. Even the traditionally partisan Toronto Star abandoned Wintermeyer in this election, endorsing Robarts instead.

75 G.E. Mortimore, "The Man who has taken Politics out of Politics," GM, 25 September 1963; MacDonald, The Happy Warrior, 138; McDougall, Robarts, 107–8.

76 "Robarts Gains New Stature as PM With Province-Wide Sweep," GM, 26 September 1963; McDougall, *Robarts*, 95–6.

77 The federal NDP was first within the movement to use television in a big way, beginning with the 1962 federal election. The individual in charge of producing television advertising for the party, Brian Huggins, suggested to Morden Lazarus that television could be very useful in dispelling the image of NDP leaders as "wild-eyed 'commies.'" Referring to Tommy Douglas specifically, he said: "It wouldn't be so much what he says as how he *appears* that will determine what influence the broadcasts have on the success enjoyed by the party at the polls. I think our ... broadcasts ... will show our team; our appeal to the heart rather than the mind." Huggins to Lazarus, 18 October 1962; Grier to Stewart, 14 August 1962, Ontario CCF/NDP Papers.

78 NDP, Ontario, Minutes of Provincial Executive, 17, 18 November 1962; Minutes of Public Relations Committee, 17 November 1962; Minutes of Provincial Council, 8, 9 December 1962, 20, 21 April 1963, Ontario CCF/NDP Papers.

79 NDP, Ontario, Minutes of Provincial Council, 20, 21 April 1963; "Draft Budget" for 1963 provincial election, appended to Minutes of Election Campaign Committee, 11 June 1963; "Provincial Election Report," 1963; Bury to R. Roberts. 3 October 1963, Ontario CCF/NDP Papers.

80 NDP, Ontario, Minutes of Provincial Council, 20, 21 April 1963, Ontario CCF/NDP Papers.

81 NDP, Ontario, "Provincial Election Report," appended to Minutes of Provincial Council, 16, 17 November 1963, Ontario CCF/NDP Papers. Socialist parties around the world were generally slower to adapt the new campaigning techniques, for both philosophical and financial reasons (especially the former). In the NDP's case, though, there does not seem to have been any significant philosophical opposition. Epstein, *Political Parties in Western Democracies*, 239–41, 258–9.

82 Ontario, Chief Electoral Officer, *Returns of the 1963 General Election*.

83 NDP, Ontario, "Provincial Election Report" and "Public Relations Report," appended to Minutes of Provincial Council, 16, 17 November 1963, Ontario CCF/NDP Papers; MacDonald, *The Happy Warrior*, 137.

84 In Tommy Thomas's riding of Oshawa, for example, only 30 percent voted in the labour wards. Meanwhile, Ontario's unemployment rate fell from 5.5 percent in 1961 to 3.2 percent in 1964. As for the Communist smear campaign, this was particularly strong in Brantford and, no doubt, elsewhere. *New Democrat*, October 1963; Rea, *The Prosperous Years*, 34; Walter Szmigielski, "Constituency Level Politics," 97, 178–82.

85 This realism was seen in the pages of the *New Democrat* after Andrew Brewin's son, John, took over as editor in late 1962. The paper began

carrying controversial articles critical of the NDP and, in general, adopted a less self-delusory attitude to the party's problems.

CHAPTER TEN

1 Pinney, interview by author.
2 Drummond, "Voting Behaviour: Counting the Change," 249; Brownsey and Howlett, "Class Structure and Political Alliances in an Industrialized Society"; McCormick, "Provincial Party Systems, 1945–1993," 349–71; MacDonald, "Ontario's Political Culture."
3 McCormick, "Provincial Party Systems, 1945–1993," 349; Gagnon and Tanguay, "Minor Parties in the Canadian Political System," 108–9.
4 Macdonald, "Ontario's Political Culture," 315 (italics added).
5 Morley, Secular Socialists, 15–17.
6 Duverger, Political Parties; Carty, "Party Organization and Activity on the Ground"; Wearing, "Political Parties"; and Angell, "Duverger, Epstein, and the Problem of the Mass Party."
7 Rea, The Prosperous Years, 33, 242.
8 Downs, An Economic Theory of Democracy.
9 Monroe and Erickson, "The Economy and Political Support."
10 MacDonald, interview by OHSS, 6 June 1972, transcript, OHSS.
11 Morton, The New Democrats, 65, 90; Whitehorn, Canadian Socialism, 50–65; McDonald, The Party That Changed Canada, chap. 7.
12 Monroe and Erickson, "The Economy and Political Support," 202.
13 Ibid; Whitehorn, "Audrey McLaughlin and the Decline of the Federal NDP," 334–5.
14 McLeod and McLeod, Tommy Douglas, 181.
15 This is not to say that the reverse was true; namely, that in hard times, support for the CCF/NDP rose. Severe recessions, as in the 1930s and early 1990s, did not seem to benefit the party very much. It may be that in situations of severe economic decline people are primarily concerned about daily survival and thus less willing to risk even their meagre standard of living on untried, radical solutions. Monroe and Erickson speculate, further, that recessions have not benefited the NDP because the party was viewed as being unable to solve economic problems, and because an extensive social security system was already in place to buffer the recession's impact and thus keep people from turning to the NDP. On the other hand, as Maurice Pinard has demonstrated for the Social Credit Party in Quebec in the early 1960s, "economic strain" – the sudden deterioration of economic conditions after relatively long periods of economic prosperity – can work to the benefit of third parties; the significant support given to protest parties generally in the 1930s, parties offering unorthodox solutions to social

and economic problems, is further proof of this. M. Pinard, *The Rise of a Third Party*; Monroe and Erickson, "The Economy and Political Support"; Penner, "The Past, Present, and Uneasy Future of the New Democratic Party," 90.

16 Nichol, "In Pursuit of the Voter," 133–4; Steeves, *The Compassionate Rebel*, 176–86; Hunter, "Social Democracy in Alberta," 58; Wiseman, *Social Democracy in Manitoba*, 65–6; McLeod and McLeod, *Tommy Douglas*, 184.

17 Beck, *Pendulum of Power*, 273, 327.

18 In contrast to this line of argument, Duverger argues that membership in mass parties is unaffected by such external forces as economic fluctuations or war. Membership, he says, is "very much more sensitive to problems that are truly party problems," especially internal division. In the case of the Ontario CCF/NDP, however, its severe loss of membership largely *preceded* the serious divisions of the early fifties, and its membership in fact began to increase shortly thereafter. Duverger, *Political Parties*, 84–5.

19 Carty, "Party Organization and Activity on the Ground," 191.

20 Wearing, *Strained Relations*, chap. 2; Drummond, "Voting Behaviour: Counting the Change"; Kornberg et al., "Determinants of Provincial Voting Behaviour," 434–5; Pammett, "Class Voting and Class Consciousness in Canada."

21 Wearing, *Strained Relations*, chap. 2.

22 See Drummond, "Voting Behaviour: Counting the Change," 241; and Wrong, "Ontario Provincial Elections." The distortions of the electoral system, as far as the CCF/NDP was concerned, were especially strong in the 1950s, when the ratio of the percentage of seats won to the percentage of votes garnered was lower than it had been earlier and in subsequent periods. It might be argued, as well, that the unusually weak link between class and voting in Canada was another factor exacerbating the CCF/NDP's decline. Kornberg et al. note that the tendency of subjectively defined working-class persons to support left-wing parties more than voters from other classes, is very weak in Canada, except in British Columbia. Had class voting been stronger – that is, had the working class been more conscious of its interests as a distinct class – the larger macro forces eroding CCF support in this period would not have proved quite so devastating to the party. Pammett, "Class Voting and Class Consciousness in Canada," 137; Kornberg et al., "Determinants of Provincial Voting Behaviour," 437.

23 Wilson, "Towards a Redefinition of the Nature of the Canadian Political System"; Drummond, "Voting Behaviour: Counting the Change," 247–8; Brownsey and Howlett, "Class Structure and Political Alliances in an Industrialized Society." An interpretation similar to

Wilson's is presented by Chi and Perlin, "The NDP: A Party in Transition."

24 The urban population of Canada as a whole increased from 54 percent of the total population in 1941, to 63 percent in 1966, with much of the increase occurring in Ontario's "Golden Horseshoe" region in the south-central part of the province. By the 1960s, this area, which contained half of Ontario's population in the 1940s, had grown to comprise two-thirds of its residents. It also led the way in terms of industrial growth, with one-third of the growth in the net value of Canadian manufacturing from 1947 to 1961 coming from this region and, in particular, the cities of Toronto, Hamilton, Oshawa, London, and Kitchener. Leacy, ed., *Historical Statistics of Canada*, A67–74; Rea, *the Prosperous Years*, 30; Kerr and Holdsworth, eds., *The Historical Atlas of Canada, vol. 3*, Plate 51.

25 Between the 1951 and 1955 elections, for example, the CCF's popular vote fell by 2.5 percent across the province, while in Toronto and Hamilton it fell by 2.2 percent. When the urban centres of Brantford, London, Niagara Falls, and the Yorks (just north of Toronto) are included, the figure jumps to 4 percent. Ontario, *Returns of the Chief Electoral Officer*, 1951 and 1955.

26 Richards, "The Decline and Fall of Agrarian Socialism."

27 Silverstein, "Occupational Class and Voting Behaviour: Electoral Support of a Left-Wing Protest Movement in a Period of Prosperity"; quote from McLeod and McLeod, *Tommy Douglas*, 211.

28 Between 1951 and 1963, the CCF/NDP's popular vote in the 11 ridings adjacent to the greater Metro Toronto and Hamilton areas experienced a net loss of 10 percentage points, compared to a net loss of 3.6 points across the province. Ontario, *Returns of the Chief Electoral Officer*, 1951–1963; Rea, *The Prosperous Years*, 134–50.

29 Gagnon and Tanguay, "Minor Parties in the Canadian Political System."

30 Rea, *The Prosperous Years*, 11–16.

31 Manthorpe, *The Power and the Tories*, 31–7; Penner, *From Protest to Power*, 80–3; Rea, *The Prosperous Years*, 17–19.

32 Rea, *The Prosperous Years*, 225.

33 Ibid, 21.

34 By this point, notes Rea: "The concern in Ontario soon shifted from unemployment to the ability of the government to provide the infrastructure investment in highways, electric power generating capacity, and municipal services needed to meet the demands of a rapidly expanding and industrializing society." *The Prosperous Years*, 22

35 Ibid, 23–4; MacDonald, "Ontario's Political Culture"; Wise, "The Ontario Political Culture."

36 Hofstadter cited in McNaught, "Socialism and the Canadian Political Tradition," 91.

37 MacDonald, *The Happy Warrior*, 345.

38 On Goodman's organizational work in Toronto during the Frost years, see Goodman, *Life of the Party*, 58–61.

39 Lewis, *The Good Fight*, 415.

40 Canadian socialists have a history of internal division going back to the early 1900s, when socialist parties of varying degrees of radicalism were badly split between doctrinaire revolutionaries and more pragmatic, revolutionary socialists. A similar division afflicted the British Columbia CCF in the late 1940s. Fox, "Early Socialism in Canada"; Gagnon and Tanguay, "Minor Parties in the Canadian Political System," 109; Steeves, *The Compassionate Rebel*, 201–2.

41 Bryden, interview by author, 1984.

42 Zakuta, *A Protest Movement Becalmed*, 109. This view is shared by Nichol, who asserts that over time the CCF, "most notably the Ontario section, had been moulded into a moderate social democratic party working in close alliance with the non-communist trade unions." Nichol, "In Pursuit of the Voters," 123.

43 The percentage of union members affiliated to the NDP through their unions fell from a high of 15 percent in 1963, to 10 percent in 1974, to only 7 percent in 1984. Archer, *Political Choices and Electoral Consequences*, 37.

44 Whitehorn, "Audrey McLaughlin and the Decline of the Federal NDP," 330; Penner, "The Past, Present, and Uneasy Future of the New Democratic Party," 96–7.

45 One must put Archer's finding in perspective though, for he himself points out that "union-party affiliation has [only] a moderately positive effect on rates of support for the NDP" and more members of NDP-affiliated unions vote for the Liberals than for the NDP. Archer, *Political Choices and Electoral Consequences*, 62, 64 (quote).

46 Bryden, interview by author, 1990.

47 See Horowitz, *Canadian Labour in Politics*, 234–52; and Young, *Anatomy of a Party*, 207–8. For a discussion of why European socialist parties – particularly the British Labour Party – have been more successful at attracting labour support, see Epstein, *Political Parties in Western Democracies*, 145–9.

48 Young, *The Anatomy of a Party*, 60. Perhaps Young's interpretation can be explained, in part, by his background. A one-time Liberal activist who played a prominent role as a spokesperson for the "liberal-minded" during the New Party development, Young was determined that the New Party become something that the CCF, in his view, was

not: namely, less pedagogic, less doctrinaire, and more broadly based. "The independent [liberal]," he told a New Party conference of liberal-minded representatives in Toronto in 1960, is someone "who has a streak of pragmatism in his nature, [and] mistrusts panaceas and those who claim to have all the answers ... The party which the independent could support is one which represents the *whole* of the Democratic Left, not merely the socialist element – for in the narrow sense of this word, the independent is not a socialist." In short, Young may have interpreted the evolution of the CCF as he did because he desperately wanted to see the CCF become less of a movement and more of a party, albeit a progressive, principled one. NCNP, Report on New Party conference, 15 October 1960, CCF/NDP Papers.

49 NDP, Ontario, Minutes of Provincial Council, 20, 21 April 1963, Ontario CCF/NDP Papers.

50 J.S. Woodsworth may, indeed, have been more the educator type, preferring to teach people about socialism than win their votes through organization, but many other top leaders in the early years earned their stripes by doing organizational work at the local level, and doing it with a particular genius and zeal. See Stinson, *Political Warriors*, chap. 1.

51 Lewis, *The Good Fight*, 447.

52 In his doctoral study of the CCF in northern Ontario, Campbell argues that academics have placed too much emphasis on the role of party leaders in "keeping the party together during the lean years between 1945 and 1961," and that, in fact, "rank and file CCFers made an important contribution to the survival of the CCF as a party." Unfortunately, Campbell's conclusions are too general and are based almost entirely on a handful of interviews. Notwithstanding the efforts of a "dedicated core of activists," the hard evidence (especially the organizers' reports, including Ames in the north) clearly points to an overall decline in activism at the local level in this period. Were it not for the tireless efforts and inspiration of the provincial leaders, it is certain that the party would have collapsed. Even Campbell admits that much of the local activity in the north was due to the efforts of Doc Ames and that the inspiration of the leadership kept the local people going during the hard times. Campbell, "'Truly Grass Roots People,'" 1, 55, 117, 131.

53 Young, interview by author.

54 Pinney, interview by author.

55 Morley, *Secular Socialists*, xvii.

56 See Michels, *Political Parties*; Ostrogorski, *Democracy and the Organization of Political Parties*, chap. 8, and "Introduction" by S.M. Lipset; and Duverger, *Political Parties*, "Introduction."

57 Young, interview by author.

58 Bristow, interview by author, 8 May 1990, Mississauga, Ontario, notes.

59 CCL, PAC, *Newsletter*, December 1951, CLC Papers. The best account of the sorts of sacrifices that CCF activists across Canada chose to make is Melnyk's, *Remembering the* CCF.

60 Epstein, *Political Parties in Western Democracies*, 102.

61 Young and Pinney, interviews by author.

62 MacDonald, *The Happy Warrior*; Shackleton, *Tommy Douglas*, 248.

63 Young, *The Anatomy of a Party*, 4.

Bibliography

ARCHIVAL COLLECTIONS

Canadian Labour Congress Papers, National Archives of Canada (NA).
Donald C. MacDonald Papers, Queen's University Archives (QUA).
Federal CCF/NDP Papers, NA.
George Grube Papers, QUA.
G.M.A. Grube Papers, Trinity College Archives, University of Toronto (TCA).
Oliver Hodges Papers, York University Archives, North York, Ontario (YUA).
Ontario CCF/NDP Collection, McMaster University Archives, Hamilton, Ontario (MUA).
Ontario CCF/NDP Papers, QUA.
Ontario Federation of Labour Papers, NA.
Ontario Historical Studies Series Interview Collection, Public Archives of Ontario (PAO).
Ontario Liberal Party Papers, QUA.
Ontario Woodsworth Memorial Foundation Collection, MUA.
Paul Fox Collection, YUA.
Toronto and District Labour Council Minutes, Labour Council of Metro Toronto and York Region, Don Mills, Ontario (LCTY).
United Steelworkers of America, District 6, Papers, MUA.
Woodsworth Memorial Collection, Thomas Fisher Rare Book Library, University of Toronto (TFRB).

PERSONAL INTERVIEWS

Bristow, Dudley.
Bryden, Ken. (1984, 1990)

Cotterill, Murray.
MacDonald, Donald C. (1984, 1990)
Pinney, Marjorie.
Young, Fred.

SOURCES (PUBLISHED / UNPUBLISHED)

Abella, Irving. *Nationalism, Communism, and Canadian Labour: the* CIO, *the Communist Party, and the Canadian Congress of Labour 1935–1956.* Toronto: University of Toronto Press 1973.

Angell, H.M. "Duverger, Epstein and the Problem of the Mass Party: The Case of the Parti Québecois." *Canadian Journal of Political Science* 20 (1987): 363–78.

Archer, K. *Political Choices and Electoral Consequences: A Study of Organized Labour and the New Democratic Party.* Montreal: McGill-Queen's University Press, 1990.

Avakumovic, Ivan. *The Communist Party in Canada: A History.* Toronto: McClelland and Stewart, 1975.

– *Socialism in Canada: A Study of the* CCF-NDP *in Federal and Provincial Politics.* Toronto: McClelland and Stewart, 1978.

Azoulay, Dan. "The CCF's Winnipeg Declaration: Watershed or Grand Illusion?" *Journal of History and Politics* (1992): 109–28.

– "'A Desperate Holding Action': The Survival of the Ontario CCF/NDP, 1948–1963," *Ontario History* 85:1 (March 1993): 17–42.

Beck, J.M. *Pendulum of Power: Canada's Federal Elections.* Scarborough: Prentice-Hall, 1968.

Brewin, Andrew. "Woodsworth Foundation." *Canadian Forum* 32 (May 1952): 34–7.

Bristow, Dudley. "Agrarian interest in the politics of Ontario; a study with special reference to the period 1919–1949." M.A. thesis, University of Toronto, 1950.

Brownsey, K. and M. Howlett. "Class Structure and Political Alliances in an Industrialized Society." In *The Provincial State: Politics in Canada's Provinces and Territories*, edited by K. Brownsey and M. Howlett, 147–74. Toronto: Copp Clark Pitman, 1992.

Campbell, Peter J. "'Truly Grass Roots People,' The Cooperative Commonwealth Federation in Northern Ontario." M.A. thesis, Laurentian University, 1986.

Canada, Chief Electoral Officer. *By-Election Report, 1954.*

Canada, Department of Labour, Economics and Research Branch. *Forty-Second Annual Report on Labour Organizations in Canada, 1953–55.* Ottawa, 1954.

Caplan, Gerald. *The Dilemma of Canadian Socialism: The* CCF *in Ontario.* Toronto: McClelland and Stewart, 1973.

Carty, R.K. "Party Organization and Activity on the Ground." In *Canadian Parties in Transition*. 2d ed. Edited by A. Tanguay and A. Gagnon, 190–212. Scarborough, Ontario: Nelson Canada, 1996.

Chi, N.H. and G.C. Perlin. "The NDP: A Party in Transition." In *Party Politics in Canada*, 4th ed. Edited by H. Thorburn, chap. 16. Toronto: Prentice-Hall, 1979.

CLC, *Can Farmer and Labour Co-operate? A Report of the Farmer-Labour Conference, June 27–28, 1959*. N.p.: Farmer-Labour Co-ordinating Council-CLC, 1959.

CLC-CCF Joint National Committee, *A New Political Party for Canada*. Ottawa: JNC, 1958.

Cross, Michael, ed. *The Decline and Fall of a Good Idea: CCF-NDP Manifestos 1932 to 1969*. Toronto: New Hogtown Press, 1974.

Downs, Anthony. *An Economic Theory of Democracy*. New York: Harper and Row, 1957.

Drummond, Robert. "Voting Behaviour: The Blueing of Ontario." Cited in *The Government and Politics of Ontario*, 1st ed., edited by Donald MacDonald, 294–316. Toronto: Macmillan 1975.

– "Voting Behaviour: Casting the Play." Cited in *The Government and Politics of Ontario*, 2d ed., edited by Donald MacDonald, 272–89. Toronto: Van Nostrand Reinhold, 1980.

– "Voting Behaviour: Counting the Change." Cited in *The Government and Politics of Ontario*, 4th ed., edited by Graham White, 238–54. Scarborough: Nelson, 1990.

Duverger, Maurice. *Political Parties: Their Organization and Activity in the Modern State*. 3d ed. New York: John Wiley and Sons, 1966.

Engelmann, Frederick. "Membership Participation in Policy-making in the CCF." *Canadian Journal of Economics and Political Science* 22 (May 1956): 161–73.

Epstein, Leon. *Political Parties in Western Democracies*. New York: Frederick Praeger, 1967; reprint, New Brunswick, N.J.: Transaction, 1980.

Fisher, Doug. "An Interesting Campaign." *Canadian Forum* 37 (September 1957): 121, 143–4.

– "The Last CCF Roundup." *Canadian Forum* 5 (September 1960): 122

Fox, Paul. "Early Socialism in Canada." In *The Political Process in Canada: Essays in Honour of R. MacGregor Dawson*, edited by J. H. Aitchison, 79–98. Toronto: University of Toronto Press, 1963.

Francis, R. Douglas. "The Ontario Woodsworth House Controversy: 1944–1954." *Ontario History* 71 (March 1979): 27–37.

– *Frank H. Underhill: Intellectual Provocateur*. Toronto: University of Toronto Press, 1986.

Gagnon, A. and A. Tanguay. "Minor Parties in the Canadian Political System: Origins, Functions, Impact." In *Canadian Parties in Transition*, 2d ed., edited by A. Gagnon and A. Tanguay, 106–34. Scarborough: Nelson, 1996.

Goodman, Eddie. *Life of the Party: The Memoirs of Eddie Goodman*. Toronto: Key Porter Books, 1988.

Graham, Roger. *Old Man Ontario: Leslie M. Frost*. Toronto: University of Toronto Press, 1990.

Harrington, Lloyd. "What's Left." *Canadian Forum* 31 (March 1952): 269–70.

Horn, Michiel. *The League for Social Reconstruction: Intellectual Origins of the Democratic Left in Canada 1930–1942*. Toronto: University of Toronto Press, 1980.

Horowitz, Gad. *Canadian Labour in Politics*. Toronto: University of Toronto Press, 1968.

Hunter, Robin. "Social Democracy in Alberta: From the CCF to the NDP." In *Socialism and Democracy in Alberta: Essays in Honour of Grant Notley*, edited by L. Pratt, 57–83. Edmonton: NeWest Press, 1986.

Kerr, Donald and D. Holdsworth, eds. *The Historical Atlas of Canada, vol. 3: Addressing the Twentieth Century*. Toronto: University of Toronto Press, 1987–1993.

Knowles, Stanley. *The New Party*. Toronto: McClelland and Stewart, 1961.

Kornberg, A., et al. "Determinants of Provincial Voting Behaviour." In *Politics Canada*, 6th ed., edited by Paul Fox and Graham White, 434–51. Toronto: McGraw-Hill Ryerson Ltd., 1987.

LABEL. "Onward and Upward with the Revolution." *Canadian Forum* 35 (June 1955): 58–9.

Leacy, F.H., ed. *Historical Statistics of Canada*. 2d ed. Ottawa: Statistics Canada, 1983.

Lewis, David. *The Good Fight: Political Memoirs, 1909–1958*. Toronto: Macmillan of Canada, 1981.

Lipset, S. M. *Agrarian Socialism: The Cooperative Commonwealth Federation in Saskatchewan*; rev. ed. Berkeley, California: University of California Press, 1971.

Lucas, Peter. "Will New Party financing threaten secret ballot rights?" *Canadian Business* 34 (June 1961): 58–62.

MacDonald, Donald C. *The Happy Warrior: Political Memoirs*. Markham, Ontario: Fitzhenry and Whiteside, 1988.

– "Ontario's Political Culture: Conservatism with a Progressive Component." *Ontario History*, 86: 4 (December 1994): 297–317.

– ed. "The Happy Warrior," n.d., typewritten manuscript. In possession of author.

MacPherson, Ian. "The 1945 Collapse of the CCF in Windsor." *Ontario History* 61 (1969): 197–212.

McCormick, Peter. "Provincial Party Systems, 1945–1993." In *Canadian Parties in Transition*. 2nd ed. Edited by A. Tanguay and A. Gagnon, 349–71. Scarborough, Ontario: Nelson, 1996.

McDonald, Lynn. *The Party That Changed Canada: The New Democratic Party Then and Now*. Toronto: MacMillan of Canada, 1987.

McDougall, A. K. *John P. Robarts: His Life and Government.* Toronto: University of Toronto Press, 1986.

McLeod, Tommy and Ian McLeod. *Tommy Douglas: the Road to Jerusalem.* Edmonton: Hurtig, 1987.

McNaught, Kenneth. *A Prophet in Politics: A Biography of J.S. Woodsworth.* Toronto: University of Toronto Press, 1959.

– "Socialism and the Canadian Political Tradition." In *On F.R. Scott,* edited by S. Djwa and R. Macdonald. Montreal: McGill-Queen's University Press, 1983.

Manthorpe, Jonathan. *The Power and the Tories: Ontario Politics – 1943 to the Present.* Toronto: Macmillan of Canada, 1974.

Meisel, John, ed. *The Canadian General Election of 1957.* Toronto: University of Toronto Press, 1962.

– *Papers on the 1962 Election.* Toronto: University of Toronto Press, 1964.

Melnyk, Olenka. *Remembering the CCF: No Bankers in Heaven.* Toronto: McGraw-Hill Ryerson, 1989.

Michels, Robert. *Political Parties: A Sociological Study of the Oligarchical Tendencies of Modern Democracy.* Translated by Eden and Cedar Paul. Hearst's International Library, 1915; reprint, New York: Dover Publications, 1959.

Monroe, K and L. Erickson. "The Economy and Political Support: The Canadian Case." In *The Ballot and Its Message: Voting in Canada,* edited by J. Wearing, 195–222. Toronto: Copp Clark Pitman, 1991.

Morley, J.T. "The Politics of Socialist Secularization: A Biography of the Ontario CCF/NDP." Ph. D. diss., Queen's University, 1977.

– *Secular Socialists: The CCF/NDP in Ontario, A Biography.* Kingston, Ontario: McGill-Queen's University Press, 1984.

Morton, Desmond. *The New Democrats 1961–1986: The Politics of Change.* Toronto: Copp Clark Pitman, 1986.

National Committee for the New Party. *Study Paper on Constitution of the Proposed New Political Party for Canada,* and *Study Paper on Programme of the Proposed New Political Party for Canada.* Ottawa: NCNP, 1960.

Nichol, Christina. "In Pursuit of the Voter: The British Columbia CCF, 1945–50." In *'Building the Cooperative Commonwealth': Essays on the Democratic Socialist Tradition in Canada,* edited by J. William Brennan, 123–40. Regina, Saskatchewan: Canadian Plains Research Center, 1984.

Oliver, Peter. *Unlikely Tory: The Life and Politics of Allan Grossman.* Toronto: Lester and Orpen Dennys, 1985.

Ontario. Chief Electoral Officer. *Returns from General Elections and By-elections.* (1943–1963)

Ontario. Department of Labour. *Labour Gazette.* (1956–60)

Ontario. Legislative Assembly. *Debates.* (1954–55)

Ostrogorski, M. *Democracy and the Organization of Political Parties,* vol. 1, *England.* 2d ed. New York: Anchor Books, 1964.

Pammett, J. "Class Voting and Class Consciousness in Canada." In *The Ballot and the Message: Voting in Canada*, edited by J. Wearing. Toronto: Copp Clark Pitman, 1991.

Penner, Norman. *From Protest to Power: Social Democracy in Canada, 1900 – Present*. Toronto: James Lorimer and Company, 1992.

– "The Past, Present, and Uneasy Future of the New Democratic Party." In *Canadian Parties in Transition*, edited by A. Tanguay and A. Gagnon, 89–105. Scarborough, Ontario: Nelson, 1996.

Pinard, Maurice. *The Rise of a Third Party: A Study in Crisis Politics*. New Jersey: Prentice-Hall, 1971.

Piva, Michael. "The Toronto District Labour Council and Independent Political Action: Factionalism and Frustration, 1900–1921." *Labour/Le Travailleur* 4 (1979): 115–31.

Rea, K.J. *The Prosperous Years: The Economic History of Ontario 1939–1975*. Toronto: University of Toronto Press, 1985.

Richards, John. "The Decline and Fall of Agrarian Socialism." In *Agrarian Socialism: The Cooperative Commonwealth Federation in Saskatchewan*, rev. ed., by S. M. Lipset, 364–92. Berkeley, California: University of California Press, 1971.

Roberts, Wayne. "Artisans, Aristocrats and Handymen: Politics and Trade Unionism among Toronto Skilled Building Trade Workers, 1896–1914." *Labour/Le Travailleur* 1 (1976): 92–122.

Robin, Martin. "The Trades and Labour Congress of Canada and Political Action: 1898–1908." *Relations Industrielles* 22 (April 1967): 187–215.

Sangster, Joan. "'Women and the New Era': The Role of Women in the Early CCF, 1933–1940." In *"Building the Cooperative Commonwealth": Essays on the Democratic Socialist Tradition in Canada*, edited by J. William Brennan, 69–98. Regina, Saskatchewan: Canadian Plains Research Center, 1984.

Shackleton, Doris. *Tommy Douglas*. Toronto: McClelland and Stewart, 1975.

Silverstein, S. "Occupational Class and Voting Behaviour: Electoral Support of a Left-Wing Protest Movement in a Period of Prosperity." In *Agrarian Socialism: The Cooperative Commonwealth Federation in Saskatchewan*, rev. ed., edited by S. M. Lipset, 364–92. Berkeley, California: University of California Press, 1971.

Sinclair, Peter. "The Saskatchewan CCF: Ascent to Power and the Decline of Socialism." *Canadian Historical Review* 54 (December 1973): 419–33.

Smith, Cameron. *Unfinished Journey: The Lewis Family*. Toronto: Summerhill Press, 1989.

Steeves, Dorothy. *The Compassionate Rebel: Ernest Winch and the Growth of Socialism in Western Canada*. Vancouver: JJ. Douglas Ltd., 1960.

Stinson, Lloyd. *Political Warriors: Recollections of a Social Democrat*. Winnipeg: Queenston House Publishing, 1975.

Szmigielski, Walter. "Constituency Level Politics: A Case Study of the Cooperative Commonwealth Federation and New Democratic Party in Brantford, Ontario." M.A. thesis, McMaster University, 1977.

Trofimenkoff, Susan. *Stanley Knowles: The Man from Winnipeg North Centre.* Saskatoon, Saskatchewan: Western Producer Prairie Books, 1982.

Underhill, Frank. "What's Left." *Canadian Forum* 31 (February 1952): 243–44.

– "Power Politics in the Ontario C.C.F." *Canadian Forum* 32 (April 1952): 7–8.

– *In Search of Canadian Liberalism.* Toronto: Macmillan 1960.

Wearing, J. "Political Parties: Fish or Fowl?" In *The Government and Politics of Ontario,* 3d ed., edited by Donald MacDonald, 238–61. Scarborough: Nelson, 1985.

– *Strained Relations: Canadian Parties and Voters.* Toronto: McClelland and Stewart, 1988.

Weisbach, Henry. "The First CLC Ontario Provincial Education Conference." *Canadian Labour* 4 (March 1959): 73–4.

Whitaker, Reginald. *The Government Party: Organizing and Financing the Liberal Party of Canada 1930–1958.* Toronto: University of Toronto Press, 1978.

– *Double Standard: The Secret History of Canadian Immigration.* Toronto: Lester and Orpens Dennys, 1987.

Whitehorn, A. *Canadian Socialism: Essays on the CCF-NDP.* Toronto: Oxford University Press, 1992.

– "Audrey McLaughlin and the Decline of the Federal NDP." In *Party Politics in Canada,* 7th ed., edited by Hugh Thorburn, 315–35. Scarborough, Ontario: Prentice-Hall Canada, 1996.

Wilson, John. "Towards a Redefinition of the Nature of the Canadian Political System." *Canadian Journal of Political Science* 7 (September 1974): 438–83.

Wise, S.F. "The Ontario Political Culture: A Study in Complexities." In *The Government and Politics of Ontario,* 4th ed., edited by Graham White, 44–59. Scarborough, Ontario: Nelson, 1990.

Wiseman, Nelson. *Social Democracy in Manitoba: A History of the CCF/NDP.* Winnipeg: University of Manitoba Press, 1983.

Wrong, Denis. "Ontario Provincial Elections 1934–55; A Preliminary Survey of Voting." *Canadian Journal of Economics and Political Science* 23 (August 1957): 395–403.

Young, Walter. "The Peterborough By-Election." *Dalhousie Review* 40 (Winter 1961): 505–19.

– *Anatomy of a Party: The National CCF, 1932–61.* Toronto: University of Toronto Press, 1969.

Zakuta, Leo. *A Protest Movement Becalmed: A Study of Change in the CCF.* Toronto: University of Toronto Press, 1964.

Index